D1243839

SOCIAL FOUNDATIONS OF CONTEMPORARY ECONOMICS

SOCIAL FOUNDATIONS OF

CONTEMPORARY ECONOMICS

GEORGES SOREL

Translated with an Introduction by
John L. Stanley

Transaction Books
New Brunswick (U.S.A.) and London (U.K.)

HX
72
,S6813
1984

Library of Congress Catalog Number: 83-12056

ISBN: 0-87855-482-3 (cloth)

Printed in the United States of America

Library of Congress Cataloging in Publication Data

Sorel, Georges, 1847-1922.
    Social foundations of contemporary economics.
    Includes index.
    Translation of: Insegnamenti sociali della economia contemporanea.
    1. Socialism.   2. Capitalism.   3. Economics.
I. Title.
HX72.S6813   1984   335   83-12056
ISBN 0-87855-482-3

Analytical Table of Contents

INTRODUCTION

vi

PART II
The Old Utopias and the New Socialist Doctrines

Part III
Cartels and Their Ideological Consequences

INTRODUCTION

John L. Stanley

Perhaps the most interesting aspect of Georges Sorel's political and social thought is the difficulty one has in attempting to classify it. Just when we think we have Sorel conveniently pigeonholed into some tidy little category (protofascist being a recent favorite), he fools us by putting forth ideas which at first seem to be in complete contradiction to all our preconceptions.

This elusiveness is partly responsible for the allegations of "shocking inconsistency" and negativism leveled against Sorel. These allegations have some truth. Anyone like Sorel born in France in the middle of the nineteenth century had numerous political traditions from which to choose, and it appears that he sampled a good many of them. As a young engineering student at the prestigious Ecole Polytechnique, Sorel expressed a sympathy with royalism and was a partisan of the Comte de Chambord in 1867. After his early retirement from the Department of Highways in 1892, he moved toward social democracy, but this attachment to a revised Marxism soon changed into a sympathy for antistatist syndicalism from about 1902 until about 1908. This was the period in which the present volume as well as *Reflections on Violence* and the *Illusions of Progress*[1] were written. After 1908, Sorel regarded the snydicalist movement as a failure and flirted once more with royalism. After 1917, he embraced Lenin's Bolshevism and even occasionally made favorable remarks about Mussolini.

This seemingly bizarre series of changes is better understood if we keep in mind the historical backdrop of Sorel's youth: France's defeat in the Franco-Prussian war in 1870 profoundly demoralized French society. The political thought of the next decade and the parliamentary immobilism of the Third Republic reflected this malaise. The inertia of liberal institutions after 1871 had provoked a challenge from the Right in which Royalists and Bonapartists formed a coalition in support of Minister of War Boulanger in his demand for a reformed constitution and a more spirited foreign policy—an attempt which came to naught. Its failure helped to solidify the multiple stalemate between the forces of radicalism and conservatism. "France is dying," proclaimed Ernest

Renan in 1882, and these words from the great religious scholar come close to summing up Sorel's own feeling about the period. Renan was moved by the French defeat to call for a reform of the educational system to teach the heroism of classical times and to synthesize French and German virtues. These sentiments were found in Sorel's first important work, *Le Procès de Socrate* (1889).[2] There Sorel drew an implicit analogy between the decline of heroic Athens at the hand of philosophers and the decline of France under Louis Napoleon and under the Third Republic. In its pages Sorel appears much more reactionary than the liberal Renan. We find a deeply pessimistic Sorel, hostile to the Enlightenment, a bitter critic of "the illusions of progress."

But appearances here are deceiving. Sorel was not a reactionary in any vulgar sense, but was espousing a new moral order that was sometimes profoundly hostile to the prevailing system of values. To Sorel, the malaise of contemporary European civilization was a moral one. But unlike Renan, he was not content to preach morality or to put forth small palliatives. He sought a genealogy of morals or what I have called a "sociology of virtue,"[3] which attempted to examine the historical and psychological roots of the moral basis of a social order and its decomposition. It was the search for the historical genesis of morals that Sorel said was "the great concern of my entire life."[4]

Le Procès de Socrate was a general indictment of philosophical teachers in ancient Athens, not merely an attack on Socrates. To Sorel, Athenian philosophers, with Socrates at their head, had replaced the preachments of intellectuals for the heroic teachings of the Greek mythic poets. In Sorel's view, such new teachings were largely ineffectual except in a negative sense, serving only to undermine the moral strength of the old institutions. (1) Philosophy had preached an abstract brotherhood of man instead of solid family institutions and Platonic instead of erotic love. The family life on which all other stable social institutions are based was thus undermined. (2) Philosophers preached the rule of experts instead of the rule of warriors and fighters. The military virtues on which Greek citizenship was based were weakened. (3) Philosophers emphasized the leisure necessary for philosophical and political activity; the ethic of productivity and energy was replaced by a morality of the weak based on consumption. It is the last two themes, the morality of struggle and of productivity, which stand as the major inspiration of the present work, *Insegnamenti sociali della economia contemporanea.*

Sorel derived this sociology of morals mainly from the work of Pierre-Joseph Proudhon, who had criticized his own social milieu on roughly these same bases. On the other hand, it was Proudhon who had emphasized the futility of war in modern society and who, instead of calling for battle, assimilated the heroism of war to the day-to-day struggles of the worker in production. The modern proletariat had replaced the Greco-Roman citizen farmer.

After publication of *Le Procès de Socrate* Sorel discovered the writings of Vico and Marx. To Sorel, Vico revealed the recurrent nature of the heroic virtues he had longed for. Vico argued that the natural cycles of history, of greatness and decline among peoples, always contained periods characterized by the heroic barbarism expressed in Homeric poetry or the medieval epics. Such recurrences, or *ricorsi,* the beginnings of new civilizations, are accompanied by a transvaluation of values, an upheaval that annihilates the old, decadent civilization with a moral catastrophe far greater than any material one; in such times, "the logic of imagination replaces the logic of philosophy."[5] The *ricorsi* embody new dynamisms, new vitalities and energies.

From Marx, Sorel discovered how he could apply the heroism of the Homeric epics to new conditions, through the class struggle. Marx's notion of absolute class separation, of the proletariat isolating itself from the mentality of bourgeois civilization, proved the key to Sorel's search for new beginnings. He embraced Marx as the one philosopher outside Proudhon who revealed a way in which a true Vicoian *ricorso* would occur in modern times. A combination of Proudhonian heroism and Marxian class struggle would pave the way for a rebirth of contemporary civilization.

Two more theorists contributed to Sorel's philosophy. From Henri Bergson, Sorel derived a psychology which revealed the nature of the heroic leaps of imagination that invariably accompany a *ricorso.* Bergson explained how such leaps could go beyond the scientific universe, whose routines threatened the vital life force, the very expression of which was necessary for moral renaissance.

In William James, Sorel found a philosophical expression of what he had always viewed as axiomatic: that the "success" of a doctrine is more important than its inner coherence. Once we keep in mind the instrumental nature of political and economic doctrines espoused by James, Sorel's continuing change of allegiances becomes more explicable[7] For Sorel embraced a doctrine only insofar as it revealed a potential for a *ricorso* and he rejected it if it was shown to be ineffectual. For example, he explained his most notorious switch, from syndicalism to royalism in 1909-10, when he said: "I do not know if Maurras will bring back the king of France and that is not what interests me in his thought; what I am concerned with is that he confront the dull and reactionary bourgeoisie in making it ashamed of being defeated."[6] As he later stated it, he had always been a traditionalist in a sense: "One can call me a traditionalist as one can call me a pragmatist, because in the critique of knowledge I attach a major importance to historical development. When I sided with Vico . . . I was in a certain sense a traditionalist."[7] Sorel's "monarchism" is a means by which he can envision a sharpened social struggle that makes possible the unfolding of virtue—that he defines in terms of the warrior ethos of courage and self-sacrifice. Each ideology is viewed in terms of its potential to uphold the *élan* of such a struggle. When it does not live up to these hopes, it is abandoned even more quickly than it was adopted.

The pragmatic nature of Sorel's use of Vico is further emphasized when we keep in mind Sorel's view that, in the realm of ideas as well as in social action, there is a "heterogeneity between the ends realized and the ends given."[8] For Sorel reality differs greatly from the ideas that we had of it before acting. Sorel's distinction between the psychological basis of the royalist actors themselves and the psychology of the observers of the royalists is similar to William James's distinction between the "religious propensities" of believers and the "philosophical significance" of those beliefs.[9] In modern sociological terms, beliefs have "latent functions," the most important of which is the role they play in struggle and economic productivity.

The pluralism between intention and result in pragmatic thought extends to historical pluralism as well. Despite Sorel's attraction to Vico, he was critical of his simplistic account of the relationships between psychological states and society.[10] Vico looked upon history almost as an organic growth in which thought and activity are brought together in an indissoluble whole: he treated phenomena *en bloc*. But to Sorel, if history developed in this fashion, there would be few chances for a durable renaissance. *Ricorsi* are produced when a body within society declares itself separate from the prevailing civilization; Vico's holistic approach to change obscures the importance of this separation; it hides the need for ideologies to coexist and compete with one another for supremacy. It is this competition which makes movements struggle in order to triumph, and it is the struggle itself, more than the outcome, which produces virtue in the hearts of the participants.

This doctrine of struggle stands at the basis of Sorel's treatment of various ideologies. One of the best illustrations of Sorel's position is found here in the *Insegnamenti* where he deals with the ideologies of liberal capitalism and socialism. In reading this work, we come to understand that Sorel admired each of these ideologies most insofar as it stood in resistance to (or at least in isolation from) the opposing ideology. The more an ideology represents struggle and the overcoming of resistance, the more it possesses dynamic elements, elements of creativity and mastery in which it represents the fight against decadence. The less an ideology embodies the ethos of struggle, the more it embodies degeneration and laxity. Each ideology contains both regenerative and degenerative components.

This striking parallelism between liberal and socialist degeneration and regeneration stands at the core of the *Insegnamenti sociali della economia contemporanea.* This work was completed in 1903-05 when Sorel had written off liberalism in France as a lost cause and had become fully disillusioned with the "official socialism" of the German and French Marxist parties. By then Sorel had turned to antipolitical syndicalism, and the *Insegnamenti* is especially interesting when viewed as a sort of *Grundrisse* or draft for his most renowned work (written the following year), *Reflections on Violence.*

While *Reflections* is Sorel's clearest statement of syndicalist action and the social myths which sustain it, in the *Insegnamenti* we find the clearest theory of the idea of class separation as a function of the rise of syndicalism. In the *Insegnamenti* we also find the most detailed analysis of the role class separation had performed in the great periods of liberalism and socialism; and it is here that we find the most profound condemnation of what Sorel calls "social solidarity" (or social unity) and the role it has played in the degeneration of the two great European ideologies.

The work is doubly interesting because not only does Sorel discuss these ideologies, but he actually uses them as tools for analyzing these very ideologies. As Sorel expresses it: "The true method to follow to know the defects, inadequacies, and errors of a powerful philosophy is to criticize it by means of its own principles."[11] Thus he announces at the beginning of the *Insegnamenti* that he will use, as much as possible, the principles of historical materialism.

In this work Sorel is not only analyzing socialism according to its own system of historical materialism; he is also examining the ideologies of liberal capitalism. Yet there is no explicit reference here to a theory corresponding to capitalism that Sorel found useful as a means of analysis, though such a theory did exist at the time and was implicit in Sorel's analytical approach. That theory is pragmatism, one of the main philosophical progeny of liberalism. Since it is through pragmatic as much as Marxist criteria that Sorel evaluates the various European ideologies, and since it is more through pragmatic criteria that he pledges allegiance to so many of them at various times, not only does Sorel view Marxism using Marxian categories and liberalism in terms of its own pragmatic norms, but each of these ideologies is (here or in later writings) examined with the other's philosophical weaponry as well.

In the present volume Sorel is explicit about using historical materialism and says nothing about pragmatism because, at the time of writing (1904-05), Sorel had gravitated to pragmatism only by instinct. It was not until four or five years later in 1909 that Sorel would discover the writing of William James, and only long after 1909 would he extoll "the utility of pragmatism." Yet this still unarticulated pragmatic thought is at least as important as Marxism in Sorel's thinking; perhaps more so. Marxism was important to Sorel chiefly because of the role it played in analyzing the historical and economic roots of social phenomena. Sorel's pragmatism is important because it provided him with an expression of the plural nature of reality and of the necessarily partial and tentative nature of all explanatory theories. Marxism is important because it emphasizes man's interchange with nature as the basis of knowledge. Pragmatism will be important to Sorel because it, more than Marxism, emphasizes that nature cannot be viewed successfully as a totality.

Liberal capitalism and socialism, as dealt with in the *Insegnamenti,* are, among other things, also philosophies of man's relationship to nature, and Sorel's own pragmatic theory of nature is important in understanding the present work. Sorel developed this natural theory quite early, long before his formal discovery of pragmatism, and it informs his entire philosophy as few other aspects of his thought do. In no small measure, this philosophy is the basis of Sorel's method of looking at all social as well as scientific phenomena. Thus, before turning to an analysis of the *Insegnamenti,* this pragmatic methodology should be discussed in detail. It is the implicit method he employs (coupled with Marxism) throughout this work.

In Sorel's eyes, the examination of ideological phenomena, like the experimental controls involved in scientific questions, is necessarily limited to partial views of phenomena. The ideology of liberalism, for example, can be seen most effectively if we look at it from a single angle, say its period of decline. We can look at other stages of the ideology at other discrete moments. This method results in a series of representations roughly analogous to single frames of a motion picture which might give a closer and more detailed view of an otherwise confused action. On the other hand, this "still frame" cannot help but distort the full portrayal of the movement by virtue of its partial nature.

Sorel asserts that knowledge of the full social or ideological "newsreel" is impossible. Methodologically, Sorel attempts to deal with the problem of totality by using what in his early writings he called an "expressive support" and later called *diremption.* The term *diremption* is defined as "a forcible separation or severance."[12] As Sorel stated it: "In order to study the most important philosophy of history, social philosophy is obliged to proceed to a *diremption,* to examine certain parts without taking into consideration all their connections with the whole; to determine, in some way, the nature of their activity by isolating them. When it has attained the most perfect knowledge in this way, social philosophy can no longer try to reconstruct the broken unity.''[13]

We can elaborate on the concept of diremption in a number of ways, and there is an anticipation here of Max Weber's ''ideal types.'' It is a method of analysis which abstracts a phenomenon from social reality for the purpose of clarification. We know, however, that the process of abstraction, by its very isolation, distorts or blurs the totality from which it is derived, and that the diremptions themselves have been changed in the process of being isolated.

Sorel is aware that, to some extent, every social philosophy or political theory must use diremption, and he seems to argue that these theories are themselves diremptions. Yet to Sorel, most social and political theorists are only half conscious of the consequences of making these abstractions. Sorel insists that we shall gain insights from diremption, that is, from abstract social theories, but we must never forget what a diremption is; although diremptions must be used, we must be careful not to abuse them. According to Sorel, most of the errors of social philosophy stem from such abuses.

At the root of the problem of social analysis is the displacement of an empirically based theory with rationalist theories. This hostility to the rationalist tradition is partly responsible for Sorel's attack on the rule of philosophers and social scientists. Rationalism places the objects of diremption in an extreme degree of isolation from the total milieu; it produces conclusions giving an appearance of logic, reasonableness, and necessity, but which are at complete odds with other diremptions derived partly from the same milieu which seem equally logical, reasonable, and necessary. When diremptions have been ''pushed far enough along the path of such antinomies, it is easy to forget the historical and economic roots from which they derive.'' When diremption becomes rationalized, it undergoes a process of reification; diremption becomes, in Sorel's words, ''without an object,'' that is, it floats free and ''comes into conditions that are irreconcilable with the nature of their formation'';[14] then we obtain distortions that are even further removed from reality than the original diremption. The insights and clarification derived from the original procedure have given way to sophistry, arbitrariness, and vagueness. In other words, by forgetting the historical and theoretical genesis of a diremption, a theorist makes the error or thinking that he can bring it back to social totality without causing further distortions. The reimmersion into the totality both results from, and in turn causes, an illusion of wholeness, a false consciousness of universality. Social diremption, like social philosophy itself, is a phenomenon that must be treated "diremptively."

Perhaps the best example of a misused diremption, in Sorel's view, is one that recurs throughout this work: the concept of economic man perfected by British political economy in the nineteenth century. For Sorel, the analytical utility of the concept of a calculating market bargainer is undeniable, but it is a great misuse of diremption to extend that concept to cover areas for which it was not intended. Nonetheless "subtle writers even worked to create a science which considered the relations of buyer-seller, capitalist-employee, lender-debtor in a market that no government penetrated." Hence a useful symbolic device was transformed into a utopia governed by the "natural harmony of mutual interests." Such utopias are wholly misguided because the "petty concerns of *homo economicus*" in no way can represent the totality of social relations. The adherents of the utopia "did not seriously examine the legitimacy of the diremption."[15]

But at what point do we know that such a diremption has been abused? Sorel's method of diremption is a pragmatic, trial-and-error method that makes each diremption a hypothesis to be tested against social reality. In this testing process Sorel comes close to replicating in social theory the philosophy of science he had developed in the early 1890s. The analogies Sorel had observed between the practices of science and those of laboring not only inspired his theory of diremption, but also affected his thoroughly pragmatic revision of Marxism.

To Sorel, as to Vico and Marx, man's knowledge of the world is derived from the act of making or manufacturing—either in the realm of ideas or in man's interaction with nature. Similarly, construction of laboratory models, in Sorel's view, effects an isolation—a diremption—from the world in the very process of our getting to understand the world through changing it. On these grounds, Sorel argues that the milieux of the scientist and of the worker become increasingly similar as science and productivity become more intense; and the more intense they become, the more they separate themselves from the realm of nature. The laboratory is "a small workshop where instruments are used that are more precise than those in manufacturing, but there is no essential difference between the two types of establishments."[16]

In other writings, Sorel calls this separation or diremption from nature "artificial nature," which he juxtaposes to "natural nature" or nature in its undisturbed or "pure" state.[17] The *Insegnamenti* does not contain specific discussion of these two natures, but the argument presumes this distinction as we shall see. Sorel argues that there is always plurality in these two realms in the industrial world. Thus the two natures represent a plural—hence pragmatic—view of understanding reality. On the one hand, the more a phenomenon is removed from nature, that is, the more nature is "artificial," the more precisely we can predict the results of our experiments. On the other hand, most natural nature, still immersed in the totality, remains comparatively vague. The physicist is thus dealing with a more "artificial" realm than the meteorologist. The result is a dilemma regarding the apprehension of totality: in natural nature the scope of our investigation is much wider, but the precision of our knowledge and the accuracy of our predictions is blurred, while in artificial nature, the scope of our understanding is more limited as our precision increases. Our knowledge of nature will thus never become total in the sense of an equally precise knowledge of all its parts. There is an uncertainty principle here which cannot be overcome. The unity of science and nature that had for Marx been alienated under capitalism, Sorel regarded as being shattered by the very process of manufacturing. Whereas Marx, and especially Engels, would overcome alienation through the establishment of an all-encompassing socialist laboratory-workshop and a unified science, Sorel insisted that, whatever the economic system, scientific and industrial production in the modern world cannot avoid being alienated from the rest of nature either through the actions of *homo faber* or through those of the laboratory scientist in the creation of experiments and controls. Knowledge of that nature cannot help but become alienated. Scientific knowledge is diremption, the analytic counterpart of artificial nature.

This alienated condition of modern industry is presented in another way by Sorel. The world of "artificial nature," the world in which nature is transformed through science and industry, is determined and predictable. But Sorel insists that this predictability and precision are insufficient to perpetuate a world of artificial nature. Left to itself, artificial nature reverts all too easily back to the world of natural nature. It "coasts" by sinking from the empirical world into the abstractions of rationalism. A perfectly predictable world is not sufficient to produce new science but invites stagnation in science as well as in society; it returns to the passive terrain of natural nature, because, in Bergson's terms, we become "enclosed in the circle of the given." Insofar as it is purely intellectual, "scientific knowledge presents itself as something alien to our person. . . . We attribute to it a dominant force on our will and we submit weakly to its tyranny."[18] Thus scientific determinism is self-negating; it becomes an adversary to continued scientific research because it affirms the "powerlessness of our creative forces; *we then have science only to the extent that we have the force to govern the world.*"[19]

To continue our practices in the realm of artificial nature, some motive force must make us "interfere" in nature; something must make us come to this nature, as it were, "from the outside"; intention must break this circle of determinism. This break comes only by bringing in a poetic dimension to the productive or scientific process. "Poetic fictions are stronger than scientific ones," Sorel says. They represent "the ability to substitute an imaginary world for scientific truths which we populate with plastic creations and which we perceive with much greater clarity than the material world. It is these idols that permeate our will and are the sisters of our soul."[20] The vision that inspires the syndicalist myth of the general strike, or assures the Marxist that his cause is certain to triumph, exists outside of science; it lives in the world of intuition, of instinct, of imagination, in a word, of creativity. It is these poetic visions that convince the inventor or producer of the moral certitude of his task. "If man loses something of his confidence in scientific certitude, he loses much of his moral certitude at the same time."[21] It is not science that gives men certitude; it is moral certitude that gives man the inner strength to wage constant war against the passive terrain of natural nature. Artificial nature, once established, requires constant struggle merely to keep even with natural nature. Artificial nature, sustained by poetic myths, means a twofold battle against the material on which we work as well as our own "natural nature"—the tendency to relaxation, sloth, and leisure. Because they are the very embodiment of such a struggle, Sorel can assimilate science and labor and assert that their successes constitute a rough measure of the virtue of a given culture. Artificial nature represents the triumph of self-overcoming as well as the triumph over external nature; natural nature represents the failure of self-overcoming; it is the terrain of surrender to our own worst inclinations and passions; natural nature is the realm of unity while artificial nature destroys that unity.

We can now see more fully why Sorel's pragmatic break with Marx alters so radically the conclusions of humanist Marxists. By dint of the necessity for continued struggle with natural nature, neither laboring man nor scientific man will ever triumph fully, never bridge the gap between man and the world around him. "We will never be able completely to subject phenomena to mathematical laws. . . . Nature never ceases working with crafty slowness for the ruination of all our works. We buy the power of commanding artificial nature by incessant labor." This command does not come easily. Marx was mistaken insofar as he believed that a utopia of abundance and leisure would ever be achieved: "The more scientific our production becomes, the better we understand that our destiny is to labor without a truce and thus to annihilate the dreams of paradisiacal happiness that the old socialists had taken as legitimate anticipation.''[22]

Readers of the *Insegnamenti* will be struck by the importance the work ethic plays in Sorel's analysis of economic ideologies. Artificial nature, as the struggle against natural nature, means a world of production. In natural nature we are no longer in the realm of production and invention, but are instead in the realm of consumption and leisure. Sorel's judgments about the ''success'' of a given civilization are based on this overcoming process sustained by work, and the same criteria are applied to the economic ideologies which emerge from these civilizations. In the *Insegnamenti* Sorel favors Marxism when it represents the struggle of the laborer or scientist, the triumph of *animal laborans* and the overcoming of Feuerbachian naturalism; he scorns Marxism when it becomes ossified into the platforms of ''official'' political parties which promise that a ''land of milk and honey'' will be delivered on the silver platter of progress.

Sorel can be for liberalism when it embodies these same ''Protestant'' virtues of enterprise, productivity, and the conquest of new frontiers. He scorns liberalism when it becomes ''democratic,'' that is, when ''petty philosophers devoured by ambition to become great men'' transform the productive aspects of liberalism into rationalist utopias in which parasitic politicians and financiers devour the natural wealth through usury and the chicanery of legislative logrolling. In the *Insegnamenti* Sorel evaluates socialism and liberal capitalism in this manner. Each of the two views has its dynamic side in which it represents a partial *ricorso;* each has fallen into decay. The twofold nature of these ideologies constitutes the theme of this book whose contents we shall now analyze in detail.

Sorel divides the *Insegnamenti* into four parts (an introduction and three parts). While many themes in each part overlap with those in other sections, the attentive reader can discern a basic theme in each part as well as a general theme for the whole book. The introductory segment announces the overall theme of the work, and it is interesting to note that a book on economic doctrine should have an especially political thesis. The *Insegnamenti* is, first and foremost, an attack on the time-honored notion of community solidarity whose Platonic and Aristotelian versions are expressed in the formulations of natural sociability and social obligation and which found its most enduring historical example in the church, ''the most perfect example'' of a completely duty-bound society ''whose mission is to preach to the ruling classes their obligations toward the poor.''[23]

Sorel stresses the great similarities found in the justifications for social unity in both the old and new political theories. Despite vast differences among various theories of sociability, the classical political theories resemble the modern Fourierian and Saint-Simonian utopias as well as Kantian ideas in regard to the permanence of the laws of nature. In much the same way as Plato attempted to apply to society the Greek philosophy of science—a science based on the need to rationalize everything by replacing the changing phenomenal world with the immutable laws of mathematics—so the nineteenth-century utopian socialists attempted to eliminate chance from human affairs. In Sorel's view, Kant too based his theories of social duty on the absolute harmony between the exigencies of reason and the methods of Newtonian physics. The Fourierian and positivist utopias were constructed in the same way as were philosophical explanations of matter. Fourier even aspired to the planetary regularity of Laplacean astronomy.[24]

The failure to recognize the difference between physical and social science, and more importantly, between natural and artificial nature within the physical sciences, meant, in Sorel's view, that naturalistic social theories would establish a social unity that would correspond to the one that supposedly existed in the physical world. Despite the great differences between physical and social sciences, Sorel regarded theories of social unity and community as corresponding to "natural nature" in the physical world.

For Sorel, this meant that utopian socialism was little different from the other social theories used to justify decadent societies. Most political and ethical theories, as Sorel later made clear, "take as their starting point . . . books written for declining societies; when Aristotle wrote the *Nichomachean Ethics,* Greece had already lost her own reasons for morality." The moral principles set forth in this work and in classical political philosophy, generally reflected "the habits which a young Greek had to take up by frequenting cultivated society. Here we are in the realm of consumer morality. . . . War and production had ceased to concern the most distinguished people in the towns."[25]

What is true for classical political philosophy, in Sorel's view, is even more true in the modern setting. Despite their pretensions to philosophical precision and abstraction, modern ethical and political utopias are characterized by the ease with which their utopian elements are carried over into programs for improving the existing order. The Saint-Simonian ideas on administration corresponded to the Napoleonic ideas of bureaucracy and social hierarchy; duty is expressed in the Prussian land law of 1794. Ninety years later, Bismarck proclaimed to the Reichstag that he intended to imbue his social legislation with the principles found in that law and stated that "it is a state concern to care for the maintenance of the citizenry who are unable to procure those same means of subsistence."[26] To Sorel, such proposals, and similar ones contained in socialist programs, demonstrated an almost uncanny continuity between the ancient and medieval philosophies of charity and social duty and the modern notions of welfare and economic right; between the paternalism of the lord of the manor who justified his social position on the basis of "natural law" and the *dirigisme* of the modern welfare state bureaucrat who justifies his power on the "right" of citizens to subsistence. The modern social welfare state, whose development Sorel foresees in this work, will be, in his view, deeply reactionary.

Not only is there a certain continuity in social policy in the old and new regimes as well as in the declining cities of antiquity, but the elite of the old regime shares many characteristics with those of the new ruling classes. Not only is the authoritarianism of the old court bureaucrats reproduced in the new society, but both elites are in decline, separated from war and productivity and become fundamentally urban in both their social attraction to the *beau monde* of salons or wealthy artistic patrons and in the consumer habits fostered by the urban environment. Sorel concludes the introduction with a fascinating discussion of the effects of urbanism on moral decadence—its resistance to productivity in virtually all branches of industry save those devoted to luxury items consumed by tourists and courtesans.

The extraordinary pessimism shown by Sorel regarding moral theories and utopias does not extend to all philosophers and theories. In part I of the *Insegnamenti* Sorel deals with the economic, social, and psychological conditions which give rise to social theories which avoid the decadent quality of the ancient viewpoints. Since decadent theories embodied the spirit and the letter of social solidarity, Sorel argues that theories take on dynamic qualities when they partake of what he variously calls the "spirit of separation" or "the organization of revolt," clearly manifested in the Marxian view of the class struggle and in revolutionary syndicalism.[27] Here we find Sorel arguing that socialist ideas, like those of liberalism, have achieved their highest degree of vitality when they have attained the highest degree of independence from the notion of social totality; that is, when they have attained their most refined diremption. At this point a theory's explanatory power is most complete.

Sorel regarded ideas as being far more important than the epiphenomena depicted by vulgar Marxists. As he states it in the first chapter of this section, ideas rely more on antecedent theoretical formations, historical knowledge, and (especially) memories of past conflicts than on economic phenomena. Thus the socialist idea cannot be explained by economic factors alone because "the attitudes that man takes in the presence of reality are highly variable according to circumstances."[28]

From Vico, Sorel derived the idea of the importance of the psychological aspects of social movements. Vico suggested that memories of past struggles were expressed in "psychological concatenations" which members of a society experienced in the passage from one regime to another.[29] The difficulty with these notions, which Sorel saw very early in his writing career, was that Vico's concept of psychological upheaval did not always square with another notion Sorel derived from Vico, the idea that "man knows what he makes," which found its way into the Marxian theory of knowledge and, in a somewhat different form, into Sorel's theory of artificial nature. In Sorel's thought psychological upheavals were connected more directly than in Marxism to moral upheavals. There was in Sorel an autonomy of moral thought absent from conventional Marxism. How was Sorel to picture a psychological state without reverting to the very intellectualism he had condemned in rationalist utopias?

Sorel found a solution to this dilemma in an interpretation of these psychological states as "myths" which he depicts as states of mind roughly analogous to those accompanying religious conversion. Myths are highly subjective, and thus inevitably partial rather than societal. Thus in anticipating, subjectively, a total moral catastrophe, as for example in the Christian vision of the second coming of Christ, the very totality of the vision forced its adherents to isolate themselves from the larger society. The more total the vision, the higher the degree of psychological upheaval, and the more partial, the more isolated was the movement carried on in its name. For Sorel, psychological concatenations or myths are self-limiting and as such they inevitably produce only partial *ricorsi*. In a word, myths "dirempted" themselves from the totality.

Added to the paradox of a total vision becoming self-limiting was the notion that the more self-limiting the social boundaries of the new movement whose members had experienced psychological upheavals, the more effective their teaching became. What started as a total vision of catastrophe ended in transforming the world precisely by dint of the isolation the visionaries had imposed on themselves. Sorel responded to the difficulty of severing psychological upheavals from the productive process by separating mythical and scientific thought. Sorel does this largely by accepting what William James was later to call a distinction between the religious and the philosophical points of view. Religious or mythical points of view see the world subjectively, or, as Sorel expresses it here, they are like "optical devices turned around before our eyes and which mute the relative value of things." They obscure objectivity and are thus the opposite of scientific thought.

But to argue for the separation, for analytical purposes, of mythical from scientific thought is not to say that there are no relations between the mythical and scientific realms—especially if the science in question is economics. The relationship between mythical and economic thought is one of the most interesting questions that arises in the course of reading Sorel's works. The most explicit treatment of this relationship is in *Reflections on Violence*, where Sorel treats the myth of the general strike in syndicalist theory. This myth allows the subject to anticipate the future in which he feels certain his cause is to triumph. The subject does this without recourse to the historical "dialectics" of Marxian "science" —a rationalistic diremption having lost sight of its own limits and presuppositions.

Yet the myth too is a diremption because it is severed from its scientific offspring. It performs in economic life what the poetic spirit of invention performs in scientific life. It allows us to break out of the circle of the given. The myth of the general strike reinforces the feelings of heroic struggle against the enemies of the working class and the forces of natural nature. Even if there is nothing intrinsically scientific in the images of conflict engendered by the myth, the myth still has a scientific function in that such a struggle is a spur to creativity and hence to productivity. The myth is not an economic product; it is not as much acted upon by the economy as *it* acts upon the economy. It performs a role analogous to that which Sorel, in the present volume, assigns to heroic Norse and Homeric tales of historic legends of searches for lost treasure. These legends and tales produced a sort of intoxication in the minds of Medieval German metallurgists; they thereby encouraged the industry which was so important to the prosperity and independence of the old German cities.[30]

Sorel only touches on the role of his theory of myth in the *Insegnamenti,* but he does provide helpful explanatory analogies to his conception of myth in his discussions of religion. He suggests that the development of mythical or religious thought can be viewed over time in the form of a bell-shaped curve in which the peak of vitality in the history of a religious belief is found at the mid-point between, on the one hand, an utterly primitive superstition which takes the form of magic, the pseudoscience which attempts to "explain" spiritual and physical totality, and on the other hand, a highly sophisticated liberal religion such as Enlightenment pantheism or Renan's relaxed Christianity, which attempted to justify itself on the terrain of the sciences by giving "rational" explanations of Biblical miracles.

In both extremes we find doctrine enmeshed in the totality of nature— in a sort of theological natural nature. The mythical or heroic period of religion, its highest point of vitality, is the point at which mystical or mythical components predominate over pantheistic naturalistic or pseudoscientific magical aspects. Exponents of this heroic religion are neither unitarians, pantheists, nor witch doctors. Nourished by holy legends and great efforts of resistance, the mystic insists on an "absolute cleavage"[31] between his own beliefs and those of others. At this point, at which "science" has been rejected, religion, ironically, most closely approximates the diremptive efforts of the laboratory scientist or the inventor. Religion comes closest to science when it has most firmly excluded science from its realm, just as science attains its most dynamic point when it excludes religion, theology, and holistic philosophy from its realm. At this point religion (like science) attains its greatest meaning for its professors, its highest explanatory power for the believer, in no small part because of its centrality in the life of the believer who must devote much effort to preserving the integrity of the faith by severing it from other ideas.[32]

In Sorel's view, like mystical religion, myth is separated from social totality and, like religion, solidifies certain ties with the world in the very process of reaffirming itself. In the case of certain religions and certain myths, these ties are with the economic world. The Nordic myths that were so important to the German miners' search for treasure have a counterpart in the faith of the early Protestant sectarians in England and America, whose beliefs strongly encouraged economic virtues even though there was no overt economic dogma in the early stages of the development of these beliefs.[33] Belief intersects with the material world at the point of economic productivity, and its vitality is measured in terms of its economic efficacy. (This is one of the themes of Sorel's *La ruine du monde antique.)*[34]

Sorel makes approximately the same claims for economic beliefs, only in reverse. Just as religion takes on a pecurliarly decadent quality when it attempts to ape scientific thinking and explain everything rationally, economic doctrine becomes moribund when it takes on the allure of a general belief system—when its diremptions have lost their empirical (hence limited) moorings and float free in a rationalistic totality. The particular example of the decay of economic dogma Sorel gives us in this section is the development of the labor theory of value and its particular Marxian applications. Sorel suggests that the labor theory of value had a useful application in early British political economy inspired by observations made in the operations of the British cotton industry. Soon this idea became transformed into a total system and deductions were made from these early observations in much the same way "as ancient physics was derived from the heavens."[35] In Marx's hands, labor is treated as a universal entity which is fairly nearly the same in all times, places, and circumstances. For instance, Marx said that there was little difference between skilled and unskilled labor and that any differences among workers were largely a matter of quantitative determination. To Sorel this universality was unfortunate. By assuming that all industries are equivalent and all workers reduced to a uniform type, the labor theory of value leads us to a homogeneous capitalism in which identical values of labor are exchanged. The result is that labor, which should be the basis of productive virtues, is now reduced to the process of exchange of equivalent values.[36] In Sorel's view, as long as socialism remains beguiled by this circular theory of value exchange, it will never be revolutionary. Instead, Marxism has remained steadfast to what is essentially a bourgeois law of Ricardo; it has merely replaced the fetishism of commodities with that of labor. "Isn't it odd," asks Sorel, "that socialism comes to regularize the order that, according to Marx, would be stabilized spontaneously and in large part in the manner of capitalist production?"[37]

What is worse, in Sorel's eyes, is that if such movements of the economy can be reduced to such simplistic calculations, Marxists are thereby encouraged to calculate other social movements through the same reductions. Marx and Engels "believed that they could (like the physicist) uncover laws as inevitable as that of gravitation."[38] As Marx himself puts it in *Capital,* "capitalistic production begets its own negation with the inevitability that presides over the metamorphosis of nature."[39] Such "scientific" predictions, if taken literally, lead to the utopian expectations of the social democrats who expect the progress of history to deliver the revolution to them. Such expectations not only discourage socialist action, but the vitality of the socialist movement becomes sapped, and the productive virtues which stem from the psychological tension that arises in the course of socialist action are replaced by a rationalistic pseudosocialist science of nature, a social "natural nature."

Elsewhere,[40] Sorel gives a perfect example of the scholasticism of the Marxian theory of value. If labor value can be calculated with certainty, the corollary theory of surplus value wherein the proprietor "steals" labor time from the worker can also be calculated precisely. By the abolition of capitalism, the precise and just compensation for the worker can supposedly be deduced. Authoritarian laws will be passed legislating the "just price" of labor in a harkening back to medieval concepts. Such concepts only lead to idyllic welfare utopias of a socialist land of milk and honey, of a consumers' paradise. In any case, they are not revolutionary, but based on a "medieval nostalgia," of which Marx was guilty at times in Sorel's view.[41] Such a nostalgia was part of the basis of Sorel's critique of the French and German social democratic parties whose scholasticism was in harmony with the current order because of their emphasis on consumption rather than production. The bell-shaped curve which Sorel observed in religious thought has now been replicated in the economic "science" of socialism. The more Marxism emphasizes the importance of the labor theory of value and like formulas, the more similar it becomes to the primitive socialism it professes to criticize. Holistic religious magic, which found its parallel in Fourier's magical visions, has now come full circle to the universalistic science of the human economy.

The question remains as to what is left in the labor theory of value that has a valid place in economic explanation. Is it possible to make a diremption from the labor theory which rejuvenates its scientific vitality and in which it intersects with the heroic myths? Sorel analyzes the positive aspects of the theory of the labor contract which "abolishes all bonds between the employer and the employee: after the presentation of his labor merchandise . . . the worker is in the same position vis-à-vis the master as a grocer is in regard to the customer who comes to buy coffee."[42] A strictly business relationship abolishes all social solidarity; employer and employee are mere buyers and sellers. Objectively, they can pursue entirely opposite political goals and organize for the struggle against one another, and this is all to the good in Sorel's view.

What is interesting about this diremption is that it relies on legal as well as economic thought. Such a market arrangement can come about only when it is accompanied by a transformation in legal arrangements. At this point Sorel sees economic theory dovetailing with "outside" (or mythical) influences that give a theory the same vitality that "outside" (poetic) inspiration gives the process of science. Sorel concludes the first part of this book by stating that the only things the proletarians can know are "the principles of juridical rules that the victorious class will impose on society after its victory."[43] In such considerations, Marxism makes an economico-juridical diremption: "It knows only the worker and takes him as he has been conditioned by the historical conditions of capitalism."[44] This is the least metaphysical and most scientific aspect of labor theory.

But by itself, this theory is no more able to produce working-class action than scientific theory can of itself generate further scientific advancement. Neither the spirit of class struggle nor the struggle against nature can be derived solely from science because, in themselves, neither of these struggles is purely scientific. Both must be inspired by a poetry. Socialism, as the organization of revolt, must be guided by a myth which "expresses with perfect clarity the principle of the separation of classes, a principle which is the whole of socialism."[45] Sorel's readers, as we have noted, were to await an elaboration of the content of the myth in *Reflections on Violence*. In the *Insegnamenti* Sorel is content to argue that both mythical and economic (as well as scientific) thought become most efficacious when they embody the spirit of separation. Myth and science—especially economic science—are inverse bell-curves of each other and achieve their highest dynamism when their peaks intersect.

But how, we might ask, can Sorel criticize the labor theory of value for its conservative implications at the hands of orthodox Marxism, when his own theory of the labor contract is quintessentially bourgeois, a bedrock of economic liberalism? It would appear that, in Sorel's eyes, liberalism and socialism have a good deal in common, and it is precisely this issue that is addressed in the second part of the *Insegnamenti*.

In Part II, Sorel deals with the parallels between socialism and liberal capitalism, pointing out that they have as much in common as they have differences, and that it is this very commonality which, ironically, sustains their separation from each other, both morally and intellectually when expressed in their dynamic forms. But commonality is also found in the degenerative forms of the two ideologies.

This section starts off with a comparison of two types of degenerative social thought, socialist utopias—especially Fourier's—and "bourgeois" democratic theories—Rousseau's in particular. Sorel maintains that there are strong resemblances between these two categories of thought which, if taken in certain ways, have particularly onerous social consequences. In Sorel's view, both sets of theories rely heavily on the notion of mathematical averages which, sometimes against the will of the inventors of these theories, bolsters state authoritarianism and arbitrary power. This authoritarianism in turn runs contrary to the productive virtues.

Sorel takes the thought of Charles Fourier as his archetypal utopian socialist. Fourier, relying on probability theory, allows passions and instincts free rein, regulating his utopian communities (or phalanxes) in such a way "as to obtain average results which translate precisely into natural laws. . . . A result will be obtained that will become independent of circumstances, and the entire society will have only to reproduce what was once produced on a small scale."[46] The uniformity of the world arises from "passional equilibriums" roughly analogous to those produced in free market theory.

In Sorel's opinion, Rousseau too was convinced by the importance of mathematical averages, which gave his theory of the general will a market orientation. In Rousseau the fatality of market relationships is transposed into the assembly in which the average opinion represents truth. Generalizing on the model of the almost completely mobile Swiss craftsman who, without roots, is able to move from job to job, Rousseau idealized *homo economicus* in such a way that "social atoms" would be obtained. The result would be a democratic government in which citizens, having had "no communication among themselves, the general will shall always result from the greater number of little differences, and their deliberations will always be good." Here, in Sorel's words, "the assembly produces reason as a prairie produces hay."[47]

In the case of both Fourier and Rousseau, we have instances of a breakdown of diremptions whose historico-empirical origins have been obscured. As a consequence of this obscuring process, economic theories (diremptions) are inappropriately applied to political phenomena. The result is that what starts out as a random multiplicity of wills and passions terminates in a passion for unity that can only be satisfied by state authoritarianism.[48] In Fourier we find a false analogy between passions and commodities. Fourier has blotted out the fact that his notion of mathematical averaging has its origins in the market, and has thus taken his passional equilibriums as an absolute mathematical truth. More importantly, he has ignored the fact that the inspiration for his own laxist moral system is found in the loose morality of the Napoleonic era and translates politically into the Napoleonic desire for a universal monarchy.

In Rousseau's case we find a political doctrine which cannot be directly translated from economic theory without grave dislocations. Assemblies are not markets; they possess political powers. The mathematical averages of the general will are not used by Rousseau as justifications for free, individual market choices, but rather for the suppression of the particular will by the city. Sorel argues that no general will is possible. In his view, no assembly can live up to Rousseau's maxim that, in expressing the general will, members of the assembly can have no communication among themselves. Rousseau has forgotten that the market orientation of *homo economicus* demands bargaining, and this form of communication is lacking in his ideal assembly. Bargaining on votes would result in the will of all, i.e., the sum of particular wills, and not the general will.

Sorel goes further than merely rejecting Rousseau's democratic theory, for he thinks that even if we reject the adequacy of Rousseau's argument and admit bargaining into the legislative process, in the manner of the *Federalist* or of American liberal pluralist theories, the transposition of market theory to the legislature fails. Not only do "pure" markets ignore legislation, but legislators all too readily ignore market conditions when power is connected to their own interests. Bargaining in assemblies means logrolling and influence peddling; tariff legislation and other restrictions come all too readily into being; the "free market" of legislative bargaining is thus a self-negating process. In Sorel's view, most legislators regard the prosperity of a group as depending on compromises with other groups to obtain a parliamentary majority. But when this majority is obtained, it can ruin any group which stands in its way and "annihilate a cumbersome competitor who is too weak to make the hungry wolves in parliament listen to reason."[49] Such a result, Sorel realized, was utterly contrary to Rousseau's idea, especially if it takes place in the representative assemblies that Rousseau scorned. Sorel's critique of legislative bargaining as an activity in which "both the revolutionary and the juridical spirit are extinguished at the same time" is covertly imitative of Rousseau. In any case, Sorel's critique of Rousseau and Fourier ranges far beyond the two thinkers and extends implicitly to a critique of Madison and of most liberal and democratic theory.

It would be a mistake to assume that Sorel is content with a criticism of the decadent moments of liberal democratic and socialist theories. Perhaps the most interesting aspects of part II consist in the parallels he draws between the two theories in their moments of greatest vitality. Here Sorel presents the dynamic aspects of socialism and liberalism not only as mirror images of their decadent counterparts, but as having strong similarities with each other.

The first similarity between the two schools is that they both attain their highest and most powerful moment when they do not extend their economic theories beyond their proper limits, that is, when their diremptions maintain their historical functions. Liberal theory was at its most triumphant stage when the idea of the free market was limited to the market and did not extend to analogies found in the political realm. "Commerce became quite powerful and capable when, and only when, nobody could see any longer what interest the state had in intervening to control it."[50] The idea of unity that had so transfixed Rousseau was now replaced by a division between economics and what Sorel scornfully called the magical power of the state. The state's old function as the great protector of industry was abandoned.[51]

Sorel interprets Marxism as possessing a general antistatist view similar to that of liberal, laissez-faire capitalism (or Manchesterism). This antistatist component of Marxism makes it, in contradistinction to socialist utopianism, the most virile socialist theory. In support of this view, Sorel points to Engels's assertion of the ultimate powerlessness of the state in the face of economic forces. If the state attempted to resist autonomous economic forces, in Engels's view, it would be destroyed; the state could only accelerate or retard development. Sorel was aware that Marx and Engels were not anarchists. But he insists that the idea of economic fatality was a far more important element in Marx's theory than was state action. For both Marxism and Manchesterism, "the combination of many events produces fatality of movement." Under such conditions, "it is possible to assign any cause to the same fact, and it is really a chance phenomenon; instead, the totality is so well determined that if anybody pretended to oppose the movement he would invariably be defeated."[52] In sum, the power of the economic theories of both capitalism and socialism lay in self-foreclosing their extension beyond economics, a self-imposed diremption.

A major consequence of the idea of economic inevitability in both capitalism and socialism is that both liberal capitalism and Marxism possess a view of historical development that foresees great sacrifice from their respective client classes. This sacrifice requires an ethic of struggle which is highly productive in the long run. Regarding liberal capitalism, Sorel argues that proprietors of most establishments had to change machinery or even abandon old enterprises altogether. Laissez-faire economics had the effect of imposing large fines on recalcitrant industries. Timidity was punished; boldness and innovation in the wrong direction could be equally disastrous. In regard to socialism, Marxist thought excuses the cruelest oppression in both past and present societies: slavery exploitation and despotism are necessary historical prerequisites to the development of capital, and capitalism is progressive.

The philosophy of struggle in both capitalism and Marxism is coupled with the view that events will develop "progressively." Free traders believe that their system will have the effect of satisfying every interest as products improve and prices become more reasonable. Similarly, for Marxists, the belief that the degradation of the working class under capitalism lays the ground for its future elevation is, Sorel argues, virtually identical to Manchesterism. To be sure, "the theoreticians of capitalism do not justify their judgments on the basis of the emancipation of the future proletariat, but this is the only difference."[53] In every other way, both theories are optimistic; both are certain that their cause will triumph. In Sorel's eyes, when this progressivism strayed from the economic realm into politics and other areas, this "certainty" degenerated into the "illusions of progress." But in its proper diremption, such a certainty has powerful psychological effects for economic practitioners—whether they be capitalists or socialists in their workshops.

Finally, both Marxism and Manchesterism regard political and historical developments as being "only a series of developments in the form of labor."[54] We have already mentioned that the idea of the labor contract is a juridical device accepted by both schools. Here we need only note Sorel's stress on the freedom the worker gains under such a system, in which the worker who has no ties to the master once his work has been performed thereby gains free labor time; conversely, the capitalist master is absolved of any paternalistic social duties to fulfill. Here we have the "perfect separation of classes through the encouragement of free labor time."

True to his own philosophy of science, Sorel insists that the self-limitation of diremption requires more than institutions, more than social "laboratory controls." For workers or capitalists to continue to rely only on the market without demanding state assistance requires extraordinary virtues not normally found among subject populations. Without the right character in the population, the free and fatalistic institutions of liberal capitalism as well as the factories run by free labor are doomed to failure.

Sorel is also aware that there are certain historical preconditions for the operation of these institutions. Free labor and free capital have, by virtue of their diremptive status, distorted the historical totality from which they have emerged. Certainly the development of the working classes is not produced as automatically as Marx believed it would; conversely, capitalist free markets and the advent of prosperity might coincide only accidently. Sorel maintains that government may play a more positive role in the development of the economy than allowed for by the Manchester school or even by Marxists. The presence of social legislation and government interference reveals the highly selective evidence cited by adherents of market fatality in support of their objections to government intervention. Just as liberal capitalism can have good and bad consequences depending on the uses to which it is put and the discipline to which its adherents subject themselves, so government interference in the economy has varying moral consequences according to its applications.

Sorel judges government intervention pragmatically, using the criteria of its effect on character and on the historical conditions under which the character develops. The historical possibilities of virtue constitute the main litmus test for the acceptability of government intervention in the economy, and to demonstrate this point Sorel takes two examples for discussion: tariffs and government legislation restricting the hours of labor (promotion of free labor time). In Sorel's view, protective tariffs can have various effects on a people, depending on their character. There are two types of protectionism: one is suitable for strong peoples, like Americans, who are growing in population and in wealth; the other is suitable for disheartened and lazy peoples with a stable population.

Sorel's other example is legislation that promotes free labor time so that the workers may develop their own autonomous institutions. It still leaves to the capitalists "the burden and profit of directing production for their own self-interest under certain legal conditions; let them leave socialism free to act on the working class, to educate it, and don't presume to 'civilize' it in the bourgeois way!"[55] On the other hand, Sorel observes that English workers use this free time in consumer and leisure activities, especially in sports and betting. Only a small and virile minority of English entrepreneurs has resisted the trend toward "laziness." This trend has increasingly gained sway among the British masses who, dominated by the desire for rest, "lack the power to think in a virile way."[56]

In both examples Sorel bases his evaluation of a people's character on the degree to which they are still willing to undertake struggles against nature and also against other classes, irrespective of the degree of government intervention in the economy. In the concluding portions of this section, Sorel renews his assertions that the index of that willingness is reflected in the degree to which a social group exhibits hostility toward the notion of social solidarity. There is a species of "symbiosis" among the three factors of social vitality, class antagonism, and productivity. As Sorel states it, "everything capitalism does to urge the workers on is a gain for socialism, whatever the opinions of ethical theorists or of the politicians always ready to encourage sloth."[57] Revolutionary socialism cannot have as its purpose the moderation of the progress of capitalism. Further on Sorel quotes Marx as saying: "The evolution of the conditions of existence for a large, strong, concentrated and intelligent class of proletarians comes about at the same rate as the development of the conditions of existence of a middle class correspondingly numerous, rich, concentrated and powerful."[58] In this quote from Marx, Sorel implies that the idea of increasing misery and especially the idea of the ever-diminishing productivity of capitalism contradicts Marx's suggestion that "there are never sufficient productive forces and . . . the capitalist class is never rich or powerful enough."[59]

We are left with the question of how these two opposing classes organize for the struggle. In *Reflections on Violence* Sorel deals with the organization of the working classes, but in the present work he concentrates on the organization of the capitalist class rather than on labor unions, for one obvious and urgent reason: "Capitalists have organized themselves in a methodical way; many people, moreover, estimate that the organization of the capitalists is progressing much more quickly than the organization of workers."[60] One type of organization in particular reflects this organizational superiority above all others: the cartel.

In the third and concluding section of the *Insegnamenti,* entitled "Cartels and Their Ideological Consequences," Sorel raises the same questions about cartels that he had raised about liberalism and socialism. While the first section of the work is devoted to the morally degenerative and regenerative side of socialism, and the second section concentrates on the similarities between socialism and liberalism in their various stages of moral development, the final part focuses on the regenerative and degenerative sides of capitalism and its corresponding ideologies and organizations, especially cartels.

In Sorel's view the cartel typifies a degenerative aspect of capitalist organization which finds a counterpart in the corruption of liberal political institutions. We will recall that in previous sections Sorel had criticized the liberal theory of legislative bargaining. In his view, capitalism, both in its corrupt beginnings and in its degenerative mature stages, is different from virile laissez-faire capitalism. Capitalism has its beginnings in a flaccid, feudal-style "collective seigneury" and it comes round full circle to conclude with an intimacy between cartels and state action. In both extremes of the continuum the power of government is harnessed to crush competitors. In both cases the virtues of laissez-faire capitalism, especially as represented in American and even German business, are being extinguished.

Sorel begins this section by discussing the institutions of the *ancien régime,* whose seigneuries resemble modern cartels in that both have had a species of eminent domain over the economic powers of their subjects, and this domain includes police and taxing powers. Both domains choose representatives to establish internal rules and defend their interests against outside forces. Just as the ancien régime's various estates were in large part cartels which deliberated and bargained on financial interests, so the cartels of modern times resolve their difficulties by sending delegates to mixed commissions, often including representatives of workers' organizations.

On the basis of this comparison between cartels and the ancien régime, Sorel comes out squarely against what we would call "functional representation." This feudalism, replicated in the industrial world, would entail the establishment of "little states": one for coal mines, one for mills, and so forth.[61] In previous sections Sorel objected to extending the diremption of *homo economicus* to the political arena. Now he reverses the argument: any extension of political analogies to the industrial regime will only succeed in corrupting both areas. Thus any form of what would later be called "corporativism" is utterly alien to Sorel's viewpoint—whether in the form of guild socialism, codetermination, or fascism. All these notions seem to share one familiar trait. They resemble modern democratic parliaments which are "not so much political bodies that legislate to realize a national ideal as they are medieval-style diets in which one undertakes diplomatic discussions among plenipotentiaries and which come to establish compromises among various interests."[62] In parliaments, corporate societies, and cartels we find the same blurring of economics and politics which Sorel had described as endemic to representative bodies where logrolling leads to systematic annihilation of uncooperative competitors. In both cases a protectionism is solidified which transforms the state into a "benefactor of all those with no confidence in their personal strength." This system has the effect of producing renewed tendencies toward "social peace, moderation of desires, and respect for weakness" which ultimately regard consensus as the highest social duty.[63]

The emphasis on the need for consensus and for bargaining in parliamentary bodies brings Sorel to an interesting comparison between cartels and political parties. In Sorel's view cartels and political parties are not only functionally dependent on consensus and solidarity, but are invariably based on systems of representation with a hierarchical structure. Here the "admiration of the electors for the elected" arises from a superstitious veneration for the representative. The representative, in turn, legitimizes his position by virtue of his increased familiarity with the "official world." This veneration is a buttress for the ideal of community solidarity.

Not only does Sorel replicate Rousseau's antagonism to representation here, but he anticipates what Roberto Michels would later call "the iron law of oligarchy," which states that even professedly democratic organizations produce leadership cadres that are self-perpetuating and nonresponsible to their constituents.[64] Like Michels, Sorel argues that both cartels and parties coopt the potential leaders of workers' movements. For Sorel these leaders were potential forces for social tension, and the "negation" necessary for social vitality. Once this vitality is sapped by cooptation, according to Sorel, social life degenerates into what Herbert Marcuse would later call "one dimensionality."[65]

Worse still, oligarchic corporativism discourages men of real talent and replaces them with men who possess "political skills." This perverse value system helps to undermine the ideal of production, which gives way to the consumers' ideal of just distribution. Hand in hand with the idea of just distribution is the erroneous notion that the spare time resulting from decreased labor time should be spent in politics. "There is no popular instinct more powerful than that which pushes man into laziness: democracy especially regards man as obliged to occupy his time in politics and has never understood the law of labor."[66]

Implicitly, Sorel appears to be endorsing Aristotle's idea of the best possible democratic regime in which the best material for citizenship is found in the agricultural population. "Being poor, citizens have no leisure and therefore do not attend the assembly, and, not having the necessities of life, they are always at work and do not covet the property of others. Indeed they find their employment pleasanter than the cares of government or office."[67] According to Sorel, the opposite view of citizenship prevails in modern democracies, where the triumph of Kantian ideals is complete and men are no longer seen as means (of production or anything else). Instead we have an "ideology of supreme ends."[68]

Sorel's strong indictment of cartels and corporativism is qualified in much the same way as was his condemnation of protectionism and social legislation in the previous section. With cartels, as with protectionism and social laws, one must take account of the character of the people with whom we are dealing. The spirit of enterprise found in the practices of the great American financiers who organized American trusts has a completely different character from the European outlook. The German cartel is not like the American trust because, unlike the German cartel, the trust is "the result of a life and death struggle."[69] In America, unlike modern Germany, "we are in the presence of a population that has preserved to the highest degree the rural, combative, and dominant characteristics which gave them a certain resemblance to feudal knights."[70] As Sorel noted elsewhere, this feudal warrior type "was pushed to its extreme in the American cowboy . . . admirable in the face of danger, insouciant, intemperate, improvident, and animated with the spirit of liberty."[71] This independent spirit made Americans "the most daring people in existence," who defend their intellectual, moral, and civic independence as surely as they defend their property. Behind the façade of democratic political institutions in America there is an aristocracy, not of birth, but of ability and energy, personified in Carnegie and Roosevelt, warrior types who look upon life as a struggle instead of a pleasure. Here is an "aristocracy of power," not the European "aristocracy of weakness."[72] The character of this aristocracy means in practical terms that even the most "reactionary" and unproductive form of capitalism, usury capitalism, has a unique character when practiced by the great American financiers whose spirit of enterprise is so strong. Sorel does not praise the trusts; he is simply stating that the historical conditions in America are such that trusts do not become a serious impediment to productivity.

The American spirit of enterprise has allowed the trusts to operate independently of the state. The few connections the trusts do have with political forces in the United States are of little consequence because American politicians "are universally regarded as rascals but have the ability not to interfere too much with the progress of business."[73] Economic and political power have sustained a separation in the United States, and this division between economic and political life makes the American economy the most dynamic and vital force in the otherwise decaying, bourgeois world. As Sorel stated in the previous section, this divorce of politics and economics is the greatest contribution of liberal thought. He has "dirempted" the positive aspects of liberalism which emphasize divided or checked power from those involving representative democracy.

The separation of politics from economics also means that liberalism can implicitly sustain a distinction between corruption and decadence.[74] Degeneration signifies the laxity of an entire culture—or a good part of it —while corruption can be confined to a small group of politicians and even, in the American case, function as a device to prevent degeneration of the larger society: corrupt politicians in America limit the extent to which the state can effectively intervene in the larger economy. In this case, the self-restraint of the state does not become a virtue; Sorel has reversed the argument of classical liberalism. Rather than private vices becoming public virtues—the standard moral justification for the free market—in Sorel's view public vices now enhance private virtues.

For Sorel the American experience also helps to confound traditional Marxian theory. The latter distinguishes three types of capitalism: primitive usury, commercial capitalism, and industrial capitalism. While accepting this typology as useful, Sorel points out that they do not succeed one another in serial fashion as some Marxists have argued. He insists that in most modern times there has been a mixture of the three. As his example, Sorel cites American trusts which, despite the advanced nature of the American economy, closely resemble usury capitalism. On the other hand, German cartels are largely marketing agreements and therefore resemble commercial capitalism.

One further element of Sorel's critique of cartels deserves mention. The social democrats of his day often cited cartels as an advanced form of capitalism because they were close in form and substance to state socialism and therefore constituted, in their eyes, a sort of final stage of the capitalist era. In Sorel's view no such interpretation is justified. Here Sorel appears to have reversed the social democratic argument. Rather than linking cartels and the state as forward-looking and progressive, he regards them as backward and unproductive. Once again the union of economics and politics, between state authority and production, can only result in the decadence of both capitalism and socialism. In misconstruing the role of the state, socialism decays, and "the degradation of socialism is everywhere accompanied by moral decadence, at least in our democratic countries."

What is the proper role of the state? There is some irony in Sorel's rejection of politics as an activity. In his complete embrace of *animal laborans,* it would appear that Sorel is totally opposed to the thesis of people like Hannah Arendt who insist on the autonomy of politics as a realm of self-revelation and fulfillment.[75] Yet in insisting that politics remain separate from the economic realm, Sorel appears to be arguing that each realm should reassume the dignity that had been denied it. For Sorel, politics would be an arena for the discussion of "a national ideal" or of "general principles," while economics would emphasize productivity without invading the political realm and transforming it into "national housekeeping," to use Arendt's term.

In other places Sorel, while not an anarchist, seems to scorn political life as such, and this scorn leaves Sorel's political thought shadowy. He argues that the pluralism of political centers of power is a good thing. But since he argues that a diremption such as market pluralism cannot be carried over into the legislative arena without disastrous consequences, the balanced equation that existed in liberalism between the pluralistic view of economics and its corresponding view of politics as bargaining is now abolished in Sorel's hands. So too is Marx's assumption that the state is little more than a handmaiden of ruling-class interests. But then what is left of government? The rather vague notion that politics should be an activity that concerns the discussion of "general principles" or "the national ideal" was not given much refinement by Sorel either in this work or in *Reflections on Violence.* It was not until 1913 and especially 1919 and the publication of *De l'Utilité du pragmatisme* that Sorel elaborated on the role of politics. Before that time, Sorel's implacable hostility to politics is inspired in large part by the traditions of French statism and centralization. In 1913, however, he juxtaposes the reality of sovereign authority in modern Europe to the memory of medieval Germanic kingships in which royalty did not execute tasks directly but remained mere "proprietors" of the crown. Surrounding the monarchies were networks of "true republics, the church, universities, religious orders, and corporations of all kinds."[76]

The authority structure of these "true republics" was based less on persuasion or force than on symbols, myths, and the ordering of groups of activities belonging incontestably to the same type and whose participants followed the opinions of men of experience and possessing "incontestable dignity." Political authority does not exist here as much as "social authority" or rather a complex array of social authorities. Such authorities Sorel calls *cités,* but they are not so much cities as institutions that are themselves highly authoritative and devoid of political power of the state. We find such authorities in science (*cité savante*), art (*cité esthétique*), society (the American business aristocracy which he calls the *cité morale*), and in socialism (the syndicalist carriers of the general strike myth). It is the authority rather than the politics of the cities that Sorel admires, because they scorn the bargaining, the persuasion, or the force of the state and limit their scope to their respective arenas of experience.[77]

That is why it is not only bargaining in the political realm that is unsatisfactory to Sorel, but even in the present volume he goes so far as to criticize it in the realm to which it is properly suited, the economic realm itself. Here as in *Reflections on Violence,* Sorel appears to condemn bargaining even between unions and management, and instead argues for a union movement that remains implacably hostile to having anything to do with the bourgeoisie. Yet Sorel's decentralized vision of socialist labor unions in the new society gave way to the reality of a labor movement with the same oligarchic tendencies and the same proclivity for bargaining he had condemned in political parties. These tendencies were already apparent to Sorel and are discussed in the last section of this work. Sorel's pragmatic myth of the general strike was already in the process of giving way to an even more pragmatic strategy of striking for more improved "consumer" benefits. In any case, Sorel's adherence to a labor movement as the motive force for a secular second-coming can only bring smiles today.

How valid is Sorel's critique of social unity in regard to its supposed undermining of productive virtues? Sorel's attack on social unity, whether of democracy, guild socialism, or (in the final section) any corporate state notions should give the lie to those who see in his thought a prelude to "fascist notions." Sorel's view of corporatism and of the state, and of social cohesion and community is generally the antithesis of fascism and owes much to liberalism. But there is no denying the powerful productive forces that social unity, in some form or another, has unleashed, especially in the modified corporatism of Japan or the profit-sharing and codetermination plans of West Germany and Sweden. The relatively unsolidaristic liberalism of the United States is appearing increasingly unproductive in comparison with these highly cohesive societies.

On the other hand, social insolidarity represents a stage in the development of a group whose conscious revolt against the existing order sustained by revolutionary myths has positive moral consequences for its adherents as is evidenced by the early stages of the Black Muslim sect in the United States. Sorel is useful to us today in the examination of sects such as the Muslims in seeing how their activities correspond to his sociology of virtue, the social and ideological bases that produce great transformations in a people or civilization. Sorel's concern with the subject of virtue has not been a prominent interest of academicians over the years, except perhaps in Nietzsche studies, and only recently have we seen a revival of interest in it on the part of philosophers with social science concerns.[78]

There is still another reason for an interest in Sorel, and that lies in the realm of social science methods. Sorel's method of diremption is a forceful supplement to Weber's ideal types, and as such provides a helpful guide to the evaluation of both social beliefs and movements. It is with these ideas in mind that the present translation is offered to the public.

Since the original manuscript of this work has been lost, the present translation was made from the original Italian publication. It thus entails the usual risks involved in any translation only in quantum degrees. These risks have been modified by the Italian language's common ties with French, and by the fact that Sorel himself approved the Italian version. In addition, I have made every attempt to check quoted sources—especially French sources—in their original form. Nearly all French sources have been translated from the original as has Sorel's "Conclusion," which, alone, is available in French. In cases where an English translation of a quoted work is available, I have quoted directly from it; in the case of the works of Marx and Engels, I have taken the liberty of inserting an English edition and page numbers in place of Sorel's own sources when possible.

I wish to thank Fernanda Douglas, Danielle Salti, Teresa Carioti, and, as always, Charlotte Stanley for their invaluable editing and advice.

Notes

1. Both *Réflexions sur la violence* and *Les Illusions du progrès* were originally published in the syndicalist journal *Mouvement Socialiste* in 1906 and in book form in 1908 by the publisher Marcel Rivière. Excerpts from both works are translated in John L. Stanley (ed.), *From Georges Sorel* (New York: Oxford University Press, 1976).
2. Georges Sorel, *Le Procès de Socrate* (Paris: Alcan, 1889).

3. See John L. Stanley, *The Sociology of Virtue: The Political and Social Theories of Georges Sorel* (Berkeley, Los Angeles, and London: University of California Press, 1981).
4. Letter to Benedetto Croce, 6 May 1907, *Critica*, 26 (20 March 1928): 100.
5. Georges Sorel, "Etude sur Vico," *Devenir Social* (December 1896): 1020.
6. Jean Variot (ed.), *Propos de Georges Sorel* (Paris: Gallimard, 1935). Statement of 14 November 1908.
7. Edouard Dolléans, "Le Visage de Georges Sorel," *Revue d'Histoire Economique et Sociale* 26 (no. 2, 1947): 106–107. Citing letter of 13 October 1912.
8. *From Georges Sorel*, p. 210.
9. William James, *Varieties of Religious Experience* (New York: Mentor, 1958), pp. 22–23.
10. Sorel, "Etude sur Vico" (October 1896):794–95 (November):916, 919.
11. Georges Sorel, *De l'Utilité du pragmatisme* (Paris: Rivière, 1919), p. 4 and note.
12. *Oxford English Dictionary,* Vol. 3, p. 394. The verb *dirempt,* first used in English in 1561, was derived from the Latin *diremere,* to separate or divide.
13. *From Georges Sorel*, p. 228, citing *Reflections on Violence,* p.259.
14. *From Georges Sorel*, pp. 235, 231.
15. Ibid, pp. 239, 344, n. 52.
16. *Social Foundations of Contemporary Economics,* p. 81.
17. Sorel deals with this question in "La préoccupation métaphysique des physiciens modernes," *Cahiers de Quinzaine* (16th *Cahier,* 8th series, 1901). This work was largely incorporated into chapter 4 of *De l'Utilité du pragmatisme* under the title "L'expérience dans la physique moderne."
18. "La science et la morale," in *Questions de Morale* (Paris: Alcan, 1900), p. 7.
19. Ibid., p. 15 (Sorel's italics).
20. Ibid., p. 7.
21. Ibid., p. 2.
22. *From Georges Sorel*, p. 369, n. 33.
23. *Social Foundations,* pp. 53, 56.
24. Georges Sorel, "Vues sur les problèmes de la philosophie," *Revue de Métaphysique et de Morale* 18 (December 1910):609.
25. Georges Sorel, review of Fouillée, *Eléments sociologiques de la morale* in *Revue générale de bibliographie* (December 1905):489; *From Georges Sorel,* p. 216.
26. *Social Foundations,* p. 54.
27. Ibid., p. 169.
28. Ibid., p. 108.
29. Ibid., p. 107.
30. Ibid., pp. 106, 313.
31. See Sorel, *Reflections on Violence,* p. 184; idem, *Le Système historique de Renan,* passim.
32. See Georges Sorel, *La ruine du monde antique* (Paris: Rivière, 3rd ed., 1933), for an analysis of early Christianity in this regard.
33. *Reflections,* p. 125n; *From Georges Sorel,* p. 335, n.7.
34. Sorel, *La ruine du monde antique,* pp. 16–17.
35. *Social Foundations,* p. 150.

36. Ibid., pp. 151-55.
37. Ibid., p. 155.
38. Ibid., p. 166.
39. Ibid., p. 168. Cf. Marx, *Capital* (New York: Modern Library, n.d.), p. 837.
40. See *From Georges Sorel,* pp. 152–53; Sorel, "Sur la Théorie marxiste de la valeur," *Journal des Economistes* (May 1897):215.
41. Georges Sorel, *Lettres à Paul Delesalle,* ed. André Prudhommeaux (Paris: Grasset, 1947). Letter of 9 May 1918, p. 139.
42. Sorel presents this view of the labor contract in *Social Foundations,* pt. II, ch. 8, p. 234.
43. *Social Foundations,* p. 167.
44. Ibid., p. 168.
45. Ibid., pp. 170-71.
46. Ibid., p. 186.
47. Ibid., p. 70.
48. Ibid., p. 184.
49. Ibid., p. 214.
50. Ibid., p. 205.
51. Ibid.
52. Ibid., pp. 199-200.
53. Ibid., p. 201.
54. Ibid., p. 200.
55. Ibid., p. 216.
56. Ibid., p. 217.
57. Ibid., p. 237.
58. Ibid., p. 289. Cf. Karl Marx, *Revolution and Counter-Revolution of Germany in 1848* (Chicago: Charles Kerr, n.d.), p. 22.
59. *Social Foundations,* p. 289.
60. Ibid., p. 281.
61. Ibid., p. 265.
62. Ibid., p. 267.
63. Ibid., p. 297.
64. Roberto Michels, *Political Parties,* trans. Eden and Cedar Paul (Glencoe: Free Press, 1958).
65. Herbert Marcuse, *One Dimensional Man* (Boston: Beacon, 1964).
66. *Social Foundations,* p. 292.
67. Aristotle, *Politics,* 1318 a 38—b 20.
68. *Social Foundations,* pp. 293, 296.
69. Ibid., p. 310, citing De Rousiers, *Les Syndicats industriels,* p. 125.
70. Ibid.
71. Georges Sorel, review of Paul de Rousiers, *La Vie américaine: ranches, ferms, et usines, Revue Internationale de Sociologie* (October 1899):744-45.
72. *From Georges Sorel,* pp. 213-14; *Social Foundations,* pp. 311-12.
73. *Social Foundations,* p. 289.
74. I am indebted to Richard Vernon for this observation.
75. See Hannah Arendt, *The Human Condition* (Chicago: University of Chicago Press, 1958).
76. Georges Sorel, "Germanismo e storicismo di Ernesto Renan," *Critica* 29 (March-November 1931), citing Renan, *Questions Contemporaines* (Paris: Levy, 1868), p. 15.

77. Sorel, *De l'Utilité du pragmatisme,* ch. 2; *From Georges Sorel,* pp. 257–83.
78. Alasdair MacIntyre, *After Virtue* (Notre Dame, Ind.: University of Notre Dame Press, 1979).

AUTHOR'S PREFACE

I have previously published under the title *Saggi di critica del Marxismo* a series of studies in which I examined the best-known theories from among those that go under the name of orthodox Marxism as constituted by the men who claim to have the right to speak in Marx's name. I did not confine myself to criticizing what to me seems contrary, either to observed and known reality or to the thought of Marx, but more than once had to explain my views on capitalism. Professor Vittorio Racca, who generously spent his time with this publication, has asked me to complement it by setting forth my observations on contemporary socialism and wanted to be in charge of translating this second work.

I have taken as the subject of my studies the transformation of social ideas from the end of the eighteenth century until our time; I have tried to conduct this investigation using as much as possible the principles of historical materialism. I believe this work will not be useless for showing what resources can be provided by Marx's methods and what must ordinarily be added to purely economic explanations to arrive at a complete knowledge of history.

At present many new problems have been posed and socialism is torn in several directions. I do not wish to enter into the discussions that have been undertaken on this subject, but it seemed useful to call attention in the "Introduction" to many questions that are very important for understanding contemporary socialism: the introduction of the notion of private property in partial collectivism, the theory of revolution, and the relationship between democracy and socialism.

Ten years of participation in parliamentary life have transformed French socialism. After the 1902 elections, it is nothing more than a noisy faction of the government majority; its representatives are not the least ardent among those politicians who are most capable of swindling and deceiving the ingenuous electorate. It was believed that the 1904 Amsterdam Congress of the International Workingmens' Association would bring socialism back to the true path, but after long and vehement speeches, the opposite result was produced. Two resolutions were voted: one, obscure and full of contradictions, was against the deviations and compromises blamed on Jaurès's friends; the other, very clearly worded, recognized that the existing conflicts between them and their adversaries are not of such a nature as to prevent unification. This result was applauded by the so-called revolutionary socialists as a triumph—it condemned their previous schism. Besides, it seems that they were only too glad to unite, as it seemed hard for them to remain outside of the government stable where there is such good hay!

After these international assizes, Jaurès does not show himself very pressed to unite with his adversaries. At Bourges, the General Confederation of Labor convened a Congress of French Workers' Organizations, and Jaurès hoped that his friends would obtain the majority of delegates, which would have allowed him to present himself as the true representative of the French proletariat. Despite the combined efforts of the Ministry of Commerce and of the Musée Social to create a trend favorable to Jaurès, he was defeated. Then he deigned to listen to the proposals for unification, knowing full well that in politics the most solemn declarations never oblige anyone except imbeciles. And then why not unite, given that the deputies of the two socialist groups are equally ministerial? There is perhaps, in the entire French Chamber of Deputies, no man more able than the Blanquist Sembat, for turning aside a possibly embarrassing question for the government. In more than one district the self-proclaimed revolutionary candidate has the support of the administrative authorities who prefer to have to deal with a rather frivolous chatterbox (such as Dejeante or Coutant) than with a representative of the Center-Right.[1]

The two socialist groups have an excellent reason to unite: they lose more and more influence on organized labor every day; they have therefore decided to recapture this influence by gaining power over the General Confederation of Labor. Divided they can do nothing; united perhaps they will succeed.

It would be a complete waste of time to follow all the developments of socialist politicians; their actions no longer belong to the history of ideas, and such slight accidents cannot possibly give rise to discussions that would interest anybody six months after they happened. What will emerge from all this confusion? This would be very imprudent to prophesy. Nevertheless it is possible to imagine that things could happen in the opposite way from what Jaurès expects; because the day on which events will have forced the workers who remained revolutionary—and not just in words—to organize separately from the rest of society, socialism will be able to take on a new life. It is still too early to discern which events in the last few years have historical importance, and so there is no interest in discussing them. On the other hand, the ideas that I would be tempted to present would have an excessively subjective nature;

we must stand a bit removed from events to be able to write history. Nevertheless, I will allow myself to formulate several opinions on the paths socialists could adopt to avoid the consequences of degeneration which harm the socialist movement today; but I will do this to illustrate my exposition rather than with the expectation that this advice should be followed.

Friends have chided me for having published my earlier book in Italy; I believe it is convenient to continue in this procedure and to submit to Italian philosophers and jurists a book that has been written to be read by men who are used to reflecting on problems of the kind discussed herein. In France the moment is not propitious for presenting scholarly research on socialism. Socialism in France is presently in full decline; no one cares for doctrines; only politics interests the country. Those of our politicians who belong to the Socialist Party have a ferocious hatred for anyone who thinks, and juridical ideas are detestable to them.

We must not let ourselves be deceived by Jaurès's clamorous invocations to justice, which he makes from time to time out of political necessity. There are few men less concerned with the development of juridical ideas than Jaurès; he is too much dominated by the idea of success, and he sacrifices everything to the agreements that ought to make him triumph. To affect the mass of the people, it is useful to give the appearance of a prophet who speaks in the name of a higher power. Gambetta invented the "imminent justice" which should ensure France's revenge on Germany, but this justice is virtually identical to that of which Jaurès speaks—it is indifferent to everything that the world calls "law." Ever since socialist leaders have acceded to power they have recognized all sorts of virtue in government force. The violently anti-clerical policies to which they have abandoned themselves completely, have allowed us to see how their minds are closed to any idea of law. They appeal to party legislation capable of crushing the minority, and think that justice does not exist for the vanquished.

It is not to politicians of this kind, estranged from all philosophical ideas, that I present my studies. I hope that in the land of Vico, I will find more competent judges.[2]

Notes

1. The Mouvement Socialiste of 15 November 1904 contains an article entitled "Revolutionary Ministerialism," but the author tells only a hundredth part of what he knows. One can assert that the profession of revolutionizing gives great freedom to those who adopt it; thus Jaurès would never dare take part in a committee on which were found the names of the Abbé Lemire, Count A. de Mun, or Jay, mixed with those of the Blanquists Groussier and Vail-

lant: I refer to the Board of Directors of the French National Association for the Legal Protection of Workers. This association was founded by the Musée Social and by the flower of the Social-Christians.

2. As the reader will observe, I have not been able to avoid all repetitions between this book and the one I published in 1904 under the title *Introduction à l'économie moderne;* but since the latter will never be translated into Italian such an inconvenience will not be very severe. There are several notable differences between my present theories and those expounded in previous publications; but although I use past articles, I still hope to learn and benefit from experience.

Boulogne sur Seine, March 1905

INTRODUCTION

CHAPTER ONE

By entitling this book *Social Teachings of the Economy,* I used the word *social* in the sense that in my opinion[1] Marx gave it in writing the preface to the *Critique of Political Economy.* I intend to discuss the ideas that developed in the public mind, that is, in strict relation to the "life of the law," as it exists in legislatures, in universities, and in the books of legal reformers—but emanating from the scientific principles of the law differently from those discussions formed in the system where jurisprudence is developed, discussions that are incapable of making the law.

We cannot overemphasize, in socialist theory, the importance of the great difference between the *legal movement* and the systems of *existing laws.* The former has often been defined by means of a language suitable only for the latter; this has been the origin of many sophisms. Perhaps it has claimed still more often to overthrow the order in which the phenomena are really presented, and the legal movement is made to depend on the growth of a ready-made law.

I try not to present a philosophy of law here; and still less to expound a system of principles from which one might deduce facts. I investigate how the economy acts on social ideas and the explanations it provides for understanding the influence it has exercised on the ideas of social reformers. I begin from a point of view almost diametrically opposed to that of the old socialists who had to *demonstrate* their theories. I propose to *explain their theories,* to show why they existed and why they have declined.

The old socialists had proposed to their contemporaries a perfect society, constructed according to a preestablished plan and realizing completely the conceptions they had formulated on human perfection. They claimed knowledge of what is suitable for the improvement of mankind, the purpose of life in the world, and the best means to use in a realization of our terrestrial destiny. At first their inventions (since they were inventors) only existed in a more or less profound obscurity; their *messianism* was presaged, in a more or less vague way, by several superior souls who had *symbolized* in their lives and teachings some of the truths that the modern genius had, thanks to them, finally succeeded in formulating. In every utopia there was some memory of Christianity,

41

because, as in Christianity, the utopia was believed to accomplish what humanity had ardently sought over the centuries.

We find something of this unique idea in Marx[2]—everything produced before the social revolution whose imminent appearance he expected belongs to "prehistory." But at least Marx does not separate the course of the centuries like a Messiah; the division would be formed from a phenomenon produced fatally from the "blind progress of the economy," from a kind of economic convergence over which the philosophical spirit can have no effect. In Marx the ideas of development, of preparation, of the sufficiency of objective forces, are otherwise much clearer than those of his predecessors; but it was impossible for him to avoid the general influences that dominated the men of his time. Like them, Marx imagined that the world had set out to know finally the true nature of man, that it would no longer be determined by the laws which eschew its will, that reason would find its expression in a regenerated humanity. All this belongs to that part of Marxism that must be rejected, having been formed only from the remains of the old utopianism.

The utopians searched for the best means of presenting their "inventions" to the public, in order to make them acceptable; they knew that the public mistrusts anything new. They wanted to prove that their plans were much easier to realize whatever was said to the contrary. To attain this purpose, they did not have better procedures than those generally employed: to describe, in great detail, the life that would be led in the utopia, and to demonstrate with a sort of "ideal experimentation" that their projects constituted a structure that was logically, psychologically, and aesthetically irreproachable. Nothing was left to chance; there was an answer for every objection. The reader became aware that he might live in such a society; and he experienced a feeling of pleasure at the idea of transforming present conditions with whatever the inventor proposed. No one would deny that we have here conjurors of a prodigious ability, and that they have produced works much more seductive than those of the economists or Marxists. Their literary ability ought to make us feel that they are deceiving us.

The utopian novel constitutes the best means of description and it is most convincing. Every reader is, at every moment, asked to compare what exists with what is promised; he lives the life of the novel's hero and is judge of the psychological possibility or impossibility of the solution. There is, however, in this procedure a fundamental vice that ought to be distrusted by every scientifically minded person: the attractive aspects are so well ordered that they give the impression of a theatrical scene in which every actor occupies a position and makes prefigured gestures determined by the director. But experience teaches us that most men are not very sensitive to some particular defect of verisimilitude that so strongly impressed people accustomed to observing but which rarely concerns literary men. On the other hand—would art be possible if we had such a mistrust of convention? That is why so many educated people will always be seduced by the utopian novels that seem absurd to practical men.

The minutia of the old accounts seem puerile sometimes, because we almost always forget that the "inventors" did not ever have around them anything but the smallest number of disciples, and that these were literati who needed diversion. It is thus rather difficult to understand why they did not limit themselves to some general indications of the future life, without composing voluminous works that could not have interested the general public. Their procedures nowadays seem so bizarre that, for a long time, the Marxists have taken it as a rule not to give any explanations on the operations of the new society. As long as socialism was directed solely to the people in laboratories, to organize them in view of the class struggle, it had no need to produce utopian novels. Socialism is now returning to these novels, since it is seeking, as in the past, the cooperation of the upper classes.

The inventors of the utopias relied on the conversion of men with force at their disposal (as had the converted princes of the sixteenth-century Reformation); or on the conversion of people who dominate public opinion and who are capable of gaining the support of powerful figures; or still on the effect of imitation that is sometimes stronger than inhibition in the world, and that could have vulgarized the given example of some colony. The number of disciples was therefore less important than the quality.

The men who needed to be convinced were in a situation rather like the princes of the sixteenth century; they were cultivated, able to reason about good and evil, the beautiful and the ugly, the just and the unjust; but their culture was that of the university—brilliant and literary. They would have been able to give some aid to legislators, and, as needed, also to vote laws; but they were neither philosophers, nor lawyers, nor historians. The argument the utopians had to employ derived from this situation; it would have been bad procedure to discourse in the name of juridical science; this would not have interested anyone unacquainted with this science, and the thesis presented in this way would have been too easily refuted by professional lawyers. This difficulty was avoided and discussed in the name of justice without, however, entering into the field of legal science. It was thus possible to hope to persuade powerful men to become interested in a reform of institutions. Instead of discussing current law in a profound way, they only touched on it; they wanted to prove that the law was incomplete, that it left too much room for violation and that it would be necessary to complete and purify it at the same time, by introducing into it new principles which had been totally neglected by legislation until then.

Presenting socialism as an *addition* rather than a *suppression* made criticism by men of science and experimentation very difficult. These men are often able to prove with much evidence that there are precise disadvantages in suppressing an institution or a rule; but it is generally impossible to know what an addition to the law will produce. It is because of this that so many formulas destined to define the redistribution of wealth were proposed—formulas that some illustrious contemporary writers have tried to reattach to three fundamental principles:[3] the right to life, the right to labor, and the right to the integral product of one's labor. This would complete the edifice of the rights of man; by combining political and economic rights a society would be organized that is completely logical and harmonious and hence conceived as perfectly juridical as our weak minds can imagine.

There is much more than what I indicate in the works of the old utopians; very frequently they seem not to take into account the prudence and tactical skill I have illustrated. But over time, the relative importance of theories is not well assessed and they are often granted a greater importance when appearing to be the most absolute—when historically they were secondary. In discussing William Thompson, Antonio Menger observes[4] that sometimes the most radical critiques of modern society are able to join forces with prudent reform proposals.

Our ancestors were not impressed by affirmations that seem very paradoxical today; very often what decides men to adopt a party is a secondary aspect of the proposed theory. How many Protestants are converted to Catholicism through reasons that the theologian sees as fundamental? What decides these converts is an emotion experienced in the presence of death, or the disgust provoked by the skeptical attitude of ministers of God; or the idea that God ought to have a single church and that the true church is that which has the most unity, etc. These are secondary reasons, but they prevail over theological ones: each one puts the center of Catholicism where it is most convenient. The same was true for the views on certain moral reforms or practical economic matters that most often made for the success of certain of the old socialist schools.

The great emotion produced by the first memoir of Proudhon on property demonstrates that until then people were not too worried by theses that to contemporary authors appear destructive of property. On this point we have the testimony of Marx who, in *The Holy Family*, written some years later, proclaimed that Proudhon had made a rigorous critique of property *for the first time.* But precisely because he centered the discussion on the citadel of bourgeois law, Proudhon will remain a solitary figure; to his contemporaries he often had the reputation of trying to attract attention by means of striking paradoxes,[5] and the Fourierists held against him the defense of the "principle of property." He took a very different path from that of the other socialists: he did not try to overcome the bourgeoisie by some utopia; little success is obtained under these conditions. He had no school, and the rigor of authority was raised against him. The first memoir was not tried through the intervention of Professor Blanqui; but in 1842 the *Avertissement aux propriétaires* (in which Fourierism was so violently attacked) was submitted to the Court of Assizes.

This first period of socialism ended on the day in which it was no longer a question of revealing to the world a sociological "invention," but of providing the working class with a *theory of imminent revolution,* and with the school of Marx and Engels this new point of view was created. I do not believe this school had the preponderant influence that is generally attributed to it; but it is certain that it made the notion of *fatality* penetrate socialist thought to eliminate (or at least to provisionally relegate to a secondary level) the idea of spreading "ingenious inventions."

In this case, there is no more need to convince the powerful, no more need to propose a humanist ethic superior to the current morality, while still full of survivals of violent cases, no more need to ask if a new state of things is really desirable—since the revolution is inevitable and imminent. But if the social upheaval cannot be avoided, it is not, on the other hand, possible to affirm what will happen.

In all previous revolutions we saw minorities organized in factions, seizing power and using the force of the state for their own greatest benefit. This can be prevented today, and it is the study of the proper means of combatting the tyranny of factions that should draw the attention of socialists. Against these factions it becomes possible to oppose an organized proletariat, that will be able to take all possible alternatives in the events in which it intervenes for its own sake. If an invention is needed, it is that of a proletarian tactic capable of permitting the whole working class to make a triumphant irruption in the political future, to destroy all traditional organizations which would serve the factions in domination, and to substitute new emancipatory mechanisms issuing from the economic conditions of their own existence.

The ideas of Marx and Engels have never been very clear on the mode of this transformation; they have changed according to circumstances.[6]

In 1850 the two friends admitted that what was needed was a long period of civil war, during which the proletariat would prepare itself to take definitive direction of society. Circumstances that no one could have predicted have allowed the Socialist parties to exert a noticeable influence on the politics of several European powers and undertake the struggles that might have been considered an attenuation of the great social wars of which Marx and Engels spoke in 1850.[7]

With great sagacity, Ernest Renan[8] notes that one never knows what he has built. The experience of revolutions teaches us that the best plans are always sacrificed to the convenience of the moment; the revolutionaries rarely conserved much of their early programs when they took power. The day on which the idea of a long struggle to be endured became preponderant, it was evident that it would be useless to discuss the best political principles for application in the future of the world. It can still happen that we abandon every expectation of a radical transformation and remain content with reforms. But if the revolutionary spirit is conserved, a single thesis dominates the writings of the school: the new institutions will emerge from the organizations that the proletariat will have made in view of the social wars. Revolutionary syndicalism will advance to the workshop functioning without bosses; its new legal order will only be composed when the *class that embodies the destinies of the future* becomes most capable of governing itself in an independent way, of understanding its own activity and of administering production.

The law will not be produced through a mechanical adaptation to all social conditions; it can only result from reason. The capitalist economy treats the proletariat as a passive thing that cannot think; the new juridical system should be the product of the thought of the proletariat refusing to accept the old notions inherited from the bourgeoisie. In the same ways that in its organizations the proletariat manifests its activity, it must carry on this activity through the creation of new laws. The most serious objection to the authors that anticipate an imminent revolution is the backward condition of this juridical construction: too often what is given to us as a breach of a labor law is only a sentimental and literary paraphrase of popular instincts having bourgeois origins.

In a work on "the day after the social revolution," Kautsky states that he is not concerned with knowing what the supreme legal principles will be. "It is certain that law and morality will have their functions in the social revolution; but it will be the economic demands that will need satisfying before anything else."[9] He has not noticed that the regime described by him does not correspond to any one "of the economic laws that the socialism of the jurisconsults has uncovered." Had he made this observation, he would have seen that these famous legal studies by Menger are useless today: these laws relate to the redistribution of wealth produced, and Kautsky is concerned with the mode of production; remuneration ought to be distributed in a manner which insures this production.[10]

The Socialist parties have not kept themselves completely outside of every legal condition, but seem to speak legal language reluctantly and employ obscure formulas. For example, read the program of the French Workers' Party:

> Whereas . . . producers will be able to be free only insofar as they are in possession of the means of production; whereas there are only two forms under which the means of production can belong to them: (1) The individual form [which is increasingly eliminated by industrial progress]. (2) The collective form, whose material and intellectual elements are constituted by the very development of capitalist society.
>
> Whereas, this *collective appropriation* can arise only from the revolutionary action of the productive class . . . [etc.].

The London Congress of the International Workingmen's Association in 1896 determined that from then on there would be convened at the congresses only "groups that would push to substitute socialist *property* and production for capitalist property and production, etc." At the Paris meeting held on 27 September 1900, of the International Congress, Jules Guesde said that "the emancipation of labor is subordinated to the question of expropriation, to the question of *transformations of capitalist property into collective property whether communist or socialist.*"

All this is obscure, but many socialists thought that it was necessary to obfuscate things even more in such a way as to be able to address to the naive voters equivocal speeches that, according to circumstances, allowed for posing as friend or foe of the property of peasants.[11] Thus the official formula that the French Socialist Party closes with is unintelligible: "The conquest of power and *socialization* of the means of production and exchange, that is, transformation of capitalist society into a collectivist or community society." It took care not to be specific and in fact Socialist deputies had previously promised not to attack small proprietors. In the resolutions voted at the Congress at Tours in 1902 (and published by Jaurès) we read that there is "only one means of insuring the order and the continuous progress of production, individual liberty for all, and the increasing well-being of the workers:[12] that is of transferring to the collectivity, to the social community, the *property of the capitalist mode* of production." It is noteworthy that the program does not repeat this distinction between capitalist and noncapitalist modes of production.

Collective property is unintelligible when individual property does not exist beside it and in greater quantity. It is easy to understand state or communal property when it is juxtaposed to individual property from whose laws they arise. For a long time, the socialists have reasoned in a very different way; they regard as primitive and as serving as the origin of the notion of private property a certain notion of collective property they apply to the territories occupied by savage tribes. This outlook is abandoned by the best historians of institutions. If individual property were to disappear in France, perhaps access to national shipyards would be forbidden to the German or Italian workers; this exclusion would depend on public rather than private law and could not be ascribed to the exclusivism of the law of property. To say that a nation is proprietor of its territory is to speak in purely figurative language.

The socialist formulas which speak of collective appropriation are not completely developed, and each notion is presented in all its glory: a future revolution is involved, often skillfully concealed and covered with thick veils as much as possible. The essence of such formulas is the word *appropriation*, which brings with it two kinds of ideas: (1) the socialist regime will recognize law since it will allow the use of a notion of separation between mine and thine; (2) this separation is connected to proprietary exclusivism. It is possible to deduce from these two premises a third hypothesis: the present laws can never be completely suppressed, since they provide the bases of the juridical system such as it is envisioned for the future. One can thus assume that socialist theory is not so absolute as we might believe at first sight. The expressions borrowed from the law regarding property have never been eliminated from socialist language; it appears that Marx did not sufficiently consider the danger presented by such a means of expression. The result was that the notion of private property would be necessarily combined in various ways with socialism.

The principal concepts of moderate socialism can be summed up in three points. First, England produced a particular type of socialism which depends most notably on feudal vestiges, which remain very much alive. Now the nationalization of land and the confiscation of income have remained a direct product of a reformist theory; at other times the product of a theory with communist origins. This socialism has the effect of demeaning landed property to return to leasehold systems of greater or lesser duration combined in such a way that the producer has the ability to take from the soil all the fruits of his labor and nothing else. As in all feudal organization or those that imitate feudalism, the notion of property is attenuated, and this attenuation can appear both as a progress toward communism and as a reintroduction of property in the communism of utopians. The socialists are strong enough to consider things under the first perspective, but they are deceiving themselves; communism is a point of departure and not a point of destination. It is not good to concentrate very much on these considerations because it does not seem that the theories on the socialization of land have any future possibilities outside England.[13]

Second, Proudhon is the author of a much more noteworthy idea based on the distinction between property and the economic environment; the socialization of this environment vivifies and intensifies private property, instead of attenuating it. Not without pain and much tergiversation, Proudhon arrived at this doctrine exposed in a more or less complete way only in his posthumous memorial on property.[14]

Third, the great mass of socialists proclaim themselves today in favor of partial collectivism: one part of the production remains in private hands, another part is the subject of a fiscal monopoly. This system is what is most pleasing to the electorate; the peasants, shopkeepers, and small manufacturers do not see any common measure between their mediocre enterprises and the immense forges of a Krupp or a Schneider. The question is knowing how to separate the production between the two types. Any theorist comforted by the abandonment of the old principles asserts that survival of private property will be an exception and will be only temporary; to me it seems instead that in the thinking of the politicians, the exception will be on the role of state enterprises (sugar refineries, petroleum refineries, the large steelworks and textile mills, etc.). In countries like France where we have many small property holders and businesses, socialism can be accepted as a political party only on this condition: giving a very large role to private property.

In a manifesto published after the elections of 1898 by the French Socialist deputies, we read: "*Faithful to the doctrines of the French revolution*[15] we want to secure to all the *free disposition of the means* and the fruits of their labor. We want to attenuate the murderous effects of the increasing tendency toward capitalist monopolies. And we are preparing for the transformation into *social property*, of the means of production, transportation, and credit, stripped of their individual owners from capitalist feudalism" (*Petite République*, 6 June 1898). Thus the production of the party is promised to the small proprietors and they threaten only a few of the great capitalists, whose number will be able, on the other hand, to be reduced or increased according to the needs of electoral politics.

It is in the elasticity of this formula that resides its legal weakness:

Proudhon's theory gives an incomparable force to law. Partial collectivization tries to imitate it but gradually subordinates the extension of private right to the caprices of the electorate.

Notes

1. Georges Sorel, *Saggi di critica del Marxismo* (Palermo:Sandron, 1903; reprinted Rome:Samona e Savelli, 1970), p. 247.
2. Ibid., pp. 148–50; 160–62.
3. Cf. the work of Professor Antonio Menger, *Il diritto al prodotto integrale del lavoro*, which was published in French translation as *Le Droit au produit intégral du travail* (Paris: Giard et Brière, 1900) with a most worthy preface by Charles Andler, the most learned professor at the Sorbonne, who is author of such profound works as the *Origines du socialisme d'Etat en Allemagne* and *Prince Bismarck*.
4. Menger, *Il diritto al prodotto*, p. 79.
5. Arthur Desjardins again repeats this accusation: "He had relied on a great scandal, and had sought scandal as an element of success; his expectations were not disappointed." *Proudhon, ses oeuvres, sa doctrine*, Vol. I, p. 46.
6. Cf. Charles Andler, *Le manifeste communiste*, Vol. II, pp. 134–36.
7. "You have fifteen, twenty, fifty years of social struggle to endure, not only to change social conditions, but to transform yourselves and make yourselves worthy of power." ("Verbal transcript of the Communist League," 15 September 1850, cited by Kautsky: *Le marxisme et son critique Bernstein*, French translation, p. 54.)
8. Ernest Renan, *Histoire du people d'Isräel* (Paris: Calmann-Lévy, 1893), Vol. IV p. 147..
9. *Mouvement Socialiste*, 1 March 1903, p. 414.
10. *Mouvement Socialiste*, 15 February 1903, p. 317.
11. During the particularly turbulent period from 1893 to the schism of the socialist party into two groups, the clarity of the declarations was always abandoned. In 1897, according to an eminent radical journal of Southern France, Jules Guesde had formulated the program in a banquet near Libourne (Gironde) thus: "The peasants are supporting socialism because they know that in this final *proclamation of property for all*, it wants to give to those who don't have it, to conserve the small property holders, to relieve the latter of those taxes that make them as miserable as the city proletariat." *France de Bordeaux et du Sud-Ouest* (7 September 1897). The Libourne moderate journal gave another version: "It is necessary that you organize yourselves in order to have this property (that is now wholly nominal): it is necessary to bring everything to the collective mass; we will liberate you from taxes, from unsecured debts, etc., and you will enjoy the fruits of your labor." *Union Républicaine* (9 September 1897).
12. Here is a good example of the manner in which Jaurès borrows ideas from all schools: "order and progress" is Auguste Comte's formula; "individual liberty for all" comes from Jules Guesde's program; "increasing well-being" recalls the oft-used formulae of the syndicalists. The motto of the General Confederation of Labor bears the inscription, "Well-being and freedom."
13. Cf. Antonio Menger, *Il diritto al prodotto*, pp. 196–211. The author writes

that the nationalization of land is motivated by the excessive concentration of property in England: he does not take account of the feudal idea which seems indispensable for understanding the importance that propaganda for the nationalization of land has had in England and in the British colonies.

14. Cf. Georges Sorel, *Introduction à l'économie moderne* (Paris: Jacques, 1902), pp. 130–31, 143–52.

15. The principles of the French Revolution are tutelary principles of individual property; Jaurès recognizes this implicitly in the declaration that he had passed at the national congress held at Tours in 1902: In the morrow of the French Revolution, the proletariat became aware that the Declaration of the Rights of Man would remain illusory without a social transformation of property. Then appears "our great Babeuf" who "has called for common ownership of property, guaranty of the common good. Communism was for *the more advanced proletariat,* the supreme expression of the Revolution"; from this we must conclude that this was not the doctrine of most of the revolutionaries.

CHAPTER TWO

To better understand the importance of change that is now operative—a change which remains obscured for the majority of socialist writers—we need to examine what Menger understands by economic law and to define the old socialism according to the nature of its famous principles. Is what occurs today a return toward older ethics or is there a completely new evolution? At first it does not seem easy to answer this question. After having nearly completely negated the ethic, socialism partially accepts private property, and consequently, to a certain extent, the legal ideas that serve as the basis of our modern codes. Is it a return to the past, to the period in which nothing but the law is ever mentioned, to the time in which society was attacked in the name of the law?

It is truly extraordinary that so many people really believed that the theories of Anton Menger could belong to the philosophy of law. The three fundamental economic rights are not rights; they define in a symbolic language—whose words are mistakenly borrowed from legal language—the ideas to which the ruling classes should aspire to fulfill all their "social obligations" toward the poor. As a result of an old custom that assumes that to every law there is a corresponding duty and vice versa, it is believed possible to call a right of the proletarian class that which is the obligation of the landowning classes according to an ethic of their own. This way of thinking is in conformity with the uses of the men of the world, but their opinions on law are almost entirely sophistic.[1]

Here is how we need to translate the claims of economic rights: the poor turn upon the rich, and make their speech: "You have in your hands all the means of production, or at least those that exert a direct influence on the national economy; if you are not the absolute masters of the state, at least legislation is unable to have any effect whatever when it is too contrary to your essential interests; you have then complete economic and political responsibility. You are also our intellectual and moral masters; you teach us science and morals, you have philosophers for research into the principles of human thought, and your professors have expressed in the books put into our hands the notions of equity, goodness, and charity. We ask you to behave toward our classes according to the principles of your science and of your philosophy: to be provident, benevolent, and just masters. You cannot allow the working classes to fall into increasing misery. You cannot endanger the future of the country by permitting anyone to gratify his greed. The greatness of the citizenry must be able to live and reproduce themselves; do not allow our children, our women, and our old people to anguish in a state of misery. You have the duty to ensure the existence of those who are unable to work; as for the men who are capable of useful and continuous work, give them occupations adequate enough to allow them to live; do not permit a mass of idlers and usurers to draw away the product of labor through taxes which do not serve the progress of the country and which enervate us.''

This idea takes different forms, according to the particular conditions of the ruling class. In Germany many conservatives have presented it in detail, in connection with the perspectives familiar to the great *feudal* and Christian lords. The people are in their eyes raised as servants or as domestics to whom the lord of the manor has obligations to fulfill. In 1884, Bismarck proclaimed to the Reichstag[2] that he intended to imbue his social legislation with the principles exposed in the Prussian Landrecht of 1794 expressed thus: "It is a state concern to care for the subsistence and maintenance of the citizenry who are not able to procure those same means of subsistance, nor obtain from any other private person what is required by special laws. To those who lack only the means and the opportunity to earn their own and their families' sustenance, work ought to be provided according to their strengths and abilities." Here is the right to existence and the right to labor regarded from the feudal and Prussian point of view; and these are "social duties" assumed by the state when there is not a local lord that has obligations to fulfill.

Above all, it is in the question of the right to the integral product that the feudal system clearly shows its character. Generally, each class accuses the other of stealing something. In the eyes of the great landed proprietors there are no greater robbers than the grain and cattle merchants and money lenders; it is these people that cause all evil and the great social "solution" would consist in eliminating them. As for the peasants, all they can hope is to be able to sell their products at customary prices, and not to be exploited by the middlemen and the usurers; the reforms that serve the great proprietors can thus benefit them also. This sentiment is most often developed in the workers who accuse all intermediaries of defrauding them. The profits that are made by crew-chiefs dealt with by contract with the landlords are considered by many socialists as thefts. This sentiment of a rather primitive order is found as strong in the agrarians as in the workers.

Sometimes the German lords raise themselves to *conservative socialism* of the highest level. They conceive of the whole country as submitting to a vast administration analogous to the one ruled by the dominant grandees of the Prussian state. Engels ruthlessly derides the illusions of Rodbertus[3] who believed in satisfying the workers by offering them a government that was, for Engels, only tolerable for the peasants of a feudal estate in Pomerania and which is wholly inspired by the bureaucratic spirit of old Prussia.

In the system of fundamental economic rights there exist many recollections from ancient Greece which, through the influence of classical culture, always act upon our own mind, on our unconscious. The Athenian republic—the model state in the *legendary history* of antiquity—was much more celebrated for its consumption than for its production. The citizens were partly maintained by the production of the mines, partly by the tribute drawn from the allied cities, and partly by the fines proposed[4] by the sycophants; public assistance had such an important part in the life of the poorer classes that, after its suppression, there was an emigration to Thrace.[5] The Athenians were available or retired mariners rather than workers;[6] there was no need therefore to be surprised if the demagogues found so much credulity among the poor when combatting the pacifist party. In expeditions much like those of pirates, the mariners attained an occupation in great conformity to their tastes. The military idea hàd great importance in Hellenic civilization.

The chief who wants to bring back victory must interest himself in the fortunes of his men. He must punish failure, but, much more, reward merit. Nothing is more offensive to the soldier than to see attributed to another the success that belongs to him. The duties of the military chief become also that of the city: he ought not show ingratitude for the old veterans who have contributed to its glory and power. It is necessary that it put under the category of needs so many obscure devotions, without which its most able generals would never have been able to triumph. Thus in ancient Greece *compensatory justice* had a preponderant function that is very surprising nowadays because our own ideas have economic rather than military origins, since our standing army has a special life of its own and remains in several respects estranged from the nation. The professors quite willingly conceive of the world according to the model of thèir own institutions; the success of pupils depends entirely on the intelligent care used by the teacher in charge of preparing them for examinations: he must show himself to be equally dedicated to all, to help the weak pupils who need additional explanations, and to distribute rewards in a way that does not stir up dispute. The quality of the teacher greatly resembles that of a general; the school is a type of camp. In both cases we are not concerned with the rights of subordinates; everything is reduced to determining *the obligation of the leaders* and to impose on the subordinates a discipline proportionate to these duties. We have a tightening relation between thse two things: the duties of the teacher increase as the obedience accorded him is more complete.

The church gives us the most perfect example of a *completely duty-bound society*. Not only is it both militant and educational, but it also directs the conscience and judges sins. Whatever question is submitted to it, the church takes possession of it only to know the purity of intentions, when it does not deeply examine the matter itself. Moral theology mixes very different things; after having treated murder, torts, and larcency, St. Thomas Aquinas examines the duties of the judge, of the prosecutor, of the defendant, of the witnesses, and of the lawyer. He then goes on to the diverse forms of calumny and offense; then deals with the obligations of merchants and of money lenders.[7]

It is partly because the church has the mission of preaching to the men of power about their obligations that it has so often taken the defense of the debtor against the creditor, reminding the latter that he ought not always to employ all the strictness of civil law. The church is the guardian of the rules of social duty. As Thamin has recognized,[8] the church is not familiar with rights, and I have noted that it has an insufficient theory of property.[9]

Every time that a philosopher addresses the men who direct matters and speaks in the name of those who form the passive element in society, he can concern himself only with teaching social obligations. He tries to arouse emotions any way he can to elicit moral sentiments; he invokes reasons appropriated from the education and conditions of the masters to bring them to understand that, if so much wealth is produced for their benefit, they ought *to do something* to improve the lot of the inferior classes.

One speaks of charity, fraternity, and solidarity or of so many other principles of the same kind, to show the rich that they have duties to fulfill. These duties remain rather vague, as long as they are not completed by other considerations borrowed from past or present organizations. It is only by those means that have a real existence that notions can be constituted completely and attain clear expression; the same ethical formulas can lead to very different practical conclusions depending on which means are being borrowed. This is why so many books on the ancient economy or on "model countries" are written; the school that claims to readhere to Le Play's ideas misuses remote examples by a history made *ad usum Delphini*.[10]

Here then is a "first system" that can be defined as follows: passivity of the workers; social duties imposed in the name of morality on the ruling and possessing classes; equitable distribution of products by benevolent and enlightened bosses who have taken their rules of determination from the practice or memory of prosperous institutions founded on duty. To this system we juxtapose another in which life is regarded mainly from the active economic side, that is, from the point of view of production, leaving distribution to the passive side. Kautsky reasons, we have seen, without asking what compensatory justice should be; he reasons according to the sole consideration of production; wages will be uneven without the intervention of an idea of difference in merit between one person and another: "The offering and the demand will always maintain a certain influence over wages in respect to different industries. . . . It might happen that certain industries are overburdened while others lack workers. To reestablish equilibrium one need only lower salaries where there is an excess of workers and increase them where there are insufficient numbers until every branch of industry has as many workers as it needs."

Distribution of wages is thus a *coercive means* to ensure the division of power in the workshops: every worker remains free through the choice of activity that suits him best. But the general marketplace in which he offers his skills, values them not according to individual merit, but according to the relative need of one or another specialty. Individual initiative on the one hand and the scale of prices on the other form the bases of the economic order, and these bases are *entirely mercantile*. The worker who will decide to attach himself to an industry and who sees his wages lowered because there are too many people having the same tastes as his, will not have to complain in the name of social duty. Whom could he ask to fulfill that duty since there are no more ruling classes?

In a socialist society, completely cleared of bosses, there can no longer be room for these old notions of social duty. If this does not appear obvious to many people, it is because few people yet conceive of a society without bosses. The bodies politic function just like the bosses in every democracy. The deputies are also bosses toward whom it is necessary in every case to address life's problems. The electoral committees of every party have so strongly disciplined the clientele that we can no longer entertain the idea of a socialist society without mixing it with recollections borrowed from these democratic usages: the state forms a cloud which hides the economy.

In the past it was less difficult to understand a regime without bosses, because it started from the hypothesis of a city where all the citizens possess moderate amounts of property. In such conditions the function of the state can be reduced to a minor thing, as long as it does not have to face strong external enemies. The citizenry then do not have much among them except those relations that depend on situations relative to their property; there can be landed servitude, but no dependence among proprietors. No one need have recourse to arbitration by public authorities and to the favors of the government in ruling on his disputes with neighbors. The tribunals are at his disposal. Nothing is simpler than conceiving of such a peasant republic that is equalitarian and almost completely free of political hierarchy.

But it becomes most difficult to understand socialism through a hypothesis of large-scale industry; one has to assume that there exists a purely *technological* organization, in which no surviving hierarchy remains. What we see in certain social institutions does not conform to this ideal. On the other hand, experience shows that one falls rapidly into a caricature of the church in which property is suppressed.

Partial collectivism constitutes an ingenious solution to the ideological difficulty:[11] if a sufficient number of free enterprises exists, ideas will be able to be formulated taking property as a principle. Thus the juridical notions will be able to continue to be constituted as now, and not fall into a more or less ecclesiastical utopianism. The workers of big industry will demand and will undoubtedly succeed in being treated as if they were proprietors of their functions, which seems to be the ideal of the employees of the state and the big corporations. But this type of proprietary relation is highly unfavorable to the progress of production. One can compare this with what would be the property of the manufacturing processes in the name of what is demanded in consolidating a technical system. Here it would only be a formal imitation of property: that is why I say that the ideological problem would be the only one resolved.

Contemporary socialism has great trouble in attaining a clear consciousness of the conditions of its new juridical life. Property is being introduced without having understood what the consequences of this introduction are. Few socialists understand how property has been generated in the course of the history of civil law, how it would be possible to conceive of a juridical regime without private property, and of what importance the development of the notion of law is in the world.

Before 1878 great efforts were made to leave the realm of utopia and advance toward practice; one relied heavily on the progress of the associations of production to resolve the social question. Perhaps the school of Buchez was not quite aware of its work: vulgarizing the idea of the cooperation of production, it illuminated the active productive and juridical side of the economy and invited the proletariat to cease being a passive body. But at the same time, it bound the workers to a life that was more religious than juridical, taking for its models the old monestaries and the indefinite development of mortmain.

Corbon[12] confesses that the association dreamed of at that time had to entail "a perfect agreement of the political and moral opinions among the associates. It was something *like a religious and socialist order* instituted in the bosom of civil society to generate it." He recognized that experience pronounced against Buchez's ideas, and that the societies that have existed have[13] operated each according to its own fashion. He admitted the principle of competition when in the minds of the founders it is a question of absorbing the entire economy in an increasingly widespread association. From a more or less ill-determined communism we reach a conception of associations similar to those in which the civil code is interested; experience teaches us, too, to pass over the field of law.

The working classes make many attempts to understand the law, and we always see the old religious theories return. Corbon[14] reports that one day the manager of a cooperative confessed to him "half blushingly" that he had not been able to stabilize the equality of pay. "It was our ideal. The inequality of income is not fraternity, but what do you want? One must make this concession to general egoism. We are thus corrupted by individualism." The old collaborator of Buchez answered him that inequality conformed to the most exact justice. "I did not need to reason at length to be right in a *superficial and groundless opinion*. But not often have I had such easy success."

The workers, used to regarding themselves as passive beings, understand with difficulty the ideas that seem natural to a company boss. For the latter, the worker ought to be paid according to what profit he brings; for workers, who have neither property nor enterprise, all those who show equal good-will ought to divide earnings like comrades.

Today we see many rich bourgeois promote producers' cooperatives; the workers appeal to the philanthropic sentiments of generous donors[15] and consequently operate in the same conditions as the Catholic convents, which compete with free enterprise, and claim to have a right to higher prices than the capitalists because of the superior idea they represent. Contemporary philanthropy gives rise to many of the most ludicrous scenes; some millionaires transform themselves into comrades and condescend to become members of the administrative council of these "democratic charitable institutions."[16] Don't we often see rich Catholics fulfill, in certain festivals, the function of subaltern in the church?

The advanced republicans in France do everything they can to prevent the people from acquiring the knowledge of socialist ideas; they monopolize the popular universities, flattering the instincts, and wanting everywhere to declaim against the bourgeois who do not fulfill their social duties. The strange puerile book published by Léon Bourgeois in 1896 under the title *Solidarity* has served as a gospel to young professors in search of popular applause: every capitalist has a debt to the nation; "here is the basis of his duties, the cost of his freedom . . . the obedience to social duty is only the acceptance of a cost in exchange for a profit."[17] There is among men a *quasi contract of association*, beyond which there is "for each living man a debt to all living men, because of and in proportion to the services given him by the efforts of all."[18] From this results the following consequence: "Social duty is not a pure obligation of the conscience, it is an obligation based in law, the execution of which cannot be avoided without a violation of a precise rule of justice."[19] Léon Bourgeois thus conceives of a sanction given by the positive law to social duty; all political order is dominated by duty and by the secular branch: here we are in theological fulfillment!

If, as many people maintain nowadays, these ideas constitute what is most essential in modern democracy, it would be urgent to declare a ruthless war against this very same modern democracy. It would oppose the movement toward law, would oppose the doctrine of social duty, and would corrupt popular thought as far as its roots, habituating it to taking for the basis of its reasonings the existence of a superior class.

It is so natural for the proletariat to regard itself as passive, and for the human spirit to ask help from the strong—instead of trying to think how to be active and strong. It is natural that the people accept without protest the inferior situation that is made for them by their ordinary advisors, as long as this situation does not cause them immediate material and very noticeable losses.

It is often noted what truly bizarre language has been used by socialist writers when an economic conflict occurs: they proclaim that popular claims are "just." Is this what should be said? How can justice intervene in a difficulty that concerns costs? Which is to say that if the capitalists fulfilled their social duty, they would give satisfaction to their manhood. The workers think this language constitutes a good method of involving in their cause all good souls and of rousing public opinion: nowadays we are concerned with the thoughts of those people armed in such a way as to be able to discern praise and blame. No one likes to be taken for a misfit, an ignoramus, and a fool:[20] How many people make grave sacrifices for the purpose of avoiding being attacked by the press? The tactic of intimidation complies with the leaders of the working classes and is therefore not a bad option; but one must, to evaluate matters from a socialist point of view, regard this notion of social duty as constituting the gravest obstacle that the proletarian movement can encounter in its path toward emancipation.

During strikes, journalists sometimes threaten the bosses, other times flatter them and appeal to their humanitarian sentiments. A great difficulty in ending strikes derives from the fact that the supervisors have been abused by the most ardent workers, and the question consists in knowing if the agitators will be arrested; there is always a request to forget everything that has happened. This solution is certainly easy—but is it not inspired by a singular sentiment of scorn for the workers? The defenders of these workers act as if their clients were irresponsible people or children playing at some foolishness. The truly paternal capitalist will not keep account of abuses that have been formulated against him; he is stationed too high up to be impressed by words or acts from a class of slaves. In all countries with slaves—is it not admitted that these people should have the liberty of avenging their suffering with crude epigrams? Social duties forbid taking these inferior beings for equals, capable of formulating injuries demanding some sort of reparation.

If there have been disturbances and trials, one tries to alleviate the seriousness of offenses as much as possible; begging the governors for numerous favors, one speaks only of the need to forget all deplorable incidents. Is this not once more to treat the workers as weak in spirit? There is no more important idea in the development of humanity than that of personal responsibility; this idea is manifested in an elementary way in criminal matters. The anarchists[21] appear to be more aware of this point than petty socialist politicians; they think there is nothing that is forgotten, and instead of asking for forgiveness, they make the accused into heroes of the working classes. If it is true, as Kautsky says,[22] that it is the revolutionary idea that has regenerated the proletariat, and if it is essential to remain faithful to the revolutionary idea, the tactic of the anarchists is the only one that has any value from the socialist point of view. The magnanimity of the bourgeoisie is a patent of inferiority bestowed on the working class; this magnanimity is solicited with parades of great eloquence by those who claim to labor for the total emancipation of the proletariat.

Notes

1. Cf. Jhering, *Esprit du droit romain* (French translation), Vol. III, pp. 14–15. Renan has stated a maxim of rather general importance from a scientific point of view on the subject of the *men of the world*. "It appears that there occurred in Babylon what would have occurred in our time if scientific charlatans, supported by the men of the world and the newspapers, in-

vaded the Institute, the Collège de France and the University faculties. With us, certain needs that are superior to the caprices of the men of the world, artillery, the manufacture of explosives, scientific industry, uphold true science. In Babylon the buffoons won out." *Histoire du peuple d'Israël*, Vol. III, pp. 179–180. Can't we say as much of our great *modern-style* socialists and of the man of the world who is so sympathetic to them?

2. Anton Menger, *Il diritto al prodotto*, pp. 22 and 24.
3. Preface to *The Poverty of Philosophy*, 2nd Fr. ed., pp. 18–27.
4. In the Kabili tribes the fines are almost entirely spent in distribution of meat, done by a population count, without regard to age or sex (*thimecheret*); the distribution of meat has the greatest importance in the life of this hard-working and very poor people; therefore the collection of fines is performed with great strictness. Hanoteau and Letourneux, *La Kabylie et les coutumes Kabyles*, Vol. II, p. 52; Vol. III, pp. 134, 170.
5. Guiraud, *La main d'oeuvre industrielle dans l'ancienne Grèce*, p. 211.
6. Cf. especially Aristophanes, *The Wasps*, vs. 235, 685, 117.
7. St. Thomas Aquinas, *Secunda secundae*, from questions 67 through 78.
8. Thamin, *Saint Ambroise et la morale chrétienne*, pp. 273, 274, 285 and 464.
9. Georges Sorel, *Essai sur l'Eglise et l'Etat* (Paris:Jacques, 1902), p. 13. One must not show oneself to be deceived by language that the Church uses when it defends its possessions; then it will adopt the language of the law of its time; thus, today, in France the defenders of ecclesiastical property menaced by the State compare the Church to an enterprise conducted by a civil corporation. It seems quite likely that in the Middle Ages, the Church should have taken care to borrow from the barbarians many of their ideas on property in order to have its possessions respected. Even the positivists have borrowed from the Church their scorn for law. But it is useless to concern ourselves with these charlatans.
10. Cf. Georges Sorel, *Introduction à l'économie moderne*, pp. 72,73.
11. The economic problem of the technical organization of State industry remains to be resolved.
12. Corbon, *Le secret du peuple de Paris* (Paris: Pagnerre, 1863), p. 128.
13. Ibid., p. 130.
14. Ibid., pp. 113–14.
15. Marx was strongly averse to this philanthropy, and did not admit that charitable institutions of the bourgeoisie could have a socialist aspect; on this point he expressed himself very clearly in his *Critique of the Gotha Programme*. I think that he had as much contempt for the generous benefactors as did Yves Guyot!
16. After the Dreyfus affair, some of the literate and wealthy Israelites gave a great deal in order to revolutionize capitalist society—which did not accord enough honors to them. Among the new foundations of that period was a so-called communist publisher that, according to its founders, ought to have overthrown the world; in the 1902 account of management appeared a commission "Comrade B, a dramatic author." This "comrade" is a millionaire! A Hebrew diamond merchant has largely commanded this institution, but it does not appear that he has yet taken an honorific post in the French publishing house!
17. Léon Bourgeois, *Solidarité*, 2nd ed. (Paris: Armand Colin, 1897), pp. 101–2.
18. Ibid., p. 138.

19. Ibid., p. 141.
20. In *Humanité* of 15 March 1905, it is stated that "the intransigence and pride [of the Paris carriage manufacturers] had triumphed through 'common sense' and 'duty' — because these bosses did not want to abandon piecework and the employment of foremen with whom they deal under contract." This journal, directed by Jaurès, is edited by the personality most visible in the University.
21. The meaning of the word *anarchist* has so many varieties that it is well to define what is meant by it: Today politicians call "anarchist" all those who incite the proletariat not to participate in the political life of the bourgeoisie; the syndicalists are therefore among the "anarchists." I believe that this meaning is the most etymologically correct one.
22. *Mouvement Socialiste* (15 October 1902):1891.

CHAPTER THREE

We have now to inquire whether it is possible for a type of regime imbued with the ideas of duty and hierarchy to be transformed into a socialist regime that knows nothing else but rights. It is not useless to examine modern history and examine closely how two great revolutions that have transformed the appearance of the world have come about. I want to discuss the revolution which resulted in the introduction of Roman law into Germany in the fifteenth century and the revolution of the eighteenth century.

Jansenn constantly juxtaposes egoism, of which Roman law would be the earliest expression, to the old medieval regime, filled with Christian ideas and which, according to him, takes greater account of social duties. Everyone agrees in recognizing that the picture that Jansenn gives us of old Germany is fantasy;[1] things did not go as idyllically as he claimed, and Roman law is not responsible for all the evils he attributes to it. We must grant this historian that since the juridical constitution of Germany has been very imperfect in the past, theology and canon law exerted enough influence so that we may be able to say that the idea of duty played a preponderant role which has vanished in the modern era.

The history of the acceptance of Roman law reveals an essential character upon which Catholic authors insist with an extreme obligingness but without determining its true importance. The new regime is contemporaneous with an extraordinary reenforcement of the power of the princes. Modern despotism was constituted in that period; the heads of state were able to make people recognize that they were above all control, as direct delegates of God and placed by Him at the head of nations. All that concerned them now was to ensure the greatness of their houses; they had squeezed the populace in a frightful way to maintain their armies. From that time on there are no more social duties imposed by religion on the heads of peoples; there are just duties of the people who were bound to bring to the temporal power, largely and sometimes completely, the veneration that the church had formerly inspired in them.

Many Catholics accuse Roman law of having produced these unfortunate results and of having produced absolutism; but it is obvious that they have mistaken the effect for the cause, as often happens among

65

ideologues. The jurists had upheld against the church the claims of the princes for whom they were functionaries; but their disquisitions are a commentary on the power acquired through a skillful policy and by force of arms. The most we can admit is that their "scientific prestige" contributed to reducing the prestige enjoyed by theologians, and has contributed to giving the princes a greater audaciousness in the struggles in which they engage to become rich and powerful. Many acts of violence remain sheltered by juridical forms; but the church had allowed into inquisitorial sophistry some juridical models that the Romanists could never expect to attain.

Gervinus has done very well in emphasizing the results of the new way of governing: Henry VIII of England, Louis XI of France, and Ferdinand the Catholic of Spain obtained especially notable results:[2] "Of these 'three magi' as Bacon calls them, Ferdinand was the master of skill; he appeared to Machiavelli as the living model of *those princes of the new school* that his perspicacity was able to recognize as the necessary remedy of that time." The procedures used were, according to Gervinus, fashioned after that of the absolutism of the church: they gave the highest positions to the professionals and were thus able to create a regular administration. But the German historian keeps account also of the new tactical methods and of the formation of permanent armies, by means of which the royal authority could always have the last word. "Ferdinand," in the words of Machiavelli, "raised himself from being one of the most sluggish princes in Europe to the ranks of the most celebrated and distinguished." Obviously it was not Roman law that produced this result.

The historical value of this royal absolutism has not perhaps been quite appreciated; and Gervinus appears to have appropriated the idea from Machiavelli that the unlimited authority of a single man had become necessary, and that, on the condition that it be transitory, this authority could lead to a regime of liberty. Meanwhile he observed that the Florentine secretary had not foreseen the abyss of evils into which royal despotism was about to hurl Spain.

I interpret this phenomenon slightly differently. In it I see proof that history does not pass through an "internal evolution" from a system founded principally on duties to a system based principally on right. A *revolution* was necessary. Violence did away with the old organizations. A number of institutions that seemed at the beginning to be as estranged from right as they were from duties, for the time being served as the material basis for the development of the new juridical ideas.

We have here one of the most notable examples of revolution, and it cannot be too closely studied if we want to understand the processes by means of which social revolution can emerge. Violence has had a predominant role; but we see its value: it is entirely negative and destructive; it is necessary for arresting one development and for permitting a new one to be born; but this is all it can do. Our university socialists imbued with the ecclesiastical spirit deceive themselves in attributing to violence the power of putting into practice the dogmas formulated by theoreticians.

In the fifteenth century the break was made in a particularly simple way, because the established powers were practically united in making all the applications of the system of social duties disappear. The ecclesiastical authorities, which according to the principles of the church should have conserved untouched the residue of duties, did not show themselves very different from the lay authorities in the exploitation of the public force. They regarded the wealth and power that the previous centuries had conveyed to them as personal private goods which they could command for their own advantage. The popes had exhausted themselves in vain fighting against this state of things; the old church became laicized and was no longer concerned to ensure the fulfillment of duties.

The true interpretation of the French Revolution ought also to be sought in the passage from a system of duties to one of right. The ruling classes did not accept social duty for themselves, but tried to impose it, in all its rigor, on the inferior classes. On the eve of catastrophe, the aristocracy became attached to its prerogatives—more so now than a few years before: their single preoccupation was settling their existence in the soft life to which they had become accustomed. The Revolutionary Assemblies claimed to have abolished this regime in order no longer to allow juridical relations based on property to exist (narrowing or even suppressing the law of testation, they believed they had made a great step toward the civil law that would completely dominate the organization of the family).

The liquidation of feudal law finds its most natural explanation when it is put in the perspective I indicate here: let us regard this law as a set of occurrences resulting from an old discipline that had imposed obligations on the peasants toward the lords, who were free to do what best suited them: they were the expression of a regime of duties toward the privileged classes. Wherever the feudal mark appeared, the contribution had to be suppressed as lacking juridical character; it had to be conserved when it was evidently the result of a simple contract under civil law. In practice the various jurists who compiled the laws on the liquidation of feudalism each brought particular views on the historical interpretation of the old laws, and their interpretations were often quite arbitrary; but it is possible nevertheless to justify the general spirit of the reform.

Violence had here a special function; it manifested itself less by means of proscriptions than of what are called the "wars of liberty"; a quarter of a century was occupied by struggles after which paled the most glorious expeditions of our old monarchs. The oppressed class had conquered its nobility on so many fields of battle that it became impossible to impose the yoke of duty from then on. All the new territorial constitutions were kept; it was agreed to indemnify emigrants because the state was unable to profit decently from confiscation in a regime based on absolute respect for property.

Feudal rights remained abolished without any indemnity; expressions of old social duties, they were unable to find defenders among the jurists. When the memories of the revolution were attenuated and there was no longer reason to fear a return attack by the ancien régime, feudal rights were no longer regarded as they had been before; one tried to salvage everything that could be susceptible to a juridical interpretation founded on a better knowledge of medieval history.[3]

The present situation offers no analogy to that of previous revolutions, and what we see is of such a nature as to baffle historians. The ruling classes, the state, and the church compete in their zeal for social reform; they all want to prove to the socialists, destroyers of the status quo, that the rich are capable of an effective abnegation; everyone is eager to fulfill his duties, all his duties. These new tendencies are not manifested solely with sermons in honor of poverty or with some unusual charitable institution, but with legislative acts and philanthropic works that demand enormous sacrifices. No one will ever understand present-day politics in France if he does not know that there is an increasingly greater number of men determined to impose on themselves hardships and pecuniary sacrifice to rescue what seems to them to constitute the heart of modern civilization. *They offer their money to redeem what is, according to their judgment, priceless from an economic point of view*, and hope therefore to arrest the progress of revolutionary socialism.

For the young French Christian Democrats for whom *Sillon* is the principal organ and Marc Sangnier the chief theoretician, the church must be saved, and nothing should seem too costly to obtain this great purpose. They accuse the republican government of neglect and blame it for not protecting the workers enough. They claim that anticlerical policies are a diabolical invention having as their object the stifling of social reforms. On the other hand they claim to be very liberal, and when the bishop of Nancy denounced "the danger to the faith and to the discipline in the French church,'' they demanded the rights of freedom of thought.[4] Marc Sangnier is very rich; he procures many distractions for the young men grouped around him. In their meetings, everyone addresses M. and Mme. Sangnier in the familiar form. I assume that in the life to come the humility of this family will be acknowledged.

At the end of the session of the Chamber of Deputies during which Jaurès attempted to revive the Dreyfus affair, the army found itself threatened by numerous scandals; the French radicals are as chauvinistic as the anti-Semites. A rather obscure deputy named Magniaude mounted the tribune and implored his colleagues to follow neither Ribot nor Jaurès, but to be inspired by the ideas of Léon Bourgeois, to study fiscal and social reforms, and thus to render justice "to the people who await it with untiring patience" (*Journal officiel*, 8 April 1903). He asked that the army be saved at the expense of the capitalists.[5]

Clericals and bourgeois radicals have found common ground in their *policy of social conservation by means of ransom*. At the Musée Social, they meet one another fraternally; the director, L. Mabilleau, is a follower of Léon Bourgeois and a freemason emeritus. One of the most important men in this institution deplored, in my presence, that the laws against congregations were of such a nature as to arrest the progress of labor legislation. I have noted elsewhere[6] the unique function of Professor Jay, a proclerical fanatic, important advisor to Millerand, one of the representatives of the really bizarre science cultivated at the Musée Social and the Paris School of Law.

It is hoped, with this policy, to take from the socialists a part of their working-class clientele, and sometimes it succeeded in attracting some labor union chiefs, discouraged with the sterility of their efforts and happy to be flattered by some powerful bourgeois. None of this is very important, but the French bourgeoisie is idealistic and believes it is on the path to victory when it has won over isolated individuals to its conception of social peace.

The direct results will probably always be ridiculous; but the indirect results are considerable because these tactics produce an eternal confusion of ideas: on the other hand the bourgeoisie tried to deceive itself, keeping its head in the clouds so as not to recognize the whole extension of the danger; on the other hand the workers have some difficulty in recognizing the absolute separation of classes when the enemy classes give themselves over to so many philanthropic displays. After the great reactions of 1851 and 1871, it would have been possible to believe that the schism between the proletariat and the bourgeoisie was definitive, because the brutality of the repression seemed contrary to every idea of social duty; but the ties were refashioned more strongly than ever. We must examine here the ideological forces that prevent the workers from understanding socialism.

First we should note the influence of revolutionary legend. According to common opinion, one would pass abruptly from an imperfect law, too favorable to the aristocratic families, to a more perfect law, favorable to the immense majority of the poor; the break would occur by changing the organs of power. Instead of allowing that they be overcome by a small number of functionaries and courtiers, one appealed to the representatives of the people and admitted that the assemblies issuing from universal suffrage produced reason just as a prairie produces hay.

Jaurès, who in general perceives the instincts of the popular spirit rather keenly, has understood what the utility would be for his "personal political power" of the skillfully fashioned legend of the revolution. It is for this reason that, despite so many other concerns, he has accepted the crushing burden of writing a history of this period. Desiring to get rid of what he disdainfully calls "pater-noster Marxists" (*Petite République*, 4 April 1903), he must try to attach himself once again to the memories that still today excite the workers to such a high degree. He is reproached for not being revolutionary and exalts the heroism of the great revolutionaries, taking Plutarch for his model (as he announced at the end of the preface to his work).

The break need not be as abrupt as it was in 1793; the modern transformation could be made through evolution, profiting from acquired experience. According to Jaurès, there would be only a difference of degree between his adversaries and himself; the conflict would only revolve around the speed imparted to the movement. To conquer the state piecemeal in order to direct it always in a way favorable to the interests of the poor and to lead it to judge in a sovereign way the difficulties presented in judging between the haves and have-nots, is, according to Jaurès, the purpose that should be attained. It is useless to rack one's brain thinking about the class struggle when one has a very convenient means for producing the transformation of the state.

To enlighten universal suffrage with harangues and newspapers is for Jaurès the immediate purpose of socialism which is thus placed on the same ground as democracy. This work will be so much easier if the ruling classes understand their social duties and realize that we have here a superior form of justice to shine upon the world. Jaurès likes to take as subjects of his discourses justice, the law of historical justice, the necessity of justice, etc.

The Dreyfus affair provided Jaurès with the marvelous opportunity to drag the revolutionary workers along the path that he intends to lead them; he has been able to concentrate on a particularly emotional case all the popular rage, rejuvenating the anticlericalism that was becoming ridiculous, *and giving shape to the idea of revolution*, at least for some time, apart from the class struggle. The aspirations of all the men whom his eloquence aroused were the conquest of the state by means of a party capable of making justice reign. The notion of the perfectly just and moral state took on an importance that one had believed to have been lost. This great struggle for the repression of offenses committed by the most violent Catholic groups was impossible without the participation of all men of good will; the state called upon to persecute culprits had to be accessible to the socialists.

Such an alliance is opposed to the conception of the class struggle. The democrats admit that there can exist parties having as their mission enlightening the public on the urgency of certain reforms; but these parties accept all the acts of political scrutiny as works of reflection. For the socialists the oppressed classes do not recognize the sovereignty of the majority and have faith only in their own juridical theories relative to the economy of production. The revolution summoned the poor to participate in the formation of laws; it had to form a poor man's party which the bourgeois democrats confuse with the socialist party. The latter tries to teach the workers that the purpose of their whole life ought to be to revolt against the owners of production.

The great electoral successes of the socialists have allowed them to exert an influence on the course of parliaments. There is nothing which removes the spirit of clarity and earnest investigation so much as the habit of sophistry, without which a party cannot have power in the Assembly. Arguments that contradict themselves, images that are confused and that give rise to the most deceptive analogies, abrupt returns to the most vulgar sentiments for the purpose of dissembling the weariness of reasonings, such are the procedures that the great parliamentary tacticians employ. The workers who form their judgment by reading the newspapers and who have a singular superstition for eloquence do not feel any need for coordinating their ideas when the masters reason in a stupid manner.[7]

Next to the politicians, there are the literati who have a great function in journalism and who decide everything according to their "common sense." The ideal of these noisy and ignorant characters would be to abolish all distinctions of legal origins and to lead the tribunals to reason no longer; they have created a whole legend around President Magnaud who, according to them, would be a renovator of jurisprudence and who, in reality, is a charlatan[8] who amuses himself by compiling the laws in the style of a small-town journalist. The literati feel for legal reasoning the same repulsion felt by the old fifteenth-century German judges when they found themselves in contact with professors embroiled in university disputes: these professors claimed vainly to introduce quasi-geometrical procedures into matters that were until then regulated by means of the light of natural equity.

It is only by putting things on legal grounds that one can give clear expression to class conflict. Mixing everything in a jumble of meaningless words, based on a so-called natural equity, the literati and politicians prevent the workers from comprehending the existence and the mission of their class. Therefore, one need not be amazed if the socialists have generally misunderstood the evolution that has led them to partial collectivization. If they had not been dominated by the "big" words of the literati and parliamentary politicians, they would have regarded the evolution beyond their own station in a scientific and juridical spirit; they would have been struck by the difference between the point of departure and the point of arrival on account of the reintroduction of the notion of private property. But because of the influence of sentiments, being incapable of reasoning about the philosophy of law, they have seen the change produced in themselves. When we place ourselves in such a perspective, what appears essential is no longer the length of the road to be traveled, but the unity of expressions that arouse the old feelings.

Many socialists believe that they have not changed much and affirm that they have conserved their revolutionary ideals; they are *unfortunately* in good faith, their good faith being the consequence of their intellectual inferiority. Between total and partial collectivism they think that there is only a difference of degree, because the same substantive *(collectivism)* is used in both cases. Here are general reasons that tend to confuse socialist thought; here is another reason which prevents socialists from emancipating themselves.

The revolutionaries[9] of the eighteenth century believed they possessed science and reproached the ignorance, pedantry, and intrigue that in their view characterized the upper classes: men who felt secure in their reasoning could not easily accept the notion of social duty; they wanted law, and all of rational law. In the fifteenth century the professors of Roman law had a deep contempt for all the old feudal constitutions; they were often criticized for being under the influence of this prejudice, misinterpreting the texts and favoring terrible abuses of power. The lords drew an excellent alternative from the tendencies of the new jurisprudence which concentrated law more around property, and they tried to give the latter the means of emancipation from inconvenient obsolete law.[10] Often, lands that peasants regarded as communal were awarded to the aristocracy; the heads of tribes became real proprietors, and their men were no longer anything but tenants susceptible of being exploited.[11] The entire revolution that the state of property underwent was dominated by this contempt on the part of tribunals for practices regarded as barbaric and contrary to all reason.

Today the proletariat does not find itself in this situation: they do not despise bourgeois civility; they envy and admire it, hoping to assimilate the ideas of the capitalist class. In previous times, two civilizations appeared, and each was aware that the levels of its development could not be reconciled; the innovators sought only to separate themselves from the old system of ideas. Today there is an effort toward reconciling the levels; the bourgeoisie goes to the people out of social duty, and the people aspire to think in a bourgeois manner. Is the problem of socialism then insoluble?

Several years ago, the Marxists made passionate and at times effective propaganda to prevent the workers from being lured by the illusions of bourgeois theories of social duty. Since the ruling classes want to discharge their social duties, it appears that the easiest means of shattering every connection with them and with the past would be to present to the proletariat as stupid and ridiculous everything which comes from the bourgeoisie. The risk of this procedure is great, since it leaves us open to discrediting all ethics: the paradoxes of Lafargue are well known and have contributed to representing Marxism as a pedantic, puerile, and even cynical literature. The joke is a weapon that must be managed very prudently when one claims to work for the education of the people.

I do not believe that there is need to resume the tactic that consists in opposing the high morality of the people to the scarce morality of the upper classes. "From the wisdom of the people," says Van Kol,[12] "arise the ideas of the morality of the future, since civility always climbs up from below." This is a misunderstood and hypocritical adulation addressed to the workers. It is not true that at present their conscience is in a position of giving ethical lessons to the world.

In the polemics raised by the application of social laws or incidentally by philanthropic works, it is wrong so often to criticize the bourgeoisie for not doing enough for the poor; such criticism has no meaning if one does not accept the theory of social duty. The bourgeoisie must be allowed to execute its plans, but one should never collaborate with it. The minor participation in bourgeois government is, at the present time, the recognition of the system of duties: a system that should disappear completely (provided socialism does not deceive itself) and which would last indefinitely if it did not encounter obstacles from the proletariat. The proletariat must *rebel against the men who want to be its benefactors.*

If the question of the participation of the socialists in a bourgeois government had been neatly posed in the terms I have used here, we would have far fewer conflicts among the socialists. When the working population is sufficiently numerous in a city to be able to take over the city council, a socialist administration can have felicitous consequences, if it goes so far as to prevent public instruction and charity from being directed so as to spread the ideas of peace and social duties. If this result cannot be obtained, if the socialist municipality cannot act in such a way as to ruin the ideas of philanthropy and unity, it is preferable for the socialists to stay home, because socialism is easily transformed into pure and simple democracy when it is governing.

The proletariat has the means for creating a life apart; it is with this intention that so many anarchists have praised the *Bourses du travail* where the workers' organizations could remain on purely revolutionary grounds. The name of Fernand Pelloutier remains joined to this work in France, because no one has understood better the importance of this separation of the new institutions from the bourgeoisie.[13] Young lawyers are besieging the *Bourses du travail* and wish *at all costs to dedicate themselves to the well-being of the people*, but insofar as the anarchists will represent the functions that they now represent, the bourgeois invasion will not have very much importance. The anarchists display much more shrewdness than the socialists, who make politics the principal object of their concern, and have understood better than they by what means it is possible to combat the prestige of the moralists, philanthropists, and of the Christian clergy, that today devote themselves so much to sustaining the system of social duties. The anarchists *juxtapose violence to beneficence*; by this means they introduce and maintain in the proletariat the idea that one must repudiate and ridicule the patronage of the ruling classes. The direction of the anarchists is often clumsy, because the use of violence is subject to many accidents and often depends on somewhat barbarous instincts. It is always unpleasant, because there is something strange in this savage means of responding to benevolence. And perhaps it has not always been analyzed, but violence escapes all analysis.

In the old revolutions, violence had a completely different meaning and was much simpler. In the fifteenth century it was produced by the princes; in the eighteenth century by the greatest majority of the nation rising up against an unbearable power; now it is necessary for violence to help reject the charity of the upper classes. The future social revolution cannot be compared, as is so often said, to that of the eighteenth century. In all cases the revolution will have a long and painful preparation, and in this preparation the violence of the anarchists ought to play a very considerable role, as long as the bourgeoisie persists in fulfilling its social duty.

It would not be asking too much to recommend to observers to direct their inquiries from this viewpoint when studying strikes; most of the time it seems that they do not understand the phenomena developing under their own eyes. The big question is not knowing what material advantage could be gained by a corporation; it is to determine to what degree the idea of social duty is rejected by the violence of the strikers. It is very wrong for the socialists to try to conceal their violence; it is pure hypocrisy on their part, and it is a bad miscalculation since violence is the most efficacious means for maintaining the separation of classes so long as there are no institutions formed in the bosom of the proletarian class strong and independent enough to ensure this separation. The philosophy of history that considers results will doubtless give the rule of violent strikers much greater attention than it is given today.

Notes

1. Cf. *Études religieuses*, January 1890, p. 47.
2. Gervinus, *Introduction à l'histoire du XIXe siècle*, French trans. (Brussels & Ostend: F. Claassen, 1858), p. 27.
3. Doniol, *La Révolution française et la féodalité* (Paris: Guillaumin, 1874), p. 169.
4. The doctrinal conceptions of these young Catholics are so preposterous that a Protestant newspaper has been able to ask if they are really Catholics. *Vie Nouvelle* (21 March 1903).
5. We should not forget that Léon Bourgeois has always remained opposed to the agitation stirred up by Jaurès in the Dreyfus affair.
6. Georges Sorel, *Saggi di critica del Marxismo*, p. 332. It is thanks to this coalition that France has been led to collaborate with the so-called Papal government in an association formed for the legal protection of workers.
7. In the discussions on the congregations, Pressensé accused Father du Lac of having betrayed the secret of the confessional as proven by the disposition of Judge Bertulus before the Court of Cassation; this judge was said to have been cautioned by the state major general that a certain "Madame M." was the "veiled woman" that had given the mysterious appointments to Esterhazy; the major general supposedly had made this statement after the confessions made by this woman to her confessor, Father du Lac. But at the same time, Pressensé informs us that the "veiled woman" was Du Paty de Clam. *Journal Officiel* (24 March 1903). What secret could the confessor have thus revealed? What stupidity!
8. We read in *Petite République* (23 December 1902) that the Committee of the French Socialist Party had asked Magnaud to preside at a lecture by Jaurès on "Justice in Humanity." Gerault Richard opened the meeting by reading a letter in which Magnaud declined this honor and made an hyper-

bolic eulogy on his ridiculous judgment. "The applause that has greeted the reading of this letter shows what esteem and what sympathy he enjoys among the militants." This proves above all that these militants are absolutely incapable of reasoning. In *Petite République* (22 October 1900), Fournière vaunted the "juridical science" of Magnaud and accused the Court of Amiens of "crippling the law in order to be able to annul some of the admirable sentences of President Magnaud." Reading these lovely things, people endowed with a caustic spirit certainly can do little else than murmur an old schoolboy proverb: *asinus asinum fricat.*

9. We find in *Petite République* (18 April 1903) an amusing definition of revolution, created by the editor-in-chief: "In my view, the revolutionary is the man who has a horror of social conventions, who always searches for the best, who always adapts his general conceptions to progress of all sorts." Here is a fine little philosophy of café society; Gerault Richard was in fact a composer of songs before he started to direct the policy of the French Socialist Party.

10. Jansenn has strongly insisted on the oppression endured by the German peasants.

11. Marx, *Capital*, Vol. I, pp. 319, 321-22 [Modern Library ed., pp. 789-90; 794-97].

12. Van Kol, *Socialisme et Liberté* (Paris: Giard et Brière, 1898), p. 240.

13. Fernard Pelloutier, *Histoire des bourses du travail.* Passing away in the prime of life from an atrocious malady and in a condition quite close to poverty, Pelloutier gave, in what he wrote, only a pale idea of what he could have produced; but when the day of historical judgment will come, we will pay homage to the great undertakings that he had begun, and this great socialist will be distinguished, while in time will be forgotten those who hold first place in our parliaments and who represent socialism to the eyes of the dazzled bourgeoisie.

CHAPTER FOUR

In social philosophy we always find ourselves confronted with this grave question: will the law be immortal? The question is rarely approached frankly, and a majority of authors even seem afraid to discuss it, undoubtedly for fear of weakening their readers' confidence in ethics. Ordinarily and implicitly, utopians assume the question is resolved in the negative, since they imagine a society in which law would become as useless as in a religious congregation.

In our times, the problem has made great progress as a result of the studies of the school of Cesare Lombroso. The most solidly acquired result of this school is this: crime is not a purely moral matter, ascribable to a spirit independent of the body. Crime depends to a large degree on material conditions; and the deviations whether atavistic or from degeneration are reproduced indeterminately in the human species. Crime is thus eternal.[1] From this results the following alternatives: either penal law will never disappear or there will always be some disciplinary statutory authority outside of law on the fate of criminals. The Lombroso school would seem favorable to this second solution, because it mainly understands remedies; but the first solution seems infinitely more likely.

Civil law draws on the one hand from criminal law and on the other from public law; if these two laws always exist, it would be strange if civil law should disappear; therefore we must also ask ourselves what would become of the state in a socialist society. Engels did not have any doubts on this point:[2] "The state has not existed from all eternity." There have been some societies that did not have a state, that did not have any notion of the state and of state authority. At a certain point in economic development which was connected to the division of society into classes, this schism made the state necessary. The classes will thus disappear as inevitably as they have come into being, and with them the state will inevitably collapse.

What appeared especially to determine Engels's belief is that he found, in Lewis Henry Morgan's description of savage society, the absence of any state organization. He thought that an institution ought to perish when it is possible to discover its origins[3] and when preponderant circumstances which have favored its first development have disappeared. For example: private property has found considerable support in the protection that magical superstitions could give to personal goods; we might think that the progress of instruction should provoke the decline of private property and perhaps even its death.

This sophism has had great influence on the historical economists who give such importance to the slightest details surrounding origins. One finds in nearly all these authors a tendency that Marx noted in the English,[4] "who love to confuse the *raison d'être* of a social fact with the historical circumstances in which it first appears." Rogers sometimes has rather extraordinary theories of this kind; he asserts[5] repeatedly that the decline of the English workman had for its principal cause the alteration of monies by Henry VIII and Edward VI. Elizabeth vainly attempted to produce a monetary reform;[6] a period of twenty years had produced effects which "have dominated the history of labor and salaries from the sixteenth century till today." But Rogers elsewhere amends this historical theory, warning the reader[7] that the well-known aphorism "to stop the causes is to stop the effects" need not generally apply.

We must distinguish between institutions and ideas. Their changes do not depend on the same kind of causes: there are institutions which disappear and it does not seem that after disappearing they can ever be reborn; one can imitate the past, but never reproduce it. As to ideas, we should nourish great doubts as to the possibility of their disappearance. It seems that ideas are like science and that the notion of progress must be applied to them. Professor Antonio Labriola seems convinced on this point.[8] Nonetheless, the fact is certain that in the passage of decisive action from one people to another in the course of history, the useful products already acquired from those who were declining passed on to those who were growing and ascending. This factor is not as valid for the products, as I put it, of sentiment and fantasy, which are also preserved and perpetuated in the literary tradition, as for the *results of thought* and especially the discovery and production of technical means, that by means of law are communicated and transmitted where they are acquired. The author draws a distinction between ideology and technology, but admits that the law of conservation certain for the latter is applied at least partially also to the former.

The problem of conservation has survived discussion so far only in regard to religion; and yet this discussion was never carried on in a scientific way. For most authors it was a question of taking sides for or against the church; they accumulated facts to illustrate a theory which was already established. Those who want to maintain the necessity and consequently the eternity of religion try to point out that it is a natural phenomenon that man undergoes as a law of his spirit or that it results from a primitive revelation[9] of which it would be possible to find traces in all countries and in the most primitive periods. Others maintain that religions are historical facts that owed their force to the ignorance of men, and that therefore one can trust that they will disappear with the progress of culture.

The question has not been correctly posed. Religions are much more modern than is often believed, and I find it very difficult to affirm that there are no people unaware of religion as Ribot contends.[10] Religions, like science and like laws, are preceded by a lengthy confused period during which magic keeps enclosed the seeds of the most disparate developments. When one examines savage customs closely and without bias, one sees that man has made many efforts to understand that he is different from a fragment of nature, that he is isolated in the world, that his destiny is different from that of the other living beings. As long as this notion of separation has not taken root, it is difficult to know whether a true religion exists.

The modernity of religion cannot serve as an argument to prove that it must disappear, in the same way as the memories our maturity are weaker than those relative to our infancy. Science is still younger than religion, and no one believes that it ought to disappear. It is true that science enriches itself constantly by way of the most attentive observations of nature, but religion finds a means of rejuvenation in mysticism.[11]

We greatly deceive ourselves on the history of religions because we place ourselves too much in the perspective of Roman history. The ancients allowed their old national religion to perish through general indifference, when philosophy acquired a certain favor. Ribot[12] thinks that religions are transformed, in the long run, into a subtle metaphysics, accessible only to the philosophical professionals—this is not seen at all among Catholics. In ancient times, the official cults were abandoned by the wealthy classes, not so that religion would disappear, but because these cults were inadequate from the religious point of view; when they had lost their patriotic significance, they became simple festivals.

The modern religious problem should be posed as follows: "Is not religion like science? Is it not made in order to be cultivated by a minority? Is it not destined to become so much more alive and more strictly religion in proportion that it is concentrated in a smaller circle separating itself from popular superstitions?"[13] Often what comes to be called "the decline of religious spirit" in the people can only be called the decline of magic. Religion is augmented unceasingly in classes estranged from magical ideas.

Renan believed that certain privileged peoples had each brought a cornerstone to modern civilization, and he was disposed to distill these initiatives in a very rigorous way. "Law owes nothing to Israel";[14] Israel has left a deep historical impression by giving a particularly strong expression to the laments of the poor. It was Greece that created[15] "the absolute standard of civilization which everyone after her would accept. . . . Greece alone discovered the stability of the laws of nature. Greece *alone* discovered the secret of the true and the beautiful, the standard, the ideal." But if these things were born by accidental historical causes in a very small country, one need not believe that they should perish.[16] The Greek work of science, rationality, experimental civilization—devoid of charlatanism, without revelations, based on reason and liberty—will continue without end.

Many people would grant science a special place, because it is imagined that science is a *discovery* of laws that exercise some function in the world in a perfectly objective way and which, enclosed in a mysterious sanctuary, are conveyed by scholars. This is an old Platonic concept. More and more we see another conception of science making headway in philosophy: one tends to regard science no longer as a natural and complete system, alien to man, but as an edifice that every generation augments and consequently has a history, and which could have been constructed in another way.

In his work on ancient Italian wisdom, Vico tried to demonstrate that we have knowledge only of what me make: Marx had been amazed by this opinion and wrote in *Capital:*[17] "Darwin has interested us in the history of Nature's Technology, i.e., in the formation of the organs of plants and animals, organs which serve as instruments of production for sustaining life. Does not the history of the productive organs of man, of organs that are the material basis of all social organization, deserve equal attention? And would not such a history be easier to compile since, as Vico says, human history differs from natural history in this, that we have made the former, but not the latter?"

I do not believe that we have so far made the best of this profound observation in order to construct a new philosophy of science. We imagine that, by means of science, we question nature and put ourselves in direct contact with it. We question only our instruments and are in contact with productive forces organized by our industry. What science knows are the instruments created by the human genius. Science takes off from the existence of the "common arts" which we learn through an apprenticeship, arts which entail rules and which are gradually perfected thanks to the reasoning of those who practice them. On this datum the mind works and pursues the transformation of empiricism which did not satisy its logical requirements in order to create science. The Greeks were weak inventors; but because of their "inventive weakness" they experienced to an extraordinary degree the *need* to rationalize everything and replace the changing or the uncertain with the immutability of science. The exceptional rationalism of the Greeks could very well have had a technological base. The spirit of invention and the spirit of system are not opposed; this is a point on which Henri Bergson often insists in his lectures.

Greek geometry did not emerge from any experimentation, but its principles derived from the rules of construction. The Hellenic architects established their edifices in stone with such precision that they had no need of laboratory controls as some of our producers do, the walls being built by means of stones joined with perfect accuracy. The art with which this was attained became the geometry of straight lines.[18] It was only in a later revision of the *Elements of Euclid* that the famous postulate that bears his name was introduced. Euclid never doubted the importance of this principle: he would have been amazed if someone had said to him that some beginning pupils would one day be required to demonstrate that on a point on the upper side of a straight line, one can trace a perpendicular line and only one!

It is much more difficult to determine the origins of the principles employed by Archimedes. I think that he had borrowed them especially from naval architecture; the carpenters who outlined the designs customarily measured curved lines and compared one with another. This is what Euclid did not yet believe possible to be included in geometry. They had to concern themselves with centers of gravity, and it is obvious that Archimedes worked on the old empirical rules, as for example when he acknowledges that the centers of gravity of two like figures are similarly placed in each of them.

At present we are a bit deceived by the magnificent results obtained in the laboratories and believe, too easily, that industry applies the laws of nature that science has discovered, when in the past it was evident that science rationalized industry. But the laboratory is a small workshop in which instruments are put to use that are more precise than those in manufacturing; there is no essential difference between the two kinds of establishments.

If there is a difference, it is to the disadvantage of the laboratories where experiments are made under highly exceptional conditions. Science, having for its object the employment of productive forces, is the practice that must be illuminated and it is from it that one must start. As long as we do not have a wide application of the methods found in the laboratory, we ought to consider the labor of scholars as having only hypotheses for results.

Are not the best and most able experimenters quite often deceived by a false interpretation of phenomena they have observed? How many times have they believed to have "seen"? If Crookes had not had blind confidence in the certainty of laboratory methods, he would not have been deceived by the mediums: the "exceptional" phenomena attributed to the mediums do not concern industry and do not have rules outside of science.

The human mind would have been able to reveal itself less exacting than it had been among the Greeks, by not demanding a total rationality analogous to that which the rigorous constructions of the Hellenic temples introduced into geometry, and which passed into all science. The ancients also, because of their rationalist requirements, were led to abandon certain sciences such as chemistry which the moderns have developed to the highest degree of perfection.

It does not appear that they saw that metallurgy could have provided the elements of a rational knowledge of bodies; even when they did not attribute a magical character to it, they compared metallurgy to zoology rather than to mechanics. The formulas they used most resembled the description which naturalists gave of the habits of animals and their management. Language has preserved many traces of this comparison.

If the Greeks had taken metallurgy as their scientific standard, they would not have regarded mathematical formulas as representing the highest truth of nature. Ancient metallurgy consisted of too much dross, wasted too much fuel, and took too little account of the duration of operatior.s, so that no one could grasp that the numbers in this discipline were other than empirical indications.

Even today, despite so much research, the perfect determinism of chemistry does not consist of anything but a hypothesis derived from physics. This hypothesis is granted to it by comparison, but it is not yet certain whether it is possible to predict in an absolute way the reaction that will be produced. Until we discover laws to establish the manner in which reaction varies with duration, there will always be a doubt regarding this determinism. Mechanics would have changed appearance had it not found at its beginning astronomy, which imposed its notion of time and introduced the concern for determining all phenomena according to duration.

Greek rationalism which depends on architecture as much as on knowledge of space, depends on astronomy as much as on the knowledge of time. Rationalism therefore depends on historical phenomena which might not have existed nor might have exercised such influence.[19] Law evolved especially in a people who had little science but who intended that its material interests be effectively protected and not abandoned to arbitrariness. The development of law was dominated by rationalism imported from Greece and ended by becoming analogous to geometry or physics.

Law had been preceded by empirical solutions born of chance circumstances and crudely consolidated by magical combinations. When these fragmentary solutions were reassembled into customs that had given birth to rules in which the mind discovered some use, law then began. On these data that men are used to finding convenient in their life and conforming to their sentiments of justice,[20] rationalism labors for the purpose of organizing a system analogous to that of science. While this departs from the "usual arts," law departs from what we could call the "social arts." In both cases practice precedes logic.

These two processes are so analogous that it often seems impossible to separate the destinies of science from those of law. Since these are two manifestations of a similar rationalist tendency of the mind, we can ask ourselves how the former can increase without the latter also being progressive. In both cases man strides toward enlightenment. But today there are grave doubts on this parallelism of the two great rationalisms, and we can ask ourselves whether juridical progress is as secure as scientific progress.

In our time, science has undergone an incredible development, because in every country capitalism was able to give to any people access to the movement of the new productiveness. Everywhere technical schools, laboratories, and universities were established in such a way as to maintain competition. Science has thus taken an unexpected geographic advance, and all peoples seem inclined to cultivate it successfully regardless of their traditions. A century ago it was believed that liberal institutions advanced at an equal pace with science, and that wherever industry was transported, it would find in its continuation the juridical guarantees of liberty. But experience has shown that this expectation was not realized. From this has arisen a great discouragement, and the bourgeoisie has ceased to believe in the inevitable progress of ideas.

Contemporary capitalism has realized considerable profits so that it no longer has anything but derision for the parsimony of the old industrialists. It finds that taxes are small matters compared to the general costs with which it is burdened. It seems as natural to it to purchase the support of threatening politicians as to pay commissions to middlemen. Parliamentary institutions that at one time were believed necessary to defend the taxpayers against the abuses of power are not defended by them too much, and are on the contrary a source of foolish expense in many countries. Capitalism is increasingly uninterested in what was once the object of its most lively concerns.

The legislative activity of parliaments has greatly contributed to diminishing respect for law. "It is not without reason that, at the beginning of the nineteenth century, the school of legal philosophy associated with Savigny protested against the idea of codifying German civil law. It realized that such an undertaking could only cause great disturbances in the country's political ideas. At present the idea of law has little influence in the world. It is not very difficult to see that the principal cause of this juridical decay of modern nations is related to the legislative activity of parliaments, whose members believe they are called to carry out continuous reforms. Legal science ends when everything depends on the chance of the will."[21]

The need for rationality, without which there is no felt need for law, seemed for a long time quite natural to French philosophers, because it existed to an extraordinary degree in France's classical century: the men of the seventeenth century did not want to accept anything that was not perfectly clear and logical.[22] From this point of view, they were analogous to the men of the classical period in Greece. The Hellenic genius can be defined as "plastic." It wanted representations whose parts could be known with exactitude and whose whole could be built with these parts, just as a temple is built with tightly joined materials. Although rationalism has greatly declined in the modern world, it still remains very strong among Latin peoples, and the clarity of their concepts is often envied by contemporary German thinkers.

In this perspective, the English are completely different from us: they are not offended by the contradictions that exist among rules whose practical advantages they appreciate—while the Latins often advance the cult of perfect coordination to the point of superstition. The defects of the English acquired extraordinary intensity in their Australian colony; it does not appear that in these countries there is a great mental difference between Europeans and Asians. This discovery is of great importance because it shows that rationalism could vanish from us more easily than is ordinarily believed, and then law could become medieval again. It would be extremely important to know if, as some believe, the Australian mind is the product of a culture completely devoid of classical education.[23]

If we wish to understand English socialism, we must note that John Stuart Mill is regarded by the Fabians as the most profound writer who ever confronted social problems. One author[24] who has taken his information from Sidney Webb tells us that the Fabians are distinguished from the democratic socialists in that the former recognize Mill and the latter Marx. Although John Stuart Mill has written some bulky volumes on logic, he is not distinguished by the logical precision of his mind, and Marx often noted the incoherence of the economic theories of this author who regarded himself a second Adam Smith. Marx was amazed that Mill was acknowledged as such an authority. "With his usual eclectic logic," says Marx, "John Stuart Mill understands how to hold the view of his father, James Mill, and the opposite view at the same time."[25] Thorold Rogers, who had been a friend of J.S. Mill, often deplored[26] that Mill had contributed to spreading in England false ideas on the most serious economic questions.

The future of juridical rationalism seems far from certain, and the problem would probably not be susceptible of solution if socialism did not intervene here. We no longer have to ask ourselves if, in the entirety of a country, this rationalism is maintained, but whether the socialist proletariat is inspired by it. Despite all the efforts to lead socialism to participate in the dissoluteness of today's fashionable morbid sentimentality, there is a very energetic resistance, and the revolutionaries have the clear sentiment that they defend the citadel of the modern world by refusing to collaborate with bourgeois institutions. Despite beckonings of the church, socialism remains obstinately irreligious because it wants to remain rationalist.

Engels exaggerated a bit when, at the end of his article on Feuerbach, he said that the German theoretical sense was conserved in the working classes and that the direct heir of German classical philosophy was the workers' movement. But beneath this exaggeration there is a base of truth. This need for rationalism, misdirected and separated from material bases, produces utopia; based on the practice of institutions, it can generate law. Law cannot be formed by itself solely through rationalism; it needs substance, institutions; everything done today with a view to creating new institutions, independent of the bourgeoisie, in the bosom of the proletariat, allows us to think that the future of law is secure if democratic policy does not extinguish the new light burning amidst the proletariat.

Notes

1. I have had many occasions to hear from a professor of scholastic philosophy that he greatly appreciates Lombroso's ideas and that they seemed to him to support the Thomistic conception of human nature.
2. Frederick Engels, *The Origin of the Family, Private Property and the State* [From Karl Marx and Frederick Engels, *Selected Works* (Moscow: Foreign Languages Publishing, 1958), Vol. II, p. 332; hereafter cited as M.E.S.W.].
3. This idea was quite common in the past; I do not believe that there is any

thing more false than this; therefore I will linger a little longer on this subject.

4. Karl Marx, *Capital*, Vol. I, French translation, p. 174, Col. II (Modern Library ed., p. 440).

5. Thorold Rogers, *Travail et salaires en Angleterre depuis le XIIIe siècle*, Fr. trans. (Paris: Guillaumin, 1897), p. 337.

6. Ibid., p. 311.

7. Thorold Rogers, *Interprétation économique de l'histoire*, Fr. trans. (Paris: Guillaumin, 1892), p. 306.

8. Antonio Labriola, *Del materialismo storico* (Rome: E. Loescher, 1902), p. 143.

9. This second thesis is not favored today; to understand how it has been able to prevail for so long, we must regard it as a means of expressing this incontestable fact: that primitive religion is incomprehensible if one does not connect it to more developed religions; generally it is the mature state which explains the embryonic state, and the degenerative state. From this it results that the most primitive states seem to have something perfect which has been borrowed from the more completely developed states, and it appears that they arise from nothing and are born in an adult state. The same illusions have made people believe in the existence of a natural right which men discover and in the existence of a priori laws of nature.

10. Théodole Ribot, *La psychologie des sentiments* (Paris: Alcan, 13th ed., 1930), p. 315.

11. Catholicism does not appear to grow old, although its death has been often announced as imminent. What contemporary history shows us in an incontestable way, and what seems to be the result of a law common to all ideologies, is that their evolution is not regular, and the movement works by means of successive rebirths.

12. Ribot, *Psychologie des sentiments*, p. 315.

13. Taine had been amazed by this phenomenon in studying modern French Catholicism: "by an imperceptible and slow withdrawal, the great rural mass following the example of the great urban mass is in the process of becoming *pagan* again. Inner Christianity through the double effect of its French and Catholic entanglement is kept warm among the clergy, especially in the regular clergy, but grows cold in the world." Taine, *Le régime moderne* (Paris: Hachette, 1891), Vol. II, pp.151–52.

14. Renan, *Histoire du people d'Israël*, Vol. III, p. 429.

15. Ibid., Vol. IV, pp.196–97 (italics added).

16. Renan, ibid., IV, p. 421.

17. Marx, *Capital* (Modern Library ed., p. 406 n.).

18. I called attention to this question since 1894 and have taken it up again in "Le système des mathématiques," published in *Revue de Métaphysique et de Morale* (June 1900:413-14). The principle of the great masters is this: with rectangular stones of the very same dimensions one can construct a wall in which the assemblies are completely parallel, which do not permit any gaps and which do not demand any shaving. Euclid acknowledges that all right angles are equal, and that if two lines are parallel to a third, they are parallel to each other; these two principles are those which express the rules of the art with which Greek walls were constructed.

19. Bergson has quite often called his students' attention to the influence

of Greek geometry on the formation of philosophy. According to him, the human mind so far has relied too much on Greek "absolute rationalism"; he thinks that a new philosophy will be born on the day in which one will take biological evolution as the basis of reflection.

20. The sources of civil law are thus found connected on the one hand to the economy (by means of the adaptations to the means of existence) and on the other hand, to political and penal institutions (by means of the sentiments of justice and sociability).

21. Georges Sorel, "La crise de la pensée catholique," *Revue de Métaphysique et de Morale* (September 1902):530.

22. Renan often insisted on this character of the seventeenth century; it is because of this need for clarity and perfect logic that the scientists of that time were poorly prepared to study the origins of institutions.

23. I do not believe that this question has been examined yet by people who have written much on pedagogical reform, which I regard as of capital importance for the future of the modern world. When one defends the Latin peoples against the apologies of the Anglo-Saxons, does one do anything else than defend some consequences of classical teaching?

24. A. Métin, *Le socialisme en Angleterre* (Paris: Alcan, 1897), pp. 192-94.

25. Marx, *Capital* (Modern Library ed.), p. 140, n.

26. Thorold Rogers, *Interpretation économique de l'histoire*, French trans., pp. 202, 213, 271-73, 278, 328, 333-35.

CHAPTER FIVE

Now that socialism is so often found linked to democracy, it becomes all the more necessary to find what relations exist between them while at the same time revealing their differences. Such an investigation cannot begin with definitions and party programs; rather, by means of ideological procedures we can demonstrate everything we want. Since socialism has often a certain democratic development, it can be maintained that it is an extension of democracy, and since it differs from democracy, it can be maintained with as much verisimilitude that it is in contradiction with it. If we want to reach scientific conclusions, we should proceed by way of a materialistic analysis, substituting the conflict of ideas with the conflict among well-established social groups, and find in society where democracy is primarily established and where socialism above all is established. Everyone agrees that the history of democracy is reduced to the influence of the great cities over the countryside.

E. Vandervelde pointed out[1] as a very noteworthy fact that "the evidence in all countries demonstrates that the increasing number of cities and their population constitutes one of the most powerful, if not the most powerful factor in the development of democracy." The Belgian author places himself on ideological ground in the old-fashioned way. To be faithful to Marxian teaching he does not see the necessity of reversing his proposition and saying that democracy is a set of aspirations of the urban masses who desire to participate in the advantages available to the rich and powerful minority. This is exactly what ancient democracy was, and we constituted all our ideas on democracy according to this example, until socialism intervened to upset them.[2]

The separation of city and countryside has been noted by Engels[3] as the most important phenomenon that would occur after the separation of the sheepraisers from sedentary occupations. Among the characteristics of civilization he noted the function of this antagonism as "the basis of all divisions of social labor." Most socialists believe that in the future all class antagonism must disappear; that socialism has uncovered the means of realizing social unity, bringing the city and the countryside together. Vandervelde has devoted a good part of his book *L'Exode rurale* to showing that in modern society the situation of the workers can be improved by establishing two types of life that were entirely too separate until now. He has thus discovered Le Play! For the most part, socialists have been solely concerned with the city and have thus confused their position with that of democracy. We ought to try, first of all, to discover the reasons why "the party of labor" has placed such great emphasis on the metropolises.

The most important labor for the wealth of countries in the Middle Ages was in textiles. When historians want to give an idea of the prosperity of a municipal center, they enumerate weaving looms that were listed in the large cities. Cloth and linen were then the most important merchandise, whose sale was almost always assured, as securities are on today's stock exchanges. Weavers were not solely creatures of urban wealth; they were also the soldiers of democracy who struggled against the municipal aristocracy to prevent it from using the public force in their own particular interest. The cities made powerful through textile manufacturing provide the most notable examples of these class struggles that Giry has shown[4] as providing the key to medieval history. To remove authority from an oligarchy to give it (or probably return it) to the craft corporations—such was the course of the terrible struggle that developed in the fourteenth century.

When the socialists began to study the means to emancipate the working classes, they above all studied the miserable conditions of the cotton industry workers, so harshly treated in England. They compared them to the medieval weavers whose history they vaguely knew. The socialists viewed the cotton workers as the chosen soldiers of the proletarian army. At the end of the preface to the *Eighteenth Brumaire of Louis Bonaparte*, Marx recalled Sismondi's observation on the difference between the proletariat of ancient Rome and that of modern countries: the former lived at society's expense while current society lives at the expense of the proletariat. Ancient democracy translated labor into profit for the inhabitants of the great metropolises. The revolution the socialists want to realize will be made by the workers to acquire the administration of their own production. The new democracy therefore ought not to resemble that of Rome: it should no longer exploit anyone. The Marxist concept always assumes that this function of democracy results from the fact that it represents what is most essential in the national wealth. This hypothesis derives directly from conditions of the medieval economy, and it is essential to know whether it can be preserved.

In the Middle Ages, security considerations led to concentrating weaving operations in places capable of being easily defended. Later the merchants who took direction of cloth weaving production found it advantageous to have within reach the workshops of what Le Play called "collective manufacture." Finally the great steam forges were established, in the beginning by persons generally estranged from technology and desirous to oversee their managers. Thus most often the best locations were not chosen, and the urban capitalists sacrificed the future interests of their industries to secondary considerations regarding the convenience of management. Also the urban regime continued to win favor contrary to all inclinations of common sense. But after a certain number of years, the bosses found that they would benefit by changing their industrial policy. They saw that in the urban agglomeration labor was expensive and that confrontations with the producers there were particularly difficult to settle. Henceforth they became partial to rural labor.

The history of the city of Lyon is extremely interesting in this respect.[5] "The urban weavers that numbered in the city and its surroundings about 40,000 looms had gradually emigrated over fifty years to the Rhone and to departments nearby. The 1900 census noted the presence in Lyon of 1,432 mechanical looms in a total of 30,368, and 8,637 hand looms in a total [much lower in reality] of 56,043." Vandervelde reports[6] that the weavers of Ghent, unable to hope to reduce the wages of their workers and needing to lower their prices to sell their wares, transferred some of their manufacturing to the countryside after 1885. "Manchester nowadays does not have nearly as many weaving and spinning mills. The weaving mills have been moved out to the countryside. They had first been moved to Stockport. . . . Stockport having become a great center, the textile mills were moved still further out." He notes a phenomenon of the same type in Westphalia, and proclaims this proposition whose importance cannot be ignored: "By all indications it is foreseeable that the industrial exodus, whose principal aspect we see today, is destined to take on a scope that perhaps will equal that of the rural exodus of the nineteenth century."

There is still another technical fact which should be taken heavily into account. In the modern world, metallurgy occupies a position it never had before; it is no longer wool that governs the world as it did in the Middle Ages, but iron. When iron manufacture is arrested, for some reason or other, it seems that the entire national economy is paralyzed. Metallurgy is becoming ever less of an urban business; it can function only with an extremely powerful plant which requires establishments that cannot possibly be built in cities. On the contrary, metallurgy seeks out the locations of mines and has no need of anything produced in metropolises.

Metallurgy gives us a kind of agglomeration whose study would offer the greatest interest to socialists who want to discover the embryo of future society in today's world. It unites many men whose lives depend on a great industry; but the city will be confused with the *enormous boroughs* constructed around the foundries and steel mills. Thus we are led to regard as a completely accidental phenomenon the hypothesis which has so long served the socialists as the basis of their speculations: if the cities are no longer the chosen sites for the largest industries, democracy which always remains dependent on the conditions of urban life tends to become separated from socialism which gravitates to where the most powerful and strongly based industry exists. From the time when possibility of this separation was recognized, it became possible to push the analysis further, looking at what the city is in relation to the countryside, when it is not the site of great industry. Thus we come to know what democracy is in itself, and rediscover the principal results to which the historical experience of classical democracy leads us.

It is not worthwhile to concern ourselves with the urban centers which were created solely for security reasons; today these reasons cannot give us the key to the relationship between city and countryside. The urban type created solely for security is the Berber "Guerlaa" of Aurès, Algeria,[7] a small redoubt which contains the supplies of its inhabitants when they leave to practice their pastoral industry. Centers of this type are always tightly enclosed and do not allow for any development. When we study the division of rural property, we must nevertheless greatly consider the ancient historical data on security; many large cities owe their birth to the necessity of uniting to avoid depredation; but we do not yet find here the economic separation of the population.

The cities and the countryside are manifestations of a breakdown in social life that does not entail any domination of one part of society over another. This procedure was used by Engels in studying the division of society into classes; he considered a division of functions that produced exploitation later on. This method has sometimes been criticized as lacking in absolute historical value, and Engels's mistake seems to be having presented his schema as a summation of the total development occurred. By this method we obtain an ideological determination of relations rather than a knowledge of the facts. The cities appear as the servants and benefactors of the countryside, while simultaneously becoming dominant and aggressive. It is not possible to establish a chronological distinction between the two periods which history would allow us to separate everywhere, but the mind has different demands than those of history.

It is hardly necessary to insist on the immense importance of the market which created the prosperity of so many cities. If, as Professor Flach believes,[8] exchange relations were unknown to primitive men, who nonetheless had long experienced mutual obligations, then the markets had been the originators of purely economic relations. The system of mutual obligations was derived from the hospitality practiced toward travelers. There was no longer any sentimental bond on the markets, and the mercantile economy could develop with all its consequences. But while producers found great advantage in exchanging their products at festivals, there emerged a class of merchants who tried to keep more wealth than was necessary.

The great maritime metropolises give the best example of this exploitation of production by innumerable types of parasites, always done in their quarrels over the division of the spoils of the producers. From the porters in the ports of entry to the commission merchants and transportation contractors, there is everywhere the same greed of predators who come to impose their services by virtue of the "customs of the marketplace." One of the great reforms of the mature capitalist economy is being rid of all these useless people.

The marketplaces are almost always centers of the spiritual orders. Generally a tribunal exists where an important market functions. The peasants protest energetically when someone wants to affect their customs and modify a legal institution that corresponds to the practices of their economic order. One also notes the importance of the places of worship, whether they came into being before or after the markets (the question of which came first is unimportant in our inquiry). Finally, the cities ordinarily contained scholastic institutions which rendered the greatest services to the people of the surrounding region but which also served to maintain urban prosperity by attracting the rural population to the center.

These spiritual institutions contribute largely to the exploitation of the countryside. Around the courts live corporations of people whose evil purposes have been noted so often that it is useless to elaborate this point; one of the benefits of the French Revolution has been that of greatly reducing the number of local courts and at the same time abolishing much starvation. At present Algeria suffers greatly from lawyers who exploit the proprietors and accumulate wealth in the city. The great religious centers have always attracted large quantities of precious metals and harbored a population of the lazy. Scholastic institutions are often much more useful to teachers than to students; they attract many intelligent young men from the countryside and, after having made them lose much time, produce weak men, parasites, or new exploiters of rural production.[9] We need a great deal of time so that people can come to understand the importance of science in agriculture and cease to be dazzled by the charlatanism of intellectuals.

Cities render great services to the countryside providing it with capital for the development of land. The Italian savings banks and public banks show how this distribution of small amounts of capital can be regularized and produce new wealth. On the other hand, one notes the destructive function of usurers who ended up by becoming lords of the whole country, especially when they combined the two types of commerce: goods and money.

The domination of the city over the countryside is shown in the most immediate way when the countryside is inhabited by princes or an oligarchy of capitalists exacting taxes from the peasants. Today the same relations still exist when a purely urban bourgeoisie possesses latifundia over which it exercises no care and which are exploited by means of managers, with the goal of drawing the greatest possible net return.

Athenian democracy provides the most notable example of an urban population that cannot live without state support, and charges the state to procure resources through taxation to come to its aid. Today the workers of the great metropolises do not ask to be paid as members of juries or of some assembly,[10] but demand from the state convenient wage labor even when this labor does not as such augment the national wealth. Australia, which has a great excess of urban population, provides us with a good example of modern democracy that recalls the Athenian democracy. Because of its agricultural production, the country is rich; the people of the city share in the profits resulting from the high wool prices paid in Europe. The English capitalists, seduced by the idea that the newly settled countries should develop as America has, loaned enormous sums both to the government and to Australian speculators. It was thus possible to undertake many luxury enterprises (in the cities) or useless ones (on the railways) and to nourish democracy at European expense. Urban democracy has—like oligarchy—always aspired to find weak people to plunder or ingenuous foreigners to rob in order to be able to live without working on those things truly capable of enriching the country.[11]

Let us now examine what constitutes a properly urban industry. To understand the function of cities, we must regard them as places of pleasure, and take into consideration the enormous part played by prostitution in urban history. Writers have hardly ever recognized the importance prostitution has had and still has in the world; people have often preferred to confuse it with inferior forms of matrimony rather than to study its own peculiar development. From this there resulted theories that were completely inappropriate and on which sociologists cannot agree.[12]

In pagan times, the shores of the Mediterranean were strewn with temples to Venus that were nothing else than cities living off prostitution. In the Middle Ages things did not change too much, and we know that until the seventeenth century Spain still set aside large districts administratively organized for legal prostitution.[13] The Jesuits had great trouble in abolishing this unique institution that most of the time annoyed nobody.

The great cities still have as the foundation of their "specific prosperity" the purchases that the "professional beauties" draw from their retinues. More than two-thirds of Parisian industry and commerce would certainly collapse if foreigners ceased to come to find distractions in the great metropolises of pleasure. What would become of jewelers, dressmakers, and milliners if prostitution did not maintain them with large orders. In spite of the recurrent laments of the moralists against the luxury of women, courtesans have for so long drawn the world to spend money on luxury goods, that it has become impossible to portray a society in which what is called "fashionable good taste" could exist without these women whose function has been so great in the history of clothing, furnishing, and housing.

The theater, the novel, and painting increasingly take on the same character as the preceding industries: people have vainly attempted to give modern drama patriotic and historical forms; it seems that we can have no other subjects but love and especially guilty love. It is what occurs in novels that increasingly absorbs nontheatrical literature.[14] As for painting, it is produced for actresses' boudoirs rather than for palaces and churches: we can call this "great painting" with a smile.

A part of the working population that has remained a bit primitive in custom and thought still loves the old melodramas where vice is punished and virtue rewarded, the old novels where unlikely adventures and sentimental romances are compiled; but the progress of the new customs tends to cause all these old types of popular literature to disappear. They are replaced by a more refined, more bourgeois literature. Unceasingly, small, illustrated folios are produced which make pornography (once reserved to the great lords) available to all social classes. The great success of the cabaret derives from this: that it is increasingly licentious and often cynical.

The true tendency of modern art is displayed in the discussions over artistic freedom; everyone seems to agree in protesting against judges who desire rigorous punishment and against the "societies for public morals," which have become truly "cumbersome"—to use the expression of the *Petite République* of 3 April 1903.[15] No one wants to accept that it is forbidden that singers and actresses give an obscene interpretation of the works they perform. This is a cry from the heart of the urban bourgeoisie, which protests against all attempts to reduce the importance of places of pleasure and diminish the function of prostitution. It is deplorable that the socialists too often follow abjectly the representatives of democracy.[16]

But we need not hide from the fact that urban luxury, whatever its cause, has had a very important role in the history of human development. We should not judge the historical value of one group of phenomena by the moral value of the sentiments that can easily be revealed in those who control society. Engels says[17] that mercantile society has done many things by "putting into motion man's most sordid passions and inclinations and by developing them at the expense of all his other faculties. The basest cupidity has been the impetus of civil society. . . . If, in the pursuit of this aim the increasing development of science and repeated periods of the fullest flowering of art fell into its lap, it was only because without them the ample present-day achievements in the accumulation of wealth would have been impossible." Science has been very useful to modern capitalists—but art? How has it been able to produce wealth? It only enriched those cities that lived in luxury, and the sources of art's prosperity have often been the most corrupt; here it is no longer cupidity that intervenes, but incontinence.

Democratic policy is greatly concerned with protecting the arts metropolises live off. It establishes professional schools of theater and luxury industries; it gives artists encouragement that can end in constituting for them a veritable right to labor; it tries to attract as many foreigners as possible with festivals to provoke a constant influx of money. Modern states have abandoned mercantile policies and, while bringing their attention to the progress of "heavy industry," are no longer very concerned with the importation of gold. In spite of this, it often happens that the exploitation of foreign visitors is still regarded as one of the most fruitful sources of income. I do not believe that the latest World's Fair in Paris was made with any other purpose than to attract rich guests.

If all the inhabitants of the city are in agreement on attracting money, many violent disputes break out when it is necessary to divide the spoils. The entire urban economy is dominated by considerations of talent; it eschews the general determinants applied to large industry. Everyone desires to draw higher salaries from the sometimes enormous benefits produced by merchants. Given that prices depend on caprice—why should not able workers who maintain the good name of the local arts benefit from these happy circumstances?

In sum, the city is contrasted to the rest of the country as a place of consumption and pleasure which is the opposite of establishment of production and severe discipline; it is still the agglomeration of talented people who live at the expense of the mass of producers who do all they can to maintain the life of society. The more that the exodus of industry Vandervelde discusses, increases, the more apparent these urban characteristics become, and consequently the more democracy is separated from socialism with which it has been confused through accidental circumstances.

But we must also consider the intellectual function of the city, which has been enormously important in history. "What," asks Vandervelde,[18] "would antiquity be without Athens or Rome? What would the modern world be without London, Paris, or Berlin? What would contemporary life be if there were not, in every one of the great centers all that the nation reckoned as the best, all who thirst for truth and justice, all who, at the moment of crisis, rise up in protest every time it is necessary to battle iniquity or falsehood?" It is difficult to establish how this spiritual and revolutionary life of the city comes about. Vandervelde has not tried to discover it, and it would be interesting to determine whether art has a certain function here that is still badly accounted for.

Democracy is presented to us as also having a spiritual function, and it is this function that Vandervelde points out in the great cities; it brings into the world *the abstract* ideas of emancipation, liberty, and equality. These ideas are presented with all the more energy to the degree that the population in which these ideas ferment is independent of large industry. For example, the Parisian worker is always quick to take part in the cause pointed out to him as just, and he is the worker of the small establishment par excellence.

The cities are therefore potent ideological hosts, and with this qualification democracy can claim an influence over socialism. But modern socialism also teaches us that ideologies are sterile; it shows us the value of institutions which alone generate juridical concepts while democracy is consumed in declamations and accusations. Sycophants appear to be one of the essential parts of the democratic mechanism, and French parliamentary socialists have exhibited a delirious enthusiasm for the abominable delation made by the minister, Combes.

One can say many good and many bad things about democracy (just as Aesop thought one could for language). The relations between democracy and socialism are complicated and obscure; but here we have been concerned above all else with their differences. I hope that my readers will not be deceived as to the true importance of this scientific inquiry. If my book falls into the hands of some courtier of Jaurès he will accuse me of being a "vile reactionary," but the opinions of sycophants do not matter to me.

Notes

1. Emile Vandervelde, *L'Exode rurale et le retour aux champs* (Paris: F. Alcan, 1903), p. 211.
2. Democracy contains a mathematical absurdity because it promises the poor that, by equalizing revenue, one can give each citizen much more than the average.
3. Engels, *Origin of the Family, Private Property, and the State* (M.E.S.W., pp. 314, 325).
4. Cf. Giry, *Histoire de la ville de Saint-Omer et de ses institutions—Les établissements de Rouen.*
5. Charléty, *Histoire de Lyon depuis ses origines jusqu' à nos jours* (Lyon: A. Rey, 1903), pp. 298-99.
6. E. Vandervelde, *L'Exode rural*, pp. 253-55.
7. Masqueray, *Formation des cités chez les populations sédentaires de l'Algérie*, p. 154.
8. Flach, Lecture at the Collège de France, 1 April 1903.
9. This has been the reproach often made of the teaching institutions founded by Christians in Syria.
10. The French Revolution, faithful to the principles of democracy, had decreed an emolument to the members of the innumerable committees and citizens that attended the departmental assemblies. Taine, *Le gouvernement révolutionnaire*, pp. 298-303. Taine calculates that if the laws of 21 March and 5 September 1793 had been followed completely, there would have been 540,000 "patriots" employed by the revolutionary committees and this would have cost 591 million francs.
11. Australian writers give the name "primary industry" to cattle raising, to agriculture, and to mining; these are the three sources of national wealth in which the people of the big cities take no part whatever.
12. This confusion is especially notable in regard to the ancient Arabs; the explanations that Strabonius gives us stem from Greek sailors who had frequented the cities where prostitution was the principal industry. Even today in the Arab Hassanyeh of the White Nile there are houses in which the women have liberty of prostitution a certain number of times per week. Giraud-Teulon, *Les origines de la famille* (Geneva: A. Cherbuliez, 1874), p. 80.
13. Cf. Emile Desplanque, *Les infâmes dans l'ancien droit roussillonais* (Perpignan: C. Latrobe, 1893), pp. 98-108.
14. Guyau thinks that the realistic novel is too concerned with commercial success; he notes that Zola boasts of having for the first time in the novel given the genetic instincts their true place, and that, according to this author,

"the genetic instincts will become the incessant preoccupation of the human race." Guyau, *L'art au point de vue sociologique* (Paris: F. Alcan, 1889), p. 158.

15. Regarding the lawsuit against the famous pornographer, Willy, author of the *Claudine* books, the newspaper greatly admired the defense presented by an exsecretary of Waldek-Rousseau who launched a political career through exploiting the credulity of the workers.

16. Jaurès said to the 1900 International Congress: "As for the Heinze laws in Germany, the Socialists have not recoiled from defending the freedom of art, science and thought." Who would ever have doubted that pornography was related to science and thought! Pornography and socialism are too often in agreement; in *Petite République* (12 November 1902) I read: "*Greek love* was inoffensive and innocent; and this same ingenuousness adorns 'the unnatural vice' with a natural grace. . . . Christianity invented sin. It invents vows of chastity, and the shame of nudity. . . . In the society of which we dream everyone will have their share of bread, *roses*, and *embraces*." This will be truly strange! A veritable bordello!

17. Engels, *Origin of the Family, Private Property, and the State* (M.E.S.W., II, 325).

18. *Mouvement Socialiste* (15 February 1899):143–44.

PART I

CHAPTER ONE

The theories that serve to interpret history for the Marxists could not be better tested than through their application to modern socialism and especially to the vicissitudes of Marxist doctrine. The true method to follow to know the defects, inadequacies, and errors of a powerful philosophy is to criticize it by means of its own principles. Marxism is worth submitting to this procedure. How have economic facts generated ideas that were in absolute contradiction with current ideas? How have men imagined a future world that they can realize by their own strength? How does it come about that the hopes of the reformers have changed so much? Here are problems it would be interesting to resolve through the inspiration of historical materialism.

In the nineteenth century socialist doctrine was presented in an entirely different way than in the past. Formerly, philosophers had imagined new societies and described their dreams as if they were reality; but few people took these literary fantasies seriously. They were generally regarded as sermons destined to show men that they would not find happiness in the money-hungry life of the speculator or in that of a noble lord; to give a printed criticism of vice and of ridiculous contemporaries; to depict an enchanting picture of a society conceived according to a plan opposed to that of existing society—these were the works of the old utopians.[1] In the nineteenth century the creators of these systems had come to believe that their concepts could be realized shortly and had come to share such convictions with many.

During the nineteenth century socialist utopias ceased to be regarded as harmless. The moment the state began to concern itself with schooling was also the moment in which socialist doctrines ceased to be isolated paradoxes and became *historical data*, whose definitions can be given in a way that is all the more certain insofar as they are diffused among the masses. Henceforth it will no longer be considered important to know how one author has influenced another: rather it will be necessary to determine to what degree a reformer will have touched a common base in the great reservoir of current ideas of his time. Thus we will be able to understand why certain men can have such a great temporary success and later fall into sudden oblivion when popular concerns change.

103

The difference between the socialists of the nineteenth century and their predecessors is so great that one often hesitates to apply the name "utopian" to the former. In a lecture given on 17 May 1901 to the students of Berlin (translated into French under the title "Socialisme et science"), Edouard Bernstein endeavored to show that Owen, Saint-Simon, and Fourier had made a profound study of the "conditions of social life of their time and of the forces that had to be taken into consideration." According to Bernstein, between these authors and Marx there exists a difference in degree rather than an absolute opposition, in the sense that Marxism allows a more restricted place for the imagination, striving more for discovery than for invention, to determine means with a more practical direction. I will limit myself to calling attention to this fact: nineteenth-century socialism presents itself as an immediately realizable plan.

As men came to better understand what the "postulate of applicability" encompassed, they became greatly concerned with the economic conditions of their time. They asked themselves how such a plan could be realized when it had been deduced (more or less arbitrarily) from the observation of reputedly essential facts. The measure of the means suitable for realizing the idea became the principal object of the meditations of socialists. It is only because the experimental verification of their conceptions had proven impossible in the past (because of the weak economic development of society) that Owen, Saint-Simon, and Fourier could merit the name "utopians" according to many authorities. I am not representing the influence of economic conditions on doctrine as Bernstein does; this influence has been much more profound and unconscious than Bernstein admits. It has acted not only on the choice of means, but also on the way in which we consider the facts to determine their essential elements. It is enough to recognize that this influence has been considerable to understand the incoherence manifested by nineteenth-century socialism. Here one finds disparate doctrines which at first glance seem impossible to put into a general framework; obviously its transformations did not result from an internal logic and cannot be explained by a concatenation of ideas. Whatever the manner in which its influence is felt, the economy is an "external force"[2] that can produce the most unpredictable changes of attitudes: a school can appear over a long period to be the most complete expression of the modern economy and can succumb when industrial processes are modified. Could this not be the explanation, to which Jaurès and Kautsky have partly adhered, for the influence of Bernstein's ideas in Germany?[3]

During the nineteenth century economic facts presented a complexity that had no parallel in any previous time: never had there appeared in such an unpredictable way and in such a compact mass technical inventions of the first order and such powerful industrial combinations. One could say that here was a regime which, like a volcano, continuously upset the regular strata in the process of formation and which created new heights.

In the realm of economic facts, men take different attitudes that are more or less strictly attached to one of the three following determinants: (1) considerations on the present world according to our idea of preparation for a better world (e.g. judgments subordinated to the principle of *class struggle*); (2) the choice of the most direct and efficacious means for withdrawing from the existing regime (e.g. revolution, democratic evolution, state socialism); (3) affirmation of the new principle in opposition to the fundamental principle of the present time (e.g. communist principle opposing the individualist principle).

The reflections associated with the first category comprise the most concrete aspects of socialism; but it is obvious that our mental habits make the most abstract things the most popular, and much more has been written on the principles of the future than on ways for acting on the present. Man begins by adopting the most abstract attitudes and returns to the practical world only by a road that is both indirect and almost against his own volition. There will never be a lack of utopian thinkers to criticize what exists, find a thousand faults with the world, and condemn it in the name of a principle; but all this does not lead to social conclusions because reality has not been attained.

Today we are ever more persuaded that socialism is not a philosophy as much as a changing movement that is about to have a place in the complex of institutions. Marxism has had the great merit of causing this way of understanding things to enter into the public mind, and this acquired idea will never perish. It equally has the merit of reuniting in a solid synthesis the three systems of the socialist mind; in this its work has not been in vain. Finally, it has placed on the first level what utopians placed on the last—whose nature (the concrete aspects of socialism) they did not even understand. This lends such great importance to the Marxist notion of class struggle, a notion whose meaning almost completely escapes professional sociologists.

The mind is not determined by economic phenomena; it constructs its ideas on the basis of previous ideological formations that arise from traditions, from the knowledge of ancient or foreign institutions, or from the history of wars and revolutions. There are three sources of evaluation that can be made on the possibility of realizing something new in society. First, tradition has a more considerable importance in the formation of the mind, insofar as it acts in a hidden way. It is the mother of social instinct; it imposes rapprochements that are sometimes irresistible; it applies judgments that are almost always stereotypical to everything that occurs in front of us. We combat its action with the help of science; but one cannot always struggle against oneself. I believe that if we do not return to the historical origins of popular social concepts, it is impossible to understand the vast differences existing among the various workers' organizations of modern states.

Second, to discuss the possibility, utility, or justice of certain reforms, we can appeal to experience only by taking examples from the past or from other peoples. The public has a very imperfect knowledge of the civilization we talk about; besides, with very rare exceptions, we are unable to understand well the lifestyles that are foreign to our own or values based on traditions different from ours. The ablest people are disoriented when they have to compare legal reasoning of foreign countries to that of the law of their own. It is always easy to solicit the truth gently to demonstrate by experience the excellence of the doctrine that is being defended. There are very few inquiries made abroad which have serious scholarly value; even the most conscientious inquiries have always been influenced to some degree by the whims of the author.[4] On the other hand, we know from the history of the French Revolution what strange ideas our forefathers had of Roman and Spartan institutions and what trifles their admiration for poorly understood antiquity made them pronounce.

Third, legends born of wars and revolutions exert the most potent influence on the public mind while at the same time this influence is the most neglected. These legends impress us strongly and take away from us almost all freedom of appreciation. For the majority of men, history is reduced to these legends that are so deeply rooted in childhood memories of strong sentimental tone, that they cannot be eradicated by reason when one reaches maturity. The historical period designated by Vico as the Heroic Age has determined the direction taken by a civilization for centuries.

Greece was nourished by Homeric legends and later by those associated with the Persian wars. In France the memory of the revolution continually crosses our minds, and leads us far astray from considerations that should derive from the class struggle. This explains the constant influence of the Jacobin spirit and the anticlerical policy to which the French Socialist Party adheres, while the German Socialists recognize the right of association for the Catholic ecclesiastics. Kautsky[5] finds that his compatriots conform better to principles and that their conduct "responds better to the position that the proletariat occupies as a class," but he recognizes that "in France, the tradition of the revolution continues to exert a strong influence," so that socialists are obliged to be ferociously anticlerical to surpass the liberals "not only by the quality of the battle but also by the vigor of the struggle."

We have not yet exhausted the causes that create the great variety of socialist ideas. Now it is necessary to examine a very important law of transformation which depends on the structure of our minds. Since socialist ideas have entered the domain of collective phenomena, they have undergone a number of successive changes that have been ascertained in all branches of social activity. I have already called attention[6] to the great importance of one of Vico's theories that shows us how humanity passed from instinctive to intellectual thought; from sentiment to reason, from empiricism to science.[7] Vico believed that an entire civilization was caught up en bloc in the same movement; but it is easy to see that there are often more contemporaneous *psychological concatenations* not found at the same stage of development. New beginnings are not all produced at the same time as Vico had imagined, and they depend on many complex causes. It is obvious that Vico was not able to predict the transformations that stem from modern political life; but these transformations tend to make warlike sentiments pass over into utilitarian compromises and thus reenter into its general formulations.

In its beginnings, socialism contained many fantasies; it was strongly influenced by popular suffering, economic crises, and political revolutions which produced a strong exaltation of the sentiments of revolt and revolutionary aspirations for a better world.[8] When socialism becomes a political party, it is impossible for it to avoid the law of transformation, and it is vulnerable at all times to sacrificing its principles to the convenience of public opinion. It is absolutely necessary for it to become "practical," which leads it to abandon simplicity and move into complexity;[9] to abandon the absolute and be content with the relative; to abandon the ideal for the sake of tangible advantages for the electorate. Thus the "social question" is transformed, to use Gambetta's expression, into "social questions" that we are forced to dispose of in series to avoid difficulty. Communism being the most unitary, most absolute, and most ideal form of socialism, ought to be primitive; but little by little this conception was abandoned on behalf of less complete solutions. Several years ago, Serverio Merlino noted[10] that many official Marxists had abandoned their theory of a homogeneous future society and were increasingly preoccupied with minimal programs, or even foreign to socialism. Kautsky himself seems shaken in his faith: he no longer believes that the social revolution will bring communism to us as if by magic, but[11] he reckons that it will be the beginning of a new era, the origin of a new development. Only after a long evolution will it be possible to abolish small rural property.

At first socialists wanted to suppress the state; now they ask that the state become industrialized, and distinguish between good and bad governments. In politics, a government is always excellent when its friends take part in it.[12] After having rapidly descended the opportunistic decline that leads to immediate results, certain French socialists thought of returning to the old revolutionary aspirations; but they were not followed by the great majority of their adherents. It appears that they have not yet understood the cause of such an event. For a new revolutionary beginning to occur, there would have had to be an upheaval like that of June 1848 or March 1871; in vain does one seek to galvanize the popular masses by making appeals to the legendary memories of the Paris Commune. The presence of General Gallifet alongside Millerand in the government seemed an excellent reason why the workers abandoned opportunistic socialism; but images cannot produce that tension and concentration of the mind of which we spoke above: only the reality in the midst of which we live can generate a new revolutionary beginning. We have a good illustration of this in Vico's theory. The movement of the mind can occur only in the sense indicated by this great thinker, and the most active sermonizing is powerless to renovate the current of the mass of people.

I strongly emphasize this general question because it is necessary to understand well the reasons why it is not possible that the socialist idea be determined precisely by economic factors. The attitudes men take in the presence of reality are highly variable according to circumstances, and the law of psychological concatenations still comes to exert a disturbing influence on the whole. It is like an optical device that is turned around before our eyes and which mutes the relative value of things.

To perform a useful task, we need to know how to confine ourselves to considering the most important socialist conceptions of a given period, to separate what is accessory from what is characteristic, and also to look for the essential nucleus in economic life. This is not always easy, because the economic structure is composed of many disparate elements inadvertently accumulated; and in addition the powerful social philosophies are never completely coordinated.[13] It seems that, if they became completely logical, they would lose a great part of their influence on the world.

Notes

1. Read what I have said about utopianism in my *Saggi di critica del marxismo*, pp. 135-37 *(From Georges Sorel,* pp. 130–31.) Vilfredo Pareto has explained very well how Thomas More created his *Utopia*: "His system is simple enough: it consists in identifying the ills of society and portraying the opposite of them." Pareto, *Systèmes Socialistes* (Paris: M Giard, 1926), Vol. II, p. 252.

2. Jehring has made great efforts to imbue juridical scholarship with the notion of external causes which he opposes to that of the logical development of the idea. In his fragment on "The History of the Development of Roman Law," he strongly insists on the importance of this perspective. "I am convinced," he concludes, "that in all branches of human consciousness, this is the road to follow in order to advance scientific research and thought."

3. Cf. the lecture by Jaurès on 10 February 1900: *Mouvement Socialiste* (1 March 1900):258 (15 March):362.

4. I have said in chapter 2 of the Introduction, above, that the school of Le Play undertakes much bad research.

5. *Mouvement Socialiste* (15 December 1902):2268.

6. *Saggi di critica del marxismo*, p. 153.

7. Théodule Ribot in his *Essai sur l'imagination créatrice* (Paris: F. Alcan, 1900) recognizes the great merit that Vico had had in giving a schema of the development of the imagination which passes through successively more rational stages (pp. 138–45.) Modern psychology has nothing essential to add to what Vico has said on this point. I believe that I have been one of the first to note in France the great importance of this law. G. Sorel, "Etude sur Vico," *Devenir Social* (November 1896):911.

8. Under the influence of this exaltation, people can no longer see things as they are; all their faculties are simultaneously excited and reduced, constrained and concentrated in a highly limited field. They are the victims of what might be called "the illusion of subjective reason," which consists in believing that one augments one's power of acting on the world and that one can attain the "mysterious principles of becoming," putting themselves beyond reality, constructing *unitary*, *absolute*, and *ideal theories*. When we want to approach reality in order to accomplish something, we find ourselves in the presence of difficulties which lead us to change our initial concepts in order to be able to act: or to adopt average solutions, or to enclose ourselves in a restricted circle, or to limit ourselves to doing things which are not hindered by the general conditions of society; to be free by limiting the importance of one's own ideal. Thus monastic institutions are developed and the communists have often attempted to realize their ideals in colonies.

9. Théodule Ribot says that "increasing complexity" is a secondary law in the development of the imagination, and connects it to rational development (*Essai sur l'imagination créatrice*, p. 142). I believe I am closer to the truth by connecting it to practice.

10. Francesco Merlino, *L'utopia collettivista*, (Milan: Fratelli Treves, 1898) pp. 21-35.

11. *Mouvement Socialiste*, 15 September 1902, p. 1639. In another article he says: "Naturally we hardly think of the immediate socialization of the means of production. *Mouvement Socialiste* (15 December 1902):2270. There would

be a period of partial collectivism, and Merlino rightly estimates that such a regime does not constitute collectivism. *L'utopia collettivista*, p. 22.

12. According to Vandervelde, the Belgian workers would not have the same reasons as the German workers in showing hostility to the exploitation of the mines by the state, because in Belgium "parliamentary institutions are not a vain appearance." *Mouvement Socialiste* (15 December):2229.

13. This is very notable in Marxism; Marx and Engels never attempted to give the definitive formula. This definitive formula of Marxism, often claimed by philosophers, will be given on the day on which Marxism dies.

CHAPTER TWO

In all of Europe at the end of the eighteenth century there arose a strong current of opinion favoring agronomic progress. For a long time French writers tried to diminish the importance of this great economic phenomenon; they attributed the prosperity of modern France solely to the beneficent effects of revolutionary legislation so that, listening to them, the modern economy would have to have been determined by political upheavals. It is likely that in the French universities we still find these "scientists" convinced that things happened this way. Nobody will deny that the sale of landed estates, the progressive crumbling of inheritance, the disappearance of feudal tithes and laws exerted a beneficent influence in France, but we would also have to take account of the spoliation of Europe by the French army, whose effects were no less "beneficial" than those of the wars of liberty.

When we compare France to other countries, we see that it has not been the only one to advance very rapidly, and that the progress had everywhere as its essential cause the improvements in methods of cultivation. Several scholars have gone so far as to affirm that the revolutionary legislation and the enrichment from the spoils of war had not done much more than compensate for the great loss of strength France had undergone during a long period of turbulence; but it is useless to pose such an issue, because it would be impossible to provide a satisfactory solution.[1]

Everyone agrees in recognizing that great technical progress had been made throughout Europe. We know what enthusiasm had been produced in this period by the mass consumption of the potato: in 1761 Turgot took under his protection the potato which thenceforth became a "philosophical product." The *Encyclopaedia* devotes a long article to it; the work of Parmentier extends from 1771 to 1778. During the revolution the potato appeared to many patriots as the symbolic food that replaced the Spartan's broth, and the Convention had no less admiration for this tuber than the ancien régime had had. Artificial experiments were enthusiastically propagated by those who prided themselves on the knowledge of economic phenomena. Dupont de Nemours, during his disfavor after Turgot had retired, introduced them to Gatinais.[2] The rental value of land that had not ceased to drop since the end of the seventeenth century and which fell to its lowest point toward 1750, rapidly climbed back up and often surpassed the values attained during the best years of the seventeenth century.[3]

Our ancestors were unable to examine economic questions as it is done in our times because they did not have any idea of industrial arts. *The picturesque side of labor* seduced them because they could not view it other than through the eyes of the *gens du monde*. Even though the articles in the *Encyclopaedia* deal with agricultural or industrial subjects or with physical sciences, they are almost always conceived in such a way as to have as their purpose the satisfaction of curiosity. We know what the judicial chamber of natural history at that time consisted of: arms of savages, Roman medals, electrical machines, and conches formed a muddle then regarded as scientific; the *Encyclopaedia* is a multivolume muddle.

An economy that is not based on a rational consciousness of technology should give a preponderant place to sentiments. Technology takes man in his labor and tries to know how he uses the instruments at his disposal. But the men of the eighteenth century did not see in all this what we regard as essential; they saw only a pretty picture which could give the subjects entertaining descriptions. If they wanted to go further, they asked how the various professional types were distinguished in everyday life. Thus studies were made on the lifestyle of doctors, teachers, merchants, sailors, landed gentry, peasant proprietors, etc. These studies illuminated only trifling secondary phenomena that arise in production and which do not permit us to see how social relations develop and change in the course of time.

Our ancestors had been greatly impressed by the devotion with which the small peasantry cultivated their land and by the negligence the great lords showed for their properties.[4] They thought that the crumbling of the large estates was basically in the area of agronomy and admitted implicitly that the *surface area of farm property is a determining factor of sentiments*. They assumed that the desires of the proprietor are sufficient for determining the mode of cultivating the soil. This concept seems quite extraordinary to us today; the function of the will appears to us much less considerable than it did to our forefathers. We must try to learn the causes of their errors.

First, there is a cause directly connected to agriculture. In old times the peasant had much free time and, this nothwithstanding, was hardly disposed to cultivate the land well; he liked idleness like a savage, and, having only imperfect instruments, often withdrew when confronted with the immense work of a good harvest. Numerous popular tales and proverbs had the purpose of reminding the peasant that he would find treasures in that fertile land which he neglected so much.[5] The will seems therefore to be the regulator of fecundity. Later Fourier would believe that with the right enthusiasm one could obtain everything that the imagination can dream of.

The most important source of the illusions regarding the will is of aristocratic origin. The notable personages were used to satisfying all their caprices: they paid no heed to expense when it came to displaying their wealth or indulging in some absurd extravagance. The poets repeated to them that their power did not extend only to tailors and upholsterers, but that they even went so far as to inspire artistic works of genius. The kings were convinced that it was their task to oversee literature and science.

Aristocratic ideas passed almost completely to the bourgeoisie. We still see people making appeals to the goodwill of millionaires to create public theaters which (according to their promoters) would undoubtedly support a new art, etc. They continue to distribute academic prizes, and the state opens up competitions in the hope that an unknown scientist will come forth with an unforeseen discovery. Despite acquired experience, law schools continue to teach that the will is sovereign in technological phenomena: according to the official professors, all laws that hinder the actions of capitalists (whether shortening the working day or increasing taxes) serve to help the progress of industry and *force* the contractors to *invent* new machinery. It is clear that there is no cause and effect relationship between the desire to reduce the cost of production or increase labor and the invention of a machine. For example, it is clear that for a long time men have desired a means of rapid transportation, without this desire having advanced the invention of the bicycle.

The illusion of the literati of the eighteenth century was strongly held by members of Le Play's school. Le Play had made some good observations on working-class families and especially on those concerned with agriculture; he observed the great importance that family traditions exerted in the countries in which it appeared to him that the peasantry enjoyed the greatest well-being. Misinterpreting his observations, he believed it was possible to create economic prosperity with reforms relating to family life. His errors have been greatly amplified by his school of followers, which has taken from his doctrines only the mania for sentimental explanations.

Le Play did not exercise any influence on the country because he came on the scene too late. He based his theory on assertions by men imbued with the prejudices of the eighteenth century. Completely immersed in the ideas of his time, Napoleon believed that his legislation on primogeniture would have great social importance; this was not the only time he had been mistaken. In 1833 Le Play was told that at the time of the Treaty of Vienna an English diplomat had said that France would never be able to improve itself because of the ill-effects of the system of inheritance established by the civil code.[6] This anecdote greatly struck him. It is entirely natural that one of those Tories that succeeded William Pitt should have spoken thus. In the eighteenth century, the fanaticism of "landlordism" had made the English commit many errors in Scotland and in India.[7] But when Le Play wrote his books he should have looked to experience and seen that the hazy forecasts of the admirers of great property had not come true. The great defect of the ideas of Le Play's school lay in its psychology. They believed that, in the last analysis, everything is explained by the general qualities that novelists recognize: enthusiasm, abnegation, foresight. These qualities certainly have an important function in economic life; but they take on different colors according to the type of occupation, and do not serve any purpose when viewed as abstractions.

The men of the eighteenth century were much less bothered by this psychology than we are, because they were not used to determining with any precision the variety of psychological capacities. To their historical study they brought an extremely abstract notion of man, and they believed that the same arrangement of sentiments reigned throughout all ages. Judging the past through their means of feeling, they had to think also that *man is uniform in all tasks*, and that consequently the workers ought to have the same sentiments as the wealthy classes *when amused by manual labor in the workshop or in the fields*. If there were a difference, it should be explained by the influence of the shadow of the past and it was destined to disappear. The fashionable agriculture of the Trianon was the most perfect illustration of the theories of the eighteenth century. In the past, the aristocracy had been very concerned with land, but had abandoned these pursuits since the reign of the Bourbons. Now there was a return to the land, but with serious purposes and enlightened by experience. Economic science tried to demonstrate that there was no other source of wealth than agriculture; continually the economists vaunted China where "the sovereign plowed the land with his own hands once a year."[8] Rousseau had shortly before celebrated the heretofore unknown beauties of nature and popularized the idea of introducing manual labor into the education of the children of the wealthy. It had to result from all this that the theories of social reform be deeply penetrated by agronomical concerns. All these theories of reform had a bucolic character and were reattached in form to the utopias of the Renaissance, which are Virgilian manifestations.

Now we find it hard to understand the ideas of this period. The French Revolution often presents a vile mixture of the tragic and bucolic. The repugnance one feels today in reading the descriptions of official celebrations of the revolution deters many people from inquiring into the historical significance of these celebrations and especially of understanding that they manifested, in an ingenious and clear way, the greatest depths of the spirit of our ancestors. Their illusions were so strong that they believed in applying the most rigorous scientific data and giving full satisfaction to the needs of the spirit while mixing their idylls with mathematic reasoning and statistics on income. Agricultural labor was still performed under social conditions replete with feudal memories, at least in most of France. We know that dying feudalism could only regard the land as a machine for producing a net income. The physiocrats, in their dissertations on net income, did not express ideas relative to the future of society, as is often believed, but ideas relative to the past.[9] In their eyes, except for the landed proprietors, there was no income; there were only annual wage payments for the necessities of life. Only the gentry had to pay taxes as coparticipants in property with the king. *Physiocratism is entirely feudal.* This explains why it perished so quickly; it ceased to be comprehended in the generation after Turgot, which, in the world of the literati, was no longer concerned with understanding the role of fiefdoms in the latest expression of French law.

On such questions of revenue Le Play was still very close to the old economists; he had wasted an enormous amount of time compiling budgets of working-class families. The usefulness of this labor today seems rather limited to us but great for those who judged it from the feudal perspective. The master needed to know whether the servant made good use of his income and whether it was sufficient to allow him to fulfill all his family duties. If the salary was too low, the master would have to intervene at certain times; the budgets compiled with care allowed the master to know what was needed to ensure the prosperity of his domestics.[10] Today these statistics do not deceive anyone; they are no longer given much scientific value, all the more because we are no longer disposed to appreciate a book just because it is laced with mathematical figures and formulas.[11]

Notes

1. Cournot thought that the French Revolution produced a delay in the progressive momentum and that, under Napoleon I, France had not returned to the level of 1789. *Considérations sur la marche des idées et des événements dans les temps modernes* (Paris: Hachette, 1872), Vol. II, pp. 246–47. Doniol, on his part, observes the great inconveniences resulting from the

revolutionary processes in abolishing the feudal regime. *La Révolution française et la féodalité*, 1st ed., pp. 347–61.

2. *Les Physiocrates*, in the Daire Collection, p. 318. There was also very much concern over the means of combatting grain diseases, and Tillet performed experiments in front of the king. G. Boyd, *Le pacte de famine*, pp. 30–31. It was toward the middle of the eighteenth century that the new methods of grinding began to be introduced into practice; the mills of Corbeil owed their prosperity to them; in 1766 official experiments proved that one could obtain 66 white flour units to the hundred instead of 23 to the hundred. Ibid., p. 60.

3. D. Zolla, *Études d'économie rurale* (Paris: G. Masson, 1896), pp. 415–17. The author has calculated the rental value of lands belonging to a certain number of big hospitals.

4. Young wrote: Every time that you encounter a great lord, even if he has millions, you can be sure that his property is badly cultivated. Oh! if I were, only for one day, a legislator for France, I would shake all these great lords. Cited in Frédéric Le Play, *Réforme sociale en France*, 3d ed. (Paris: H. Plon, 1864), Vol. I, p. 278. Young wrote this in regard to the Prince of Soubise and the Duc de Bouillon. As for wonders produced near the Ganges by small-scale farming and admired by Young, see P. Leroy-Beaulieu, *Traité théorique et pratique d'économie politique* (Paris: Guillaumin, 1896), Vol. II, p. 161; this author thinks that for us such wonders are no longer realized because the peasants have been given to believe that "labor is servitude."

5. La Fontaine, *Fables*, Book V, 9: "Le laboureur et les enfants."

6. Le Play, *Réforme sociale en France*, Vol. I., p. 266.

7. The creation of great estates of the *Zemandars* in Bengal was true folly. Laveleye, *De la propriété et de ses formes primitives*, 2nd ed. (Paris: G. Baillière, 1877), pp. 352–58.

8. Alexis de Tocqueville, *L'Ancien régime et la révolution*, p. 272.

9. It seems to me that this concept is in complete contradition with that of Kautsky. *Mouvement Socialiste* (1 October 1902):1749. But I cannot come to understand the history of the physiocrats without this theory. In recently-published fragments written by Marx we find him noting that the physiocrats gave a feudal appearance to bourgeois society.

10. Proudhon, *De la justice* (Paris: Garnier Frères, 1858), Vol. 2, p. 359.

11. Claude Bernard in his *Introduction to the Study of Experimental Medicine* (New York: Dover, 1957, Henry Copley Green, trans.) combats the pseudo-mathematical prejudices that were still imposed on physiologists 40 years or so ago.

CHAPTER THREE

The wars of liberty gave extraordinary impetus to the civic feelings of the French people who had seemed to be in a slumber since the classical period.[1] The return to antiquity that sometimes seems bizarre in the revolutionary period was not just a fantasy; it arose from the most powerful force of the time. It is insufficient to do as Marx did, who, in the early pages of the *Eighteenth Brumaire*, said that the men of this time needed a mask to disguise from themselves the narrow-minded character of their "bourgeois" struggles.[2] We should at least add that this evocation of antiquity was the only means our ancestors had for comprehending the enormous responsibility that governments were obligated to assume. It is because the necessities of war made *the modern state return to the ancient city* that one could speak like the Spartans and the Romans without seeming ridiculous.

Now man will become the Roman *citizen*, simultaneously soldier and farmer. Due to this classical evocation, the ideas that emerge from the rural economy come to be mixed with those that arise from war and therefore acquire a new forcefulness. Thanks to this union, bucolic conceptions are established well into the middle of the nineteenth century as an appendix to the spirit of the revolution. Nothing less than the revolution produced by the railroads would be necessary to make these bucolic ideas disappear. In fact, they would not disappear completely and would remain concentrated in the university world, nourished by the classical culture and by the "religion of 1789." The day on which this world made its noisy entrance into the socialist party with Jaurès at its head, we saw the reappearance of many concepts we thought had disappeared forever.

To study the history of these ideas, it is not enough to say, as Plekhanov has,[3] that the theorists of that time, pretending to reason on the basis of abstract man, were really thinking in terms of the Third Estate from which they translated political or economic needs into dogmas of natural right. The question is much more complex than the Russian writer thinks. It is evident that the eighteenth-century philosophers were unable to construct the ideal of the desirable city, except with the elements they had on hand—populating it with men like

117

them and assuming the realization of their most cherished hopes. This is obvious and hardly deserves attention. What we should emphasize is that the thinkers of this period always portray a *rustic* society, and that the heritage of the Roman republic dominated their ideas on law and the state.

The man on whom this philosophy is based is a *proprietor of abstract land*. The neo-Roman citizen is so grand that the material conditions of production and exchange are nothing in comparison to the internal powers presumed to derive from his virtue. Juridico-economic determinants are suppressed and remain only abstractions, conforming to the aspirations of people who have read Rousseau at length. "Natural man" is a Roman transported to the eighteenth century, who lives happily in his little farm, always quick to defend his rights and to take up arms to rush to the defense of the fatherland.

It is for this ideal peasant, fabricated in imitation of classical antiquity, that the *Declaration of the Rights of Man* was drawn. The peasant wants to be master in his house; he intends to cultivate his fields as he pleases. Whether he is rich or poor, he wants to have an equal opportunity to share in his heritage. He needs the police to obtain security; he fears heavy taxes extracted for the pleasures of urbanites. It is these desires that the many French constitutions claim to satisfy, and for which there is still enthusiasm among the professors. Lucky idealists: the kingdom of heaven is guaranteed to you.

We do not err much when we apply the distinction philosophers made between innate and acquired laws. According to this doctrine one cannot place property among the "natural and inalienable rights of man," as was done in 1789. Anton Menger says[4] that generally admitted theories "have been constructed by putting oneself principally in the perspective of the wealthy classes." The Austrian professor is too abstract and is not concerned with the preoccupations of the men of 1789. These men did not theorize on the basis of a man deprived of all means of acting on the world. They understood (better than our contemporaries) that such a being would have been absolutely undetermined and *devoid of rights*. We should not forget the rural characters of the neo-Roman city whose realization was assumed. The citizen was a farmer-soldier. Our modern bourgeois socialists too often forget this detail; they no longer have the poetic sentiment of the countryside, and besides attack the army. They have only scorn for men who concentrate in their persona all the epics of the wars of conquest. Their discourse is therefore devoid of all reason.

The theory of the rights of man lead scholars to no longer distinguish the field from the persona of its proprietor; they considered property as an *extension of the self*. The eighteenth-century economists often repeated that labor is the main form of property; indeed it is the first material manifestation of our human force, the first individual characteristic imprinted on things, the first extension of the *self*. From labor one proceeds to the appropriation of products and finally to the appropriation of natural instruments. This theory of property that was accepted by only a few authors before 1789 became in a certain sense "official" after the revolution, without historians having clearly perceived what gives it this importance.[5]

The sophistic character of these doctrines lies in the fact that they overturn real relations; they claim to explain property as emerging from the self, that is, from our conscious activity. But first we must know why this self already encloses *in the unconscious state* all the principles that in their development beget the relations of property. It encloses them in the self for historical reasons which philosophy should analyze, and not accept as an eternal principle of human nature. These inversions are familiar to all those who study the evolution of ideas with Marxist methods;[6] in their eyes it is only the interior that clarifies the exterior, but it is the exterior that permits us to understand our ideological constructions. The theoretical citizen has been conceived of with property; it is therefore natural that we find property in all his external manifestations.[7] Once the ideological inversion is realized, philosophy tries to create the external world by the power of thought, which results in all kinds of contradictory conclusions.

Since production is not taken into consideration in the study of the legal relations of men, economic determinants are regarded as secondary. Material inequalities are not commensurate with the virtue of the "new man" and could not be taken into consideration; class distinctions can find no place in natural right. When we read the works written to justify the present regime, it is amazing to see how often their authors begin with principles that seem in keeping with revolution and nevertheless arrive at highly conservative yet arbitrary conclusions because of their lack of economic considerations. Quite different conclusions could have been reached.

The system of the rights of man could not be completely realized except if all citizens were *truly* landed proprietors; many projects for social reform arise from this conception. It does not appear that the crumbling of inheritance will come to realize this universalization of property; the question of whether there is a tendency in this direction or whether, on the contrary, there is some concentration of rural property has been widely discussed. Those who uphold the former thesis estimate that we must leave things alone since natural evolution is taking a desirable direction. Those who uphold the thesis of concentration claim the need to intervene to remedy a state of affairs that is deteriorating every day. In the eighteenth century several observers were impressed with the lifestyle of the peasants in certain parts of Switzerland, where some lands were enjoyed in common. Not long ago de Laveleye tried to demonstrate that the solution to the social problem could be found through generalization of the *Allemand*.[8]

The theory of the extension of the self can also lead to communism. If one suppresses all considerations of historical development to explain the relations of production, property becomes only *a scenario constructed by humanity* so that we can conveniently represent the *drama of life*, or an instrument we create to act upon nature. All this can be changed at any time since it is accidental; and all this ought to be changed when *the needs of our spirit* are modified, or else when we conceive of other means of manifesting our activity.

Psychology knows only states of consciousness and does not understand that one limits the extension of the self because of conditions that depend on economic forces and the development of production. The moralist avoids as much as possible the prosaic terrain of material factors to reach the high summits of the ideal and finds himself completely disoriented when he wants to theorize on property or on production. He began by suppressing property to speak of the universal duties of man, and he is no longer able to find it again—despite the efforts he later made in the pursuit of reality. He is in a situation diametrically opposed to that of the jurist who, wishing to formulate the rights of the citizen, assumed property as a given and later discovered it everywhere. The poet of nature is imbued with sentiments of love that revert men back toward childish perspectives;[9] he cannot understand how the tender sentiments he praises, and which appear to him as the most noble of our existence, can be rejected and tyrannized by the material conditions of production. In his eyes, society is only truly human when it is composed of loving people and includes only communism as the most complete basis of fraternity.

One can attain another type of communism combining the theory of the extension of the self with pseudojuridical considerations on the state. According to the idealists, property has no determinant whatever. It is everything we can possess, everything that can be obtained through our activity. Its limits depend on accidental causes; *it is* by nature *indefinite*. We are used to thinking that the state has the right to claim wealth not privately owned, everything that does not have regular antecedents in civil live (for example, mineral wealth and floods produced by the sea). This *routine* is so confirmed among us that we have transformed it almost mechanically into axioms of natural right. Property being indefinite and accidental cannot therefore be attributed to anything but the state, like all wealth with no true owner. This doctrine has had immense consequences in modern social philosophy; many authors have not dared go into it very deeply and have been content to claim property revenue for the state. This doctrine, adopted by John Stuart Mill, became very popular among the English because it is combined with feudal vestiges that exercise an influence on the minds of this people.

Since the history of primitive institutions is better understood nowadays, people have generally abandoned these considerations of abstract right to base the claims of the state on proven facts. A dossier was produced as if there were a trial between two fictional parties, *collectivism* and *individualism*, arguing before a court: one claimed to prove that property was "tribal property" in the first instance, and private property was regarded as a usurpation due especially to violent or immoral means.

In the formation of the theories of these sociologists, we must note the great influence of certain now-vanished productive relations, originating from the old extensive agriculture whose ideological consequences persisted in philosophy as well as in public opinion. In the old agriculture, land was regarded as the inexhaustible source of wealth, whose quality persisted indefinitely while the effects of human labor disappear almost completely after a year. Man is therefore only a temporary proprietor; the true proprietor should be a permanent *persona*. The sociologists, having found in the course of history numerous manifestations of familial or communal property, have been led to think that the family and the commune (entities that endure) were legitimate possessors of an order markedly superior to that based on individuals who exist for a short period. Legal practices have made us think that there are possessions which do not matter for the acquisition of property. It is therefore possible to admit that primitive tribal property always remains the regime based on law, whereas private holders never had anything but a precarious or fraudulent possession of the common domain.

If the domain of the commune is inalienable, the same should be true of the property of the people, who are and have always been sovereign. In making their political sovereignty recognized, they claim their property which had been invaded illegally. The memory of Roman agrarian laws has also helped to strengthen this outlook. With a highly intensive agriculture, such a doctrine would lose most of its value. In this case, what would be important would be the immense accumulation of improvements that previous generations have brought to the soil, and which form an inheritance received only under certain conditions by those who till it today. From that moment there appear the fictions of debt contracted to the past, by a semisocial contract, etc.[10] on which it is useless to insist; it is enough to indicate agronomical origin.

Notes

1. See what I have written on this subject in Georges Sorel, *La ruine du monde antique* (Paris: Rivière, 1925), p. 119, passim.
2. Here is a case in which purely economic explanations are singularly erroneous.
3. Georg Plekhanov, *Anarchism and Socialism*, French trans. (Paris: Galéries de l'Odéon, 1896–97), p. 46.
4. Anton Menger, *Le droit au produit intégral du travail*, p. 46.
5. André Lichtenberger, *Le socialisme au XVIII siècle* (Paris: F. Alcan, 1895), 9–10; *Le socialisme et la révolution française* (Paris: F. Alcan, 1899), pp. 182–84, 297.
6. *Capital* (Fr. ed.), Vol. I, p. 350, col. 2. Cf. p. 34, col. 1, n.2.
7. In the second part of *Capital*, Vol. III (Moscow: International Publishers, p. 616), Marx criticized Hegel's theory of property: "Free private ownership of land, a very recent product, is, according to Hegel, not a definite social relation, but a relation of man as an individual to 'nature,' an absolute right of man to appropriate all things. . . . 'External things are more extensive than I can grasp. By thus having possession of such a thing, some other is thereby connected to it. I carry out the act of appropriation by means of my hand, but its scope can be extended' (p. 90). But this other thing is again linked with still another, and so the boundary within which my will, as the soul, can pour into the soil, disappears. 'When I possess something, my mind at once passes over to the idea that not only this property in my immediate possession, but what is associated with it is also mine. Here positive right must decide, for nothing more can be deduced from the concept.' This is an extraordinarily naive admission of 'the concept,' and proves that this concept which makes the blunder at the very outset of regarding as absolute a very definite legal view of landed property—belonging to bourgeois society— understands 'nothing' of the actual nature of this landed property. This contains at the same time the admission that 'positive right' can, and must, alter its determinations as the requirements of social, i.e., economic, development change." It does not seem to me that Marx sufficiently demonstrated the error of Hegel, who claimed to make theory walk submissively in the shadow of practice and who manifestly presupposes property in the acts which are destined to generate it.
8. Laveleye, pp. 299–314, 375–78. In regard to the influence of Switzerland in the eighteenth century, cf. Lichtenberger, *Le socialisme au dix-huitième siècle*, pp. 342–45; Benedetto Croce, *Studii storici sulla rivoluzione napoletana del 1799* (Rome: Bretschneider and Regenberg, 1897), pp. 107–12. We know that the village of Mardyck, near Dunkirk, preserves institutions dating from Louis XIV: all families have the right to extract 22 acres from the common lands. If the idea of a similar endowment to all families that are formed can be realized, there would be an internal and continuous colonization

that would keep workers in the fields. Louis XIV gave Mardyck the constitution that still exists in order to maintain a population of sailors.

9. It has often been noted that love produces in man a veritable retrogression to childhood; this is particularly noticeable in bucolic poetry. Besides, it seems that in this poetry love finds its most complete expression; there are few men in whom the spectacle of nature does not produce erotic excitement. (See my "La Valeur sociale de l'art," *Revue de métaphysique et de morale*, 1901.)

10. Léon Bourgeois, *La Solidarité*, (Paris: A. Colin, 1896), pp. 101, 115–40. The idea of solidarity has assumed great importance in our day because of protectionism.

CHAPTER FOUR

A few years after the tempest of the French Revolution, Fourier published his utopia, that we need not regard either as simple fantasy or as an economic system susceptible of scientific discussion. We need to find a historical explanation for it. Fourier's books give a faithful description of the customs and aspirations of the new proprietary classes: they are frivolous, deeply interested in luxury and good cuisine; caring little for moral rules; and they want amusement and are highly desirous of immediate diversions. These characteristics are found among the Harmonians, and one of the strongest arguments Fourier thought he could bring his readers was showing them that in fewer years than are normally necessary to establish a serious industrial business, he would introduce them to the happy regions of the new life.[1] He keeps returning to this point; his contemporaries were overexcited by revolutionary upheavals and had the souls of speculators. The wars of liberty brought with them a great flow of money; the country conquered by France ("officially" liberated) had been making contributions in a very conscientious way. Says Kautsky:

> Not only did the soldiers despoil countries at their pleasure, but what they took was only a trifle in comparison with the enormous sums the generals and commissioners extorted, partly for themselves, and partly for the treasury which in turn was pillaged by avid suppliers and statesmen. After the fall of the Jacobins, the war became good business, the best at that time. It was through war that there poured into France the treasures amassed under feudalism and which lie inactive in the churches, in the monasteries and the money boxes of princes, as well as the wealth of the Dutch and Italian commercial republics. . . . The great fortunes grew like mushrooms and looked for advantageous investment. . . . The army obtained all these advantages. And if we want to understand the political importance the army came to have, we should not forget its impact on the economic development of France.[2]

Money was easily earned provided one had a slightly alert intelligence and that one spent it cheerfully. These two characteristic traits are found in Fourier's ideas. It is well known what gluttons men of this period were; fine cuisine was one of the grand preoccupations of the *parvenus* of that time. Fourier is possessed by this understanding and desires to make the art of cooking one of the bases of his organization. He wanted to develop the appetites of the Harmonians in an extraordinary way and at the same time teach them to make subtle distinctions among highly similar dishes. "Gastrosophy" became for Fourier the object of meditations that replaced those of philosophy. In the past it was believed that refined taste ought to be applied especially to the fine arts; Fourier applied it to the preparation of food. He noted with scorn the absence of gastronomical principles among Frenchmen; that in a single dinner, even if prepared very carefully, more than fifteen errors were committed that would be noticed even by a baby Harmonian.[3]

The luxury of apartments and clothing after the revolution reached a very high and ridiculous level; in Fourier's Phalanxes we find the taste for ostentation almost always observed in societies that have become rich in a great hurry. The sumptuous parades and great reviews passed from the Napoleonic world into Harmony;[4] the theater and the church figure symetrically in the plan of the Phalanx. According to the Napoleonic idea, Catholic ceremonies are a species of opera.

Fourier spends much discussion on new sexual customs. I will not stop here to speak of the combinations by means of which he claims to procure the love of poor youths to rich old women, nor of the bizarre allusions to unnatural sexual practices. The prospect of being one of the Antinous and Phyrnes[5] leaves no doubt: in Harmony every erotic fantasy is admitted (Cambaceres who was the archetype of the old revolutionary-become-establishmentarian was said to have had slightly oriental tastes). We should devote more attention to the vestal virgins;[6] the prince or princesses of the blood (who are the same as our present king and aristocracy) go to the army to seek a mate. In the oddest way, this concept of sexual union similar to that of the animals resembles Napoleonic behavior; the emperor hardly placed more dignity in his matrimonial proceedings and regarded a woman as a reproductive machine, that is, as a *beast of burden*.

The love relationships provide us with exceedingly suggestive approaches as to the customs of the period; for example, here is an after-dinner welcome given by Gnidiani for two travelers: "Following them are two groups of dancing girls; and of Bachantes who scatter themselves throughout the room. . . . The love dignitaries, fairies and sylphs, genies and magicians, arrange groups based on *occasional attraction*."[7] We have here only a sketch, the author not having wanted to describe what occurs in the *court of love*. We know that in the early morning they were in the habit of having "backyard romances . . . where all the intrigues of the night are settled."[8]

We have here a slightly embellished description of the public balls that were so successful at the beginning of the nineteenth century and on which officials spent so much money. Compare the passages in which Fourier speaks of amorous relations to the following passage from a great academic admirer of these customs: "It was to please these bedecked and plumed heroes that women wore their transparent gowns decorated with gold rings, unique and ironic vestige of so many more serious imitations of antiquity: that was their way of returning to nature! The Spartan dream of a common happiness disappeared and a new dream began to glow in people's souls, that of a France good to live in. Only such an army wanted great wars, striking rewards and honorific distinctions, a court and a ruler."[9]

On economic questions, Fourier only knows the echo of eighteenth-century agronomy; he pushes all the illusions of his predecessors to extremes. He believes that nature has given man everything he needs to be happy and that his evil derives from an error of judgment—an error that consciousness of the true laws of nature would allow us to correct with no difficulty. Our ancestors were not as startled as we are by such optimistic paradoxes. The bucolic stories had created in them habits of mind that we do not understand easily; in their eyes, evil was a simple accident, contrary to the desires of nature, a nature which is always fecund, generous, and rejuvenating.

Human labor is inspired by the memories of the Trianon. To make the hypothesis of the passion for attractive occupations more acceptable, Fourier normally selected his examples from horticulture. Experience shows that the avid gardener is attached to rare plants with a singularly jealous ardor; and in Fourier the most extraordinary species are produced. Before one could obtain all varieties from the great impresarios of flower raising and fruit growing, the producers of flowers and fruits sometimes gave themselves over to the most Machiavellian practices to obtain an unknown plant for their region; they often went to a great deal of trouble to steal (or have stolen for them) a bulb or plant. Fourier thus showed himself to be a very good observer in speaking of attractive labor in the garden and in believing that we devote ourselves to it with great pleasure; but he did not observe that this labor did not count, so to speak, in production.[10]

In Fourier's system it is useless to concern ourselves with the organization of workshops from which abundant and high-quality goods are produced. In Harmony it is sufficient to give free rein to the passions that a deceitful civilization had claimed to repress. The workshop is organized by itself and in the most perfect way; production will become limitless when it is directed by fully enthusiastic foremen. Inventions are produced by the sole fact that someone wants them produced. Breeders will transform animals as easily as if they had outlined fictional animals and stylized the forms of nature. It is a true *messianism* that Fourier describes, and, like all true messianists, he construes new animals perfecting the ferocious ones: tigers are employed in the postal service that would be operated in a way greatly superior to that dreamed of by our contemporaries. Fourier's zoological inventions are ridiculous; but it would be wrong not to take them into consideration because they are intimately connected to his system. It appears after all that the domestication of wild beasts is a very general idea among messianists. We might ask whether Fourier is inspired by the Hebrew prophets or whether his ideas are original; I would be disposed to accept the latter hypothesis, and to regard these inventions as the natural product of the idea of the omnipotence of the mind, an idea still dear to many.

Fourier's success would be incomprehensible if we did not take into account the wars of the French Revolution. The government of 1793 had done everything possible to destroy the army of the monarchy and very little to organize the new forces. Meanwhile, undisciplined bands had spontaneously produced the most formidable instrument of war the world had ever known. Why cannot all labor be made as agreeable as the military had become for the soldiers of the revolution who were left to themselves, after being regarded as horrible things and subjugated to a slave-like discipline by the men of the ancien régime?[11] Why cannot geniuses come forth in organized industry with persons equally enthusiastic for the same purpose when we have seen so many illustrious leaders who have risen from the lowest rank of the army—leaders who would have remained unknown if the ancien régime had continued to prevent the development of natural abilities? Why mistrust combinations of the passions, when the revolutionary bands led by improvised captains who had been acclaimed during their tragic adventure, had such a marked superiority over the German troops, trained in Prussia and led according to the pedantic rules of a pseudoscience?

The superiority of enthusiasm over regular administration could have seemed much more obvious to Fourier's contemporaries, since the empire was dead because of administration and regularity. It lost power the moment the old enthusiasm diminished; the imperial government was very far from having as many eminent warriors as the revolutionary anarchy had. The philosophers had pretensions of producing human happiness with their institutions, the fruit of purely intellectual labor by highly knowledgeable and reasoned people: they talked a great game. Fourier translates well the disillusions of many of his contemporaries when he inveighs against those who have only pompous phrases and against the inventors of meaningless concepts. What does "popular sovereignty" mean, if it is given to men who need bread? Here is a reflection made by thousands of Frenchmen: that constitutions, laws, and official pronouncements do not produce happiness.[12] It was natural to ask oneself whether the wrong path had been chosen; the experience of the armies was there to show what attractions among men whose passions are exalted can do. Fourier's mistake was to believe that cuisine, musical opera, and vulgar love could replace the exaltation that results from war whose nature is entirely unique. Enthusiasm seems to him able, in every case, to produce the same kind of effect, and he did not understand the psychology of war.

To understand how Fourierism could have deceived so many people, we should note that it never ceased to modify itself, especially under the influence of Considérant;[13] but the secret of its power was in its appeal to blind instinct which never ceased to move men before 1848. In a fierce article directed against Fourier's successor, Proudhon denounced the absence of scientific value in the Fourierian school: it appeared to him to be made up of charlatans and dupes. He showed that the sect never drew back from any palinode to flatter public opinion.

In 1830 Considérant affirmed: "We are not Christian!" in order to flatter the anticlericalism of the day. Later he tried to profit from the Christian reawakening to make Fourierism appealing to believers: "Agreements with the heavens have been made; they wanted to prove that Fourier was the successor of Jesus Christ; priests and Jesuits were flattered" (*Peuple*, 11 February 1849). Popular tendencies toward associationism were very strong around 1848, but they were full of evangelical memories; what was then called "associationism" resembled the convent life more than an interest group. The Fourierists benefited from this state of mind, and did not hesitate to claim that the workers' society should be fashioned in imitation of the Phalanx's. They had reason to stabilize a reconciliation between the two institutions because both were purely sentimental.

Today Fourier has still a certain prestige among those who believe in the efficacy of magical forces in social questions. They are quite numerous—starting with the surfeit of ingenuous Marxists who have a boundless faith in the miraculous effects of the conquest of public power, and ending with the sentimentalists who are concerned with cooperation and public education in order to confuse working-class ideas and who expect to make a conservative revolution or revolutionary conservation. True Marxism desires to come closer to science in a more or less felicitous way, but, after all, it has observation and reason on its side. Fourier is an evocator of spirits, as chimeric as any spiritualist.

As Proudhon says in the article previously cited: "Everyone has heard of the self-proclaimed theory of Fourier, of the science discovered by Fourier, of Fourier's system. Such is the great mystification of the century. Despite the enormous quantity of writing that this halucinator produced, there is neither theory nor science nor system in Fourier: I challenge Considérant and all his school to quote three propositions of this greatly vaunted science which have logical coherence." Fourierians' state of mind is analogous to that of many Protestant pastors who believe in doing scientific theology, despising Catholic superstition, and who believe in transforming the world by revealing the "true significance" of the words uttered by Jesus Christ nineteen centuries ago. Nothing is more crazy than this liberal Protestant idea. To imagine that an uneducated Hebrew carpenter could have revealed to the world moral theories whose definitive meaning shall be found only in our time is a greater absurdity than anything that can be found in Fourier. Protestant theological science is on exactly the same level as the social science of the inventor of Phalanxes.

It has often been noted that there is an *absolute opposition between the Marxist and the Protestant mind.* This opposition is revealed in a very obvious way in many passages of Marx's work, and we should keep this in mind if we want to understand the deepest inclinations of Marxism. Since he was accustomed to analyzing everything that was scientifically analyzable, Marx was unable to understand the conduct of men filled with Christian fervor and who, in practice, seemed to take such little account of their precepts; he saw only "magical" sentiments placed before the eyes of these "sober virtuosi,"[14] a mystical veil which prevented them from logical reasoning. He had nothing but repugnance for a system that claims the use of reason and science but which is basically only dreaming and magic. Here we can ask whether Protestants exert some effort to maintain this mystical veil; everyone who has had any dealings with the world of Protestant ministers has the feeling that there is a great deal of hypocrisy in liberal Protestantism. The Protestants are ardently involved in the cooperative movement and an influence on the idea of cooperation is attributed to Fourier. It is not without reason that many Marxists mistrust cooperatives. In the functioning of these associations there is something contrary to economic science, something irrational that a mystical veil hides from the inexperienced masses.[15]

Notes

1. For example, he said in preparing a collection of essays in 1822 that in 1827 there would already be a distribution of "sovereignty of the regions to be colonized." *Théorie de l'unité universelle*, 1841 ed. (Paris: Bureau de la Phalange), Vol. I, p. 370. We note these "sovereignties" that recall the fiefdoms distributed by Napoleon in foreign countries.

2. Karl Kautsky, *La lutte des classes en France en 1789*, Fr. trans. (Paris: Jacques, 1901), pp. 104–6. The German author would perhaps want to accept Jacobin hypocrisy. Would despoilment be perhaps the work of only the Therimidorians and the Directory? To employ a phrase dear to Kautsky, I will say that his is a "too idealistic hypothesis." According to the author, the love of glory would be explained only by utilitarian considerations. Ibid., p. 105. It appears to me that there is a very different explanation!

3. Fourier, *Nouveau Monde industriel et sociétaire* (Paris: Bossange Père, 1829–30), p. 300.

4. "The kitchen and the theater are the two places whose attractions lead [the child] to the regime of the passions."

5. Fourier, *Unité universelle*, Vol. II, p. 237. Following Proudhon, I have already called attention to what Fourier called "the love of the saints." We must insist a bit more on this question because for a long time I have recognized that all human contact is dominated by sexual relations; this principle, which seems to me to be of capital importance, I have proposed calling the "psycho-erotic law."

6. Fourier, *Nouveau Monde*, p. 272.

7. Fourier, *Unité universelle*, Vol. III, p. 382.

8. Fourier, ibid., Vol. IV, p. 537.

9. Alfred Victor Espinas, *Philosophie sociale au XVIII siècle* (Paris: F. Alcan, 1898), pp. 191–92. It is curious to see a French professor write such discouraging things. The author is a positivist, an anti-socialist and an anti-clerical. Several years ago they sent him from Bordeaux to Paris in order *to kill Marxism*. He has only succeeded in making a fool of himself. This scholar has confused Marx's friend Engels with Engel, the Berlin statistician (Espinas, *Histoire des doctrines économiques* (Paris: A. Colin, 1891), p. 332).

10. Professor Gide notes that the work of gardeners is very painful. *Oeuvres choisies de Fourier*, "Preface," p. xl. He has failed to see that Fourier wishes to discuss house gardening and not professional horticulture.

11. Like many writers of his time, Fourier rose against the reforms of the Count of Saint-Germain. French people "had been persuaded in 1787 that a Frenchman should tremble before a Prussian and that you had to beat someone in order to make him into a good soldier. The minister, St.-Germain, almost succeeded in returning to such a system." Fourier, *Unité universelle*, Vol. IV, p. 371.

12. Fourier had as much scorn for the "ideologues" as Napoleon had.

13. Fourierism did not penetrate the general public until much later; in 1830, according to Victor Considérant, "only three or four people thought of making Fourier's discoveries known. *Contre M. Arago* (Paris: Bureau de la Phalange, 1840), p. 14. About 1840, Fourierism became very important; at this time Saint-Simonism had fallen into such disfavor that Louis Blanc felt

the need of affirming that he was not a Saint-Simonian. *Organisation du travail*, 4th ed. (Paris: Cauville Frères, 1845), p. 106. Considérant is greatly concerned with the popularization of the ideas of a practical order of Fourierism; 22 May 1848 he claimed for his friends the merit of having considered mortage credit, and Proudhon commented ironically on this claim. *Solution du problème social* (Paris: Guillaumin, 1848), p. 209; he energetically defended the right of property and the right to labor. Thus he expected to arrive at a practical compromise between the bourgeoisie and the proletariat.

14. Marx, *Capital* (Modern Library, pp. 825–26; cf. pp. 91–92). The German text says: "nüchternen Virtuosen des Protestantismus" (4th German ed., p. 718). He applies this expression to the Massachusetts Puritans, who had put a price on the heads of Indians. According to Marx, we find here an example "of the Christian character of primitive accumulation." Charles Bonnier, the principal theoretician of the Guesdist Party, wrote in *Socialiste* (27 October 1901) regarding Pressensé: "We see the enormous ignorance which a good Protestant can attain in the greatest security and confidence of his own value."

15. Professor Gide, aside from being a highly chimerical spirit, is a very zealous Protestant with a certain fondness for Fourier. He avoids as much as possible the folly of the system and the immorality of love in the Phalanxes; naturally he ignores the homosexuality of the Harmonians. Preface to the *Selected Works of Fourier*. We have here a fine illustration of the opposition noted between the Protestant mentality (even the best ones) and the critical mind.

CHAPTER FIVE

The French Revolution initiated a new era in business management. The spirit of enterprise was much more developed; newly arrived men easily succeeded in contracting great financial operations. We should connect these speculations to the wars of liberty, not only because these wars provided means for speculation, but also because there are many profound analogies between the psychology of warriors and that of the great money managers. One can very accurately call American financiers "captains of industry." All those who have read carefully the fine book by Paul de Rousiers on America have been struck by the resemblance between these men and the conquistadores: passionate and unscrupulous, with an invincible energy. Under the Empire, the mentality of the generals who despoiled the churches did not differ by a jot from that of those who equipped the army; Soult, Suchet, and Messena did not differ greatly from Ouvrard.[1]

The concept of law differs completely according to whether it is presented from the point of view of the peasant or the capitalist. For the peasant, property is above all something familial; it is a "marriage between man and the earth." The home must remain stable so that society can possess a truly juridical constitution. For the capitalist, property only constitutes a legal code to get income; the title to property has no essential difference from a title of credit.

The liquidization of national wealth greatly weakened respect for property. Those who survived the ancien régime claimed that the society could not rebuild itself on the basis of a *false and illusory property*; they thought that the only honest solution consisted in returning the lands to the old families, with the reservation of an indemnity to the temporary possessors.[2] In this way, the rural domain would not be absorbed by finance. The Restoration government adopted the opposite solution: indemnifying the old property holders and leaving the land in the hands of the buyers. This was the most politic solution, but it was dedicated to the abandonment of tradition. Ever since, we have seen many economists uphold the necessity of doing away with the regime based on real estate contracts in order to *mobilize property* and permit sale by means of titles more or less analogous to those the seller of movable objects sometimes gives the buyer before delivery of the merchandise so that the latter can immediately make this merchandise marketable. If land is viewed as a commodity like any other, we must admit that all property is acquired like a commodity by means of the industriousness of its holder or by means of labor. From this is born the theory which bases property on labor, a theory which comes from England and acquired all its importance in France after the great revolutionary cataclysm.[3] I have been trying to show above why this occurred.

During the first half of the nineteenth century, businessmen were above all men of imagination. Many writers have noted the odd enterprises financiers undertook during the crisis of 1825 (the search for the pharaohs' treasure in the Red Sea, for example). We have often heard of some English merchant who sent a shipment of ice skates to Brazil. There is no need to ask economists of this period to probe the mechanism of production; generally it appears secondary to them. What interests them is the balance sheet, the speculator's state of mind. They do not deign go into the workshop and they confine themselves to speaking with management. We discover procedures analogous to those of the old rural economy: this economy *only* took account of the surface area of possession and of the enthusiasm the peasant had for his land. Today one is concerned only with the importance of capital and with the ability of the businessman. On the one hand the statistics and on the other hand the psychology of the chief gives us here more or less everything that the economist considered in this period.

All the socialist literature before 1848 speaks continually of financial and industrial feudalism; this formula surprises contemporary writers who have up-to-date information on the history of institutions and who do not see a great analogy between the origins of feudalism and capitalism. If we examine what happens in the workshops we would not think of feudalism, but of penal colonies; one would compare the factory to the penal dunking as popular language does.[4] If anyone established an analogy between modern industry and feudalism, it is because he was struck by the imbalance of forces between the men called to struggle on the terrain of free competition. Here are several extracts from a celebrated document in which Considérant, in a truly remarkable way, summarizes the most current ideas of his time:[5]

> It is on this great field of battle that one side is educated, hardened, armed to the teeth so that they have a great supply of materiel, munitions, and war machines and who occupy all positions; the other side, despoiled, naked, ignorant, hungry, are obliged to live from day to day and keep their wives and children alive and to implore their very adversaries for any badly paid work whatever. What is true for the great classes, for the proletariat

deprived of everything, and for those possessors of capital and of the instruments of labor is equally true for the weak and for the strong in all classes. . . . Analogous phenomena take place in the class of the possessors of the substance and the instruments of labor. The strong dominate there as inevitably and swallow up the weak just as unpityingly. And if the first result of this struggle under such monstrously unequal conditions, which are flattered with the name of "industrial liberty," is the immediate reduction of the proletarian masses into collective servitude, the second result, just as forced as the first, is the progressive crushing of small and medium-sized property, the obliteration of small and medium-sized industry, and of small and medium-sized commerce, under the weight of big property and under the colossal wheels of big industry and big commerce. Who encroaches upon everything, who becomes master of everything if not the big speculators, bankers, and at every point *the big capitalists*?

A little further on he shows us a society divided into two classes. England already shows the constitution toward which France and Belgium have been evolving: "The concentration of capital in the hands of a small aristocracy; the reduction of the middle classes; the semi-annihilation of the bourgeoisie, both politically and socially; increasing pauperism and proletarianization"—this is the new feudalism. It is interesting that we find in Considérant the three theses of the *Communist Manifesto* that, according to Vandervelde, would become obsolete:[6] capitalist concentration, submission of the state to capitalist class rule, and increasing misery. It is therefore completely useless to discuss the value of the "Marxist theses," of these so-called discoveries of Marx when he limited himself to transcribing opinions current among the revolutionaries of Marx's time into the *Communist Manifesto*.[7]

It would be highly desirable were the term *financial feudalism* to disappear, because it tends to maintain deeply confirmed prejudices and prevent advancement to scientific inquiry. It is always harmful to denote contemporary phenomena by means of images borrowed from a vanished epoch. If we stop referring to industrial feudalism, the constitution of the great enterprises will be seen in a new light: we shall see there a different consequence of technology, and no longer only *a uniform manifestation of the power of money*. Concentration ought to be determined and limited by technological considerations and should no longer be regulated by an abstract law.

What dominates the thought of the old socialists is the terror that their "aristocracy of wealth" inspires. In their time, they did not yet know about centralizing small savings; the financial markets, circulation, and credit still assumed primitive forms. The chief bank was only in a position to endure the current crises which annihilated the small speculators. Recent experience has come to show how much the archaic forms of the financial markets are unfavorable to the average situation: I am speaking of what occurred in Germany after legislation on the stock exchanges. The big banks have become concentrated and have notably increased their capital in order to function.

The finance aristocracy created by the regime in many respects resembled the aristocratic nobility of the past: the routine, the stubbornness, the pride of nouveaux riches are no less than those of their predecessors. The old nobility was criticized for not being concerned enough with improving their domains. They had lived with a most imperfect form of production, having regarded the countryside as a place of rest. They had been a scourge for their neighbors, for their tenant farmers, and especially for their land—therefore everyone applauded the disappearance of these vampires. The new aristocracy decided to copy all the vices of the old nobility.

The big financiers are rarely good heads of enterprises: they do not appreciate technical questions, they depend on chance, and are deceived by charlatans who exploit them.[8] Many financiers are so aware of their incapacity that they are unable to decide whether to complete an agreement and prefer to buy when adventurers have already put it into practice. At that point they can become aware of the products to be realized but are obliged to buy at exaggerated prices plants which must almost always be completely reconstructed. Owing to the intervention of such pirates who choose the very best business arrangements many excellent enterprises become worthless after a few years. It is true that financiers do not heed this final result if they succeed in selling stocks on the exchange.

About sixty years ago the ignorance and haughtiness of money managers recalled the memory of the ancien régime. In today's great banks a bureaucracy has been established which puts a check on the ludicrous fantasies of imaginative men. This bureaucracy has a function analogous to that of the old officers coming from the lower ranks and assigned to maneuvers, sailing alongside officers of the nobility who were assigned to battle but did not understand navigation. It is not without great difficulty that this technical bureaucracy gained hold of a certain authority; it was long treated with the deepest contempt by the new princes of finance.

The men of the eighteenth century had been greatly concerned with means employed to bring the most worthy men into business; they had criticized the landed aristocracy for removing talented people from important state positions. We become aware at an early point that the sons of the newly rich were most often incapable of keeping positions acquired from their fathers; the problem of the consequences of inheritance was raised in both industrial and political matters. In addition, the experience after the revolution had demonstrated that popular elections did not always give more felicitous results than did the ruling house. The social question would have been resolved if, removing all consequences of heredity, one had been able to classify all candidates according to merit.

Our entire educational system has been conceived with a view to resolving this problem. We assume in the world a quantity of unknown geniuses we must foster; and therefore we must multiply the number of schools. In order to classify talent a complicated system of examinations is invented. But any talent that has obtained official sanction must be placed in a position able to prove its power. From this there results a bitter contest between the possessors who do not have diplomas and the graduates who aspire to possession—the graduates regarding themselves as destined to manage industry. This doctrine was exposed several years ago in the French Assembly by followers of Jaurès in regard to a proposal for a state sugar refinery:[9] "The bourgeoisie with capital wishes to suppress all initiatives, all activity on the part of the bourgeoisie without capital and entering into public service. Well, we are convinced that if you made an appeal *in favor of the national interest*[10] to all the intellectuals, to all the forms of activity and self-denial contained in this bourgeoisie which, lacking capital, has been *expropriated* of all economic activity—you could develop the industrial activity of France in the world even under monopolistic form." I believe that the orator speaking of "expropriation" wanted to say that those educated but unemployed bourgeois are deprived of the rights of labor they possess in the profession for which they have received their diploma. Like all candidates, these people want to accept the position that they solicit—through abnegation.

The doctrine of intelligence thus leads to a variety of communism, but a highly authoritarian communism. There cannot be justice in society as long as the means of production are not entrusted to its most able members. Private property, inadvertently distributing the instruments of production, produces an infinite waste of natural forces; it is a true act of rebellion by the inferior instincts against intelligence. Demanding well-paid employment for themselves, the "intellectual proletariat," so dear to Jaurès, claims to have no other purpose than to defend the interests of future civilization against bourgeois barbarism. They speak so forcefully and eloquently that they often succeed in persuading workers, especially the men of the world who subsidize them.

The defenders of property present an objection that, although it does not rise above cracker-barrel empiricism, is not without some force.

They say that if there is error in the choice of these men of talent, and if social production is unified under their direction, this error will produce an infinity of evils—whereas today there are multiple combinations of good and bad which maintain errors within tolerable limits. With armies in which, as in France, there is a great deal of initiative, there are more victories than with armies which march under unified direction, because it is rare that this direction is able to fulfill its function.

The only satisfying solution would be provided by theocracy. The power of this solution on the human mind is so great that it never ceases reappearing in history, dressed in all sorts of different ways. It is most natural that the people attribute their woes to the ignorance, inexperience, or evil of their masters, and that they should place their hopes in a government in which science, intelligence, and virtue are the requisite conditions for directing business. It is also natural that, in this reformist path, people take things to their logical conclusion and desire everything which depends on an infallible will. According to a common law of human illusion, we end up taking this desire for a possible reality. Plato asked for the city to be subject to philosopher kings; Rousseau believed in a general will of the people that could not err; the Saint-Simonians ended by placing all power in the hands of a high priest.[11] I am not speaking of the church, which has been less theocratic than the philosophical and socialist sects.

These procedures have not provided happy solutions. "Theocracy," says Renan,[12] "does not want to see that human affairs will always be managed imperfectly and that theocratic organization will not bring the wisest people to power. Judges in a theocratic tradition will have the same faults as secular ones. It is not worth the trouble to make changes." This is true not only for religious government, but for all those who claim to bring back power to an infallible source. The experience of countries in which democracy rules shows us that the "general will" (which cannot err according to Rousseau) produces deeply corrupt administrations. The example of the American regime is well known.

Despite experience, the illusion always persists that there is a deep-seated reason that relies on fundamental laws of logic. But how do we measure the wisdom, intelligence, and virtue of our aspirants? This is impossible, and all the procedures proposed by the charlatanism of the social alchemists appear ridiculous in short order. To believe that socialist reform of the world will consist in the multiplication of examinations is a stupidity that appears ridiculous to everyone except to the doctorates in philosophy! And then what is to be done since one cannot do without chiefs? Intelligence will reduce the mystery of the moral order to the mystery of an infallible will in charge of choosing.

Here is the primordial logical origin of that tendency that has led so many men to proclaim the necessity of an unquestioned regulatory power and to accept blindly the choice of an absolute leader nominated by universal suffrage to whom is entrusted the mission of transforming the world according to the dictates of reason.

But has the problem been posed well? This is disputable. It is one thing to have leaders that deliberate through their own solid knowledge; it is another to have simple functionaries concerned only with a part of labor, and whose work is valued according to proper merit. The polemic that took place apropos of the intellectuals offers considerable interest in this regard. The Guesdist editors of *Socialiste* did not contest the importance of the results obtained by all the philologists, chemists, and mathematicians who are distinguished in their areas of specialty. They protested against the pretension of submitting all questions, *of any kind*, to a brilliant committee of scientists, and against the constitution of a new oligarchy based on intelligence. When we are limited to appreciating specialized work, we should no longer take account of the person, but only of the product. Even by recognizing that the adversaries of the intellectuals were sometimes inclined to paradox, we should state that they have remained basically faithful to the teachings of Marx.

Notes

1. Suchet has left behind the reputation of a man with more integrity than the other generals, but this reputation has probably been usurped. Jaubert de Passa, who was in 1814 the under-prefect of Perpignan and later a correspondent of the Academy of Sciences, tells us in his memoirs that Suchet carried away some precious wagons that he watched over with the greatest care; he did not want to give help to Soult for fear that this treasure which, it is said, originated from an indemnity paid by the archbishop of Tarragona to prevent the French Army from plundering his city, would be robbed. Ph. Torreilles, *Le Roussillon de 1789 à 1830 d'après les mémoires et la correspondance de M. Jaubert de Passa*, pp. 25–26.
2. Ph. Torreilles, *Mémoires de M. Jaume* (Paris: Bureaux de la Revue, 1895), pp. 148–49.
3. Marx says that in a fully developed bourgeois society, people can make the earth the "primitive material of money. . . . It dates from the last third of the seventeenth century, and the first attempt to put it into practice on a national scale was made a century afterwards during the French bourgeois revolution." *Capital* (Modern Library ed., p. 101).
4. Fourier, *Nouveau monde industriel*, p. 51 (Cf. Marx, *Capital*, Vol. I, p. 184). When the comparison with feudalism became popular, this figurative language appeared to produce many consequences; thus profits were sometimes compared to feudal law, sometimes to tithes; it followed that their disappearance, it was believed, could have been decreed by a legislator; thus even the penalties were compared to the penalties imposed by a particular

judge and appeared contrary to the principles of modern law. A propos of the decree of the provisional government reducing the hours of the working day, Proudhon mocked the men of 1848 who believed they could resolve salary questions by an act of authority and who expected that half of the loss would be borne by the capitalists (reducing the working day from eleven to ten hours but requiring payment for ten and a half hours): "Imagine these novelists of the Terror who in 1848 take the manager for the feudal lord, the worker for the serf, and labor for a *corvée*!" *Solution du probléme social* (Paris: Lacroix, 1868), pp. 27–29.

5. *Democratic Manifesto* reproduced in *Ere Nouvelle* (February 1894):160–64. The anarchist Tcherkesoff calls attention to the similarities that exist between this document and the *Communist Manifesto*.

6. *Revue Socialiste* (March 1898):327–41.

7. We also find the same concerns in Fernand Pecquer as I have shown in *Saggi di critica del marxismo*, p. 305.

8. Everyone who has followed the history of electricity companies in France remembers the skill with which Creil conducted his fantastic experiments: able people, helped by wise members of the Paris academy of sciences, took advantage of the good will of the House of Rothschild which was, they say, robbed of a million francs by these bandits.

9. *Journal officiel* (26 January 1897):117.

10. We must understand: it is obvious that if the intellectual proletariat becomes the dominant class, its interest will become officially the national interest— but it will not cease to be a class interest for all that.

11. Since his first essay on property, Proudhon has sided against the pontifical infallibility of the Saint-Simonian clergy. He never abandoned this position. He protested equally against the determination of merit by means of election. *Oeuvres*, Vol. I, p. 98.

12. Renan, *Histoire du peuple d'Israël* (Paris: Calmann-Lévy, 1898), Vol. V, p.102.

CHAPTER SIX

Modern socialism dates from the great reaction that followed the events of 1848. I have often called attention to the importance of the change that occurred at that time in the realm of ideas, and it is essential to show clearly the characteristics separating the present times from the past. The conditions of a new conception of socialism had already been forming for a long time; but very few men succeeded in freeing themselves from the existing ideology. Marx had judged the 1848 revolution harshly; at the beginning of *The Eighteenth Brumaire* he wrote: "Hegel remarks somewhere that all facts and personages of great importance in world history occur, as it were, twice. He forgot to add: the first time as tragedy and the second time as farce. Caussidière for Danton, Louis Blanc for Robespierre, the Mountain of 1848 to 1851 for the Mountain of 1793 to 1795, the Nephew for the Uncle. And the same caricature occurs in the circumstances attending the second edition of the *Eighteenth Brumaire*!" There is no need to believe that Marx said this to be witty, as was often the case in his historical works. He wished to illuminate the following important fact: that the men of 1848 did not understand their own life; they reasoned about a world constructed from their imagination by means of data from the past, and forgot reality. He compared the Frenchman of 1848 to that mad Englishman of the Bedlam Asylum who believed he lived at the time of the Pharaohs and complained of the hard labor in the Ethiopian mines.

The broad burlesque of the 1848 revolution deserves close examination, so that we can better understand what the revolution was from the perspective of the ideas of that time. We call "burlesque" any person who pretends to perform a function out of proportion with his nature; who wishes to pose as a hero, while showing that he is only a poor philistine; while being an ass, he wants to wear the pelt of a lion. It is the opposition between pompous manners and the innermost nature of the soul which makes us laugh and which establishes eternal comic characters: a man who preaches moral rigor and succumbs to the first temptation; a father exercising absolute power in his household, continually invoking the wisdom of the ages, who becomes involved with a schemer whose cunning he is the only one not to understand; an ignorant, venal, and cowardly magistrate who speaks like an ancient Roman hero. These types would not provoke laughter if the spectators were susceptible to pity for their misfortune and if they were able to suppose that they too could find themselves in a similar situation one day. For a comedy to be funny it is necessary that the spectators not view themselves as belonging to the same humanity as the author's victim. Molière took great care to present things in such a way that his young contemporaries could not think that in their old age they would be as absurd as the preceding generation.[1]

Forty years ago the men of 1848 aroused a great deal of wonder. We speak respectfully of their honesty; but their heroic attitudes provoked mirth, and, if mercy had not been discreet, we would have been amused at the coup d'état of Napoleon III. An older world ended in 1848 and a new world began. The past had become incomprehensible for those who had not known the reign of Louis Philippe. The old republicans of 1848 were able to support the illusion that they were powerful men because they played the role of the men of 1793, but the revolutionary legend seems very antiquated to their young successors. The survivors of the Second Republic did not understand that the powerful upheavals of 1848 had determined a *ricorso*—they had come at a time when the psychological consequences of the revolution were extinguished. The revolutionary traditions were no longer maintained except by artificial means. When the veil had fallen and reality appeared, we asked ourselves if these heroes had not been a bit whimsical; they were at least quite ridiculous. The new generations could not believe that the old ones had been so ingenuous, and accordingly they were in a position to render mockery natural. I have written elsewhere[2] that

> The historians of our century have not shown well the great separation that existed between the periods before 1848 and those following it. The French Revolution is much more notable for the continuity of ideas than for the destruction it brought about. The eighteenth century had passed through it and finally ended in 1848. During the first half of the last century, people continued to believe in the goodness of man. They constructed utopias to believe to return humanity to happiness and at the same time were rationalist and "sensitive." Although much blood had been spilled, our ancestors regarded themselves as profoundly human. After 1848, there began the "century of the iron men," the age of men who disdained philanthropy and vaunted their power; the reign of Rousseau which had begun about 1762 (the publication date of the *Emile*) lasted almost a hundred years.

Before 1848, people had been too preoccupied with rejuvenating religion according to Rousseau's ideas. That is, making it rely on their tender feelings and especially on their feelings aroused by the spectacle of nature. The aridity of the Protestant doctrinaires of the Reformation and of Catholic reformers of the seventeenth century had become odious to everyone: people thought only of addressing the heart. Throughout Europe there was an awakening of Christian sentiment. There emerged philanthropic societies that were sometimes imbued with Christianity, sometimes content with a more or less nebulous deism.

Socialism before 1848 participated extensively in this great current of ideas; we find in the Gospel and in the works of the church fathers the most extraordinary ramifications. When Louis Philippe succumbed, the clergy loudly proclaimed its love for the people. But this ardor did not last long; there was a misunderstanding between socialists and the church. After the reaction, the situation became clear: socialism was no longer Christian; on the contrary, it often affirmed its hatred for Christianity.

After 1848 there began, rather unexpectedly, an era of great economic prosperity following the construction of railways. The bourgeoisie had faith in its "scientific power" over nature and it adored the science[3] which seemed a fit substitute for religion and philanthropy. From this was born a new literature devoted to reacting against the old and empty idealism. It claimed to work on human documents to produce the natural history of man. The theorists of realism affirmed the need "to observe well, to reproduce everything that is provided by observation, rejecting what issued from other sources."[4]

The completely new character of the bourgeoisie which was called "scientific," "practical," and "realistic" is most clearly revealed in its social philosophy. In the past, the great question had been to look for the fundamental principle that would justify all legitimate authority. That is why so much importance was given to the editing of legal declarations and to everything regarded as constitutional in the system of laws. The utopians believed that a society conforming to reason would be easily realized, and that historical accidents would provide a thousand opportunities of which people of goodwill would know how to take advantage (that which is ideally rational should, in the eyes of a pure idealist, be what is produced most naturally).

The Second Empire reveals a government with no concern for this primordial law so venerated before 1848. It conserved certain parliamentary forms, but also retained the power to appeal to the confidence the masses had in it when it found itself embarrassed by criticisms of detail used by representatives of the bourgeoisie to oppose it. The masses have only the right to answer "yes" or "no" to the question of whether they want to support the government; whether they prefer an order that is perhaps mediocre, but secure from the adventurism of coups d'état and civil wars. The appeal to the people assured the supremacy of the executive power over the organs of control, and thus tended to extinguish all justice from the administration of public affairs.

No government obtained submission as complete as that of Napoleon III. The church, which had displayed considerable docility under his predecessors, was his most faithful ally. There were several difficulties between the bishops and the state with regard to the Roman question, but these conflicts were a far cry from those of Louis Philippe's time. They did not try to knock down the emperor, but only to exert on him a threatening pressure to force him to support the Holy See. The church was no longer concerned with the legitimacy of power; it wanted to obtain satisfaction for its interests. Even today it has continued this policy and abandoned the royalists in France when it estimated that there was more to be gained by an alliance with the Republic. The controversial republicanism of Cardinal Lavigeriée and of Leo XIII can surprise only those who believe in the rebirth of idealism in present society.[5]

This transformation of public opinion is connected to the changes produced in capitalism. Marx[6] observes that under Louis Philippe the government was directed only by interests of a small fraction of the bourgeoisie: "Bankers, stock exchange kings, railway kings, owners of coal and iron mines and forests, a part of the landed proprietors associated with them—the so-called finance aristocracy. . . . The industrial bourgeoisie proper formed part of the official opposition. . . . Its opposition was expressed all the more resolutely the more unalloyed the autocracy of the finance aristocracy became." He notes that Grandin, the Rouen industrialist, and Faucher, both highly indisposed toward popular demands, were, in their role as representatives of the interests of the bourgeoisie, implacable opponents of the Guizot government.

Permit me to reproduce here several explanations[7] that I have already given in the *Rivista popolare di politica, lettere e scienze sociale* of 15 July 1899:

> At this time, the haute bourgeoisie remained confined within wholly obsolete traditions from the industrial point of view. It wished to concern itself solely with exceptional business transactions whose profits would be reserved exclusively to a small group, failing to understand that the function of modern capitalism is to develop all the productive forces of the country in an abundant way, and that this function can be accomplished only on the condition that the petite bourgeoisie and small proprietor share in the new wealth in securities.

Capitalism, swallowed up in this way, was unable to lead the country into the open road of advanced industrialism; there were immense resources whose value needed to be brought out. The laborers remained unemployed and everyone complained of a stagnation of business which seemed scandalous in the presence of the astonishing discoveries in science.

Claiming the right to labor was said to be a social question,[8] while no one knew too well what that meant. It was a question of changing the political direction of the state, redoubling the forces of government, that is, doing what an inept capitalistic system was unable to do. We had to cover the country with railways and call the small exchanges for the benefit of new speculation. Through this policy all France should profit from progress.

The Empire was often rash and uninspired; but its work generally succeeded. It was helped in its undertakings by the wealth provided by California mines, and found auxiliary intellectuals in the financial world. What it did was perhaps not difficult, but Louis Philippe did not dare do it and the misoneism of the haute bourgeoisie would still have stopped him for a long time.

After 1848, a new life was given capitalism which took on a development no one could have expected in the past. Temerity no longer knew any limits, and the old countries were no longer self-sufficient in their activities. The great financiers threw themselves on those who had not yet entered into the modern movement to revolutionize their industry. They asked themselves more than once whether they were not showing too much temerity, after having long been too prudent. Nevertheless, the most painful crises did not succeed in slowing the ever-accelerating and imposing pace of the new capitalist chieftains. The old banking houses had ceased to exert a dictatorial influence on the market. The highly imaginative financiers succeeded in accumulating dispersed savings in such quantities that their institutions were able to free themselves from the old tyranny of the financial magnates.

The oldest part of the *Communist Manifesto* is that in which Marx says[9] that capitalism can no longer direct production and compares it to the "magician incapable of mastering the underground forces he has invoked." Today we are surprised that people could believe that capitalists were incapable of directing productive forces as weak as those existing in 1847. This example shows that if the prophetic profession is always harmful, it is especially so in economic matters: *the economic future is the mystery of mysteries*. This idea was current in 1848, and Louis Blanc affirms[10] that, after his installation at Luxembourg, he received many letters from capitalists "insistently calling for the tutelary intervention of the state in industries, that appeared lost if the state did not hasten to support them. One thing that is generally ignored and of which I will provide irrefutable proof, is that the idea of publishing the plan of a vast social reform before the convening of the Constituent Assembly was suggested to me by the vehemence of the solicitations that came to me in great numbers not only on the part of the workers but *more still* on the part of many businessmen reduced to an unspeakable poverty—a poverty of ancient origins."[11]

The capitalists of the Second Empire no longer felt this terror of personal responsibility; they had faith in their individual initiative and confined themselves to asking that the state make the development of productive forces easier. At first it is surprising to see such a highly spontaneous state of mind prevailing with such energy under a government as authoritarian as that of Napoleon III; but we should note that this government had a notable tendency to limit its sphere of action to questions of trade and of policing, which are largely foreign to production. Railways, French enterprises abroad, transoceanic navigation, the renewal of the city, and the encouragement of credit for the great corporations were the main concerns of imperial policy.

The new capitalism felt strong enough to act on its own; *it had no need of external help except for its foreign activities*. It needed a government that removed the obstacles that hindered commerce and which maintained order. From the economic point of view, the state acted only to facilitate trade; from the political point of view, it was concerned only with police power to ensure material order. The same formula, "laissez faire, laissez passer," became the motto of the world,[12] the new ideological superstructure perfectly fitted for the new economics. Henceforth there would be no more principles, no more fundamental law, no more doubts about the legitimacy of power: there was only scorn for such metaphysics. From then on metaphysics was deeply despised.

This transformation holds many analogies with the theories Proudhon had developed with such insistence: "We do not want to understand," he wrote on 31 March 1848,[13] "that labor is synonymous with individual liberty; that the government exists only to protect free labor, not to regulate or restrict it. When you speak of the organization of labor, it is as if you proposed to pluck the eyes of liberty. . . . There is no need for any organization of labor at this time. Individual liberty has as its object the organization of labor. What we need, what we demand in the name of labor, is reciprocity, justice in exchange; it is the *organization of credit*."

Not surprisingly, the most celebrated socialists of that time disappeared rapidly from the scene. Vidal (who died in 1872) and Pecqueur (who died in 1887) lived forgotten amidst a society which they did not understand and which did not understand their language. Louis Blanc was concerned with history and politics; only Proudhon remained relevant because, with his viewpoint of a man of genius, he understood the great difference between production and exchange and was prepared to follow the movement unfolding before his eyes. But a great transformation would also take place in him; he would no longer appear as the great wrecker of the social order but as a philosopher, moralist, and reformer specializing in certain questions.[14]

Notes

1. In the past it seems that *Tartuffe* was presented as a farce and not as a bourgeois drama; the latter interpretation is nonsensical. We should note that the traditional garb of ridiculous characters strengthens the comicality by increasing the distance between them and the spectators; it is with good reason that Sganarelle's unlikely dress is conserved, because the deceived husbands can thus laugh freely.
2. Georges Sorel, "Proudhon," *Pages libres* (4 May 1901):399–400. I have already noted this transformation in the *Saggi di critica del Marxismo*, p. 54. See also my *Ruine du monde antique* (Paris: Jacques, 1902), pp. 229–33.
3. Brunetière, *Discours de combat* (Paris: Perrin, 1900–3), p. 12.
4. Ibid., p. 29, cf. p. 35.
5. For a certain number of years now we have been told that there is a return to idealism: this seems highly doubtful to me; the history of the Dreyfus Affair would have been different, it seems to me, if such a return had been serious; the great error of the proponents of revision was to believe in this idealism which existed only in the imagination of some of the literati. Brunetière, who after 1896 celebrated the rebirth of idealism with such fanfare has been a resolute opponent of the revision of the Dreyfus trial and this for very prosaic and grossly utilitarian reasons.
6. Marx, "The Class Struggles in France," M.E.S.W., I, pp. 139–40.
7. Cf. Sorel, *Saggi di critica del marxismo*, p. 54, in which these observations are briefly summarized.
8. In order to understand the tendencies of the people of this time, we should take account of the pacific policies of the King. I have written previously: "Every time that France has gone through a somewhat too long period of peace, she has lost all political direction and has exhausted herself in internal quarrels. It was often repeated in Louis Philippe's time that 'France was bored.' . . . France does not know what to think when she is not at war. . . . Under Louis Philippe, France had tried to get over her boredom by concerning herself with socialist fantasies: we are amused in reforming the world when we think of conquering it with armies." *Rivista populare di politica* (15 March 1902).
9. *Communist Manifesto*, p. 19.
10. Louis Blanc, *Le droit au travail*, p. 9. He announced that one day he would publish the pamphlet which he had written on the state of industry. "I will publish these letters [of the capitalists] testifying to the death of industry based on competition. Nothing is more decisive but at the same time nothing is more tragic." In the *History of the Revolution of 1848* he repeats the same affirmation (Vol. I, p. 143) and cites a letter regarding a proposed acquisition.

11. Sometimes industrialists have an interest in having the state acquire their establishments; it seems that many alcohol distilleries in France several years ago would have been pleased with an installation of a state monopoly.
12. The imperial government would have practiced commercial freedom on a larger scale than it had, if it had not found it necessary to prevent discontent among the great masses.
13. Proudhon, *Solution du problème social*, pp. 91–93.
14. For an elaboration of the questions dealt with briefly here, see the second part of my *Introduction à l'économie moderne.*

CHAPTER SEVEN

The utopias written before 1848 were concerned above all with the "captains of industry"; first they depicted a rural republic whose citizens are proprietors or beneficiaries of goods sufficient to ensure their leisure and happiness. Next utopians searched for the means to run the great enterprises by men of exceptional ability. Then they tried to conceive industries in which the associated workers lived outside the owner's firm and asked which "virtues" they should have to secure the good conduct of business. But all this appeared puerile as soon as large-scale capitalism acquired a clear consciousness of its powers and showed that it had no need for advice from philosophers on agriculture or on industry.

Utopians were moved to examine the condition of the proletariat, but almost solely from a philanthropic point of view. There was abundant writing on the misery of the workers, noting the abuses of industry and showing how excessive and poorly paid labor led to the degeneration of the poorer classes. Many sanitary regulations were proposed which were designed to save the future of new generations, but all this was foreign to the true industrial question, because it was only concerned with *certain* excesses, without trying to determine the characteristics which distinguish the worker in large-scale modern industries.

Modern socialism is solely concerned with the proletariat and designates by this term not the poor, but the man who, not owning the means of labor, lives by income earned in manufacturing. The proletariat is a "living instrument" in the great ensemble of forces organized by manufacturers following a scientific plan. One no longer wisely and eloquently rambles on about the faculties of man, his destiny, fraternity and solidarity, or on knowing whether the labor of the workshop is more or less conducive to the development of civic qualities or speaks of rights and duties. To understand the proletariat and anticipate its future, we must resolve a purely technological question which presents great difficulties and which philanthropists find it convenient to ignore.

Large-scale modern industry was for a long time observed through the cotton industry; there scientific mechanization produced its most notable results for the first time. On the other hand, cotton spinning exhibits so little intelligence or foresight in its relations with workers that capitalism was accused of ruining the future of the race. The writings concerned with the moral and physical influence of labor for the most part referred only to this industry. The great battles which gave rise to factory legislation in England were fought for the women and children employed in the cotton mills. The nineteenth-century economy was for a long time determined by the study of phenomena produced in this branch of production; one could say that it was derived from cotton as ancient physics was derived from the heavens.

Observers were rapidly struck by a change in the laboring process: the former infinitesimal division of labor, whose marvels Adam Smith had celebrated, seemed useless in the new workshop; there was a "despecialization" of the worker[1] or, as Ure stated, an "equalization" of labor.[2] Economists have not examined closely what the division of labor celebrated by Adam Smith consisted of; one has often confused *fragmented labor* with *specialized occupations*. In a period when it was impossible to construct mechanisms analogous to ours, the best solution for obtaining *rapid and fairly precise* movements was to require them from the human organism.[3] People can succeed in training their limbs in such a way that they come automatically to execute determined movements with surprising exactitude. This is only possible on the condition that a very limited displacement of the hand is required of each individual, and this renders it necessary to decompose the labor of a large number of people into parts; each one becomes, for the fulfillment of his tasks, a much more perfect mechanism than what obtained two centuries ago.

The progress of *kinetics* and of the construction of machines has, by means of geometric combinations of solid figures, permitted the discovery of solutions quite superior to those achieved by the division of human labor. Man had been automated; instead, there was then a splitting: on the one hand we had a mechanism following geometrical laws, while on the other the worker was liberated from the servitude of his automation—which had been imposed on him in a manner quite contrary to the laws of his constitution. The study of all the defects attributed to the ancient division of labor should be based on the shortcomings of rapidly executed automatic movements. Today sportive exercises largely reproduce the old shortcomings already noted in manufacturing—sportive mechanization seems to produce especially deplorable psychological results. In England they have begun to recognize this.

It is believed that all labor made on cotton in the modern factory can be reduced to a uniform type and that the various workers are (from a technological point of view) only *loci* in which given quantities of labor are manifested more or less rapidly and energetically. As diverse as the variety of the jobs is, one would only have to consider the duration and intensity of a mechanical effort. In the past attention had been paid solely to the quality of the worker, and that is why so much importance was given to the virtuosity acquired in fragmented labor. Now all qualitative differences were attributed to peculiarities of the machine, and human energy was considered from the perspective of quantity. Marx regarded the transformation as already completed in 1847 (based on Ure's descriptions which were a bit exaggerated for the purpose of demonstrating that factories were favorable to the intellectual progress of workers). "What characterizes the division of labor in the automatic workshop," he says, "is that labor has there completely lost its specialized character. . . . The automatic workshop wipes out specialists and craft-idiocy."[4]

Many economists hastened to erect this "despecialization" into a fundamental principle: they believed that the numerous facts that contradicted the principle, which became ascertained in industry, were simple accidents or survivals which would disappear before the force of the general principle. This was regarded as a great force acting in a fixed sense, while contrary facts depended on varied, secondary and temporary causes. This reasoning was common in the eighteenth century: physicists had the good fortune to discard the exceptions revealed in imperfect experiments; but often, too, they were too hasty in accepting things with contestable formulae as natural laws. This method, which produced grave problems in physics, is still harmful in social science. But in the early nineteenth century they did not distinguish the method suitable to each science from those suitable to others. It was believed that the "despecialization" was sufficiently advanced because it was necessary right away to base the entire economy on it. It was feared that the theory would soon go beyond practice if it did not quickly take part in suppressing facts contrary to it. It was decided that in all operations of production it is possible to find something in common, a "fluid element" which presents itself everywhere as identical and which is manifested in various spheres of work with differences of a purely quantitative order.

The analogy of this doctrine with that of calorimetrics is obvious, and it has likely exerted a certain influence on Ricardo's contemporaries. There is no need to note what revolution was produced in science by the idea that heat and cold are not physical qualities, and that all bodies contain quantities of heat that try continuously to pass from one body to another. Said Marx later:

> If, then, we leave out of consideration the use-value of commodities, they

have only one common property left, that being products of labor. But already the product of labor itself has undergone a change unknown to us . . . . Along with the useful qualities of the products themselves, we put out of sight both the useful character of the various kinds of labor embodied in them, and the concrete forms of that labor; there is nothing left but what is common to them all; all are reduced to one and the same sort of labor, human labor in the abstract. . . . All that [the residues of each of these products] now tell us is that human labor-power has been expended in their production, that human labor is embodied in them. When looked at as crystals of this social substance, common to them all, they are values.[5]

One could really believe that it is a question of calorimetrics. It is likely that it was the force of analogy that had prevented the economists from seeing for a long time the difficulties confronting the reduction of skilled labor into unskilled. Like Proudhon, Marx estimated that this did not present any difficulties, and he marvelled that writers had been able to find one:[6] "Is this not a case of saying, following the German proverb, that one cannot see the forest for the trees?" In order that this reduction be as obvious as he thought, it would be necessary that the skilled worker be paid at twice the rate of the unskilled, cost twice as much to train, and produce twice as much. But it is impossible to make these comparisons if one does not consider the prices paid for the wage earners and the prices of selling commodities. Thus we have only two empirical relations that correspond very exceptionally to any sort of rule. Marx observed[7] that "the distinction between skilled and unskilled labor rests in part on pure illusion or, to say the least, on distinctions that have long ceased to be real and that survive only by virtue of traditional convention." We see curious examples of the absence of any reasonable moderation in this comparison: "The labor of a brick-layer in England occupies a much higher level than that of a damask-weaver. Again, although the labor of a fustian cutter demands great bodily exertion, and is at the same time unhealthy, it counts only as unskilled labor."

It is obvious that the skilled worker is not, under all properly economic perspectives, "an exact multiple" of the unskilled worker. Marx was not impeded by this difficulty, because he thought that skilled labor does not occupy "a large place in the total national labor." This is true or false depending on the question at hand. The ideas Marx took from the English economists who followed Ricardo prevented him from directing his research on the economies of the higher-paid employees: workers who are better paid and stimulated to produce a great deal are not at all exact multiples of more poorly paid workers, as the instance of America proves.[8]

This theory of despecialization has had considerable influence on socialist ideas. Proudhon maintained that in the future society ought to be conducted by rules of remuneration according to the duration of labor: in the *Contradictions économiques*[9] he exposed a theory of the constitution of value based on this principle which appeared to him "the purpose of progress, the condition and form of social well-being, the principle and end of political economy." It does not appear that he ever varied on this point: he was content to perfect the exposition of his ideas. In the *Capacité politique des classes ouvrières* he affirms that all human labor can be expressed as average labor and should be regulated according to this valuation:[10] "That is, what a man of average strength, intelligence, and age can give of service to the production of values in any industry or profession, knowing well its condition and various components. . . . Since the child, the woman, the old man, the valetudinary or weak man cannot generally attain the average of the vigorous man, their work day will be only a fraction of the official, normal, legal day, taken as the unit of value. . . . Thus the rights of strength, talent, even character, as well as those of work, are controlled: if justice makes no personal exceptions, neither does it fail to recognize any ability. . . . But I repeat that for this liquidation to work, good faith must help in the evaluation of tasks, services, and products. Everyone must subject himself to the justice meted out, with no consideration for pretensions of variety and personality, with no consideration of title, rank, privilege, honorific distinctions, or celebrity—in a word, of opinion. Only the usefulness of the product, the quality, the work and its expenses should be taken into account."

It seems that Marx had long wavered on this question. In *The Poverty of Philosophy* he scoffed at Proudhon:[11] "After all the determination of value by means of labor time, which is the regenerative formula of the future according to Proudhon, is only the scientific expression of economic relations in contemporary society, as Ricardo has clearly and precisely shown." In *Capital* there is an oft-cited passage in which Marx examines various important types of societies: he considered what would happen in "a reunion of *free men*[12] who work through the common means of production and who employ, according to a determined plan, their numerous individual forces as a single sole force of labor." It is obvious that a socialist society is being dealt with here, but (in this as in so many other instances) the author gives no formula, in contrast to those socialist theoreticians who know beforehand and make use of the sole power of reason, how to regulate the distribution of the products of labor as needed. Marx says that "the mode of distribution [die Art dieser Vertheilung] varies according to the productive system of society and the *level of historical development of workers.* Let us assume that the portion accorded to each worker is proportional to his labor time, in order to make this state of affairs parallel to mercantile production." We must understand this as follows: that such a mode of distribution *could* suit present society if we pass to socialism with our present factory system and the present degree of development of the workers. But it is surprising enough not to find more precise indications for defining the reason for the hypothesis.

Schaffle noted the doubts on the strength of the doctrine of *Capital* and that in 1877 there appeared in *Vorwarts* an article in which it was asserted that "socialism neither seeks nor sees in the Marxist theory of value any measure of distribution."[13] Probably in this case, as in many polemics on this question, there has been a misunderstanding: it is obvious that as individual exchange disappears, it is no longer necessary to fix the *value* of commodities produced by isolated contractors. It is on this detail around which all the discussion against Proudhon revolves.[14] Marx attacked Proudhon and regarded him as a utopian because he claimed to conserve commerce in commodities by perfecting it. Proudhon conserved the capitalists then, which Marx did not want to allow, but the worker's labor still should be evaluated, leaving the freedom of his profession to him who works by taking into account the needs of the market. There are no more private commodities: labor remains a proletarian commodity. The principle Proudhon wants to see actualized in a mercantile society can well be applied in socialist society, as we shall see.

In 1875 in his *Critique of the Gotha Programme* Marx gives us a solution that is both clear and important, inasmuch as he wrote confidentially to his friends that in these writings he had no need to take popular prejudices into consideration.[15] He insists that this program does not contemplate a completely communist society: such a society is not deemed impossible, but its realization is subject to so many conditions that it is not worth talking about. The law socialism should realize is defined as follows:

> What dominates here is obviously the *same principle that today regulates the exchange of commodities* in proportion to which identical values are exchanged. No one can give anything but his labor, and only the individual means of consumption can figure among the goods of the individual. As to the division among producers, the dominant principle is the same one as for the exchange of equivalent values in matters of commodities: the same quantity of labor of one form is exchanged with the same quantity of labor of another form. The theory and the practice did not come into conflict as they do today; now the exchange of equivalent values, when dealing with

commodities, is found realized only wholesale. The equality consists here in the employment of a common measure, labor. The same equal law is an unequal law for unequal labor. It ignores class distinctions, but tacitly recognizes, as natural privileges, the inequality of individual capacities and consequently of capacity of production.

As Marx says, it is still a "bourgeois law,"[16] but is it not odd that socialism should regulate the order that, according to Marx, would be spontaneously stabilized and largely in the manner of capitalist production? Ricardo would have uncovered the essence of exchange and socialism would only legislate according to capitalist principles revealed by him. There is a mystery here that has hitherto not been elucidated satisfactorily.

Notes

1. "The textile industry presents a good example of despecialized production, and marks the highest point of the modern development of factory labor." Paul De Rousiers, *La question ouvrière en Angleterre* (Paris: Firmin-Didot, 1895), p. 387.
2. Ure, *Philosophie des manufactures*, French trans. (Paris: Mathias, 1836), Vol. I, p. 33. Marx studied with great care Ure's book, whose French translation was published in 1836.
3. I have indicated this explanation in my *Saggi di critica del marxismo*, p. 352.
4. Karl Marx, *The Poverty of Philosophy* (Moscow: Foreign Languages Publishing House, p. 161). Ure wrote a veritable apology for industry: he finally went so far as to claim that "the faculty of the worker is subject only to an agreeable exercise" (p. 199). Marx much later called him "the Pindar of manufacturing" (*Capital*).
5. *Capital* (New York: Modern Library ed., pp. 44–45).
6. Ibid., p. 220 n.
7. Ibid., p. 221 n.
8. The references to which Marx resorts to prove the small importance of skilled labor are a bit old, the most recent being from 1844! It seems certain that in a progressive economy, wages are not at all in a constant ratio to industrial labor, and that great efforts are needed to improve wages through their energy and ingenuity. The American labor unions are not at all unfavorable to increasing productivity, and in this differ sharply from the English trade unions. *Bulletin de la Société d'encouragement* (April 1900):640 (August 1902):320; *Journal des économistes* (May 1904):329.
9. Proudhon, *Contradictions économiques* (Paris: Lacroix, 1867), Vol. I, p. 101.
10. Proudhon, *Capacité politique des classes ouvrières* (Paris: Dento, 1865), pp. 94–96.
11. Marx, *The Poverty of Philosophy*, p. 91.
12. *Capital*, Vol. I (Modern Library ed., p. 92). We should note that here "liberty" should be understood in the sense of intellectual capacity: free

men are those who think with their heads and act according to their reason.

13. Schaffle, *Quintéssence du socialisme* (Brussels: Librairie du Progrès, 1880), p. 98.

14. Engels has said often that after the socialist revolution, there would be no more *values*, since there would be no more *commodities*.

15. I believe that Marx often sacrificed the scientific rigor of his doctrine in favor of his capacity as party chieftain that he imposed on himself, and that he often had to accommodate the fanatical communists. Sorel, *Saggi di critica del Marxismo*, pp. 310–19.

16. We even know nowadays, according to the Marxist theoreticians, the regime of free competition ought to be applied to labor. The ideas of Kautsky would have seemed *atrociously bourgeois* to the communists in whose name Marx wrote his 1848 *Manifesto*.

CHAPTER EIGHT

To resolve this enigma we ought to examine a very important theory of Marx's that allows us to penetrate the very core of his system. At first sight, it appears that there is no means of reasoning about the future world and defining its legal principle.[1] It is on this impossibility that the confutations the Marxist school has often made of the various social utopias are based. One could not even take in bourgeois society theses on law and "purify" them by means of a more or less scientific discourse to construct fundamental rules of the future. Since it appeared to Marx that Proudhon reasoned in this way, he attacked him passionately. The partial conservation of property seemed to Marx a strange way to produce socialism. To perfect the system of exchange was equivalent, in his view, to defending commercial capitalism, the most essential of bourgeois principles.

Marx did not want socialism to borrow anything from the bourgeoisie and started with a rule he enunciated in various ways and which can be formulated as follows: "When a class that makes its life separate eventually triumphs and becomes legislator, it imposes as legal that which was the essence of its own life, thus carrying out the law according to the philosophy made by reason of its principal mode of acquisition." In the *Critique of Hegel's Philosophy of Right*, published in 1844, he had already said[2] that if a class becomes revolutionary it emancipates all of society, but assuming that society is in the same social condition as that class. Thus the bourgeoisie emancipated everyone who had the wealth and education of the bourgeoisie. In 1847 he affirmed in the *Communist Manifesto* that all philosophy depends on the conditions of life of the dominant class. He replied directly to his adversaries:[3] "Your very ideas are but the outgrowth of the conditions of your bourgeois production and bourgeois property, just as your jurisprudence is but the will of your class made into a law for all, a will, whose essential character and direction are determined by the economic conditions of existence of your class."[4] "The ruling ideas of each age have always been the ideas of its ruling class."

The proletariat have conquered its masters and possessing legislative powers, will abandon[5] all bourgeois traditions, and therefore the theories

157

that were discussed so stubbornly in capitalist times and which formed the essence of the so-called natural laws will disappear by themselves. ''In the conditions of the proletariat, those of the old society are virtually swamped. The proletarian is without property. . . . Law, morality, religion are to him so many bourgeois prejudices behind which lurk in ambush so many bourgeois interests. All the preceding classes that got the upper hand sought to fortify their acquired status by subjugating society to their conditions of appropriation. The proletarians cannot become masters of the productive forces of society, except by abolishing their own previous mode of appropriation, and thereby also even other previous modes of appropriation.''[6]

Marx wants to justify communism against the defenses of the triad: nation, family, and property. This was the great concern of the socialists, who generally extracted themselves from the embarrassment with subtle rather than convincing arguments. Marx's explanations are not always very convincing either. But we shall see that, applying his principles, one is led to a clear idea of the intensity of the proletariat in carrying out the revolution. It is by this method that we will examine in considerable detail socialist ideas on the family, private property, and the state.

Some years before, Pecqueur replied to P. Leroux:[7] ''Every individual will be free to love this or that country, this or that boundary on the globe—this is his *actual homeland*; every individual will be free to love, to adore, and to associate in the greatest intimacy with individuals of both sexes as he prefers, and those that are bound to him by blood ties—this is his *actual family*; he will be free to consume anything his resources permit, that is, the remuneration he receives in his job—this is his *actual property*. There shall still be a homeland but no nations; there shall still be a family but no inheritance; there shall still be property but no proprietors.'' We can easily find some weak echoes of these ideas in the *Manifesto*, which proves that these ideas were very popular at that time. But the question is so important for the understanding of Marx's principles that we should examine the special reasons that dominated this part of the *Manifesto*.

The German workers that constituted the majority of the Communist Party had to regard themselves as without a country. National feeling was not very strong in Germany and was to awaken only after the unexpected triumphs of 1871. The movement of 1813 did not go beyond the university world and had been rapidly crushed. In 1847, the German living abroad was an abandoned man, without diplomatic protection, something similar to the medieval Jew. Thus Marx could write without straining the truth too much: ''The worker is without a country. He cannot be deprived of what he does not have.''

In 1847 it could be believed that once more Europe might be upset by great wars. In 1793, those that were called "patriots" fervently welcomed the revolutionary armies and helped them to expel tyrants; they were true internationalists. The meaning of the word *patriot* had changed. In 1847 it would not have been possible to label as patriots those German workers who would have assisted the French to combat the kings and princes of the German Confederation. The recurrence of the wars of liberty should have added to the ideas naturally born of the conditions in which the communists found themselves, to reenforce the concept of internationalism. Today very few people conceive of the social revolution on the model of 1793, and I doubt that in Germany there are socialists ill-disposed to fulfill their duties as soldiers:[8] Babel has always affirmed that they would carry out these duties with absolute abnegation—the war of 1870 has overstimulated nationalism on both sides of the Rhine.

As to the future, Marx remains vague, saying that the proletariat will constitute a nation, but not in the manner followed by the bourgeoisie—obviously the workers' ideology was still far from clear on this. Still today one can find the strangest contradictions in socialist writings on this subject. Thus Paul Lafargue, Marx's son-in-law, says that "capitalist exploitation produces a new idea of nation, larger than that dreamed by the medieval papacy. The international union of workers is the new idea of fatherland that the proletariat brings to the world." This is a paradox of an intellectual.[9]

The French socialists have always been obliged to have a high regard for the patriotic sentiment of the nation, and one often sees this phrase from a speech by Jules Guesde in 1896 at the tomb of the soldiers killed in 1870: "I come to salute those who die for a fatherland which has yet to be conquered." It seems that he too allowed himself to be led astray that day in confusing the revolutionary tradition with the new exclusively proletarian conditions. Almost all French notions of patriotism come from the wars of liberty, and the French working classes have received them from the bourgeoisie. Jaurès was completely dominated by these memories when he cried: "The true Frenchmen, those who love their country in its great revolutionary and humanitarian tradition, always oppose to the promoters of coups d'état the admirable words of the men of the Revolution: 'We have a fatherland since we have liberty.' "[10] Why should the proletariat not have a country on the day its deputies exercise an influence on the government?

Popular ideas have changed so much that today the notion of internationalism is devoid of meaning; there is a partial internationalism just as there is a partial collectivism.[11] Charles and Pierre Bonnier say this explicitly:[12] "The socialists are individualists about certain things and collectivist about others, but above all are nationalist and even internationalist. In regard to all forms of production or of possession, it is enough to ask if it belongs to the individual type, for example, or *if it would not be better to be collectivized*. To demand nationalization of everything that has not yet been nationalized would be absurd: it would be still more absurd to want to retain in national form that which is already international." This way of thinking is a far cry from the principles of Marx.

The proletariat has not yet formed its own concept of national life, and it is content to amalgamate some bourgeois notions with some wish for the improvement of wages. Thus internationalism for the worker consists most often in subscriptions destined to help foreign strikers. A class is not ripe for taking power when it has not acquired a clear notion of the function of the nation abroad. It is strange that in 1847 Marx had not been greatly impressed with the inadequacy of workers' ideas on this point; it seems that he had not considered the bases of the theory of the state very closely. Today, better informed than Marx, we have the right to say that the proletariat is still very far from being able to realize a proletarian revolution since its ideas on questions of nationality come to it from outside. Its active participipation in bourgeois politics can only serve to confuse its ideas.

On the question of the family, we do not find much more satisfactory explanations, and this is particularly serious, since all historical experience teaches us the importance of ideas relative to the family. The *Manifesto* asserts the proletarian has no family[13]—must we understand by this like Pecqueur, that the essence of the present-day family is inheritance? Here is the way I believe we should understand Marx's thought.

1. For a long time, the principal feature distinguishing concubinage from lawful marriage has been removed from the relation to goods. But the proletarian having nothing, not having to make marriage contracts, does not easily know how to distinguish free union from legal matrimony. At present many workers' societies assimilate "mate" to "wife" and do not recognize in the latter any rights when she no longer cohabits with her husband.
2. The craftsman and the peasant are married as soon as they are established, that is, by becoming independent heads of an enterprise; the prosperity of the workshop and farm greatly depend on the direction of women. In 1847 Marx regarded small industry and small farms as marked for death.

3. He must have known the types of families established in Germany, that Le Play admired so much; their customs are based on the preservation of the hearth. The proletariat, being unable to practice this preservation of the home, was deprived of one of the most necessary conditions for the family to attain its full realization.

Thus the victory of the proletariat was to be translated into the destruction of the present order. In the *Communist Manifesto* there are obscure passages on this matter such as:[14] "The Communists have no need to introduce the community of women, it has existed from time immemorial." I do not believe, nonetheless, that Marx ever dreamed of advocating sexual promiscuity; we must take account of the prejudices he had to respect among the members of the League of Communists.[15] He therefore appears very reserved, but note that among the transitory measures divorce does not appear, and that he undoubtedly regarded it as a bourgeois measure.

Kautsky distances himself considerably from the thought of his master when he reproaches the bourgeoisie for not having created[16] more elevated forms of the family to replace the present one based on the couple. Would the bourgeoisie be thus charged with preparing the new proletarian institutions? In this we recognize one of the returns to utopianism so frequently found in Kautsky's writings.

From this we can deduce that the proletariat has not completed the preparatory work necessary for it to assume rule. Morality depends so strictly on sexual relations, that we can say that a class that has no clear ideas on the family has no ideas on morality. It appears that Marx never closely examined such questions. Property being estranged from the proletariat in large industry should disappear,[17] though it is not very easy to know how the *Manifesto* conceives the remuneration of labor. It is likely that Marx adopted somewhat vague formulas to appeal to all voters. Marx asserted[18] that communism would not destroy property acquired through labor, since modern industrial development had already demolished it.

Marx was especially impressed by the "iron law of wages":[19] "The average price of wage-labor is the minimum wage, i.e., that quantum of the means of subsistence, which is absolutely required to keep the laborer in bare existence as a laborer. What, therefore, the wage laborer appropriates by means of his labor merely suffices to prolong and reproduce a bare existence. We by no means intend to abolish this personal appropriation of the products of labor, an appropriation that is made for the maintenance and reproduction of human life, and that leaves no surplus wherewith to command the labor of others.''[20] Only the remuneration would be better and poverty would no longer result from the cupidity of capitalists.

In 1847 Marx had projected the iron law of wages into the future, according to each the satisfaction of his needs regulated according to production.[21] His thought changed later on this matter; he no longer viewed the law of wages as the essence of present society. His research for the writing of *Capital* led him to give priority to considerations of quantity of labor, and under the influence of these considerations he wrote the *Critique of the Gotha Programme* in 1875. During his sojourn in England, he had observed how the workers understood wages, and was convinced that they understood them according to the Ricardian theory he had perfected. He had thus the right to assume that this was the beginning of the socialist world.

According to certain writers, wages will probably survive the social revolution. Vandervelde says this,[22] and surrounds this confession with a variety of pompous phrases about the future. Anticipating that "the reach of our minds will be immensely developed and refined," the worker will remain salaried and only the boss will have changed. We find here an illustration of Marxist theory. The revolution is conceived as produced by intellectuals desirous to conquer political power and impose legal rules suitable to their particular mode of exploiting the labor of the proletariat. They hope to become bureaucrats. The social revolution will thus be produced for the benefit of functionaries. Bureaucracy, parliamentarianism, and the rule over the people through the action of men who have acquired a liberal education—this is what Vandervelde dreams of. It is an infinitely bourgeois ideal. Society is regarded from the point of view of the bosses and not from that of the proletariat.

Notes

1. We do not mean formulating future law codes, but only determining a principle that, *without ever being formulated by jurists*, is nevertheless the *real and hidden reason* for all their judgments on justice for those who concern themselves professionally with it. The reader is asked never to fail to take into consideration this viewpoint: in legal matters, Marx is no more utopian than he is in economic matters.
2. Cf. Georges Sorel, *Saggi di critica del marxismo*, p. 218. In that work, I recalled the opinion of P. Violet to the effect that the new constitution of French property had been in imitation of the possessions of the peasants. The new law was thus the reproduction of the law of the society to the advantage of what the revolution made.
3. *Communist Manifesto* (M.E.S.W. I, 49).
4. Ibid. (M.E.S.W., I, 52).
5. Ibid. (M.E.S.W., I, 52-53).

6. Ibid. (M.E.S.W., I, 44).

7. Constantin Pecqueur, *Théorie nouvelle d'économie sociale* (Paris: Capelle, 1842), p. 885.

8. *Petite République* (1 October 1900) relates that an English delegate to the International Socialist Congress of 1900 went to place a crown on the bust of Kruger, exhibited in the Transvaal pavilion at the exposition. This delegate was a simple imbecile or rather the representative of English socialism.

9. *Petit Sou* (6 January 1902). It would nonetheless be unjust to make Marx responsible for all the writings of his family. In *Petite République* (4 April 1900), J. Longuet, a nephew of Marx, noted admiringly that "all the members of the Independent Transvaal Workers' Party, a majority of whom are English, battle for the defense of the young Boar Republic."

10. *Petite République* (2 February 1901).

11. For many socialists, internationalism is confused with the love for peace, and at the 1900 Congress the deputy, Sembat, proclaimed that socialists had been instruments of internationalism in not voting for credits for the China expedition.

12. *Devenir Social* (November 1897):916. These two brothers are ardent Guesdists.

13. *Communist Manifesto* (M.E.S.W., I).

14. *Communist Manifesto* (M.E.S.W., I, 51).

15. Andler has observed that the transitory measures were certainly imposed by members of the League of Communists. *Le Manifeste communiste*, Vol. II, p. 160.

16. Cf. Georges Sorel, *Saggi di critica del marxismo*, p. 304 (see *From Georges Sorel*, p. 166). Engels seems to have had peculiar ideas on the family; we are sure that he had a natural son to whom he bequeathed nothing. Kautsky was in a good position to know Engels's mode of life and his ideas about women. But it seems that Marx had always lived as a good German *pater familias* without engaging in "free love" in the name of a so-called higher law.

17. *Communist Manifesto* (M.E.S.W., I, 47).

18. Ibid.

19. Ibid. (M.E.S.W., I, 47–48).

20. Ibid. (M.E.S.W., I, 49): "Communism deprives no man the power to appropriate the products of society; all that it does is to deprive him of the power to subjugate the labor of others by means of such appropriation."

21. It is obvious that the celebrated communist formula "to each according to his needs" is nothing else but the law of wages, prodigiously widened, sufficiently to become a new principle. In both cases the life of the worker is regulated by his needs.

22. Destrée and Vandervelde, *Le Socialisme en Belgique*, 1st ed. (Paris: Giard et Brière, 1898), pp. 282–83. It does not cost the author much to assert that he aspires "to the anarchic community overflowing with fraternity and wealth." But this very remote ideal should not prevent us from considering what is maintained by the present. In the preface written in 1892 for the German translation of the *Poverty of Philosophy*, Engels censures Rodbertus of Pomerana, the naive admirer of Prussian bureaucracy, because he preserves wages.

CHAPTER NINE

The inextricable difficulties amidst which contemporary Marxism struggles derive especially from the fact that the social revolution has not arrived according to predictions of Marx and Engels. When Merlino began to attack what he calls the "catastrophic conception" of socialism, everyone understood that we are dealing with a question of the highest order, and the official representatives of the socialist party have made the greatest efforts to dissimulate at least the gravity of the problem raised. Marxism, considered as a sociological theory of modern capitalism, can continue to live and has not ceased to illuminate the social question well, but Marxism as a system of socialist politics has not survived the disappearance of the catastrophic conception. The efforts made by the political system to make itself independent when this conception became untenable have been in vain: "In what, according to the Marxists," asked Merlino in 1898,[1] "would the fundamental point of their doctrine consist?" According to Arturo Labriola, the essential point of the doctrine would not be the theory of value, nor of rent, nor the materialist conception of history, but the theory of social catastrophe. This theory would be so important that to deny it would be to deny the very essence of socialism.

In Marx's thought this catastrophe ought not to be a desired revolution which can or cannot be made according to whether it is found more or less advantageous to adopt a violent solution or a gradual one. He assumed that capitalism would be brusquely halted by a crisis, acting automatically, killing its powers of direction. A Marxist who understands Marx could therefore not pose the questions that Kautsky dealt with at length in his articles on the social revolution. He seemed to abandon the idea of any catastrophe and said:

> We should no more wait for the collapse of contemporary society from a financial crisis than from armed insurrections. In this respect also, the situation is entirely different from that of 1789 and 1848. Then capitalism was still weak, the accumulations of capital were mediocre, and capital was rare and difficult to find. . . . The decaying feudalism allowed all sources of revenue to dry up—so much so that governments derived less and less money from the countryside and had increasingly to resort to borrowing.

> This would lead to a financial crash or to concessions to upwardly mobile classes, but either case led to political upheaval. An entirely different situation prevails today. Capitalism does not neglect production as feudalism had. . . . The increase in public debt . . . would, with difficulty . . . lead to bankruptcy or even to a serious financial crisis. Financial crisis would no more lead to revolution than would armed insurrection.[2]

All this has only the most distant relation with the "business crisis" envisioned by Marx: but Kautsky no longer wants to know about this famous economic catastrophe. One can grant him that in the future there perhaps will be revolutions;[3] that is, the legislative works of a class that has suddenly become a ruling class and which profoundly alters the social order. In the past there have been many revolutions. We can grant him that the time of deepest reforms has probably passed[4] and that we will see nothing analogous to what was produced in England by the ten-hour laws. Moreover we can grant him that countries will not pass gradually to socialism by means of progressive concessions by the ruling classes.[5] All this is true enough, but what do all these assertions lead to? According to Kautsky, to desire and to expect a revolution. The revolution will impose itself because we have no other means of realizing the plans for the future invented by Kautsky. But what difference is there between Kautsky and the old utopians? One difference is that the latter often addressed themselves to princes, while Kautsky was concerned with representatives of universal suffrage. The fundamental idea of the social revolution disappeared from Marx's disciple.

Marx and Engels believed they had suppressed utopia, directing their attention to the examination of the present. In the facts that developed under their eyes, they believed they could uncover (like the physicist) laws as inevitable as that of gravitation. They allowed themselves a single hypothesis: that the working class would not be too difficult to put in motion when all normal resources of government would be paralyzed during the crisis. Is this a utopian hypothesis? The world in 1847 was replete with revolutionary reminiscences. The events of 1871 reenforced again in Marx and Engels the idea of an easy rising of the proletariat. There was no choice to make in circumstances when the forces of men matter so little and events precipitate with the rapidity of an almost irresistible torrent.

As for the results, they would not be completely indeterminate and of such a nature as to surprise the heads of the revolutionary classes. Marx believed that he could deduce from his rules that the proletariat would be organized in a certain way. Previously it had been possible to argue against the utopians that things most probably would not come about as they had dreamed they would; that revolutions demonstrate the power-lessness of man still better than ordinary history. Marxism can lay claim to the title of "scientific socialism" if it truly distinguishes itself from utopianism on this point.

Marx's socialism is not scientific in the sense that it would provide the best means for attaining the triumph of the new ideas, nor because it corresponds to some mysterious law leading to ultimate justice. It is not a question of choosing among various attitudes, nor of a hypothesis on a better world, but only of the means of knowing the principles of juridical rules that the victorious class will impose on society. The question is whether Marx and Engels were able to determine this scientifically. If this is so, the philosopher of history will keep the name "scientific socialism" for their system. We need to designate it with an expression that accurately categorizes the mind of Marx.[6]

The reasoning that helps Marx determine the future of law cannot be conclusive if one does not assume that the proletariat is about to become revolutionary and that before long society itself will become revolutionary because of the elimination of the dominant classes. It is with this condition only that one can understand how the essentials of contemporary working-class life can be transformed into juridical rules for the socialist world. In present-day discussions, these fundamental conditions of the doctrine are too often forgotten. If one does not assume a revolution is near at hand, produced from economic emergencies, nothing more can be said on the future law and we lapse into utopian fantasies. The enigma we noted at the end of the preceding chapter is resolved in the catastrophic hypothesis: socialism no longer has to make a choice among various solutions; it is what capitalism has made of it, and in a certain sense, it realizes a bourgeois law that results from conditions of life during the bourgeois era.

From then on, Marxist theoreticians were no longer concerned with finding the "good" organization of the laboratory; the socialist world would inherit the completely organized workshop from the hands of capi-talism. The capitalist era will have created for its successors the mater-ial conditions of the new production: collective labor and communal utilization of the new instruments of production. This plan that the utopians sought with such ingenuity should not be sought; it is realized automatically by the sole play of forces that keep capitalism alive: the search for the highest possible profit leads the contractors to create what the most stubborn inventors of systems had vainly imagined in fantastic ways.

We need not be surprised if Marx forcefully argued against the article of the *Gotha Programme* which said: "The German Workers' party, *in order to prepare the way to the solution of the social question*, demands the institution of societies of production with state cooperation and under the democratic control of the working people." To him it seemed absurd to proceed to such a preparation instead of allowing the capitalists to do their work and develop the sentiments of class struggle in the working masses. Nothing is clearer than the class struggle, nothing is more imaginary than this transformation of industry and agriculture into a vast cooperative struggling against capitalist enterprises.

"In Lassalle's imagination," said Marx, "there is the conception that, with state support, we can construct a new society as easily as a new railroad! What is most serious is not that this specific concern is inscribed in the program, but that the perspective of the class struggle is abandoned in order to adopt the perspective of sectarian agitation."[7] It is not the state that can prepare the economic conditions of the new regime; it is the single inevitability of capitalism. This is a fundamental thesis of Marxism.

Capitalism acts on society in two ways: first it creates the modern workshop that develops into the collectivist workshop. Therefore it forces the working class to organize itself and leads it, through the struggle undertaken by the bosses against them, to attain the capacity for self-emancipation. In the penultimate chapter of the first volume of *Capital*, Marx gives this idea a somewhat paradoxical formulation: "Capitalist production begets its own negation with the inevitability that presides over the metamorphoses of nature." There is "through the play of the immanent laws of capitalist production" a progressive centralization of capital, and at the same time is developed the collective form of the process of labor, the reasoned application of science to technology, the methodical exploitation of the land, and the transformation of machinery. On the other hand, the same mechanization of production disciplines, unites, and organizes the ever-increasing mass of workers.

The utopians claimed they were concerned with *man*. All those who are inspired by the ideas of the revolution hope to see the social transformation spring from a development of the laws of the "citizen." The citizen as it has already been seen is an ideal farmer, an abstract proprietor, a pure spirit who consents to employ material means, obliged as he is to think sometimes of the necessities of his body. Marxism puts all this aside; it knows only the worker and takes him as he has adapted to the historical conditions of capitalism.

The worker is an element of the workshop; there he imprints his individuality with a certain quantity of work, but the labor of all the workers of the same workshop is arranged without him having to concern himself with it. The workshop has an objective existence;[8] it is "the material condition already prepared for his labor."[9] Capitalist domination results from this: the power of the masters derives from the extraordinary capacity of this machinery, from science, and from the enormous natural forces monopolized by the "bosses."[10] The work plan appears as the property of the boss. Capitalism disappears when the latter's presence is no longer necessary. This same passivity that exists in the factory is found in history: it is in the presence of a complete and finished organization that the proletariat establishes itself; the activity of the proletariat would exist only in relation to itself, in its preparation.

We know today that things do not happen as simply as Marx assumed in 1847. The capitalist movement has not progressed with the rapidity that he ascribed to it. But this has no great importance from the point of view that concerns us, provided that the "fatal" character of capitalism is maintained; this is essential. It at least would be necessary that in the eyes of the working classes this fatality appear as inevitable. But it seems that the progress of the democratic idea, resulting in the infinite power of the state, buries the notion of economic fatality. The workers' movement was excessively simplified by Marx; at present we are obligated to confess that we do not yet know everything we need to do to raise the proletariat to the capacity assumed by the revolutionary hypothesis. All we can say is that a popular socialist education should be maintained in an unreduced way on the terrain of the class struggle. The principle of Marx remains sound; but the application is more complicated than he had believed. The spirit of class struggle is not automatically produced because of conflicts over salaries. Experience teaches us that these conflicts can be resolved so as to produce social peace and place the solidarity of classes in bold relief. In order that *the spirit of separation* be produced and, above all, maintained, we need institutions capable of generating and developing it. It is on this point that Marx's teaching is most defective.

Socialism is the organization of revolt, and revolutionary-style syndicalism is so when specifically socialistic. Cooperation does not put this sentiment of struggle into operation; it does not nourish the socialist idea. For this reason today's socialists give much less importance to cooperatives than they once did. Nonetheless, we cannot be completely uninterested in these issues: (1) why socialism utilizes all conquests of the capitalist era and (2) why it can participate in the experiences that take place around it to know better the economic capacity of the working classes. Marx had given productive cooperatives great importance, but he deceived himself in giving them the value of institutions that oppose the production by capitalists to the production of partners, forced cooperation to free cooperation.

This contradition is striking at first sight, because verbally it is what would be found between contemporary capitalism and the future society.[11] But when one applies the present case, we need not limit ourselves to juxtaposing two definitions, that is to say, to regard things from the abstract point of view. We need to penetrate the soul and see with what *spirit* these cooperatives function: whether they are truly associations of free men who think independently and agree among themselves, or associations of bosses who direct workers and think for them. Everyone now agrees that the cooperation of production returns, almost always, to the latter. Thus Kautsky maintains[12] "that all attempts at cooperative ownership, however little they succeed, end sooner or later by inclining toward capitalism." He does not place cooperation in production beside consumer cooperatives[13] among the institutions created by the contemporary proletariat.

This error of Marx's should make us extremely prudent and put us on guard against a form of utopianism which attributes to nascent institutions an importance they do not possess. Also we should not limit ourselves to considering, as is often the case, the value of an institution as an additional force, added to those already at the disposal of the socialist party. If we want to stay on Marxist ground, we should regard all things from the perspective of the *separation of classes*. Each new institution is an attempt whose purpose is to produce this separation, and if the attempt fails, we must ask ourselves whether the mistake is ours or whether it was inevitable. It is important to know whether the spirit of class struggle can be maintained when the expectation of a proximate revolution has been lost.

It was often believed that this was impossible and that Marxism was decisively struck down forever. Nonetheless it seems that things are becoming complex. The revolutionary idea that was believed to have been exhausted is revived among certain strata of the proletariat, and for this reason there is a certain spontaneous reappearance of Marxism. After the discouragement develops, the notion of class solidarity arises.[14] Resolving the enigma presented by Marxism, we arrive at a paradoxical result: Marxism calls itself "scientific" because it breaks all connections with utopianism, but this break cannot be realized unless it takes as its basic hypothesis what is manifestly contrary to observation or to all likelihood. Marxism bases its determination of future law on the imminence of a catastrophe and on the perfect preparation of the proletariat become capable of dispensing with the capitalists. There appears to be an insoluble contradiction between the scientific temper and reality.

This difficulty can only be resolved by means of the theory of social myths that I have presented at the end of my book *Introduction à l'économie moderne.* The catastrophe may not ever happen, but it is a myth which expresses with perfect clarity the principle of the separation of classes, a principle which is the whole of socialism. Even though they have tried to express this catastrophe under the form of the general strike; even though they have reenforced the power of action of the myth—it does not change. The notion of the general strike, so strongly rejected by so many Marxists, should be received enthusiastically by them, because it translates the catastrophic idea in a perfect way and corresponds closely to the emancipation of the workers through their own action.

The great mistrust that the German Social Democrats show for the general strike[15] comes from the fact that (without daring to admit it) they deem the working classes of their country, who are accustomed to being directed from above, as not being ripe for self-government. It is a consideration of a practical order that governs their spirit on a question that has nothing to do with practical matters. Their mistrust proves also that they have never fully understood Marx's principles and that the theory of classes has remained somewhat obscure to them.

We should not be too surprised that Marx himself had not elucidated such questions. The more one studies his work, the more one recognizes that he did not reflect on morals and on the state deeply enough. It was therefore impossible to understand well the relations between political and class struggles, and realize the level of preparation of the proletarian spirit. We should not regret too much the insufficiency of his study on this question because Marx was the first, by closing himself in his doctrine (and often being unilateral), to conceive of the class struggle. But today we should analyze the phenomena that he neglected, and especially consider his formulas on action and propaganda (as is too often done in Germany), instead of concerning ourselves with his philosophy of law which is the single essential part of his work.

Notes

1. Serverio Merlino, *Formes et essence du socialisme* (Paris: Giard & Brière, 1898), p. 264.
2. *Mouvement Socialiste* (15 October 1902):1880; cf. Sorel, *Saggi di critica del marxismo*, p. 300.
3. *Mouvement Socialiste* (1 September 1902):1541.
4. Ibid. (15 October 1902):1867.
5. Kautsky (loc. cit., p. 1859) shows us that he had believed in the possibility of this transformation. Gladstone appeared to him to be the man who symbolized this policy of concession.
6. One too often forgets that Marx is first and foremost a *philosopher of*

juridical history; all of his most important perspectives are subordinated to the concerns that derive from this.

7. The "sectarians" for Marx are the "theoreticians."
8. *Capital*, Vol. I.
9. Ibid.
10. Ibid.
11. Cf. Sorel, *Saggi di critica del marxismo*, p. 350.
12. Kautsky, *Politique agraire du Parti Socialiste*, French trans. (Paris: Giard & Brière, 1903), p. 7.
13. *Mouvement Socialiste* (15 October 1902):1862.
14. We will return briefly at the end of this volume to the question of what can be done to utilize this revival of Marxism.
15. Lagardelle has gathered together in one volume (*La grève générale et le socialisme* [Paris: Cornély, 1905]) the opinions of the most notable social democratic writers on the subject of the general strike. Jaurès's opinions on this question are quite varied according to political exigencies, and it should have been essential to place this fact in evidence in this book: when he believes he needs the syndicalists, he speaks in such a way as to make them believe that he is favorable to the general strike. At the 1900 Paris Congress of the International, Jaurès seconded Briand's motion favoring the general strike; according to the stenographic report he abstained at the time of voting, saying that Portugal (which he represented) had not given him any mandate in this question; according to the official report, he had voted for Briand's motion. Lagardelle very frankly adopted the idea of a general strike, and this is an important fact because his journal, *Le Mouvement socialiste*, is so open to syndicalists.

PART II

The Old Utopias and the New Socialist Doctrines

CHAPTER ONE

In the preceding part I have examined completely developed doctrines which have experienced the influence of their time and, going beyond the time of their complete development, can be known and defined in all their details. We should now think about generally vague and often incoherent notions formulated by politicians according to circumstantial necessities which politicians do not even try to understand very well. To attain a certain rigor in our exposition and discussion, we need to adopt a new method and compare the theses, that we find dispersed and incomplete, to Marxism, which is still living as an explanatory principle and which will remain the backbone of contemporary social philosophy until it is replaced by a stronger doctrine. This is the method always followed in writing the history of ideas; we must borrow the guidelines of the school whose thought has reached the highest level of maturity.

Some time ago, Jaurès wrote on the subject of an article by Kautsky:[1] "The particular impression we get from Kautsky is evidently one of uneasiness. . . . He would like to say that the proletariat should confine itself to a class action so strictly defined that there should never be a sharing of efforts—especially with those of bourgeois liberalism. But the dialectic of history takes unexpected reverses: it reproduces, at a higher level of proletarian development, forms of action that one might believe obsolete. These are truly incomprehensible words; this manner of walking forward while returning back is indeed admirable. On the other hand, there is some truth here: the socialist politicians act as if Marxism had never existed and the mass of workers let them or even applaud them.

The great success of Marxism in France, considered as a political-social system, arose from its completely revolutionary constitution; its catastrophic idea was perfectly suited to men nourished by memories of the Paris Commune. The most notable Communards have not played a large role in the propagation of Marxism in France, but I am concerned here only with the legend of the Commune, a legend far removed from its actual history, and according to which a rather incoherent revolt provoked by wounded patriotic sentiments was transformed into a great action of the social revolution being prepared by the proletariat. This

175

example shows us that it takes very few years to create a legend and that this legend can take a greater expanse even when its witnesses are still alive. These witnesses of history can also become the "guarantors of the legend."

The function of the Commune would have been much less important if the Thiers government had not practiced a barbarous, atrocious, and stupid repression.[2] This civil war placed "the plebeian workers, having a rudimentary organization, face to face with the old French bourgeoisie. No assembly had ever represented so perfectly the middle classes, the tradition and the general spirit of provincial France as the Assembly of 1871. The struggle, devoid of all political decorum and without any ethical concern, was developing as a struggle of violence. The people were defeated; great proscriptions would follow the defeat; and henceforth, every anniversary of the fall of Paris is the occasion of conflicts between the socialist workers and the authorities, so much is the legend maintained intact in the new generations."[3]

The lesson of these things is beneficial; under the Empire all efforts to develop the mutualist idea failed. Proudhon's theories, so strongly marked by juridical and moral concerns, were considered reactionary. Socialism was unable to avoid the very laws of transformation of which I have spoken above in the first part. It had to undergo complexity and practice, to adapt to the conditions of life of a society that stubbornly refused to die, in order to guide its adherents in electoral politics, since few were uninterested in purely political questions and in the battles among the various bourgeois parties.

In its beginning, Jules Guesde's journal *Egalité* did not consider the possibility of arriving at anything but a revolution; and when the Guesdist Party published its program in 1880, it presented it in the following terms to its readers:

> It matters little [that the program] is incomplete or moderate,[4] as long as it contains the principal aspirations of the working class as they have been worked out by that class. This is not a program that consists in a compilation of reforms; it is not the entrance of some socialists into Parliament that it has in view; it is not some parliamentary action which we should plan. We should search only for a means of reuniting the working class now scattered in the various bourgeois parties, to separate the working class from those whose interests are diametrically opposed to its own, and *to organize it in a distinct force* capable of shattering the present social fabric [*Egalité*, 21 July 1880].

Reforms were formulated to give a concrete and elementary aspect to socialism; "by means of what [the working class] itself conceives, we will lead it to what we conceive."[5] Very soon a polemic was underway between reformists and revolutionaries, represented respectively by *Prolétaire* and *Egalité*. Guesde said that his group aimed at an economic reform which was not possible without the *violent capture of political power* by the revolutionary proletariat,[6] and reproached his adversaries for wanting "to fragment the purpose in order to render it *possible* for the capitalist order" (*Egalité*, 22 January 1882). A split took place at the Saint-Etienne Congress. The Guesdists, expelled in the wake of various intrigues, met again at Rouen and immediately occupied themselves with rendering their program more unrealizable: they added to the political section the advocacy of the elimination of public debt; instead of demanding only the revision of the concession contracts for railways and mines, they called for nothing less than their annulment. In an article published after the congress, Guesde said: "Absorbed in its goal of collective appropriation and in its revolutionary means, the Workers' Party is *not going anywhere but to the barricades*, while with the power once decreed of covering with the proletarian banner every type of radical or opportunist rubbish depending on the various localities, the era of electoral successes is completely open" (*Egalité*, 15 October 1882).

In 1883 there appeared a commentary on the program, edited by Guesde and Lafargue. Minor compromises were judged with the greatest severity. The "Possibilists" (or moderates) are criticized for being preoccupied with local interests in the course of the recent electoral campaigns: on the one hand for having spoken of finishing a large street in which a local district was interested, on the other for having promised to focus on the construction of an irrigation canal. But little by little this revolutionary ardor was lost. The commentary on the party program was republished with many corrections and the historical introduction was completely suppressed. Previously the necessity of affirming centralization was proclaimed "frankly and scientifically" (*Egalité*, 11 December 1881), when the Possibilists seemed to be the only ones in a position to win municipal offices, with the intention of realizing their ideas by means of local autonomy. But after the Guesdists had succeeded in the elections, they attributed extreme importance to municipal offices. Finally in 1892 and 1894 they attempted to win peasant votes by means of an agrarian program.

The evolution seemed complete in 1896 when Millerand gave his Saint-Mandé speech. He confined himself to demanding the development, through state operation, of a few large industries, beginning with sugar refining. To assert completely that he had buried revolutionary socialism, the author avoided mentioning the names of Marx and Engels, while glorifying the memory of Benoit Malon! The Guesdists did not protest, and Lafargue confessed shortly after that he and his friends were mistaken in not having "publicly criticized" the Saint-Mandé program (*Socialiste*, 30 July 1899). In this period they believed that they would always be able to determine at the propitious moment the arrest of the reformist movement and lead the proletariat back to the old ideas. Experience has proved them mistaken. Not only can we do nothing against the inevitability of developments ruled by the laws of psychological upheavals which tend to pacify the instincts and make us seek immediate results, but besides remarkable facts were presented to Guesde's adversaries which gave them the benefit of revolutionary colors.

When the Dreyfus affair began, popular passions were quickly aroused; it provided a magnificent opportunity to reunite all of those who had to satisfy some grudge against the army or the church. The people went instinctively to the side which seemed to embody the revolutionary spirit, without taking care to find out whether they campaigned with the enemies of their class or whether the revolt against reactionary forces conformed to Marxist dogmas. At first Guesde was very violently Dreyfusard; afterward he changed and thought it more useful for his party to stay aloof and invoke the principle of class separation. This showed the weakness of reason in the historical movement. Jaurès, who took little heed of theories, became the leader of the great majority of socialist workers, and had he not been too desirous to be a "statesman," he would have been their uncontested chief. The Dreyfus affair brought about a return to the old concepts of 1848, and led socialism in directions more democratic than Marxist. The notion of class struggle experienced an important diminution when its most ardent partisans walked the same roads with wealthy and harmless bourgeois who became terribly revolutionary in words, for the purpose of frightening the ministry.

Here was a true partial *ricorso*, an awakening of hatreds closely connected with leagues of revolutionaries against the nobility and clergy. This *ricorso*, which is foreign to socialism, shows that the creation of the idea of class struggle is not as simple as Marx thought. The Marxists did not know what position to take; Jaurès became the true revolutionary in the eyes of the masses. Onto their affair was grafted the struggle against religious associations; the great majority of the proletariat is fanatically anticlerical. Jaurès understood that by throwing himself wholeheartedly into this dispute, he would have carried the workers with him and would have placed Guesde in a difficult situation. The battle against the church cannot be presented as an episode in the class struggle; on the contrary, it mixes the classes and is unsuitable to Guesde's way of thinking. His foe expects to create great embarrassment in his party and perhaps also to disintegrate the solid army of partisans that have remained faithful to him.

Jaurès relies[7] on class collaboration, carrying out anticlericalism to maintain that Kautsky was wrong in criticizing his ministerialism. Jaurès's argument seems difficult to refute because, here again, class collaboration satisfies the revolutionary instinct of the people. To refute Jaurès it is necessary to prove that socialism can be in contradiction to this instinct and Kautsky would probably not dare to attempt such a demonstration.

The "professors of Marxism" cannot explain the conduct of the party by basing themselves on Marx's principles. The inquiry on the effect of the Dreyfus affair opened long ago by the *Petite République* among the most important foreign socialists showed results of a deplorable weakness: everyone approved of Jaurès's position except Liebknecht, who was a limited man who never understood much of Marxism. But the reasons given were solely in terms of the old baggage of humanitarianism. Thus in a question of the highest importance the Marxists show themselves incapable of understanding their own actions. Another inquiry has been opened on anticlericalism in *Mouvement Socialiste*, but the results have not been any more brilliant than the preceding ones.

The same Kautsky who is the great theoretician of official Marxism is embarrassed in not finding some passages in Marx to invoke in favor of his opinions on current questions. Nevertheless, he is the past master in the art of commenting on the smallest fragment of a phrase. In his article on the clerical question he finds nothing to quote from his master. He examines the question in Germany and *from the point of view of the electoral interests in his party* asks whether it is possible to separate religious from political matters in such a way as to bring peasants and Catholic workers to vote for the Social-Democratic candidate. For him, the question is not treated as a matter of principle but as a question of electoral astuteness, which is all the more necessary inasmuch as the Catholic proletariat is increasing in Germany and is resisting the efforts of socialist propagandists.

The difficulties these propagandists find in their way are such that many people ask themselves whether there is need to reform labor union organization: "neutralizing" it for the purpose of attracting Catholic workers, thus taking them away from clerical institutions. Kautsky does not share this viewpoint.[8] It might happen that the "neutralization" could have the consequence of giving an antisocialist tendency to the labor union movement. Besides, this tactic is only a "diplomatic procedure" destined to deceive the Catholics; the attitude advised by

Kautsky in religious matters may be meant to numb the vigilance of the Catholic clergy. Kautsky distinguishes[9] between simple religious faith and collective religions historically formed "which represent a social product"; only the former is regarded as a "private matter," which leads us to believe that Kautsky would not be hostile to an anticlerical policy if it did not appear harmful to German conditions.[10]

While the great leaders of orthodox Marxism don't know what to think about questions that impassion present-day minds, the "little Marxists" do not lack ideas and sometimes perhaps they have too many. Sometimes they apply Marx's concepts in a completely unpredictable way. I couldn't choose a better example than that in *Mouvement Socialiste* of 1 October 1902. A young lawyer asks if anything new from a socialist perspective can be said about prostitution. He maintains[11] that prostitutes form a true feminine proletariat: they sell what they call their "pleasure power," just as workers sell their labor power; that there is a prostitution contract analogous to the labor contract. These considerations are really comforting for organized labor, which Marx distinguished so accurately from the *Lumpen-proletariat*, and which he never had any idea of comparing to those women of easy virtue who entice passers-by! After this great "Marxist" effort, the author is visibly worn out and does not succeed in finding which type of surplus value emerges from the employment of pleasure power; he cuts short and digresses. He claims that in both selling situations there is an injustice because there is "for the worker a certain loss of freedom, while for the prostitute there is a certain loss of soul."

I would not have cited this nonsense if I had not judged it suitable for characterizing the state of mind of our young intellectuals, crammed with a bit of literature and a bit of socialism—and especially if it had not been welcomed by a review aptly regarded as representing the Marxist doctrine in France.[12]

Notes

1. *Petite République* (2 January 1903).
2. "La crise du socialisme," *Revue politique et parlementaire* (December 1898):601.
3. Recent experience has shown there was some exaggeration in this view. The legend of the Commune is in full decline.
4. This program had been written in London by Marx and Guesde. According to Malon, the latter had great difficulty in having it accepted by his group. *Revue Socialiste* (January 1887):48. There were already reformists with whom it was necessary to compromise, but the Guesdists only compromised unwillingly, as experience has shown.

5. In an article of the 30th of the preceding June we find the same idea; the program has the goal of adding purely working-class claims; revolutionary claims. Working-class parliamentarianism would have the same sterility as bourgeois parliamentarianism; we need to convince the proletariat of the "impossibility of making the economy of 1789 a workers' economy."

6. The program says, "This collective appropriation can only arise from the revolutionary action of the productive or proletarian class." Malon informs us that Guesde had insisted with Marx that the revolutionary affirmation be explicit (loc. cit., p. 53).

7. *Petite République* (2 January 1903).

8. Kautsky, *Politique et Syndicats,* French trans. (Paris: Giard & Brière, 1903), pp. 25–26.

9. *Mouvement Socialiste* (15 November 1902):2047.

10. This is rather likely in that he does not find much to say on the anti-clerical policies of the French socialists. I believe on the other hand that Kautsky misinterprets the Marxist formula. To say that religion is a private matter is equivalent to saying that it ought to be regarded from an American point of view.

11. *Mouvement Socialiste* (1 October 1902):1790.

12. Not only has this article been included, but since *Mouvement Socialiste* has published a reprint from it that has been included in its editions, one could believe that the *Mouvement Socialiste* has embraced this theory! We may assume that it is this leaflet that inspired in Turot, a highly visible official socialist, the idea of writing a book with the title, "The Proletariat of Love."

CHAPTER TWO

Present-day socialism seems to have returned to old-fashioned concepts inspired much more by pre-1848 ideas than by Marxist theories. This is a complex phenomenon which has many causes. It is said that the Dreyfus affair and the anticlerical movement have produced new revolutionary political currents, that they have mixed diverse classes in a common action, and that we find ourselves in a position quite different from what Marxism assumes. On the other hand, utopias are not simple mental games, and they are tightly moored to real bases which normally exist in society. It is almost certain that they can never disappear completely. It is essential for us to return to the questions treated in the first part of this book to demonstrate how utopias are coordinated into a system.

In a previous work[1] I have shown that modern utopians are dominated by intellectualistic concepts and that for them pure logic has the value of social science. They regard as the decisive reasons of history the abstract sentiments of an epoch and act as if they believed the world was created by the will. They always give first place in their thought to considerations relative to proof, and end by admitting that a system is faithful to the fundamental laws of the mind and should procure the happiness of humanity if it is so well protected by syllogisms as to make it impossible to prove its falsity. The big question is not of knowing the facts well, but of satisfying the needs of a rigorous logic. It is a sort of scholastic aesthetic which serves to judge the value of utopias; if this aesthetic is satisfied and if the construction is irreproachable, happiness should be the result.

Pareto, in his last work, has given remarkable examples of the kind of thinking employed by utopians to construct their defenses made out of "definitions" and demonstrations. Enfantin, responding to those who feared the arbitrary authority of the Saint-Simonian priesthood, said:[2] "Abuse is possible because the priesthood is powerful, but if we assume that the couple which by *definition* and by *function* ought to moralize, instead uses its power to demoralize, a vicious circle is produced." This argument should not impress us; it appeared irrefutable to the many mathematicians recruited by the Saint-Simonians and it corresponds perfectly to the tendencies of the mathematical mind which were more powerful at that time.[3]

If we wish to get to the heart of the matter, we must discard all the expository material put together by the utopians and look for specific characteristics of the institutions they regarded as desirable. It is always in light of concrete relations that we must consider social philosophy. What is noteworthy in the great modern utopias we are examining is their *unity*.

1. The unitary fanaticism is obvious among the Saint-Simonians. If so many of their contemporaries did not avoid the error these adversaries of all liberties committed, it is because each and every one of them was under the influence of the memories of the revolution. During its great wars, France was often like a besieged city, in which all the citizens' efforts are strained toward a unified purpose and are directed by a dictatorial authority. We had a type of *siege communism*, to which Lichtenberger has called attention,[4] that had considerable influence on certain theories maintained in that epoch, and later mistakenly regarded as constituting the origins of socialism. These more or less communist theories have had only a very small influence on the history of ideas. The later utopians do not go back to the communist dreams which could flourish during the French Revolution, as much as to the legends spawned by the revolutionary dictatorship and the Napoleonic administration. It was believed that there was a derivation of ideas, whereas it was rather an affinity of sources.

Saint-Simonians were inspired at least as much by Napoleonic practices as by religious traditions. Their religion served solely to justify the emperor's absolutism which they wanted to carry over into the industrial domain. Napoleon was not far from regarding his authority as having a sacerdotal character; he would have liked to make the church and the university the organs charged with teaching loyalty and obedience.[5] In the great revolutionary epochs, the great requisitions made to secure the manufacture of military equipment, transportation, and agriculture did not always produce brilliant results; gigantic efforts often led to deplorable setbacks. But under Napoleon it was no longer so. Despite many accidents (memories of which disappeared in the imperial legend) the war administration was seen undertaking operations in the face of which the industries of the time seemed to amount to little. One could not be too surprised at sometimes finding corrupt or incompetent functionaries; they were the inheritance of a period in which corruption and incompetence had been the general rule. The genius of the emperor could not reform everything in a day, but these accidents did not damage the principle.

Since Napoleon could do such great things with very imperfect means —why could not a government that benefited from his experience, from the good traditions that he had left the administration, and especially from the schools that he had created—why could not this government undertake a great transformation of industry according to a unitary plan?[8] Competition was suitable for the periods in which craftsmen dominated industry; the loss of a small manufacturer was of little importance. But when it was necessary to bring to completion gigantic operations (greater than those Napoleon ever thought of), the need for a unified and enlightened direction was strongly felt. The Saint-Simonians translated into a bizarre but all the more surprising language the ideas that were latent everywhere.

2. The democratic utopians showed no less aspiration toward unity. They reasoned more or less in the following way: After having been the *faithful* of the church and the *subject* of the king, man had matured; able to direct himself and become a "citizen." But this development always took the same direction, that of submission to authority, and never with the presupposition of total rupture with the past to obtain *freedom*. This explains the unique attitude of Rousseau in the *Social Contract*, which seems written to justify the "suppression of the particular will" by the rule of the city.

The philosophers believed that after suppressing the bonds that had until then connected the "faithful" to the church and the "subjects" to the crown, they would find abstract man, natural man, the being that would have manifested himself in history up until then if he had not been repressed by tyranny. In reality they found only themselves, their desires, the customs of their time, and especially the results of classical education. The church had its theology, royalty based its absolutism on an interpretation of imperial law and the Old Testament. It was believed necessary to justify the New City with a theory of natural law, and it was believed possible to make this theory without subjecting it to the influence of the past. This was impossible.

Our ancestors believed that it was possible to found a new positive law on general principles that defined the new regime. Especially important to them was the "determination of true principles" to formulate constitutions, that is to subordinate social life to a theory of the central organ. This was the grand purpose of the deepest thinkers of that time. France was very rich as far as constitutions are concerned, and it still does not lack misunderstood spirits who know how it would be possible to produce public happiness with some article of law. Experience has not been favorable to these ideas. Since Napoleon's time, many people asked whether there was something to be done on the economic side of things.

The unitary concepts were so strongly rooted in people's minds that no one could be persuaded to abandon them. On the one hand the Republicans wanted to use the strength of the old state, reforming it democratically; on the other hand the Saint-Simonians wanted to create a new state which was completely administrative and economic.

3. In Fourier's works, the idea of the state is not explicitly placed at the base of the new organization. But we must not let ourselves be deceived by appearances and take Fourier for an anarchist, as has sometimes been maintained.[7] His appeal to princes, his admiration for the universal monarchy dreamed by Napoleon,[8] the exact discipline that the functioning of his Phalanx presupposes, should not be ignored when studying his work. We know through experience that where no regular penal organizations exist, the means of speedy repression are constituted spontaneously. In the Phalanxes the instincts would be given free reign in this respect as in others. I do not know whether anyone has noted until now how Fourier's thought depends on ideas that his contemporaries had produced on the calculation of probabilities.[9] We know that in the early nineteenth century (as well as in the eighteenth) it was thought that considerations of this kind could be applied to anything. Results which depend on chance can be determined with great accuracy using only a limited number of observations. Therefore, according to Poisson, it was sufficient to perform seven experiments on gun shots to obtain good average results on the type considered.

Rousseau was convinced that since there are no associations in the state capable of imposing perfect opinions on men, the average opinion represents truth. Few people indeed would have dared in this period to dispute the value of universal consensus regarded as proof of certain moral theses. But the calculation of probability shows that it is useless (and also virtually impossible) to proceed to an inquiry on mankind; the average could be obtained with sufficient approximation, asking questions of a limited number of citizens. The popular assembly can therefore be deemed sovereign, since it will give expression to human reason.

Fourier is also concerned with organizing his Phalanx in such a way as to obtain averages which translate precisely the natural laws; there must be a sufficient number of individuals so that every type is represented in sufficient numbers. With a number that is too limited nothing could be expected from the attempted experiments. If successful, a result will be obtained that will become independent of circumstances, and the entire society will have only to reproduce what was once produced on a small scale. The uniformity of the new world results from this: that the passional equilibriums ascertained once only in relatively numerous groups are expressions of the natural law.

The application of the three great utopias could not have been realized except by means of a mechanism that the authors had very carefully hidden, that is by means of a power of absolute coercion that did not leave room for a reasoned discussion and which did not allow the individual to defend himself through the law. If democracy has not become despotic everywhere, it is due to the fact that it has never been able to suppress completely the institutions which temper authority. The three modern utopias present this notable peculiarity: each corresponds with sufficient exactitude to a simple type, and they can be reduced to the three types which we must consider when we wish to try to make a general framework of social ideas. I have already indicated this system in the September 1898 *Socialistische Monatshefte* (p. 401): we shall return to it here to make it more precise.

1. The first moment includes everything relating to *magic*, taking this word in its widest possible sense. All at once man confuses himself with nature: he does not know how to distinguish himself clearly from animals and plants; everything that exists appears to him a *mass of wills* among which all differentiation is difficult; totemism derives largely from this concept. Magic never disappeared from society and Brooks Adams[10] regarded the medieval Christian clergy as a body of magicians. This viewpoint is quite inadequate, but meanwhile we should take account of the true organization of the miracle in the history of religions.[11] In human thought, there are many concepts other than those of religion that are based on these old tendencies to put the will everywhere.

The magical character of Fourierism has already been revealed in the first part: it was faith that was demanded of the members of the Phalanx;[12] without the help of faith none of them could have attributed the slightest value to their master's strange reasoning by analogy. We must not forget the astronomical aspects of Fourier's system if we want to evaluate it precisely; astronomy is not superfluous but an essential element of the system.[13] We know that Fourier remade the heavens, and that the moon especially was demoted far back into the Milky Way to be replaced by five younger satellites. Finally, according to him, the planets were animals that procreated. All this is more than fantasy: it is *magical fantasy*.

2. The second moment to consider is the ideological consequences of association. Man withdraws completely from nature and no longer considers anything but his relations with other men. In this association the economic side does not exist or at least it is a later addition. It is man

with man; the realization is abstract. To reconstruct this moment, we should transport ourselves to the countries in which this observation has been most able to produce the general ideas that correspond to it. We should focus our thinking on Athenian democracy, especially as it appeared to the ancient political theorists.

According to Vico, the spectacle the Athenians presented in which they united in order to make laws in the common interest led Socrates to form categories by means of a procedure that gathered that which is the same in every individual. And Plato, having observed that the united citizens abandoned their particular interests in order to will the good, was led to the concept of *Ideas*. In each case it seems obvious that Greek logic was constructed to give a perfect precision to oratorical proofs and to lead particular instances back to generalizations.[14] It seems likely that the necessity of discussion in the agora had a greater role than science itself in the formation of Greek philosophy.[15] What Auguste Comte called "metaphysics" corresponds to the philosophy that emerges from this public life in which every decision must be proven with a logical system and based on incontestable assumptions. The democratic utopia of our forefathers is replete with this spirit and this is so much more natural as it was the work of men nourished by the classical philosophy of natural right.

3. In the third moment man returns to nature but is no longer a part of the grand totality; he interposes between nature and himself a mechanism he has imagined. He has become *mind* by way of his passage through the second moment, and he conceives material forces as inferior to him. He believes himself called upon to *dominate the world before which primitive men trembled*. The basic relations of democracy and modern industry are dominated by this consideration: democracy can claim a large role in the formation of present attitudes of science toward matter. Matter spiritualizes man, and the wise men who regard themselves as materialists are no less spiritualist.

In ancient times things were not presented as clearly as they are today; ancient man barely believed that he was able to invent tools of labor. He owed them, as well as fire, to divine beings whose memory he blessed. He could not have changed what these superior beings had taught his ancestors. This occurs because magic still holds man enthralled. When intellectual emancipation takes place, men will come to give the past a limited importance; the finest inventions will be treated disdainfully and procedures will be incessantly revolutionized.[16] Now he can control his instruments and throw them away with contempt as soon as he no longer needs them; he is only concerned with science.[17]

Industry brings us to what Auguste Comte regarded as the third stage of humanity; but Comte was unable to account for the causes that produce the ideological systems that he considers and that explain them. He had based his theory of the three stages on his observations of European history: the medieval church, the philosophical Renaissance, and contemporary science provided him with the three types. He did not note that theology presupposes a previous philosophy already highly developed. The Stoics tried to create a pagan theology, but without success; only Christianity succeeded in this task. What is primitive is the magical element that can also be highly developed, while religious ideas are not very much developed and there is no theology. The third moment is in strong opposition to the second; the way of thinking of lawyers and democratic theorists is quite the opposite of that of men of knowledge and industry. The positivists are always strongly opposed to philosophers who contest all authority, who make all discipline impossible, and who only appear to be capable of producing weak negations. Jurists who upset the repose of a country to defend the interests of an unjustly condemned individual seem almost criminal to them.[18]

At the end of the eighteenth century a strict discipline was introduced in the laboratories and, to direct the laboratories men were sought who were in a position to prove their technical ability. Political legislation under the pretext of respecting the philosophical principles of classical democracy reduced the power of authority and created an electoral regime which opened the highest offices to people without talent nor morals. Such an anomaly seemed monstrous to the utopians who invoked the authority of science.[19] They also happened to have much more sympathy for the periods in which magic dominated than for those dominated by jurists and philosophers. In the former at least men were in regular contact with nature and the discipline so necessary to capitalism existed everywhere.

Auguste Comte maliciously attacked all theological survivals and claimed to utilize ancient formulae to maintain discipline artificially. To ensure against any reawakening of the Christian spirit, Comte looked for symbols in fetishism—that which is most defunct in the religious spirit. Those who have preserved the traditions of the eighteenth century and who do not admit other principles than those of 1789 are equally scornful of religious beliefs (which appear to them as magical survivals) and socialist utopias (whose charlatanism, ingenuousness, and pseudo-scientific character are clearly perceived). I need not recall what Yves Guyot has often written on this subject; he cannot understand that the philosophical ideal of the French Revolution belongs to a system of social utopias.

The ideas that enter into a utopian system are presented in the natural state, under completely different conditions than those we must consider here. Each kept on its actual ground, they fulfill a function whose usefulness no one would contest: the interpretation of the world made from the standpoint of the will is going to produce a legendary, heroic, or lyrical body of literature; philosophical idealism serves as the basis of criticism of established institutions, customs, or ideas;[20] science has too preeminent a place in modern industrial history to make it necessary to insist on its usefulness. But all these notions can also become sophistical when used to reconstruct society en bloc, in conformity with hypotheses chosen according to our sentiments and transformed into principles. It is then that utopias are produced.

In our modern civilization all parts of the system coexist, and today we see many people who, vaunting 1789 and the eighteenth century, launch themselves in turn on the path to utopian socialism. Several years ago Joseph Reinach wrote: "Democracy is already so advanced on the path of *retrograde progress* that those among us who remain stubbornly faithful to the spirit of the great eighteenth century are regarded as reactionary" (*Matin,* 19 April 1895). Since contemporary sociologists regard confusion as a characteristic of their science, they do not miss such a good opportunity to mix all the parts of the utopian system in the most amusing manner.

Saint-Simonian concepts still dominate the minds of all the great French writers; indeed they are spread by men who have ambitions analogous to those of the Saint-Simonians. Sociologists are boastful of their science and highly desirous of despoiling industrialists of most of their profits, in order to improve the conditions of their friends. They dream only of the dictatorship of the intellectuals and . . . the sycophants. Their democracy is only a means of capturing the ingenuous confidence of the people and seize power.

Marxists have long ignored warnings in the face of the fact that unitary prejudices have greatly contributed to the decline of their doctrine. To speak of unity in economic society is to focus discussions on the *heads of production,* while revolutionary socialism claims to be concerned only with the hands of production. But how can unitary prejudices be avoided when participating regularly in parlimentary undertakings? It might be necessary for parliament never to concern itself with economic or social laws; then perhaps it would be possible to maintain itself outside of the direction of production. But for several years parliament has presumed to dictate laws on national production.

Notes

1. Sorel, *Saggi di critica del Marxismo*, pp. 157-64 (cf. *From Georges Sorel*, pp. 141-45).
2. Vilfredo Pareto, *Les systèmes socialistes* (Paris: Giard & Brière, 1902-3), Vol. II, p. 205. Rodbertus also, admitting that the state is a "social providence," shows that the state can't help but regulate perfectly all social activity (Vol. I. p. 286). Pareto's truly magisterial work cannot be recommended too highly.
3. Isn't it the same order of ideas that is the basis of the thinking of so many geometers whose ambition would be to create a purely logical geometry, without taking facts into account, and who ask ingenuously if there is not a geometry that is more general than that of Euclid, since one can reason mathematically on notions different from his? One can give geometric names to these notions with as much reason as that which one gives names borrowed from legal language to institutions imagined by the utopians. It is not by chance that Saint-Simonianism and non-Euclidean geometry were established more or less at the same time. *La science de l'espace absolument vrai* by Bolyai was published in 1832; Lobatchefski's memoires from 1835 to 1838.
4. Lichtenberger, *Le Socialisme et la Révolution Française* (Paris: Alcan, 1899), pp. 253-79.
5. Professor Emile Bourgeois said so well that "the University was an order, like the Order of Malta [that had] a dogma . . . that was summed up in an imperial catechism honoring two divinities: God and the Emperor, a very simple gospel of that crusade destined to establish the ideas and the love for the benefits of imperial government among future generations." *La liberté d'enseignement* (Paris: Cornély, 1902), p. 81. We cannot overstress the influence that the imperial dogma had on Saint-Simonanism and especially on Comtean positivism.
6. Michel Chevalier, when he was a Saint-Simonian, launched an appeal to the engineers, industrialists, merchants, requesting them to provide the information "necessary for outlining the general plan for the works to be done and the factories to be established in France, and to place this plan in harmony with the general plan of the Mediterranean organization." Pareto, *Systèmes socialistes*, Vol. II, p. 196.
7. Gide would be disposed to give this label to Fourier because he did not make any appeal to the police-state. Preface to *Oeuvres choisies de Fourier*, p. xxxi.
8. "The intention of the universal monarchy is that which is most sensible in the views of Bonaparte. . . . No one better than Bonaparte has had better means of conquering and conserving the scepter of the world. This would have happened if he had not been diminished by the French spirit." Fourier, *Unité universelle*, 1841 ed., Vol. IV, p. 407. On the other hand, he was not repelled by the use of violence, although he is generally quite reserved on this point.
9. On the other hand, Fourier does not seem to understand what makes the hypothesis possible. He explained everything with faculties analogous to those of the scholastics. The passion for "the idea of unity" is a very comical invention.
10. Brooks Adams, *The Law of Civilization and Decay*, "The force that gave beginning to an independent clergy was equivalent to magic." On the persistence of practices having a certain affinity with magic cf. Georges Sorel,

La ruine du monde antique, p. 263. It is very difficult to believe that slavic Christianity is very superior to a magical religion.

11. Renan noted that in his time there was a recurrence of miracles in Italy but that they succeeded only in the Papal States. *Vie de Jésus*, p. 496.

12. In 1842, Proudhon observed that the propaganda methods of the Fourierians again instilled dogma in the disciples, without ever caring to illuminate their minds on the difficulty of reconciling these dogmas with their personal ideas. *Avertissement aux propriétaires: Oeuvres complètes* (Paris: Lacroix, 1868), Vol. II, p. 58.

13. In his work against Arago, Considérant seems to make good use of this cosmology, but this is easy. Professor Gide would have us believe that the extravagances of Fourier can be separated from the system; he thus commits an enormous error that falsifies all his conclusions. Preface to Fourier's *Oeuvres choisies*, pp. x-xi.

14. The syllogism is the juridical instrument par excellence.

15. The unique form assumed by Greek geometry that contributed to the stifling of scientific progress seemed to depend on this "logic *of the literati.*" Its proofs often seem highly confusing to the modern mathematicians.

16. Marx, *Capital*.

17. I would like to call the attention of the philosophers to the very great importance of these considerations for understanding what the religion of the future can be. The instruments of labor have such an important function in modern life that one can no longer conceive of a naturalist religion. Hartmann and Haeckel don't seem to have ever reflected on this matter.

On the other hand, since man creates his instruments and no longer receives the world from on high, everything tends to seem clear in the world; with every mysterious veil being swept aside, doesn't religion perhaps become ridiculous? Such was Marx's opinion (*Capital*). But we must see also whether or not religion has other sources.

18. Lafitte, Comte's successor in the positivist papacy, could not understand that a whole country could be completely upset in order to stop the judicial error committed in the Dreyfus Affair.

19. Pareto, *Systèmes socialistes*, Vol. II, p. 5. The intellect is said by Auguste Comte to be a disturbance (p. 205). The need for discipline in society may have been suggested to the Saint-Simonians by the observation of industry and at the same time also by the *imperial* history of the Empire. The antithesis between the regime of the laboratory and that of modern society had impressed everyone at that time (see Marx's *Poverty of Philosophy*).

20. It is by virtue of this characteristic that the Saint-Simonians and the positivists distinguished between history in "critical" periods and history in "organic" periods; it is true that all of those periods whose history was well known at that time were "critical" (Greece after Socrates, Europe at the end of the Middle Ages).

CHAPTER THREE

Marx formulated a conception of the formation of utopias quite different from mine. He thought they could have their *raison d'être* in a certain period and that, their time being elapsed, they could only be reborn as individual fantasies. In a circular published by the Workingman's International he expounded his view:[1]

> The first phase of the proletariat's struggle against the bourgeoisie is by a *sectarian movement*.[2] That is logical at a time when the proletariat has not yet developed sufficiently to act as a class. *Certain thinkers* criticize social antagonisms and suggest fantastic[3] solutions thereof, which the mass of workers is left to accept, to preach, and put into practice. The sects formed by these initiators are abstentionist by their very nature, i.e., alien to all real[4] action, politics, strikes, coalitions, or, in a word, to any united movement.[5] These sects act as levers of the movement in the beginning, but become an obstruction as soon as the movement outgrows them—after which they become reactionary. . . .[6] Contrary to the sectarian organizations with their vagaries and rivalries, the International is a genuine and militant organization of the proletarian class of all countries united in their common struggle against the capitalists and the landowners, against their class power organized by the state.

To combat ideological tendencies whose return it feared, the International did not admit in its ranks any section having a philosophical or religious program.[7] It had refused to accept Bakunin's Alliance as long as it had taken the title of "section of socialist atheists"; sections of young Christians in England and the positivist proletarians of Paris were treated in the same way. "Therefore," the circular continues, "the International's rules speak of only 'simple workers' societies,' all aiming for the same goal and accepting the same program which presents a general outline of the proletarian movement, while leaving its theoretical elaboration to be guided by the needs of the practical struggle and the exchange of ideas in the sections, unrestrictedly admitting all shades of socialist convictions in their organs and congresses."[8]

Marx conceived things quite differently from the utopians: ideology seemed to Marx incapable of directing the present social movement; men having very different ideas from one another should unify to collaborate, and theory was only a series of sketches *formed by chance* following the fate of the circumstances of the practical struggle. To act against the bourgeoisie and borrow nothing from it—this is the whole of socialism. The ideas this action produced could vary greatly among socialists without preventing their true unity.

The facts did not correspond to Marx's expectations, since sects multiplied in the same International but he did not regard them as vital and treated them with disdain.[9] "Just as in every new historical phase, old mistakes reappear momentarily only to disappear forthwith,[10] so within the International there followed a resurrection of sectarian sections, though in a less obvious form." This last appraisal is highly optimistic, since the International was going to perish right after the conflicts provoked by the sectarian Bakuninist sections.

To justify its tactics, the Alliance claimed that[11] "to make the working class the real representative of humanity's new interests, its organization must be *guided by the idea that will triumph.* To evolve this idea from the needs of our epoch, from mankind's vital aspirations, by a constant study of the phenomena of social life, to then carry this idea to our workers' organizations—such should be our aim. [Lastly there must be created] amid our working population a *real revolutionary socialist school.*" This is a complete return to the procedures of the utopians: the social problem is posed as a physics problem, and the solution is sought by means of inductive reasoning that ought to lead to the discovery of laws from which applications would be derived.

This idealistic procedure angered Marx because it tended to subordinate the proletariat to an aristocracy. "Thus the autonomous workers' sections are in a trice converted into *schools*, of which these gentlemen of the Alliance will be the masters. . . . To them the working class is so much raw material, a chaos into which they must breathe their Holy Spirit. . . . [They want to pose] before the working masses as a hierarchy of a secret science."[12]

Analogous ideas expressed in a more violent way are found in the circular of 21 July. I will not insist any more; it is enough for me to have indicated with what lucidity Marx recognized the *bourgeois character of utopias.* Utopian ideologies are always based on the fundamental distinction between *intellectual leaders and thinkers* on the one hand and the governed and indoctrinated workers on the other. What we are witnessing in France shows that Marx had perfectly determined the law of all socialist utopias. But it is strange that having strongly recommended to the workers that they get involved in politics, he did not recognize that he recommended that they place themselves under the direction of people who would have followed Bakunin's principles,

principles that were those of all the previous revolutionaries, and that must lead back to the rebirth of sectarianism. The experience of the last thirty years shows how Marx deceived himself on the future of utopias.[13] We are led to ask how Marx could ever have believed that their time was ended forever.

His error lay on the inevitable character he attributed to the formation of the idea of class struggle. The old social unity that had allowed society to be compared to an organism had been broken in the most advanced countries, and it appeared to him that this unity could never be re-established. In England's great industrial metropolises, workers and bosses indeed live isolated from each other. Le Play, who examined workers' lives from an entirely different point of view, stated with deep regret that all bonds between workers and bosses had been broken.[14] "The founders of the coal businesses have ruthlessly uprooted the workers from rural life and crowded them into urban masses without even providing that moral direction that until then had been reputed to be indispensible for the existence of a civilized people." He deplored the developing social antagonisms in England and relied on a few experiences to hope for a transformation of industry by means of a return to the usages of the old patronage.

Le Play's hopes have not been realized; Marx had foreseen the future better than he had. But there is a great gap between antagonisms based on interest and those of class struggle. Marx believed that the former would always be transformed in the direction of socialism and his predictions have not been completely realized. England, which he had chosen as the classical land of modern capitalism, has not exhibited the full development of the class struggle, and Kautsky grieves about this bitterly.[15] He also goes further: he maintains[16] that from Gladstone's time this country had experienced a stage "of attenuation of social antagonisms in preparation for social peace." This is the same as asserting that for a long time the idea of class struggle has been extinguished in this country. According to him, one would now have to go to Germany to find the true type of socialist movement.

The class struggle is obviously not as simple as Marx believed, and in many cases what is mistakenly called thus is only a simple dispute relating to material interests that could be regulated. The capitalist movement appeared to Marx as inevitable. The utopians imagined that this movement could have been changed by governments well disposed to the people. Where Marx saw *economic fatalism*, the utopians saw a set of accidents susceptible of control by the *political will*. For a long time it seemed that Marx was indisputably correct, but new ideas have been set forth in the past several years among socialists. The industrial syndicates (as we shall see in part III of this work) have led many people to return to ideas that are close to those of the utopians.

The strongest disagreement between Marx and the utopians was that relating to the role of reforms that could be attempted by a liberal government. Marx had expressed his fundamental ideas on this point in the preface to *Capital*. He said that the social antagonisms observed in England are reproduced everywhere and that especially in Germany, despite its traditions, there is absolutely no escape from the fatality of capitalism. Reforms can have only one single advantage, that is, they can facilitate the intellectual and moral development of the proletariat and consequently avoid the damage of a savage revolution. Reforms are appraised by Marx as important for the *spiritual nature of society* and not for its economic construction.

Victor Considérant started from a completely opposite point of view in the *Democratic Manifesto*. He examined the damage which would be incurred in modern society, proclaimed himself opposed to any revolutionary solutions, and sought social peace. "There is only one means of avoiding these new revolutions,"[17] he said, "it is the serious recognition of the right to work and the organization of industry on the basis of the triple association of capital, labor, and talent. This organization is the task of modern democracy." Everything that recalled struggle seemed to him so contrary to nature that he had adopted the idea of a government directed by the people in the hope of seeing the conflict that existed among the parliamentary parties disappear.

"Let us talk about organizing the interests and the rights of the workers," continues Considérant[18] "of introducing order, justice, and true liberty in the industrial workshop, in the regulation of production, distribution, and the sharing of wealth; let us speak of uniting there the interests of the possessors and proletarians, of soldiers and officers; let us speak of making machines work for the capitalists and for the people, and not for the capitalists and against the people. Finally, let us speak of organizing the association of classes in national unity, and the association of nations in humanity." The aim to be achieved was the realization of the "new rights, the democratic rights, and Christian rights, the equality and the unity, which were proclaimed to the world by the French Revolution" but which had remained until then confined to the domain of pure theory.

One would believe that he is reading some article of Jaurès or of Millerand.[19] In the French Socialist Congress held at Tours in 1902, which was under the direction of these two politicians, it was believed necessary to return expressly to the idea first expressed by Considérant on the origins of claims. Deville claimed the idea because he recognizes

Babeuf as a precursor, and the text of the declaration of principles drawn up by Jaurès says: "Socialism proceeds together with the movement of democracy[20] and of the new forms of production. Historically and since the morrow of the French Revolution, the proletarians are agreed that the Declaration of the Rights of Man would be illusory without the transformation of property." Contemporary socialists have come to believe that the gradual conquest of political power can lead to a continued transformation of the economic order, and thus they reject the fatality of capitalism that Marx regarded as incontestable. In this way, we have returned to Considérant.

Notes

1. "Fictitious Splits in the International" (5 March 1872). Reproduced in Saul K. Padover, ed. and trans., *The Karl Marx Library*, Vol. III. *On the First International* (New York: Random House, 1973), p. 209.
2. There is no need to believe, as has often been the case, that Marx is condemning the "fanaticism" of the old socialists here; indeed, we see a bit further on that Saint-Simon, Fourier, Cabet, and Robert Owen are sectarians and in the "Critique of the Gotha Program," Marx still applied this name to Lassalle's disciples; sectarians are men who claim to apply their theory of social organization: they are doctrinaire utopians.
3. We should understand this word to mean: produced by the imagination.
4. "Real" as opposed to "ideological."
5. "Coalitions" means here "unions; united movement, organized action."
6. In the *Manifesto* we find the same idea: "By degree they sank into the category of the reactionary conservative Socialists . . . differing from these only by more systematic pedantry. . . . They therefore violently oppose all political action on the part of the working class. . . . The Owenites in England and the Fourierists in France respectively oppose the Chartists and the Reformists" (III, 3). To be "reactionary" for Marx is not to believe in the class struggle and to hope for some sort of reconciliation between capital and labor.
7. "Fictitious Splits in the International," pp. 197 and 200. On pages 201–202 it says that no organization will be admitted that imposes temperance on its members. Today socialist parties no longer seem to understand the importance of these rules; thus, many societies of free thinkers are affiliated with the Belgian Party. *Mouvement Socialiste* (1 November 1902):1932.
8. "Fictitious Splits," pp. 209–10.
9. Ibid., p. 210.
10. Here is a law that would have been useful to make more precise; perhaps Marx thought of that reappearance in the farcical form of which he spoke in the opening of the *Eighteenth Brumaire*.
11. "Fictitious Splits," p. 216.
12. Ibid., pp. 216–17.
13. To the people who had shown how often Marx had been mistaken in his historical predictions, Kautsky responds that Marx and Engels were not at all

mistaken when they considered the economic movement for a long enough period of time "but that they sometimes may have been mistaken on the form and rapidity of the movements protracted by the space of several months." *Mouvement Socialiste* (15 October 1902):1877. They therefore predicted well what was most unpredictable and predicted badly what is most easily predictable! Cf. Sorel, *Saggi di criticia del Marxismo*, pp. 51-56.

14. Le Play, *Organisation du travail*, 3rd ed., p. 184.
15. *Mouvement Socialiste* (15 October 1902):1890.
16. Ibid., p. 1859.
17. Reproduced in *Ere Nouvelle* (February 1894):178.
18. Ibid., p. 177.
19. In one speech Millerand said, "My friend Joseph Sarraute has demonstrated that the notion of class struggle united with the present social system *was as false as it was damaging* if it is isolated from its complimentary notion: the solidarity of the classes." *Reveil du Nord* (5 December 1902).
20. The democratic movement is particularly suited to produce utopias, exalting faith in social reforms which can be expected from the State.

CHAPTER FOUR

We shall now examine the economic conditions that gave such celebrity to Marx's systems, and try to determine what modifications occurred in the economy which have facilitated their decline. One of the first things that is so striking is that in Marx's time the political economy of the Manchester school was flourishing. It is noteworthy that two apparently opposite theories could base the causes of their success in the same economic conditions. But two social theories can differ on their hypotheses on the future and agree on the greater part of their scientific findings: capitalist society conforms to the natural order, or it must disappear to make way for socialism—are hypotheses that nobody can transform into demonstrable theorems.

Almost always when a comparison between political economy and socialism is established, it is to oppose these two subjective views on the future. Nothing interesting comes from this. But it is not the same when we reconcile the ideas of Marx and the Manchester school regarding the phenomena developing before their very eyes; then we find surprising similarities between the two economic theories. This could not be explained if we did not admit that the common aspects of the two systems result from phenomena that then exerted an enormous influence on the world. Further on I shall discuss certain similarities between the two that exist in the concept of the labor contract. I will not dwell on the importance that Marx and his contemporaries attributed to large capital because at that time everyone agreed on this point. But it is very useful to note that the idea of economic fatality was strongly expressed by the two schools in the same way.[1]

I have often noted that this movement has the necessary character of natural movements only because of the action of free competition, raised to the highest power. Because of the mixing of so many diverse actions that encounter one another in every direction, there is no longer anything that can be related to the will, and the result has all the appearance of a physical phenomenon.[2] *The combination of many events produces the fatality of the movement*: if we examine an isolated fact it is not possible to assign any cause to the same fact, and it is really a chance phenomenon; instead, the totality is so well determined that if anybody pretended to oppose the movement he would be inevitably defeated.

All the capitalists are obliged to try to improve their machinery, reduce their selling price, open up new pathways—not because they tend to imitate each other, but because whoever should stop would be reduced to bankruptcy. It is well known with what vivid imagery Lassalle has described this rigidity of capitalist society, this system of relationships that led to forging everything together with an iron chain.

Engels asserted, with as much vigor as the most classic economists, the powerlessness of the state, thus separating himself from Lassalle, who appealed to the power of the state as the only means of loosening the bonds that bind the world of the workers: "The reaction of the state to economic development," he wrote on 27 October 1890,[3] can assume three forms: "it can act in the same way, and then the movement becomes more rapid; it can act in the opposite direction and then in the long run, *in the large nations*,[4] it is destructive to itself; or it can suppress or favor certain tendencies and, in this last case, it is easily reduced to one of the first two." In his *Anti-Dühring* Engels asserted[5] that, except in the case of conquest, political power gives way to economic movement, or else is overturned if it persists in struggling against the economic movement.

It is therefore natural that Marx's historical concepts often come close to those of the economists, particularly those of G. de Molinari. As Rouanet writes:[6] "Both schools see in the historical process only a series of developments in the form of labor; both schools limit economically the mentality [of the man] condemned not to emerge from the material progress accomplished by productive forces." It has also been noted with what harshness Engels spoke of the oppressed people of past ages; their suffering seemed to him negligible in light of the progress accomplished by virtue of their oppression.[7] I attribute great importance to the examination of sentiments of this type: they provide the best means of penetrating into what is most fundamental in a doctrine. When we discuss abstractions it is possible to make artificial comparisons, but we cannot be mistaken about differences regarding sentiments. The sentiments that relate to the oppositions manifested in labor are probably the social sentiments par excellence, those that the historian should try to determine to know the past.

Here are the terms in which Engels discusses the subject of ancient slavery in *Anti-Dühring*:[8] "It was slavery that first made possible the division of labor between agriculture and industry on a larger scale, and thereby also Hellenism, the flowering of the ancient world. Without slavery, no Greek state, no Greek art and science; without slavery, no Roman Empire. But without the basis laid by Grecian culture and the

Roman Empire, also no modern Europe. We should never forget that our whole economic, political, and intellectual development presupposed conditions in which slavery was as necessary as it was universally recognized.

"Where the ancient communes have continued to exist, they have for thousands of years formed the basis of the cruelest form of state, Oriental despotism, from India to Russia.[9] It was only where these communities dissolved that the peoples made progress of themselves, and their next economic advance consisted in the increase and development of production by means of slave labor" which led to a superior form of development. Labor being rather unproductive in previous times, there was need for a small minority that dealt in commerce or governed the state or was occupied in art or science to exploit a mass of slaves. Political freedom for all is only really possible in countries where machines give everyone enough leisure to participate in the general affairs of society. Thus Engels found it highly ridiculous that Dühring transformed the philosophy of history into "a jeremiad on the contamination of all subsequent history consumated by this original sin; a jeremiad on the shameful perversion of all natural and social laws by this diabolical power, *force*."[10]

In his book on the agrarian question, Kautsky appraised the effects of economic programs in a way that deserves to be related here. He would have the Socialist Party oppose the simple workers' movements that aimed only at immediate material ends.[11] "The Socialist Party knows well that all economic progress in the world of capitalist economic production becomes right away a cause of the degradation and poverty of the people affected by it. But it also knows that it would be still more dishonest to impede this progress which does not have as its only effect the degradation of the working class, but which also lays the ground for its future elevation." We can believe that the Socialist Party would not see any disadvantage in a policy that would automatically sacrifice the country to the city by preconceived judgment because[12] "industry is the most important mode of production in a capitalist society, [because] it is not the peasantry but the proletariat that is the vanguard of modern social evolution."

This way of thinking is completely Manchesterian. The theoreticians of capitalism do not justify their judgments on the basis of the prospect of the emancipation of the future proletariat. But this is the only difference. It seems idle to continue to detail the similarities between Marxian and Manchesterian political economy. This undertaking has often been done, and it has been shown how Marx was inspired by ideas current in the England of his time.

Free trade constitutes the nucleus of Manchesterism; the progress of free-trade policies allows us to gauge closely the progress of Manchesterian political economy. There was a time in which almost all economic literature was devoted to questions of tariffs. This should have been the case since it was in international exchange matters that state intervention always seemed to have the best motives. It is based on traditions that are difficult to eradicate. Over many centuries, the state had to protect its merchants from competition from abroad, and today one still justifies the existence of powerful fleets saying that without military force able to make the flag respected, it would be impossible for nationals to engage in commerce in many half-civilized countries. Also, nations attempt to impose on weak countries treaties that open the way for exports. Foreign commerce was thus viewed as dependent on state force, and presently there are still many enlightened people who regard English imports into France as a type of tribute paid to England. Under these conditions, free international exchange was more difficult to realize than the liberty of labor within the nation.

The destiny of free trade has been the same as that of Marxism. The two doctrines, after having been regarded as the last word—the former of capitalist economics, the latter of socialist economics—are now relegated to the domain of history, although they have not yet been substituted with doctrines that embrace all the problems they tried to solve. As with all the socialist doctrines, present-day capitalist economics is composed of fragments that cannot satisfy any reasonable mind and that have no other merit than expressing the practices of various politicians. Manchesterism is found very often at the basis of contemporary economic theories, just as Marxism is found at the basis of many socialist theories that are attacked as being exempt from Marxist influence.

Manchesterism like Marxism has been criticized for its narrowness of ideas, its materialism, its powerlessness in dealing with law. But it does not appear that the "correctors" of these doctrines, in turn, have attained notable results. German professors believe that their university science puts them above the two schools. G. Schmoller asserts that a "pure disciple of Adam Smith, like a pure disciple of Marx, cannot be treated with the same standards as the 'others.' Those who do not remain on the terrain of modern research and of the sage methods of our time cannot be useful teachers."[13] The pretense to a superior science that the German professor utters here is ridiculous; his science has as its purpose to demonstrate the exactness of the views that the Hohenzollerns have adopted in their social policy.[14] His science is what Yves Guyot calls "the servile science" (*Siècle*, 11 November 1902), but it is indisputable that

Schmoller is much closer to actual practice than either the Manchesterites or the Marxists. Here we are not concerned with knowing who is scientifically correct but with knowing who has adapted most completely to present trends.

Notes

1. Here I am obliged to reassemble observations which already appear in my *Saggi di critica del Marxismo*. It seemed necessary to do this to give a clear idea of Marxist economics.
2. Cf. Sorel, *Saggi di critica del Marxismo*, pp. 76–83 (see *From Georges Sorel*, pp. 120–23).
3. *Devenir Social* (March 1897):235. Cf. Sorel, *Saggi di critica del Marxismo*, p. 120.
4. Indeed only in the large countries does there exist a complete enough combination of capitalist forces so that fatality can be the result.
5. *Devenir Social* (August-September 1896):732.
6. *Revue socialiste* (May 1887):491. Cf. Sorel, *Saggi di critica del Marxismo*, p. 117.
7. *From Georges Sorel*, p. 172.
8. Frederick Engels, *Anti-Dühring*, 2nd ed. (Moscow: Foreign Languages Publishing House, 1959), pp. 249–50.
9. Today one hardly admits any more that the agrarian communities in Russia are very ancient. Milioukov, *Essai sur l'histoire de la civilisation russe* (Paris: Giard & Brière, 1901). In Java collective property, that De Laveleye believed primitive, dates only from the nineteenth century. Rienzi, "La propriété foncière à Java" in *Revue Socialiste*, May 1896). But these factual errors have no importance at all for the subject treated here.
10. *Anti-Dühring*, p. 253.
11. Kautsky, *La politique agraire du parti socialiste*, French trans., p. 25. In regard to the lumping together of the small parcels of land that sometimes is to the disadvantage of the rural proletariat because it reduces the surface area that is abandoned to pasturage on the boundaries of the parcels, Kautsky says: "This is one of the cases in which the interests of a proletarian group are in contradition to the economic development that the socialist party could not prevent" (p. 134).
12. Ibid., pp. 27–28.
13. Cf. Schmoller, *Politique sociale et économie politique*, French trans. (Paris: Giard & Brière, 1902), p. 321.
14. Ibid., p. 3.

CHAPTER FIVE

The preceding comparisons should help us find the essential factor in the modern economy which has allowed Marxism to acquire, suddenly, an importance so great and at the same time so ephemeral. What is particularly difficult to understand in Marxism is the absolute class separation, which one must assume from the beginning as an incontestable experimental datum. This separation appears all the more shocking insofar as one admits at the same time the fatality of social movements and the irreconcilable struggle between the two parts of society. Such a hypothesis is in contradiction with the biological analogies by means of which we describe a necessary social evolution. In a highly complicated organism, we may admit the coexistence of antagonistic forces, the growth of one organ at the expense of another, a certain freedom of movement, and an independence of the parts. But all this remains quite limited; any exaggeration of this independence of the parts is regarded as a monstrosity or a sickness.

The Marxist conceptions appear to assume that society is made up of two beings belonging to two different species, that society is a monster like those invented by the designers of the Middle Ages. If we abandon the biological for the political point of view, everyone admits easily that there are conflicting interests in society; but if these oppositions become too strong, there would be legislative intervention. Such is the opinion of at least the great mass of people concerned with social policy. Marxism denies the power of reform and appears to contradict common sense.

About fifty years ago special economic conditions existed, and at this moment the notion of absolute "insolidarity" could be espoused without seeming paradoxical. This is used to demonstrate the success of the free-trade doctrine. Commerce became very powerful and efficient; no one could see any longer what interest the state had in intervening to control it. It was admitted that trade was able to open all the sources of production needed to satisfy consumer demands; it was believed that every country could create all the wealth necessary to its inhabitants to develop all their foreign trade. Under these conditions it seemed that the state should abandon its old function as the grand director of industry.

Protectionists observed that things did not go entirely as the free-traders assumed: that foreign trade could not flouish except when all the national industries were also flourishing; that without that, it might happen that after having spent its savings in acquiring goods cheaply, a country would find itself deprived of the possibility of maintaining its artificial and natural productive forces and would sink into poverty. But free-traders responded that if these objections had any value in the past, they no longer did now that capital had become extremely abundant, its uses were more varied, and one industry was always being substituted for another.

At one time it was necessary to take a thousand precautions to ensure artificially the life of manufacturing enterprises that were not yet strong enough. Industrialists were sometimes subsidized; generally privileges were given them, enabling them to obtain raw materials at a low price and in sufficient quantities; draconian policing rules were established so that the workers would always be numerous and disciplined; efforts were made to reserve for the industrialists markets over which the state had every power, and to open those over which foreign policy had influence. In the end, all this seems old-fashioned. Protection in many cases served to protect laziness, neglect and avarice of the owners who refused to keep up with progress and numbed themselves in their old family traditions.

Free-traders maintained that the suppression of protectionist legislation would have the effect of satisfying every interest: as products became better priced, life would be easier and workers' demands less sharp; as factories improved to English standards, we would see profits and salaries raised, bringing them close to those of England; with the increase of abundance, low prices, and purchasing power, the prosperity of the country would be greater. The argument of the free-traders was reduced to this: if France had industry as strong as England's, it would not need protection and would profit from the many advantages derived from modern industrial progress; the question remains as to whether this imitation of England was possible by means of freedom, whereas it was once believed that progress was only possible with state assistance.

It is obvious that such a transformation most often required enormous sacrifices: not only did the proprietors in most establishments have to change their machinery, but sometimes they also had to abandon old enterprises[1] and undertake others (for example abandon their wood-burning iron foundry for coal). It was not certain that this could have been done, or that the old defective means of production could always be substituted with newly perfected ones: local conditions, labor difficulties, and lack of capital could arrest the progress the free-traders regarded as so easily realized. The free-traders assumed that these fears were childish after capitalism had reached a high level of development.

They thought that every country had more resources than were necessary to shift industries, that science would provide means of reducing the expenses of production, means appropriate to local conditions, and that consumption would be strong enough to absorb the quantity of merchandise that would be periodically thrown on the market by foreign and domestic manufacturers organized entirely for accelerating their output.

The industrialists who displayed too much caution would suffer such strong losses that their neglect could not last long. Whereas the old economic legislation had favored progress by giving direct or indirect rewards to entrepreneurs, the new legislation reverted to imposing large fines on industries too little disposed to embracing progressive methods. The old policy suited poor countries where capital was difficult to accumulate and capitalists were timid; the new policy suited rich countries where capital was abundant and capitalists daring. It was not assumed, as the utopians had, that production was ruled by the will, but people were not far from assuming something similar. It was assumed that (at least within the limits of prudent reforms) one had the right to regard the supply of capital as infinite.[2]

Free-traders opposed producers to consumers, maintained that the state should consider the interest of the latter and let the former adjust their interests as well as they could, and concluded with insolidarity between the two groups. We will understand this insolidarity better if we examine what occurred in England during the transition from protection to free trade. English social legislation is inspired by the same considerations as those of free trade and is equally based on insolidarity, in this case the insolidarity of owners and workers, instead of between producers and consumers. English politicians admitted that in both cases one could throw oneself into great adventures without harm, and in both cases experience seems to show that they were right in upholding insolidarity.

What perhaps encouraged statesmen in their audacity is that there is a tradition of insolidarity in England. As Kautsky says,[3] in no other country has the bourgeoisie been more inconvenienced than in England, but in spite of this it is there that "capitalist production has developed first and most sharply." Therefore one could think that the bourgeoisie would have found the means of getting out of trouble alone, as it had done in so many other circumstances. The Tories who had so often in the course of the two previous centuries acted against the interests of the commercial bourgeoisie, threw themselves furiously onto the path of social legislation.[4]

The reduction of the working day succeeded because mechanization had progressed sufficiently and was in a position to permit the rapid transformation of factories and the substitution of the old factories with new, more powerful ones; capital was looking for new means of production and could sacrifice outmoded machinery; commerce was in a position to absorb the overproduction which resulted from new modes of labor.[5] Here again the state put a type of fine on backward industry, but this penalty would not have been enough to generate the results that occurred; it only acted very indirectly on the progress of industry. This fine could have had the same result that the suppression of protection sometimes produced—ruin industry instead of accelerating its progress.

At the beginning of social legislation in England, there were grave doubts about the future. Ure, one of the main opponents of this legislation, properly admitted,[6] it is true, that science was capable of providing capitalism with instruments of heretofore unimagined power, because the capitalists consented to pay the necessary price. Since strikes had led cotton manufacturers to perfect their machinery, one could assume that the law limiting the working day could have the same result. But it was still necessary for the richer entrepreneurs to find advantages in committing themselves to this hazardous route of feverish production.

If we want to understand the state of mind of the economists of this time, we must examine their writings on the subject of compensation. According to Michel Chevalier, the savings consumers would make in buying foreign goods at low prices would be partly used to form capital, and from there national industry would be activated.[7] "The protectionist system is also judged solely on this basis." He compared, not without good reason,[8] the effects of free trade to those of mechanization, that, after transition crises, had produced such advantageous results. In one case as in the other, there would be in the minds of certain optimists inevitable compensation.

Marx attacked the theory of compensation that could not be logically sustained, and that, notwithstanding this, seems so obvious when we question certain contemporary statisticians. Carroll Wright, for example, who lives amidst the most daring people in existence, and who is witnessing an unheard-of industrial development, has no doubts about compensation. Wage earners, he says, have been able to ascertain the introduction and application of new inventions; and these bring along an increase in outlets for production.[9] The mechanism of compensation is always the same; the savings realized would be transformed into capital used to accelerate the progress of industry. I doubt that there are today serious economists who defend the theory of compensation as a doctrine that is true in itself; the incontestable facts invoked in its favor show that there existed powerful external causes of industrial development.

Progress has been independent of the "genius" of legislators who established free trade and made social legislation. It has been independent of the "genius" of English textile producers who tried to save on their expenses, who had the good fortune to have perfected machinery within their reach, sufficiently abundant capital to enable them to use this machinery in such a way as to bring large profits, and a clientele to absorb the products.

To accurately interpret the facts, we must note that there has been a period in which capitalism could be regarded as infinite and in which insolidarity existed to such a degree between it and the remainder of the country that it was impossible not to be concerned with its interests. Capitalism was strong enough to face all difficulties on its own (only insofar as the difficulties were not too great). It was with good reason, therefore, that Marx thought that the working class could develop independently of the capitalist class. From the state he demanded only free time for the proletariat, holding that the proletariat would have known enough to devote themselves to organizing autonomous institutions in which the revolutionary spirit would be formed. Taking his experience in England as his point of departure, Marx estimated that the eight-hour day was the great target toward which they should lay claim. He cited[10] approvingly two declarations made in 1866 at a Baltimore Congress and at the Congress of the International in Geneva, in which it was said that every effort to emancipate the proletariat must fail if the duration of the working day was not reduced. He was not concerned with knowing how capitalism would adapt to this regime. Imbued with the then current ideas on the infinite power of production and consumption that virtually possesses modern society, it seemed obvious to Marx that this transformation could be realized without great difficulty.

Of all the procedures of social reform, nothing is more socialist than the reduction of labor time, since it does not mix the worker's life with that of the bourgeoisie, does not increase the importance of the state as an economic organ, and strongly appeals to the "sentiments of independence" of the workers. At the time in which English social legislation was promulgated, the idea of self-help was very strong in England. It was natural to apply this idea to everyone, to workers as well as owners, and to leave to individual initiative[11] the goal of determining the most useful way to use free time. The same standard could have been applied to industry in the form of taxes to invest in workers' housing or some other philanthropic measure; but such measures are not as favorable to socialism since we cannot expect great progress in working-class organization to arise from them.

Notes

1. One of the greatest criticisms that is leveled against protectionism was that it caused men to choose enterprises that were different from those that conformed to nature. "The protectionist system had the effect of imparting to the national activity a direction that was different from that which would have been chosen if the citizens had been allowed their freedom." Michel Chevalier, *Examen du système commercial connu sous le nom de système protecteur*, 2nd ed. (Paris: Guillaumin, 1853), p. 83. The author assumes as obvious that an old industry can always be replaced by a new one.
2. This can explain how so many free traders fell into optimistic utopianism. Cf. Pareo, *Systèmes socialistes*, Vol. II, p. 46. Marxism did not fall into utopianism because, contrary to what the optimistic economists were doing, it did not pretend to give advice to the heads of industry. It asserted only the "inevitability" of movement.
3. Kautsky, *Politique agraire du parti socialiste*, p. 184.
4. It seems that in England there is at this time a tendency toward solidarity; "imperialism" has no other meaning: unity is manifested first against the outside. Kautsky notes that free-trade ideas have lost ground (*Mouvement socialiste*, 15 October 1902, p. 1858). This would be a rather natural consequence of imperialism. He also notes that the conservatives no longer have so much sympathy for the working class (p. 1850); this is due to the fact that the Tories understand better than in the past the solidarity of national wealth and find it harmful to sacrifice the interests of industrial production to their rancor.
5. Marx gives some interesting explanations on this overproduction. He cites various reports of English inspectors stating that productivity is still increasing more rapidly than the number of laborers employed. From 1838 to 1850, the number of English cotton manufacturers increased by 32 percent; from 1850 to 1856 by 86 percent. According to an 1872 journal, the old steam looms allowed a textile worker to make four pieces, while with two modern looms, one worker can make 26 of them; the spinning machine with five attendants could produce seven times more than such a machine produced with three hands in 1841. *Capital* (Modern Library ed.), pp. 455, 456n.
6. Cited in Marx's *Capital* (Modern Library Ed.), pp. 476–77.
7. Michel Chevalier, *Examin du système commercial*, p. 99.
8. Ibid., p. 120.
9. Carroll Wright, *The Industrial Evolution of the United States* (New York: Scribners, 1913) p. 348. According to Professor Levasseur, a European weaver manages three looms producing 108 meters of cotton cloth in ten hours, while an American manages eight looms producing 288 meters; with the Northrop loom a worker (who operates sixteen of them) produces 576 meters and even 691, bringing the number of strokes from 200 to 240 per minute. *Bulletin de la société d'encouragement* (February 1900):263.
10. Marx, *Capital* (Modern Library Ed.), p. 329.
11. Kautsky assures us that in the socialist society "individualism, that is, the tendency toward the complete development of the personality, will become stronger and will be developed in proportion as education, well-being and convenience are made general." *Politique agraire*, p. 215. This will depend greatly on the importance that the state will take; an authoritarian democracy is hardly favorable to this individualism.

CHAPTER SIX

The postulate of insolidarity has remained more or less undiscussed in the Marxist school until now; no one has applied himself to examining the conditions concerning it. Marx did not have to defend it at length since it was included in the doctrine of free trade in a way which was almost as inevitable as it was in the revolutionary doctrine itself. People were so used to speaking of the class struggle that they came to believe that the economic base of the class struggle would not change any more than the speeches would, speeches made by so many socialist disquisitions on this theme.

Therefore we need not be surprised at the scandal that arose from a speech given by Millerand to the Saint-Etienne Chamber of Commerce in which this minister asserted that he did not separate the defense of the overall interests of industry and his sympathy for the workers' lot: "I have never taken into consideration a labor bill without considering the repercussion it could have on the interests of the owners." These words seemed scandalous to one of the most distinguished young representatives of French Marxism: Hubert Lagardelle said[1] that this was the manifestation of "socialism suitable for the social conservatives and other partisans of social peace." He certainly expressed an opinion conforming to Marxist tradition, refusing to take into consideration the solidarity that the minister asserted existed between workers and owners.

Lagardelle observed not without reason that the conservative press had emphasized the importance of this ministerial speech, contrary to the custom of socialist writers. Lagardelle's amazement arose from the form in which Millerand expressed his ideas. We can read at any time in socialist journals and newspapers that the reduction of the working day is no less advantageous to the masters than to the workers, an idea which assumes the solidarity between masters and workers. A dozen years ago a great change occurred in French commercial policy, which had never been one of free trade in the English way. But for a long time our governments thought it useful for the prosperity of the country to negotiate treaties based on moderate tariff laws. After 1892 the victory of the protectionists was complete, and hardly a single legislative session goes by in which some new tariff is not judged necessary to save some branch of agriculture.

Socialist deputies have not escaped this trend; their electoral interests have prevented them from seeing where they were going. Nothing was so amusing as reading the *Petite République* during the discussions of the import tariff in Germany. They could not find terms expressive enough to praise the noisy attitudes of the social democracy and to lash out at starvers of the people. They thus give a good example of the audacity of the politicians, since Jaurès is far from being a free trader.[2] Taking the opportunity from a note in this journal, Yves Guyot said: "We congratulate the German socialists. . . . We should remember that in 1894, at the time of the discussion over the grain duty of seven francs, the French socialists did not oppose this tax. . . . Jaurès preferred to give speeches in honor of a grain-importing monopoly." (*Siècle*, 18 February 1901). The Belgian deputy Lorand was even more severe: "At present, thanks to the silence and to the cowardice of many republican candidates, the protectionist trend has become so irresistible that no one would even dream of reversing it, and we even saw Jaurès making proposals worthy of the German agriculturists in favor of bread shortage" (*Aurore*, 8 April 1902).

To understand present social ideas, we must abandon the old points of view. There is no longer any need to take as our point of departure the economic conditions that permitted free trade to obtain a partial and temporary triumph. We must instead take as our premise those economic conditions proper to the protectionist regime. Capitalism is no longer as rich as it once was or, better still, it is more timid; or again the outlets for products no longer seem to have the flexibility once attributed them. Prudence is imposed on everything: in the composition of import tariffs as in the framing of social legislation, and Millerand proclaimed this prudence necessary in his Saint-Etienne speech. In all periods it was admitted that one had to proceed with moderation. But it seems that in recent years legislators have felt a greater need for transition. In France, laws related to reducing the length of the working day take on curious precautions; their application is subdivided over a long time so that the interested parties would be unable to attribute their losses solely to these regulations. The effects of this legislation will thus be confused with many other causes.[3]

If in former times the history of free trade had been tied to the history of social legislation, today we see a new form of social legislation arising from protectionism. From 1879 to 1881, Bismarck reformed the German tariff structure. Immediately thereupon there commenced his social reforms with an injury insurance plan, a health insurance scheme, and pensions—what could be called the "Bismarckian trilogy" that Charles Andler believes reckoned on Colbert's maritime inscriptions and by means of which the Iron Chancellor believed he could suppress all the causes of socialism. "Thus," says Andler,[4] "Prussian rule is completed; it does not allow any power to be lost. . . . New tariff legislation had bound together the agricultural and industrial powers that were being squandered. Here, meanwhile, we have protectionism broadened to the living forces of the nation. All protectionism borders on state socialism. Colbert had already shown an example of this." There would be great reservations in regard to the influence of Colbertism on Prussian legislation which can be explained much more simply with the ideas of the Junkers; but there are deep similarities between protectionism and social legislation. Is it not noteworthy that in France since the triumph of protectionism in 1892, the Chamber of Deputies has unceasingly produced labor legislation?

Protectionism invokes the principle of national solidarity and did not wait for Léon Bourgeois to throw itself into great disquisitions on this subject that is so apt to prompt eloquent emotional appeals. "As to the *principle of national solidarity*," wrote Michel Chevalier in response to the protectionists in 1851,[5] "there is no contesting its beauty, its truth, and its fruitfulness. A theory of political economy that refused to take account of it . . . would be false, because it would *negate one of the essential attributes of man*, one of his most respectable movements, one of the most energetic and useful social forces. . . . Sociability, in turn, finds its point of departure and its purpose in the sublime sentiment that religion and philosophy cultivate above all things, calling religion charity or universal brotherhood, and the love of humanity." Our contemporary solidarists could not express this better, and I do not believe I take too much of a risk in asserting the economic basis of their doctrine. Certainly reasons of solidarity are not the reasons protective tariffs have been adopted; but the solidarist theories serve to justify the facts. It is also in the name of solidarity that social legislation is justified.

In the same work, Michel Chevalier tries to prove to the protectionist industrialists that they do not provide any good arguments against the claims of the communists of 1848. If the industries that are in danger have a right to a profit that permits them to stay alive—how can we not admit that remuneration for everyone ought to be in proportion to his needs? If it is necessary to guarantee to the owners a minimum sale price—how can one refuse a minimum well-being to the workers? "If the right to labor is recognized for manufacturers' profits by the fact of the protectionist system—why cannot the right to labor be established for the workers' profit?"

Every time a protectionist measure is demanded, the considerable interests of the numerous wage earners is unfailingly asserted. Bismarck held these arguments in high regard.[6] Among us, various socialists demand that one should not be content to protect the worker in an indirect way, by guaranteeing profits to business, but that workers should be given a direct, material advantage.[7] Many times it was claimed that the working day should be regulated in a special way, particularly in the protected industries. Socialist protectionism is translated in a brutal way into roles that limit the number of foreign manual laborers in public works undertakings. At a conference held in Paris on 16 January 1899, Vandervelde,[8] amidst the applause of his audience, forcefully threw himself against the parliamentary bills destined to restrict the use of Belgian manual labor in France and said that undoubtedly "every socialist deputy would respond with our motto: 'The world to the workers.' " Shortly afterward Millerand, once he became minister, issued a decree having the very purpose that the above speaker had denounced as nationalist. I do not believe that anyone protested against this measure.[9]

Protectionism persuades interest groups that their interests depend on the government, and that it is necessary to organize for the purpose of establishing agreements with other groups having different and sometimes even partly contrary interests, to succeed in obtaining laws favorable to their own demands. It is through the path of log-rolling that tariff legislation comes into development. In such compromises, the questions of material interests are brutally posed and resolved. One can annihilate without the slightest scruple a cumbersome competitor too weak to make the hungry wolves in Parliament listen to reason. Thus the day on which the sugar beet producers found that the port distillers who used grain were hurting the sale of their products, a tax was placed on grain. Today the Southern wine producers would like to suppress sugar beet alcohol, etc.

Protectionism develops this notion that the prosperity of a group depends on the compromises to which it agrees with other groups in order to obtain a parliamentary majority. When this majority is obtained, one can do anything; one can ruin the people who stand in the way. The weakest elements are deprived of any rights. Such compromises can be concluded between representatives of property interests and those of the workers; for example, between groups of small proprietors that distill their own wine, and socialist parliamentary groups in France. In these exchanges of influence the question of principles never arises. I need not emphasize the demoralizing consequences of this system which often resembles genuine piracy. I need not even dwell on the consequences of the illusions of those who relate the entire economic prosperity of an industry to the political influence of its representatives. I wish to call attention to a fact that touches the very principles of the doctrine.

In these parliamentary compromises for the defense of material interests, the notion of social solidarity is brought to its highest level. These compromises put this solidarity in action in a slightly lower but more energetic form. We have here in full flower the combination of interests that Lagardelle criticized Millerand for having proclaimed at Saint-Etienne. Next to the factual solidarity which is often cowardly, we have created a highly visible legal solidarity which politicians are obliged to take into account in every country subjected to a protectionist system. In Germany, the representatives of Marxist orthodoxy refuse to abandon their indefatigable opposition to government protectionist policies. The arguments they bring to bear on the question are often very similar to those of the Manchesterites, and this should not surprise us. But the fundamental reason for their opposition is the necessity of keeping alive the principle of class struggle as opposed to that of *intentional solidarity*.

There are two types of protectionism: one suitable for strong peoples who are increasing in population and wealth; the other suitable for disheartened and lazy peoples with a stable population. Americans would probably have been unable to develop so many natural means of production if they had not enjoyed a highly protective tariff. Generally one regards the German tariff as having even there a serious influence on the extraordinary development taken by industry beyond the Vosges. This protectionism is what List had foretold, and it is always this that the defenders of the tariff laws claim to want to introduce. The free-traders accuse them of wanting to protect the lazy and incompetent in view of ensuring a future to proprietors or industrialists that cannot put themselves on the level of modern science. If a country wishes to provide for a large population, it is necessary for it to be able to make the most of all its mines and land, to have many factories, to produce as much as possible for its own inhabitants. A purely agricultural population will perhaps lose some enjoyment if it is forced to buy objects manufactured in the country. But if there is a sufficient number of manufacturers to provide for all its needs, the population can gradually become double what it would be in a purely agricultural system. This consideration has a good deal of value.

By virtue of exceptional historical circumstances, England possesses industry that thrives particularly on exports. The country has abandoned its agriculture[10] and accepts a marked regression from the point of view of rural life (much land at one time under cultivation having been returned to health). But is this a situation that can be repeated in many countries? England has more than compensated for the rural regress in population because it has found an enormous foreign clientele to buy the products produced by a prodigiously wealthy capitalism. The example of England has often been cited to prove that free trade is the most suitable regime for a strongly progressive economy. But this example only proves that there can be a *coincidence* between free trade and the prosperity of a great nation. The insolidarity existing in England renders impossible any proof of a cause and effect relationship between the social phenomena produced in this country.

Just as there are two forms of protectionism, there are two social policies: one is strictly related to the progressive tendencies of the proletariat and consequently favorable to the development of socialism, while the other is conservative. It would be very useful to use different terms to designate two policies so different in spirit. We should only designate under the name of "legal protection" of workers the latter or conservative policy which, after all, has already taken this title officially and is especially recommended by the clerical party. It always assumes the existence of a protection exercised by a part of the bourgeoisie. The former policy is based on the *perfect separation* of classes. It leaves to the capitalists the burden and profit of directing production for their own self-interests under certain legal conditions. Let them leave socialism free to act on the working class, to educate it, and not presume to "civilize" the working class the bourgeois way.

We can account for English social legislation by means of an image of Proudhon.[11] This likened large-scale industry "to a *new land*, discovered, or suddenly created out of thin air by the social genius and to which society sends a colony to take possession of it and to work it for the advantage of all." These types of new lands were often discovered in the course of the nineteenth century, and English capitalism has generally been able to take possession of them before other countries were in a position to compete with it. From this has resulted an incredible prosperity which has created conditions suitable to allow free trade and social legislation.

Proudhon deemed that over these colonies, the associations, by dint of immorality, tyranny, and thievery[12] "seem to me absolutely necessary and right. The industry to be carried on, the work to be accomplished, are the common and undivided property of all those who take part therein. The granting of franchises for mines and railroads to companies of stockholders, who plunder the bodies and souls of the wage-workers, is a betrayal of power, a violation of the rights of the public, an outrage upon human dignity and personality." All this is very nice. But it would still be necessary that the worker companies (of whose organization the French author dreamed) be able to cultivate this "new land." The knowledge we have of the character of the English worker shows us how this conception would have been unattainable in England.

I have had occasion[13] to call attention to this fact: in England the greater mass of men is far from being animated by the spirit of initiative so often vaunted as universally diffused among Anglo-Saxons. Only a weak minority possesses this great energy. Without these daring captains of industry, England would again become a backward country. List wrote[14] that the British government had produced the education of the country by means of its protectionist laws. It would be more precise to say that the English capitalists have created England and that today they still maintain its greatness despite the resistance of the masses. The masses express their passion for laziness in various forms, each suitable in the course of a different period, sometimes borrowing the pretext from their Christian beliefs, sometimes becoming fanatically philanthropic, today involving themselves in socialism in a most grotesque way. These forms can only deceive a superficial observer; the basis is always the desire to rest and the lack of power to think in a virile way.[15]

"On this new land," said Proudhon, "society authorizes colonization only with the reservation of respecting certain provisions dictated by the general interest. If the concession is abandoned to the capitalists, it legitimizes the state in being able to impose charges in money or in kind. I consider, for example, as a charge in kind the shortening of the working day; and as a money charge, the obligation to participate in workers' pension plans. In his social legislation, Bismarck, imbued with the feudal spirit, did not admit the first system, and Andler noted this attitude without explaining it perfectly. "Measures of supervision, of industrial hygiene, of limitations on working hours . . . Bismarck always rejected all these reforms."[16]

The social security institutions can be employed for the purpose of fostering social peace, while the other legislative system does not lead to this result. It was this consideration particularly that guide Bismarck. At the International Congress of Commerce and Industry that convened at Ostend in 1902, there was extensive discussion on the question of social peace, and Ettore Denis (a Belgian-style socialist) appeared to believe in the efficacy of compulsory insurance to reconcile the social classes (*Débats*, 20 September 1902). Raffalovich denies this result.

A French observer who attended the 1902 Dusseldorf Congress of the partisans of social security wrote in regard to German institutions:[17] "Here is the terrain on which Bernsteinism blossomed, the Jaurism across the Rhine. . . . These old rebels are presently the most tenacious defenders of social insurance. They learn business. The conduct of their unions and their own party show the effects of this knowledge. As one of them told me, they are making the revolution in detail.'' They are making the revolution, but it is not capitalist society that is being revolutionized, but socialism itself. They are working to make socialism independent of the class struggle and, believing that they remain socialist, prove that they have lost all consciousness of the separation of classes.

To lead the flower of the working class to enter into the administration of solidarity controlled by the state is an excellent way to combat the idea of class struggle. We have seen analogous effects produced in France ever since the trade union militants began to go into public administration. However little they are being treated as specialists whom bureaucrats must consult and are receiving a bit of the luster of the state, their revolutionary concepts begin to soften. They believe that while waiting for the universal social revolution to materialize, there is a certain form of spiritual and partial revolution which is visible in the respect shown them. We should note that in the program of the French Workers' Party published in London in 1880 by Marx and Guesde, Article 7 of the economic section (putting the aged and disabled workers in the care of society) did not exist originally. This shows the rigor with which Marx attempted to reject the notions of solidarity and worker protection.

The results obtained from what I have called "progressive" legislation have not been felicitous in England. Kautsky says[18] that the English workers "use their free time unwisely; that football, boxing, racing, and betting are the things that stir their passions and which *absorb all their free time*, all their intelligence, and all their resources." Therefore it is to be asked whether this social legislation, which imposes such severe burdens on capitalism and which relies on the belief in individual energy, has produced the effects that Marx expected of it. If one accepts the word of Kautsky, who unfortunately agrees with what many serious observers say, it seems that this immense effort has been in vain. If this is so, we should regard the reduction of the working day as a burden analogous to those which result from the parasitism that flourishes in England in so many ways, but which until now has not enjoined to prevent this country from prospering.

There is no passion more violent in the man who lacks elevated aspirations than the desire to do nothing and to spend money in frivolous occupations. The democrats favorable to the clergy who try to rob socialism of its followers by promising still more than the socialists (by ostentatiously proclaiming their love for the people) have taken advantage of this human characteristic. They never fail to demand rest for the workers; they vaunt the happy lot of the population that dispenses with many working days; they push the labor inspectors to perform zealously. Their goal is certainly not the progress of the working class. Sometimes it was believed that their agitation could finally stand to benefit socialism. At present we must abandon this illusion.[19]

The same measures relative to the working day can have very different consequences in different countries. We have here a fine illustration of the principle that legislation is not susceptible of being evaluated literally, and it is for purely legal reasons that it should be evaluated according to its real contents. The progress of the working classes is not produced in as automatic a manner as Marx believed, and it will take many efforts on the part of socialists to ensure that the proletariat may derive advantage from the legislation on the reduction of the working day. If the result were the development of idleness, as clerks and philanthropists hope, this legislation would be an element of decadence.

Notes

1. *Mouvement Socialiste* (18 January 1902):98–99.
2. Jaurès was still the principal editor of the *Petite République* and had not yet established his socialist shop so much enjoyed by his rich stockholders.
3. This cunning of social politicians is quite adept; a capitalism that has become as timid in politics as in business is well suited to such slyness; in the past, in England, according to Marx, one did not take so many precautions. *Capital* (Modern Library ed.), pp. 521–22.
4. Charles Andler, *Le Prince de Bismarck* (Paris: G. Bellais, 1899), p. 256.
5. Michel Chevalier, p. 39.
6. Andler, *Le Prince de Bismarck*, p. 227.
7. Protectionists admit that it would be just to protect the national labor against foreign manual labor (cf. the report of the deputy Turrel to the French Chamber of Deputies, dated 2 April 1892); the law of 8 August 1893 prescribes matriculation measures for foreigners and has for its object according to its title "protection of national labor." Cf. *Journal des économistes* (March 1903):472.
8. *Mouvement Socialiste* (1 February 1899):68.
9. At least I do not find a trace of it in *Mouvement Socialiste* that has so often battled Millerand, nor did it appear in a resolution of the 1900 Socialist Congress. Here, therefore, is a form of internationalism that has been definitely buried.
10. During the great struggles undertaken between manufacturers and landlords over the corn laws, "insolidarity" appeared in a perfectly clear way, because no one could doubt that the free entry of grain would not completely disturb agriculture. This spectacle had certainly exerted a considerable influence on Marx and contributed greatly to the formation of his theory of classes.

11. Pierre-Joseph Proudhon, *General Idea of the Revolution in the Nineteenth Century*, trans. John Beverly Robinson (New York: Haskell House, 1969), p. 221. This book was written in 1851.
12. Ibid., p. 219.
13. Sorel, *Saggi di critica del Marxismo*, p. 103.
14. Frederick List, *Système national d'économie politique*, French trans. (Paris: Capelle, 1851), p. 507.
15. German socialists cannot come to understand the way of thinking of the people who call themselves "socialists" in England. "It sometimes appears," writes one of them regarding a proposal for social reform imitating an Australian one, "that everything in England conspires to make the worker fall into one illusion after another. He says that European socialism must guard against the 'Anglo-Saxon illusion.' " *Mouvement socialiste* (15 December 1902):2222. There is a great difference between Germany and England that results from their opposite ways of conceiving *effort*: the English are retrograde while the Germans are progressive.
16. Andler, *Le prince de Bismarck*, p. 266.
17. *Musée Social* (November 1902):396. In the beginning, the social-democrats showed great hostility to the Bismarckian laws; that is why the author sees rightly as a grave symptom the present enthusiasm for these laws.
18. *Mouvement Socialiste* (25 October 1901):1891.
19. See the very clear opinion of Kautsky on this point: *Mouvement Socialiste* (15 October 1902):1848. At present the leaders of the organizations founded by the Christian democrats in order to struggle in the aforementioned way against socialism say that anticlerical policies arrest the progress of workers' protection. They have gone so far as to cause this coarse sophism to penetrate *Mouvement Socialiste* (15 August 1902):1449.

CHAPTER SEVEN

When a decade ago the various Socialist parties came to face the agrarian question, they encountered unexpected difficulties and found that they had to bring to light the notion of social unity against which Marxism had been established. "In view of the May 1892 municipal elections," writes Zevaes,[1] "when it was shown that from the shop-workers socialism had largely 'won the city,' the Workers' Party insisted on starting propaganda among agricultural workers. This was the capital and resounding work of the party's tenth national congress held in Marseilles from the 24th to the 28th of September 1892." This first essay did not cause much of a stir, but at the congress held at Nantes in 1894 the program was made concrete in a complete and definitive way with a list of things to be considered and a report that indicated its direction. The Germans who were already discussing the special measures to be adopted for agriculture seized upon the French documents, and Engels finally intervened in the debate to recall the principles of the doctrine.

In no part of the economy as much as in agriculture does one find examples of progressive social legislation. In every period the state has intervened to help the passage from one form to another, when the dominated class could not come to free itself without its protection. Thus in Germany and in Russia serfdom was abolished and feudal canons liquidated under the aegis of the state. Gladstone wished to apply to Ireland a policy of transmutation of property analogous to that which had been followed in the suppression of Russian serfdom. Although property right in France has been clearly determined for a long time, the laws of 9 February 1897 and 11 March 1898 have modified, in favor of tenant farmers, the situation which resulted from the *retractable* contracts of domain[2] in Brittany (created by virtue of ancient usages and from the law of 6 August 1791) and from the vine-growing rights[3] in the area around Nantes. In this last case, the intervention of the state was so extraordinary that almost all the proprietors claimed that their rights could be traced to the sale of the national wealth created after the nature of rents from vintners was made the object of a sovereign interpretation of the *Conseil d'Etat*. In Brittany it was decided that the farmers who worked the land by themselves and who had renounced the option of

221

giving it up, claiming payment for their labor of improvement, will be receiving partial payment. They will be content with receiving surplus value. In the Nantes area four years were given to the vine workers to reestablish the vines, and during this time the proprietor could not take the suppression of the vineyards as a pretext to annul the rent.

It seems that no one would ever contest the legitimacy of state intervention, that this field has always been favorable to the development of agriculture. Marxists could never under any pretext associate themselves with proposals designed to impede or retard the progress of the productive economy. But should they not associate with interventionist measures that bourgeois doctrine regards as good and that are obviously favorable to the progress of cultivation? Engels did not contest this, but he never wanted to admit that one could claim to call "socialist" a policy that relates to principles entirely different from those of socialism.

What seems to have particularly impressed Engels is the influence that the organization of the agricultural proletariat of East Prussia had on Germany: "Sow the socialist word among these workers," he said at the conclusion of his article,[4] "give them the courage and the unity, and it is the end of the Junker rule! The great reactionary power, which is nothing else for Germany than Russian Czarism is for all Europe . . . sinks to nothing. . . . That is why the victory of the agricultural proletariat of East Prussia is much more important than that of the small peasants of the West or the middling peasants of the South. It is there in East Prussia where the field of our decisive battle lies." To win this proletariat, there is no need for a change of attitude. The large landholdings are apt to be socialized just as much as the great factories;[5] in one case as in the other it is necessary to concern oneself with the *arms* and not the *head* of industry.

But what of the countries where the agrarian problem is present in a completely different form; what of countries in which farmers own moderately sized lands; or what of renters? Engels adamantly refused to admit that they could join the party.[6] The party could fight with them against feudalism; but there could never be a blending. "If in our party we can admit individuals from every social class, we cannot tolerate groups with capitalist interests, or middle-class peasants or average bourgeois."[7] "As long as there have been large or small peasant holdings, they cannot exist without hired hands. If it is thus simply stupid on our part to promise the small peasants that they will be maintained as small peasants, it is almost *treason* to promise the same thing to average or wealthy peasants." It seemed absurd to him to defend renters under the pretext that they are forced to exploit their workers at the rate at which they themselves are exploited: "And why," he asks,[8] "would not our great landlords also wish . . . to ask for socialist protection to exploit peasant workers on the basis of the 'exploitation of which they are themselves victimized' by usurers, stock exchanges, annuities, or the price of grain?"

The great difficulty of the agrarian program arises from that it is almost impossible not to take account of the interests of the heads of enterprises, while socialism has taken it as a principle never to take them into account. The difficulty exists also for the small proprietor whose material situation is often as bad as that of the proletariat and sometimes worse than that of the urban proletariat, but which has a juridical solution that is difficult to reconcile with the socialist concept. Engels observes[9] that the most effective measures that can be taken on behalf of the small proprietor are general measures relative to the poor classes, or at least measures "that serve rather great landed property." He vigorously resists the idea of promising to the small peasants that they can keep their possessions. To compromise on this point[10] "would be to *lose the dignity of the party*, lowering it to the level of a long-winded *anti-Semitism*." All that can be promised[11] is not to use violence and to lead the small proprietors to collectivism through the path of cooperation. The party should therefore make every effort to favor the life of agricultural cooperatives.

The question has not been greatly clarified by subsequent publications. Engels believed[12] that the Nantes program was a draft that should have been heavily revised. After his death it seems there came about a kind of understanding to keep the difficulty in the dark. The 1896 London Congress of the International declared that the agrarian program should be determined in each country, and the 1900 Congress of the International, which dealt with so many things, did not even deign to concern itself with agriculture. This subject was less interesting than conditions in Armenia or South Africa! Since then, nobody seems to have remembered what Engels wrote. Yet his doctrine applied perfectly to the question of socialist participation in government. But no one there had ever seen an assembly with such a slight memory of Marx and Engels. This Congress was more inspired by the spirit of the old utopians than by the Marxist spirit.

In 1899 Kautsky published a fat book on the agrarian question. But we do not find many precise answers to the questions asked of the socialists. The author is in the same embarrassment as Engels. He does not wish to hear about measures that could have the effect of protecting the small peasants as heads of agricultural enterprises, because he thereby feared opposing the technical progress that would be, according to him, the passage to large property. He recognized[13] that the peasants do not attach any importance to the extension of the social laws made for the urban proletariat: "They don't want the laws at any price. What they asked is the protection of their particular mode of enterprise against economic progress. And this the Socialist Party cannot give them." Thus his conclusion is discouraging. He says that the demands which he can support[14] "are too small to become the basis of a vast party program. These small means are already frequently employed in the progressive countries, and in their application, the Socialist Party is only distinguished from the other parties by its great disdain for the rights of private property all the while that it is in conflict with the general interests of a rational agricultural policy."

Kautsky is, like Engels, particularly concerned with destroying the influence of the East Prussian nobility. He does not know what to say to the peasants in other parts of Germany. He would like to see the schism between proprietors and proletarians realized. But this is very difficult to bring about[15] since just *the hope* of owning some property is enough to change the state of mind of the men in the fields. Kautsky believes that the most suitable tactic consists in not fostering illusions on the future of small agricultural enterprises. The solidarity among various categories of the peasantry is manifested almost paradoxically on questions of tariffs. It would seem at first sight that the small peasants who generally consume all their grain, ought not to have any interest in the tariff protection that so greatly benefits the great proprietors. Nevertheless, experience shows that in countries with universal suffrage, the countryside generally nominates protectionist deputies. The small peasants are no less desirous than the large landholders of seeing prices rise.

It is the peasants who are right rather than those economists who want to show the peasants that their interests are opposed to the wealthy grain harvesters. Every time that the price of an important commodity declines, the countryside finds itself greatly impoverished, because the well-to-do classes cease to provide work and employ only the amount of manual labor strictly necessary to ensure the next harvest. In the countryside things do not develop as in the great capitalist factories. In the latter, if a crisis greatly reduces profits or if there is need for large new investments, the product is not distributed to the stockholders. On the other hand, rural proprietors restrict their personal expenses as little as possible; but they greatly restrain expenses made for the land. The small peasants and workers understand this and know that they have an overall interest in the high earnings of great agricultural enterprises.[16]

Kausky is not very sympathetic to rural cooperation. This cooperation has as its primary object to facilitate the sale of products in the cities and has sometimes obtained results that are noteworthy from this point of view. "If," says Kautsky,[17] "one favors sales to the city of milk, eggs, and meat, the consumption of these items diminishes in the countryside, where these foods are replaced by potatoes,[18] liquor, and a bit of coffee. The savings of the peasant increases; but his power and that of his children decreases." Nevertheless, we know from a very large number of examples that enrichment (which seems suspect to Kautsky) obtained in this way is translated into great agricultural advances in our Latin countries as well as a very noticeable increase in well-being.

Cooperation can hardly be formed exclusively among men of the same economic class. Milk makes butter the same way whether it comes from a large or a small establishment. *Interests that are made similar in regard to a particular aspect of the economy* group themselves together to cooperate, and this cooperation remains independent of social differences. It would be otherwise if the association had to unite in a single grouping all the economic activity of its members (as has occurred in the urban producers' cooperatives). But *in the countryside, cooperation is always fragmentary*. This mixing of people belonging to different social classes has strongly impressed the conservatives, who have seen in rural cooperativism a means of establishing social peace.

What the socialists can do to conform to the directions of Engels is to aim at the application of social policy to the people of the countryside. This is what Kautsky tried to indicate in his book, but it is not very easy to see how we could transfer laws made for factories to the countryside. One could not, on the other hand, proceed to this generalization without asking what are the *general reasons* that justify these regulations. Here there can be no question of workers' hygiene and of the extra work of the operators of extra rapid machines and the accidents resulting therefrom.

In the discussions which took place on proposals to reduce the working day, it is surprising that one did not take due account of the experience of sports. The "kings of the bicycle track" every year notably exceed the old records. Everyone knows that this progress depends on mechanical improvements of the vehicles and on changes in training machines. We do not see such phenomena in athletic exercises. This experience shows that the productivity of individuals does not vary within certain limits, while "social productivity" (machines operated by men) can increase quickly. Unlike modern industry, agriculture does not have the possibility of quickly finding new means of production that permits it to do in eight hours what it formerly did in twelve, and even when science provides these means—does agriculture have the money to put it into operation?

I do not see very clearly how compensation could be produced here. Not only does agricultural productivity ordinarily increase slowly, but again, when it can take a great extension we find that consumption is quickly restricted. The history of French viticulture gives convincing proof of this. After the ruination of the vines by the blight, the large proprietors made admirable efforts to reconstruct the old source of wealth. They performed costly experiments; they struggled against the administrative absurdity that, in the name of science, claimed to arrest the popularization of the proposed measures. In certain departments (Herault, for example) the great landowner showed qualities analogous to those shown in large-scale industry in the most advanced countries. P. Leroy-Beaulieu, himself a vine-grower, takes this regime as typical and extols the scientific and intellectual superiority of the great proprietor.[19] But there was faith in the infinite expansion of the market. They tried to do what large-scale industry had done—produce an enormous quantity of merchandise at a very cheap price. This caused a great crisis in wines, one that will probably end only with the destruction of the vineyards that give the most common wines. Never, as far as I know, has large-scale industry suppressed textile looms that produced the most common cloth.

French writers in charge of discussing social questions do not ordinarily make necessary distinctions, and, according to the case, estimate that the reduction of the working day increases or decreases production. A government circular of 17 May 1900 even asserted both things at once:[20] a law restricting labor time would have as a consequence arresting overproduction and stimulating production! But when dealing with agriculture it seems that there is no possible doubt. Social legislation analogous to that for the factories would have very grave consequences for selling prices. On the other hand, we know that the same phenomena are produced in small industries which often suffer from social laws. Here again, we find solidarity between workers and owners. It is necessary, when examining a rural law, to reflect carefully on the consequences it could have on the prosperity of the leaders of an industry. It is not possible to consider only the *arms* when dealing with agriculture; it is also necessary to take account of the *head*. Thus we rediscover the doctrine espoused in the Saint-Etienne speech of which we have spoken.

Kautsky has received the "eight-hour doctrine" from his masters and cannot abandon it. He agrees[21] to the ten-hour day in summer and six-hour day in winter so that the average does not change. At the beginning of the application of the English laws on the duration of labor, many people maintained that the worker was more tired then before. [22] This could be because professional habits are not revolutionized in a day and because a long education is needed before men can utilize their powers of attention without the fatigue caused by fear.[23]

In the countryside, it is highly probable that, if the limitation of the working day were compensated by the intensification of labor, we would end up with that premature exhaustion that one claims to oppose in order to spare the future of the race. The agricultural worker almost always performs a *technologically simple labor* similar to journeyman labor. It doesn't seem that a man would benefit from doing a day's march in five hours instead of six. The experience of sports shows how much exhaustion is caused by increasing speed. It is certain, on the other hand, that the peasant wastes a great deal of time. But anyone acquainted with agricultural labor knows that it is not very easy to convince him to waste less, to tighten up the loose ends of his working day, as Marx says. The means that succeed in the long run in factories do not apply easily to the countryside.

Should we consider the reduction of the working day as a means for giving work to larger numbers? This was the purpose American workers put forth when calling for an eight-hour day.[24] It is also the purpose English miners seem to aim for. But already in the extractive industry appear the inconveniences of a regulation that could work against its own end because of the seasons: "In winter," observes De Rousiers,[25] "at the time when, under the present regime, the miners are working the entire week, one would need to call for new workers, and this would mean employing more men during the dead season of the summer."

The countryside generally lacks manual workers during certain periods, and no one would dare maintain that labor could be distributed in a regular way. This lack of manual labor in certain seasons motivates the use of agricultural gangs that give rise to so many abuses in all countries with large proprietors. It is especially because of the trouble that they caused to peasants that the laws on keeping the Sabbath were abrogated in France. Finally, let us note that Charles Bonnier has declared that "to speak of the eight-hour day in the fields is a peculiar kind of utopia" (*Socialiste*, 24 November 1894).

The people who accept as a postulate that the agricultural worker ought to be a proprietor attribute great importance to regulations on the working day; (I do not think Kautsky would share their ideas). In countries with strong feudal traditions, the creation of a class of small property holders does not present much of a problem. It can be based on the same principles of the old law and also on known practices. Thus it was first in England that the law obliged proprietors to attach a property of four acres to each peasant worker's house in addition to his wages.[26]

It is necessary that these workers have time available to obtain profit from their little field. When they are near the great landowners too long, all the work falls back on the shoulders of women and children who turn out to be much more overworked than in the workshops. We must refer to considerations of this kind when we try to understand the true import of the reduction of the working day among the miners. Miners are peasants who generally have preserved the taste for agricultural labor and who would like to improve their lot by cultivating a garden.

Many conservatives recommend the construction of factories in the country so that workers can alternate labor in the factories with that on the land.[27] This is only possible by making the work day in the factory of moderate length. I do not believe that the conservatives are mistaken in thinking that this system reduces the existing antagonism between capitalists and workers who could then hope to become proprietors. I do not insist on this point and refer to this fact only to demonstrate with a new example how the notion of solidarity develops as soon as one goes from the city to the country. We find by means of a sort of counterproof the relation that binds solidarity to the impotence of capitalism. In the large cotton industry, *capitalism appeared as infinite, and solidarity as nothing.* Here we find a strictly limited capitalism, and a very potent solidarity.

Notes

1. Zevaes, *Aperçu historique sur le Parti Ouvrier*, pp. 63–64.
2. The proprietor can allow payment for the buildings, the tillage, the orchards of fruit-bearing trees; according to the law of 6 August 1791, the farmers also had the right to obtain payment for labor; but generally they renounced this option.
3. The farmers had an hereditary and transferable title: they had to maintain the vine-growing lands and give a portion to the proprietors. They asked what their rights were following the invasion of the blight that had destroyed the vines.
4. *Mouvement Socialiste*, "La question agraire en France," 15 October 1900, p. 466.
5. This comparison that Engels makes seems somewhat contestible to me because the great factory is provided with all the progress of science while the great Junker property is often cultivated in a backward way.
6. Engels, "Agrarian Question," pp. 454–55.
7. Ibid., p. 463. Engels had already observed (on p. 453) that the exposition of the French program spoke of "keeping rural property in the hands of the peasants, although it claimed at the same time that this property is inevitably destined to disappear."
8. Ibid., pp. 453–54. He notes with a certain bitterness that the French socialist deputies had proposed a scheme for the nationalization of grain imports analogous to that of the famous Count Kanitz.
9. Ibid., p. 458.
10. Ibid., p. 462.
11. Ibid., pp. 454–60.
12. Ibid., p. 462.

13. Kautsky, *La politique agraire*, p. 26.
14. Ibid., p. 199.
15. Ibid., pp. 20–22.
16. I have already presented similar observations in "Etudes d'économie rurale," *Le Devenir Social*, January 1896, p. 31.
17. Kautsky, p. 27.
18. It would be quite appropriate to ask if, among the "intangible theses" that make up the Marxian heritage according to Kautsky, we might find this: that the potato "produced scrofula" *(Poverty of Philosophy)*.
19. Leroy-Beaulieu, *Traité théorique et pratique d'économie politique*, Vol. II, pp. 12–15.
20. This does not give a high idea of the ability of people surrounding Millerand; as for Millerand himself, though he is a very able politician, he has a remarkable ignorance of economic matters.
21. Kautsky, *La politique agraire*, p. 106. When I speak of the "dogma of eight hours," I do not exaggerate at all. At the 1902 French Socialist Congress, Deville (one of the first popularizers of Marxist ideas in France) in the minimum program proposed not to call for a reform that seemed very far off and limited himself to demanding "measures tending to come near to the eight-hour working day" (Stenographic account, pp. 52–53). Kautsky was disturbed that Deville, after such a crime, could have been a socialist candidate from Paris. *Mouvement Socialiste* (15 October 1902):1868.
22. Marx, *Capital* (Modern Library ed., p. 454). Marx did not always clearly distinguish a true increase in fatigue from that which was due to a change of routine.
23. Mosso showed how writing can produce enormous emotions among the semiliterate. On the first impressions produced by the first rapid looms, see Marx, *Capital* (Modern Library ed.).
24. Vigouroux, *La concentration des forces ouvrières dans l'Amérique du Nord* (Paris: A. Colin, 1899), p. 242.
25. Paul de Rousiers, *La question ouvrière en Angleterre,* p. 320.
26. Marx, *Capital* (Modern Library ed.), p. 788.
27. I have observed that peasants placed in this situation become much more ardent and attentive to labor in the fields. The factory has taught them the value of time, and they tighten up the loose ends of their day on the farm as much as in the factory.

CHAPTER EIGHT

To give a more precise account of Marx's theories, we must now examine the juridical theory he constructed to represent the relations between employer and employee. We cannot master a social question thoroughly if we do not examine its juridical aspects. Marx went to a great deal of trouble to establish the doctrine of the "sale of labor power" which we will now discuss. It is strange that its true value is not appreciated by a majority of Marxists. In the doctrine set forth in the first volume of *Capital*, we find subtleties of exposition which have no great importance. There is useless discourse on surplus value and surplus labor, while Marx's originality consists in his unique idea of the labor contract.

Let us review briefly this concept.[1] Workers sell to the capitalist a commodity, *labor power*, which has its market price like all commodities. Having become a purchaser of this "thing," labor power, the capitalist unites it with the raw materials bought from merchants. The product of this mixture legitimately belongs to him without anyone having anything to see in his accounts.[2] "He is as entitled to it as to the product of fermentation in his cellar." The capitalist has harvested a profit, but respecting all legal principles.

The individual who is estranged from all philosophical considerations can be indifferent about whether an action refers to one juridical category or another. But this indifference cannot be appropriate for those who, through reading Marx, have become accustomed to studying problems thoroughly and attempting precise definitions. In books by jurists there are purely scholastic distinctions; moreover, it occurs that, despairing of being able to reduce all contracts to classical types, various jurists have ended up by placing everything that is difficult to classify into the category of "unnamed contracts"—an extraordinary way of solving the problem. The difficulty lies in that we should establish a greater number of legal levels; but for the present question we need not enter into these discussions.

Lawyers dealing with the economy recognize that it is not unimportant whether a contract is placed in one class or another. Thus sharecropping appears differently to us according to whether it is viewed as an

231

association or as *rent*. If it is an association, it can yield noteworthy results and be recommended as an economic form highly appropriate to specialized cultivation. If it is a rent at a variable charge in kind, it constitutes an almost always mediocre, and often rather bad, form. In many cases it is[3] "the worst of all regimes since it rewards neglect and old habits while at the same time it imposes a tax on vigilance and on activity in labor. Indeed, this sharecropper undergoes only half of the loss, whose sole cause will be the bad management of his enterprise, and collects only half of the gain that an improvement of effort could produce." Paul Bureau concludes[4] that sharecropping can be a lease or an association according to "the special quality of the sharecropper and especially of the landlord." This shows the schools of jurists that classify sharecropping in one or another category are right, "but in different hypotheses."

The French civil code has placed the labor contract in the category of rent, and we should observe that Article 1780 places domestic servants and laborers in the same category. There is something servile in the idea of this contract. The code has taken care to proscribe the obligations that would have had the effect of establishing serfdom. It was even believed that a one-year limit should be placed on the duration of labor obligations.[5] It is likely that, if this clause was not kept in the code, it was because it was cumbersome for the service of domestics.[6]

Presently the landlord does not have the right to bring back his domestics or his workers by force. But the sailor, after having signed up on the crew, can no longer desert, and is subject to disciplinary punishment. His enlistment has preserved the character of a partial and contractural servitude. Kant regarded the domestic servant as an acquisition by the head of the household. The contract to rent domestic service belongs to the mixed law that regulates "the possession of an external object as a thing and its use as a person." He found it natural that the master could force someone to return under his power in case he fled.[7]

In the course of strikes that arise in small factories many bosses still regard their workers as a kind of domestic servant. The Catholic masters believe that they are required to look after the faith and habits of their workers as they do for the people of their household. The workshop is in their view still a sort of large family, a *clan* whose head has moral duties to fulfill. In the countryside the idea of a clan is much more natural than in the city. The serf is very much the "master's man." The tenant farmers who pay rent in kind are truly people of the clan, and Le Play regards them as "the best kind of worker":[8] he lives in a house and cultivates a small plot let to him by the big proprietors, and gives them the manual labor they need. Those institutions called "patrist" have had as their goal generalizing the system of tenant farmers and transferring this system to industry.

The old socialists had been vividly impressed by how many servile remnants there were in the idea of renting labor. Pecqueur claimed to reduce all industry to two kinds: workers *lending* their labor in exchange for a salary, and proprietors *lending* their houses, lands, and capital.[9] "Everything is reduced to these two moments: renting one's labor and renting the material of labor. But what a difference between these two types of rental! To rent one's own labor is to begin one's own slavery; to rent out the material of labor is to establish one's own liberty. This gives birth to the idea that labor is man. The material is not part of man, and yet takes the place of the labor of the man who possesses it by the fact of human law, and earns him a share of the wealth as if he had put his labor into the creation of that wealth. . . . The *material* element which can do nothing for the creation of wealth without the other element, *labor*, has the magical virtue of being fertile for them."[10] Pecqueur's exposition is obscure and confusing because he was too concerned with sentiments to give his thought a juridical form. I retain only this fact: that he considers the rental of labor as a moral decline.

The philanthropists who don't want to follow Le Play's ideas and who pride themselves on their liberalism—especially law professors—have taken the notion of association from the utopian tradition and propagate it without caring to know to what degree it corresponds to the facts. Economic facts will have to bend to the demands of the Idea. They are sure that society is full of vices and that chairs of political economy are created in the university, not to teach a science of observation, but to teach men how they ought to direct themselves. The notion of association greatly pleases them by virtue of its obscurity and because of the memories linking it to a fraternal and superficially Christian utopianism.

One could argue with them uselessly that all solidarity—recalling more or less complete association such as profit sharing—is "in direct contradiction with the necessary organization of [large-scale] present-day industry, and relies on ideas and principles contrary to the facts," as Paul Bureau says.[11] This objection could not touch many professors who proclaim that contemporary society is unintelligible. To make it intelligible, they demand that this same society should possess a regulation on the distribution of products. This postulate necessarily assumes that production be organized under the form of association. The present "anarchy," being *unintelligible for the professors*, can be only an accident or an appearance.

The sale of labor power abolishes all bonds between employer and employee. After the presentation of his merchandise and payment for an agreed price, the worker is in the same position vis-à-vis the master as a grocer is in regard to the customer who comes to him to buy coffee. We find that Marxism here—and this is an essential point—is close to so-called Manchester economics. This school never wanted to accept the ideas of Le Play's school on the social duties of the captains of industry. Orthodox economics refuses to admit sentimental considerations in buying and selling a commodity in the market. It cannot understand how fraternity and solidarity could be introduced in established market relations between brokers and grain proprietors. According to both the orthodox economists and the Marxists, what happens with labor power happens with grain brought to the marketplace. Business is transacted on an open and abundantly provisioned market where there can be no consideration for people.

The difference between Marx and the orthodox economists is principally on the historical interpretation of the labor market as it is presently organized. About thirty years ago, nearly all economists agreed in regarding the present system as the final improvement of the long evolution that had led in 1789 to the definitive recognition of the "true principles" on which rationally constituted societies should rest. They admitted that all was not perfect in this system any more than it was in parliamentary constitutions. But they thought that nothing more than "improvements" need be brought to bear. Marx, on the other hand, thought that the present world characterized by capitalism *should perish* and be replaced by a society based on other principles that would be established in opposition to today's.

If the similarities between orthodox political economy and Marxism did not seem as great as they really are, it is because economists have never tried to give their doctrine a juridical form. They have not tried, as was possible, to go back in a precise way to the sales conditions of the labor contract, which the code calls a rental contract and which in literary publications is often regarded as analogous to a social contract. This is not dealt with here as a mere legal subtlety. We are dealing with it to give an account of the possibility of the class struggle. If employer and employee are buyers and sellers of a commodity having a market price, they can pursue entirely opposite ends on the political spectrum and organize for the struggle of one against the other. At least in large cities, a buyer is not concerned with the opinions of his grocer. If, on the other hand, the employer is the head of a clan or if he is the partner of his employees, there can exist between them disagreements regarding their interests. But such disagreements, sharp as they may be, are not class antagonisms.

In the present crisis in Marxism, the role of the professors has not been small. The university students who incline toward socialism bring with them ideological baggage irreconcilable with Marx's views. Paul Lafargue said something with a good deal of truth when he maintained that the professors could not come to understand Marx's work. It is indeed certain that the notion of the sale of labor power on the market in the manner of the sale of a commodity almost completely escapes them. Since they are unaware of the importance of this basic legal thesis, the rest of Marxism can only appear to them in a confused form.

To show how unclear the professorial doctrines are, let us take several opinions from the preface by Professor Charles Rist, of the Uiversity of Montpellier, to the translation of a book by David Schloss. It would seem that the author should reason as Marx does since he (Rist) says:[12] "The worker has become a purveyor of labor ever more similar to the purveyors of other merchandise. One can maintain that the distinction, so poorly made in the past between servant and worker, tends to be increasingly realized." This assertion does not prevent Rist from reasoning as if there were a *purely ethical* question here.

During strikes, the workers always demand the unification of rates among different firms in the same locality, taking the highest rate as the basis of this unification. There is nothing unnatural in this; they act as would any merchant who points out to his clients the prices of his competitors when their prices are higher than his own. There is a serious interest that the rates be uniform in the same locality, because then relations are established more correctly on the basis of the principle of labor power. And indeed there is an interest that the rates be established in a truly proportional way. But I do not see how the question can be asked as to whether we have come to "introduce in the distribution of wages among workers of the same profession more justice and equity."[13] These modifications are very important for relations among workers and for the idea of class. But I do not see why the masters would be obliged by natural justice to favor the development of the idea of class among their workers! Obviously the author has sunk into the incomprehensible language of ethics.

When a renter notifies his landlord that he is leaving his apartment if the landlord does not install electric lights, as is normal in modern homes—are we going to ask what part justice plays in all this? Thrifty housewives do not want to buy all kinds of meat in the same butcher shop; they have one supplier for beef, another for mutton. Is there anything in the housewife's procedure which concerns justice or equality? The merchant may find that he does not like the housewives' way of looking for the more advantageous stores for any specialty; but I have never heard it said that the merchant claims the *right* to force his clients to change their shopping methods.

The author poses some strange questions:[14] "Do the modern forms of salaried contract give a larger role to justice?" He does not believe that we are on the right path to the solution: "the procedures of remuneration (rewards or profit sharing) are only some of the numerous means used by the industrialist to lower his sale price." It would be truly strange for the head of an industry to work to increase them! Insofar as I can understand what Rist says, what is disturbing is that the same effort would always be less paid, which is contrary to justice. Should the master be similar to our Heavenly Father who rewards his children according to an eternal rule?

Since capitalist fatality does not resolve the question of justice, the professors will have to intervene,[15] and the author manifests the hope[16] that we can "come to a system in which new profits, when we will have an increase in productivity, will be distributed more equitably." Such language is criminal, since there are things that a law professor should never say and which ought to be left to professors of rhetoric. The law is not composed of wishes but of rules that are preconstituted. When we do not know what rule to propose and justify, the jurist cannot promise that he will perhaps find it tomorrow. The law is not a program of philanthropic financiers.

Awaiting the discovery of the famous solution, Rist thinks that "the solid doctrinal ground on which the working class can and should rally today is that of a minimum wage for every profession. This is both the simplest and surest *theory*." Since it is a theory and it is on solid doctrinal ground, it would have been easy to provide some justification. Rist gives us none. In the program for the French Workers' Party the clause on the minimum wage was introduced over Marx's objections: in 1881 Joffrin did not want this demand to figure in his electoral manifesto presented to the Paris Municipal Council. It gave rise to a lively debate during which the paper *Prolétaire* recalled that Marx had said that the minimum wage was a scientific absurdity. Guesde did not deny Marx's assertion.[17]

If we want to understand the problem, we must examine the sentiments behind this demand for a minimum wage. It is very popular in England and that is most natural: the men who wish to gain the confidence of the workers of this country, workers who do not like to change their habits, could not choose a better theme. For Rist, modern industry presents this disturbing aspect:[18] "the worker is forced even despite himself to provide a certain energy." But the day on which this situation will have ceased, capitalism will no longer have any reason for being, and it will be pushed *from forced cooperation to free cooperation.* We have not yet come to the point at which men *accept through reason* the fundamental law of their nature: the law of the progressive increase of labor.[19]

The savage wants only free time. It is enough for a person to enter a factory to see that, if the boss did not employ a thousand ruses to accelerate production, work would progress very slowly. The failure of numerous producer cooperatives derives from the fact that their members believe in being able to rest from time to time. In those that succeed, labor is more ardent than in privately owned workshops. The great work of capitalism is not only material. It should not only bequeath powerful productive forces to socialism; it should leave a new man who has finally understood labor. Everything capitalism does to urge the workers on is a gain for socialism, whatever the opinions of ethical theorists or of the politicians always ready to encourage sloth.[20]

Notes

1. Cf. *Saggi di critica del marxismo*, pp. 194–96.
2. Marx, *Capital* (Modern Library ed.).
3. Paul Bureau, *L'association de l'ouvrier au profit du patron* (Paris: A. Rousseau, 1899), p. 32. This book cannot be too highly recommended; the question dealt with here has been definitely examined. The author displays the sureness of view of the jurist, the great knowledge of the economist, and the perspicacity of the observer. The professors of our official faculty do not resemble Paul Bureau who is a professor in the Catholic faculty in Paris.
4. Paul Bureau, *L'association de l'ouvrier,* pp. 33-34.
5. In 1843 the administration relied on this provision to maintain that the participation in the profits inaugurated by Leclaire was illegal. "The worker should remain entirely free to fix and regulate his salary and should not come to an agreement with the boss; it is this toward which M. Leclaire tends today. . . . Through profit sharing, the worker binds himself to the master beyond a year, which is prohibited by article 16 of the law of 22 Germinale of the year XI." Report cited by Roger Merlin, *Le métayage et la participation aux bénéfices* (Paris: Chaix, 1900), p. 343.
6. Jurisprudence allows a domestic to obligate himself to serve someone until the latter's death; consequently there exist numerous testimonial dispositions.
7. Kant, *Metaphysical Elements of Justice,* trans. John Ladd (Indianapolis: Bobbs-Merrill, 1965) p. 63.
8. Frédéric Le Play, *La réforme sociale en France* (Paris: H. Plon, 1864), Vol. II, p. 89. He points out some "intelligent establishments witness to the piety and devotion of the ancestors [which] put within everyone's reach, *above*

possession, worship, private instruction, health services, and moral recreation." Cf. *Saggi di critica del Marxismo*, p. 357.

9. Pecqueur, *Théorie nouvelle d'économie sociale* (Paris: Capelle, 1842), pp. 411–12.
10. It is difficult to read this passage without thinking of many Marxist writings where the same idea is developed. I have been struck by the analogies that exist between this doctrine of Pecqueur and a passage in the *Manifesto* where living labor is juxtaposed to accumulated labor.
11. P. Bureau, *L'association*, p. 122.
12. David Schloss, *Les modes de rémunération du travail* (Paris: Giard & Brière, 1902), p. xliv.
13. Ibid., p. xvii.
14. Ibid., pp. xxvi–xxvii.
15. This intervention is justified by reason of intelligibility. Today "the new redistributions are made solely under the pressure of unconscious forces." Ibid., p. xliii. An intellectual could not do otherwise than to rebel against this.
16. Ibid., p. xli.
17. Cf. *Egalité* (15 January 1882), and an article by Malon in the *Revue Socialiste* (January 1887). It seems to me that Guesde embraced this clause in the Workers' Party program because of the great influence Lassalle's writing had had on him.
18. Schloss, *Les modes de rémuneration*, p. xlii.
19. Proudhon forcefully insisted on this law whose importance appears to me greater every day.
20. We should mistrust what is found in the official documents in regard to labor. Several years ago the working day was reduced to eight hours in the workshops in the post office; it was said that an experiment had proven that productivity had not diminished at all; but ever since that time the facts are in full contradiction with that "experiment." I believe that the same thing could be said of all "experiments" of the same kind made in all state workshops.

CHAPTER NINE

We should now inquire as to why reasonable men like Charles Rist can maintain such obviously unreasonable ideas of the kind I have examined. Causes of a general order contribute to this unreasonableness, causes that also act to push socialism toward new doctrines.

1. Marxist ideas assumed *specialization* and *uprootedness* in the working class. Workers did not feel any difficulty in going from one type of work to another,[1] from one city to another. Moreover, it was assumed that capitlalism was so rich, daring, and clever that nothing would stand in its way for a long time. When the worker can thus choose his boss without too much difficulty, the corporative idea disappears rapidly in him. It therefore does not appear to have any influence in America where these three conditions are found realized to a great extent. It is completely different when opportunities for work are not certain: then (a) the corporative and local idea appears or (b) the idea of bonds that connect the worker to his workshop emerges. These two ideas never disappeared in any part of Europe in Marx's time. In England the corporative idea retained all its forcefulness in certain trades, notably shipbuilding. Marx seized on *corporative claims* to transform them into *class demands*, but he thereby went infinitely beyond the English point of view as contemporary experience demonstrates: no country rejects Marxism more than England.

The workers show in many ways that they believe they are attached to their workshop by an undefined bond. They therefore claim that strikes do not break the labor contract, that the owner is *legally* bound to take them back, and that no one has the right to come and substitute himself for him.[2] Departing from this observation, some clever bosses have dreamed up various means of giving a more regular form to these ties so as to increase the power of discipline. Many paternalistic institutions arise from this: profit sharing[3] and finally the famous workshop councils.[4] All this results in creating the idea that the worker has a certain right over the enterprise.

2. There is a completely different kind of idea that derives from feudal concepts. The human mind has a tendency to explain authority according to a theory analogous to that of feudal regimes. There is nothing sur-

prising in this because we know that the feudal system is found among a large number of barbarian peoples. The man of the people willingly assimilates authority and property, and this leads democracy to bizarre ideas. Thus one finds it quite natural that a deputy or mayor not re-elected to office should receive compensation; he could not be deprived of his authority without his "acquired rights" being taken into account. To many people it seems strange that the French Revolution, having surrounded the authorities with elective councils or rather having rendered them elective, did not establish an analogous regime in business.

In 1838 Pecqueur gave a precise formulation to this thinking: he said[5] that "the mode of election and competition which is so fruitful and so social" had been applied so far only in political and administrative matters; that "election is in our political customs, in the general tendencies in Europe and in modern civilization" and is "the great vehicle of regulatory power of the enlightened and wealthy classes"; that similar means should be applied to industry as to politics. He imagined that no business would delay in transforming itself into societies of share-holding corporations: "Representative government will be the form of industrial economy as it is of political economy. There will be elections in the factory as there are elections in associations, on social grounds as well as political grounds."[6] Elections will have to be connected to the capacity of the taxpayer as the liberals of the time demanded. Finally, he hoped that they would succeed in forming a curia of universal suffrage and in admitting into the assembly of shareholders delegates "in charge of representing the workers more or less as the Third Estate once did with two other bodies constituting the Estates General."

Pecqueur's projects could appear perfectly reasonable in the period in which they were published, at a time in which people did not yet know—as they do today—the vices of parliamentarianism. These ideas have been revived today by one of those false philanthropists who, having considerable wealth, wants to become a benefactor to humanity —though being an unbearable tyrant to all those obliged to submit to his will. The Count of Chambrun, who, having had the good fortune to marry a colossally rich woman, and deciding to become a celebrity, created the Musée Social to defend this conception of constitutionalist industry.[7]

It did not have immediately much success, but today the Musée Social provides ideas to the Ministry of Commerce. This has been the principal and possibly paradoxical result of Millerand's ministry. This influence was quite noticeable when the Association for the Legal Protection of Workers was organized. The Catholic politicians succeeded in obtaining

French membership in an association in which the Holy See was treated as a government.[8] *La Rivista internazionale di scienze sociali e discipline ausiliarie* celebrated this event as very important, and not without reason (August 1900, p. 658, and December 1900, p. 520). We therefore should not be surprised if the ideas of the Musée Social are often found in official French publications.

3. Modern industry is based on mines and railroads. These two types of enterprise are formed by stocks and administered by bureaucratic hierarchies. They have generally organized pension services for workers and employees. French railways and mines are state concessions. The word *concession* has two distinct meanings; but the public pays no heed to these distinctions. For the mass the word *concession* consists of something feudal and one imagines rather freely in the parliamentary world (in which the notions are completely primitive) that the state has preserved a kind of eminent domain in such a way as to be able to legislate in favor of workers and employees. A law has already been passed on the pension funds for miners, and a bill has been submitted to the Senate benefiting railway workers.

Until 1867 limited liability corporations could not be established in France without government authorization and were subject to surveillance. These regulations, written for the purpose of protecting the public against excessively audacious financiers, still allow for the application of the feudal notion of concessions and for regarding them as fiefs on which the concedent preserves a right of wide surveillance. We understand, therefore, how the idea of proposing a law of compulsory profit-sharing in corporations could have arisen. In 1892 a bill was presented by Naquet, who later, as administrator of a dynamite corporation, had to settle very serious accounts with legal authorities and who today gives doctrinal advice on socialism.[9]

Theoretically, the limited liability corporation is governed by the stockholders, but in fact, under normal operating corporations, these stockholders are only stockholders with a variable income. Everything depends on the chief officers[10] and a few of the very largest stockholders. And especially in the railways these officers are content to exert their influence to procure advancement or gratuities to their white-collar protégés. The people who deal with the "higher social economy" do not know any of this, and believe that *reason* is produced in the general assembly (just as it is assumed it is produced in the academy). They regard wages like shares of interest and therefore, if the company agents are coparticipants, they are like stockholders. One is impelled to ask oneself why they would not have any influence over services.

Some wishful thinkers devoid of any knowledge of business, would like the workers to send delegates to the general assembly. Undoubtedly they assume that in these assemblies the stockholders really discuss the true interests of society. They would be quite surprised if they knew how things unfold there. Someone else, more practical, would like labor leaders to have over administration an influence analogous to that of the large stockholders. It seems that the directors of the large associations of miners and railroad employers work toward this purpose. Basly seems to have succeeded, and presently he holds the miners under his authority, not so much as deputy and mayor of Lens but as influential personality in the mining commission leadership.

There are very few writers who dare give a clear expression of their thought. This last system is presented to us as one in which a new authority is imposed on the workers. This authority acts in its own interest as a manifestation of the emancipation of labor! The fiction, the eternal deceit which mistakes the boss elected by a group of people who come together for some common interest[11] for the representative of the masses is here produced in all its glory. Whoever does not want to be taken in by appearances and wants to get to the bottom of things recognizes that all the formulas of present-day socialists are in contradiction with Marxist theory. Undoubtedly these formulas can be reconciled with nebulous declamations on the class struggle. But when we try to give juridical expression to the economic bases of contemporary ideas, we see that they presuppose a *tight solidarity between the capitalist and his workers*. The idea of the sale of labor power is abandoned by all those who claim to be adapting socialism to the conditions of practical life.

We end up with a type of state socialism[12] which has as its purpose giving guarantees to workers or transforming them into bureaucrats. About twenty years ago, Paul Brousse, Bakunin's old friend,[13] caused a great uproar in France by claiming the need to push wage earners into the bureaucracy before reaching[14] "the still unknown state which will be brought about, for the producers, by the common ownership or social appropriation of the means of production." He maintained that his projects for the organization of public services greatly surpassed the "utopianism" of Marx,[15] and he was not far from regarding Marx as a beginner compared to himself. Guesde violently attacked Brousse, and rightly so this time. But presently socialism has rapidly evolved in the Broussist direction—Brousse could boast of having given as long ago as 1874 to the Brussels International Congress a formula which requires no changes today (*Petite République*, 22 December 1902). Belgian socialism has for a long time adopted Brousse's opinions. Vandervelde, who at the International Congress established himself as Doctor of the Class

Struggle, has no other ideas than those he has taken from Brousse and from De Paepe.

It has often been announced that a rapid solution to the problem of capitalist anarchy was needed,[16] and this solution was a system of public services which anyone can understand. In their 1883 writings on the Workers' Party program, Guesde and Lafargue proclaimed that they did not intend that industries wrung from the capitalists would be exploited bureaucratically. They demanded that they be restored as corporations which included workers as stockholders. It is clear that this is utopian: it means entrusting the discount rate of the Bank of France to clerks and office apprentices or railway tariffs to an assembly of employees and manual workers! Brousse must have considered such a program with great pity and must have been persuaded the future would prove him right.

It would not appear that the situation is very different from that of 1851 when Proudhon asked how one could operate workers' companies, to which he wished to entrust the railways. "The laboring class," he said,[17] "is still by the narrowness of its view and its inexperience in business incapable of carrying on such large interests as those of commerce and great industry [and in consequence cannot attain its true destiny]. Men are lacking in the lower class as well as in the democracy. We have seen it all too clearly for three years. Those who have reached the greatest celebrity as officials are the last to merit the confidence of the people in matters relating to labor and social economy. Ask the Parisian associations, enlightened by their experience, what they think today of the crowd of little great men who recently waved the banner of fraternity before them." Proudhon thought it necessary to appeal to members of the bourgeoisie and to offer them honorable positions; "There is not an exact and capable clerk who would not leave a precarious position to accept an appointment in a great association."

Proudhon was aware of the unpopularity of his program, since he continued with this declaration: "Let the workers consider it; let them get rid of a mean and jealous spirit; there is room for everybody in the sunlight of the Revoluton. They have more to gain by such self-conquest than by the interminable and always destructive squabbles inflicted on them by their leaders, who are sincere no doubt, but incompetent." This situation should, according to Proudhon, last only for a short time, as long as it would have been necessary for the apprenticeship of leaders arising from the proletariat.

Enlightened by the many failures experienced by workers' corporations, numerous socialists think today that workers are incapable of creating a bureaucracy themselves and of attracting experienced businessmen to it. They think that popular sovereignty is the most beautiful thing in the world, but with the qualification that it manifest itself by means of the absolute authority of leaders who by some means or other have officially become their representatives. The bureaucracy should be reformed, but meanwhile we must make use of this great traditional mechanism. It will be rendered docile to the impulses of government, changing personnel where necessary. But preserving the old artibrary authority that it holds.

In 1883 Guesde[18] criticized the system of public services for consolidating the hierarchy, and reproducing and "aggravating the entire monstrosity of the salariat." Since our state socialists hope to be at the head of this bureaucracy and to be in a position to utilize it for their own interests, Guesde's consideration is not the sort of criticism that frightens them very much.

In the capitalist workshop, the worker experiences only an accidental, fragmentary, one might almost say apparent, subjugation. When he has accomplished what was entailed in the contract for the sale of his labor power, he is free. Without this freedom no socialism is possible. In the public services, submission would have to be permanent and total (we can call it "real"). Every day the socialist journals remind functionaries that they are obliged to act in the way the government proclaims desirable and combine this with denunciations of bureaucrats whose wives go to church too often and send their children to Catholic schools!

In this system man must be the faithful vassal of government. But would it not be, once again, an old feudal concept that would reappear? In 1851 Proudhon advised the workers to take technical directors from the bourgeoisie; now the socialist bourgeoisie wishes to persuade the workers to take it as master. The investiture that these masters will receive from universal suffrage will make them more terrible lords than the present-day capitalists against whom so much antagonism is directed.

Notes

1. Proudhon regarded an education directed to this end as an ideal. "Nothing prevents the apprenticeship of the worker being directed in such a way that he embraces the totality of the industrial system instead of choosing a particular case." *De la Justice dans la révolution et dans l'église* (Paris: Garnier Frères, 1858), Vol. II, p. 336.
2. Denis Poulot tells us that in his youth the foremen of machine workshops usually did not find a worker who consented to finish the work begun by one of those greatly renowned workers who were called *grosses culottes*. These men claimed to have the right to enjoy themselves when it pleased them. *Question sociale: le sublime*, 3rd ed. (Paris: Marpon & Flammarion, 1887), p. 151.

3. De Courcy strongly encouraged the insurance companies to practice profit sharing, which he mentioned as a means of keeping the agent tied to the company.

4. In the monograph of Julian Weiler on *La Grève de Mariemont et les conseils de conciliation et d'arbitrage* (Paris: Guillaumin, 1889), we see that these councils have been formed *solely* for the purpose of rendering discipline easier.

5. Pecqueur, *Des intérêts du commerce, de l'industrie, de l'agriculture et de la civilisation en général sous l'influence de l'application de la vapeur*, Vol. II, pp. 241–45.

6. Pecqueur's language is rather bizarre; political economy is here the political administration of the country; the "political grounds" are the circumscribed areas (departments, districts and municipalities) which form an electoral unity.

7. It is not said whether he did something to constitutionalize the Baccarat glassworks of which he was one of the major shareholders.

8. A congress was held at Colonia in 1902; the annals of the *Musée Social* announced that "the governments of France, Belgium, Hungary, Italy, the Vatican, Sweden and Switzerland were represented" (October 1902):337. The Italian government undoubtedly believed it had to *imitate* once more the foolishness of our own government.

    Owing to this rather intimate union between the Ministry of Commerce and the *Musée Social*, we encounter many members of the clerical party in the juries of the 1900 Exposition; when the government opposed the services rendered by certain religious congregations that it wanted to suppress, the answer given made much of the high rewards that were granted to them by this jury, nominated, it was said, by an anti-clerical government! It is possible that the *Musée Social* judged it prudent not to draw any more attention to its alliance with the Ministry of Commerce, because in its publications I found no more information on Congresses after 1902.

9. He is one of the oracles of reformist socialism, and an organ of eternal justice.

10. As a result of quite special circumstances which depend on the recruitment of these high personnel, we find that the high officials of the French railways make it "an entirely military point of honor" to defend the company interests. When we can attend the discussions between these agents and the bureaucrats charged with defending the interests of the state against the railways, we are quite surprised to find that this same point of honor is not found among the state officials.

11. According to the *Voix du peuple* (the organ of the French Confederation of Labor), the Basly's union included four percent of the miners (18 January 1903). This did not prevent Jaurès from identifying Basly with the "mining proletariat."

12. It seems to me most important to classify the different forms of state socialism; the more "pure" is that which is conceived on the model of the Prussian bureaucracy and which allows no external restraint. In France we are always dealing with a mixed system in which professional politicians play a greater role.

13. It can seem paradoxical that an ex-anarchist has become an apostle of such reformism; it seem that Bakunin was surrounded by men who were filled with

memories of 1793 rather than by true socialists; as their predecessors had been good employees for Napoleon, so they were not slow in proposing as an ideal the conquest of public offices.

14. Cited by Jules Guesde in his monograph: *Services publiques et socialisme* (Paris: Oriol, 1884), republication, p. 31.

15. In an obituary article on Marx. *Prolétaire* (24 March 1883). Bernstein notes this fact in his lecture to Berlin students on 17 May 1901. Cf. Sorel, *Saggi di critica del Marxismo*, p. 145.

16. I cannot resist the temptation of citing some curious observations of Jaurès on this subject: "This proves, once again, that today's anarchic regime of production cannot assure the workers any guarantee. . . . The crisis of arms manufacturing is only one episode of the great capitalist crisis that is today manifested in one place, tomorrow in another." *Petite République* (12 June 1902). This crisis has nothing imputable to capitlism; it results from the hurriedness with which the government wished to transform its rifles. It has been aggravated by politicians who, for electoral reasons, delayed the beginning of discharge (military). On the observations on the influence of the state in France on crises cf. *Saggi di critica del Marxismo*, p. 371.

17. P.J. Proudhon, *General Idea of the Revolution in the Nineteenth Century*, trans. John Beverly Robinson, pp. 223-24.

18. Guesde, *Services publiques*, p. 32.

PART III

Cartels and Their Ideological Consequences

CHAPTER ONE

Public opinion is nowadays greatly concerned with cartels and trusts. But these institutions are discussed in a haphazard and often mysterious way, impressing the imagination of ignorant people with large numbers. Questions of this type can only inspire descriptive monographs; but this cannot satisfy the curiosity of the majority of readers. We are asking what influence these new ways of doing business can have on the future of society. Such questions are evidently insoluble, but one can try to find out how new conceptions of economic order are formed and how socialist ideas are transformed under their influence. This is all I propose to outline in the present chapter. Let us begin by establishing several distinctions necessary for understanding the various aspects in which the question is posed.

1. The producers are always lamenting the profits that commerce makes at their expense. Their claims are not always without foundation, since speculators or even simple brokers frequently have profits superior to those of the heads of enterprises. The buyers place manufacturers in competition with one another and are sometimes able to push their prices down to such a low level that manufacturers are exposed to working at a loss. The public only benefits from a part of this dip in prices. The producers can defend themselves by means of agreements limiting their competition in many different ways. These various procedures are based on a very old and popular concept which can be called "goodwill." The merchant has long had the habit of regarding the clientele of an establishment as a value subject to sale. When one merchant takes the place of another, he must pay not only for the merchandise that is in the store, but also for the privilege that seems to be yielded by his predecessor, the "right to the clientele." In his comedy *Monsieur de Pourceaugnac*, Molière has a doctor say: "His illness . . . is a piece of furniture which belongs to me and that I count among my effects" (act II, scene 2). This is a comic exaggeration of a very old practice.[1]

If we consider economics under this aspect of a competition for "ownership" of clientele, it is easy to understand that many agreements can be made for the purpose of limiting the pressure the buyer exerts on the producers. These producers can determine the areas in which each will operate; they can agree not to sell below a certain minimum price which is fixed from time to time according to the circumstances of the market; finally they can have an understanding to reduce their production, and this is a very practical measure because if the shops are overstocked, no obligation will be worth much outside of the imperious necessity of selling.

All these agreements arise from the idea of property, but they can lead to consequences that go much beyond private law. The point of passage to another regime is often difficult to determine. The courts have often found it difficult to decide whether agreements among producers constituted a restraint on the freedom of labor or were merely simple combinations of legitimate interests. The silk industry at Saint-Etienne gives us a curious example of this difficulty: after 1848 the manufacturers,[2] wanting to defend themselves against the demands of Parisian buyers, made an agreement which fixed payment and delivery. They were denounced and condemned as guilty of conspiracy. In 1894, after an industrial crisis, various manufacturers of velvet promised not to carry out certain labor below a certain price, so that they could retain workers whose wages were greatly reduced. In an opinion of 1 August 1900, the Court of Cassation recognized the legality of this agreement, because it applied to a limited category of textiles and would only have transitory application.

Here the agreement was reduced to a level between proprietors without general importance and consequently not calling for the control of justice. This agreement was judged to belong to private law, because the industrialists did not cede an eminent domain over their property to a corporation and thus did not sell what was no longer in commerce. After the French Revolution, it was necessary for the land to be free of feudal rules and for industry to be free of them. The same principle applies in both cases. But this principle is much clearer in the first than in the second. This theory of freedom is made in the general interest of consumers, so that they may benefit from all the inventions of individual genius which were shackled in a thousand ways.

2. The cartel at Longwy shows us another fundamental system based on completely different ideas. Some cast-iron producers, closely unified because of competition, began to share their means of commercial activity to gain an important place in the national market. Constructed after the Franco-Prussian War by means of modest local resources, the Lorraine blast furnaces had great difficulty in attaining prosperity. Agreements among a certain number of establishments were made in 1876 for the purpose of increasing sales at low cost. The results having been excellent, the number of adherents of the cartel increased. The

Longwy establishment does not find itself in a position to dictate laws to its clientele; on the contrary, it is frequently obliged to make sacrifices to preserve the clientele. Mostly it prevents buyers from taking advantage of the precarious situation of certain foundries to obtain unreasonably low prices. During the period of high prices that the metallurgical industry went through in 1899[3] when cast-iron was worth from 100 to 110 francs abroad, the cartel carried out its contracts faithfully and priced its goods from 62 to 65 francs to its domestic clientele. When the decline of prices occurred, those that had concluded contracts during the period of peak scarcity raised all sorts of difficulties not to keep their obligations. The cartel did not dare to be too demanding and compromised.

This moderation seemed strange to many: to compromise on the high prices when decline occurs after having delivered at low prices during the increase looks foolish, especially since in Germany[4] the cartels were very demanding and encumbered the factories with often unusable cast iron. Villerupt Laval-Dieu, a member company of the cartel, protested and denied that the association has the right to modify contracts. This claim was natural inasmuch as the complainant transformed part of its cast iron and therefore had to look askance at something that favored the steel manufacturers, who were competitors. The Briey Tribunal, with a judgment of 14 February 1902, judged the Villeraupt Laval-Dieu claims to be wrong. The judgment states that the cartel had compromised "in presence of an absolute necessity and for the purpose of conserving the clientele of its members, that the purpose of the cartel as it was conceived by its founders is, in origin, to conserve a 'faithful clientele,' and that it would be to go against its purpose if it had exasperated its customers by demanding a rigorous fulfillment of the contracts they had declared impossible to execute."

"Is this disinterestedness?" asks Paul de Rousiers.[5] No, it is self-interest rightly understood, it is the enlightened concern for keeping, first of all, a prosperous clientele. It would probably be more precise to say that the Longwy cartel was much less concerned with immediate benefits than with the future, and that it was therefore more industrial than commercial. The spirit of the commercial man is always close to that of the speculator who risks everything on the decision to obtain quick returns, counting on chance to arrange something for the future. Industrialists always think of ways to aggrandize their means of activity and voluntarily sacrifice today's profits for tomorrow's prosperity. The Longwy cartel is not the lord of the marketplace:[6] in 1899 French production of cast iron was 2,567,000 tons, of which the department of Meurthe and Moselle alone accounted for 1,565,000 and the cartel sold 454,000 of it, or 58,000 more than in 1898. At a given time it was almost the only seller of cast iron in France insofar as the great establishments absorbed local production. But when the crisis passed, competition resumed.

3. In Germany we also find sales bureaus; but they resemble the Longwy cartel only in form. The German cartels claim to dominate prices completely: "The German sales offices," says Paul de Rousiers,[7] "are a means of ensuring discipline in the syndicate, the result of the development commenced by the agreements. The German industrialists never felt the need to constitute a sales office for its own sake. On the contrary, it is a constraint to which they have subjected themselves to prevent the members from making agreements for the purpose of escaping their obligations. And they arrived at this conception only later and gradually. While the Longwy cartel goes back to 1876 . . . in Germany one had to await the year 1885 to find the first attempt to sell through a single agent. . . . The Longwy cartel has its self interest as its purpose, while the German sales bureaus are only means for attaining another end."

At Longwy they try to gain a respectable share of the market. In Germany they want to appropriate the market and govern it in an absolute way. We find ourselves placed on the ground of privileged corporations. The way of thinking of the defenders of the cartels leads them to view economic problems in political terms. For example, they say[8] "that according to the natural order" the selling price ought to consist in the cost of production increased by a slight profit; that the producers alone are able to determine these *necessary and legitimate* prices; that speculators claimed rights that belonged solely to the producers. Other times they speak[9] of establishing a wise industrial policy and placing production in exact relation with consumption. All their vain talk is based on the hypothesis that it is possible to create a beneficent authority in the economic order.

Thus we depart from private law which appears only at the origin of agreements. It is an object of general interest or of interest to the government that cartels have in mind. The organization of cartels is received with great enthusiasm among some men who call themselves conservatives and among others who call themselves socialists. From the feudal point of view, the cartels are *collective seigniories,* as were medieval communes. These seigniories have eminent domain, exercising police power over the economic areas belonging to them and receive duties from all those who must resort to their services. Democracy does not differ on this point from feudal thought as much as we might think. Rousseau conceived of the *Social Contract* as a recommendation to a collective seigniory. There is, he says[10] "the total alienation of each associate, together with all his rights, to the whole community." Every day we see discussed in France the question of knowing whether children belong to the family or to the state, or at least in what the state's eminent domain over children consists.

The difference between the feudal point of view and the democratic perspective could be minimal if modern democracy had not become unitary, while for Rousseau it was dispersed into many restricted groups in the medieval fashion. From this change of extension and internal organization there arise new tendencies which are so emphasized that we end up by no longer seeing the analogies that exist on the theory of power in feudal and democratic points of view. At present, what is especially impressive is that the feudal people uphold the need to abandon much initiative to the local economic barons, while our democrats are particularly disposed to abolish these forces to return centralized power to the state.

Many socialists view the progress of cartels with pleasure, because they think that the state will sometimes engage in struggle with these feudal powers, and that the state will be forced to destroy them to enlarge itself. Once the monarchy triumphed, its rule suppressed the abuses of the small lords and subjected the country to its equalitarian leveling. Such phenomena could be reproduced in the economy: the state would not have to create a communal economy itself; it would be already prepared, and it would only have to adapt it.

It is therefore not surprising that various schools of socialism quite distant from one another are interested in cartels for reasons that have nothing to do with economics or affinity with their political opinions. From this result many questions that appear bizarre at first. As an example, we ask ourselves—what are the effects of cartels on consumers, on the salary of the workers, and on the future of the country? In a word, we ask whether cartels, in their special sphere, practice "good government," not requiring central state intervention, and whether we can allow them to function under a decentralized economico-political system without any control. Such questions would be impossible if there were not something of a very strictly political nature in the cartels.

The German industrial cartels find themselves in direct contact with the government for the support that they give its foreign policy. The sugar cartel has been particularly cited as the most curious model of this system. Before the Brussels convention, various European states awarded prizes for the export of sugar to facilitate the access of national producers to the London market. In Germany this legislation was reenforced by a cartel. The refiners guaranteed the manufacturers a minimum price on the Magdeburg market or for all the sugar used in internal consumption. This price was very profitable (about 32 francs per hundred kilograms). They agreed to sell refined sugar for between 68,10 and 73,10 francs (including the 25 franc tax). On 1 August 1901, the difference between refined sugar for export and that destined for internal consumption imposed on the natives a "tax" of 16,35 francs per hundred kilograms, which the refiners and manufacturers shared. Assuming that these figures can be taken as average, it has been calculated[11] that the German population had paid 100 million to the sugar industry and that half of this enormous sum was earned by the refiners. It is very likely that these calculations are exaggerated, but it is certain that Germany had paid dearly for the wealth of its sugar industry.[12]

Often in Germany a cartel gives rewards for exports to the industries that transform the material the cartel produces. Paul de Rousiers cites[13] various cases of this type: in 1888 the rolling mills subsidized the export of metal wire; in 1892 and 1893 the coal producers association came to the aid of the foundries of Westfalia; Sayous tells us[14] of the formation of a Dusseldorf office in 1902 for the regulation of export rewards: "For the contracts carried out in the second trimester of that year, the coal association paid 1,50 marks for every ton used; the cast iron association 2,50 marks not including the sum promised by the coal association; for wrought steel and iron beams, the total return is 10 marks per ton." This system of rewards seems destined to be consolidated[15] after having been adopted by temporary right to clear the market.

The results of this policy of export at any cost have more than once been paradoxical. It has been shown[16] that German builders are better off by going to Holland to buy exported tin and then bringing it back to Germany paying tariff duties. The tin sold in Holland for 180 marks, while it sold to nationals for 200 marks at the station at Essen.[17] Many facts of the same type have been noted in American trusts: the native consumer must provide all the profits and export is made at cost and even below. This system is too closely connected to the policies of the German Empire not to continue to develop in that country. Not long ago Russia demanded[18] that an international agreement intervene to prevent the cartels from subsidizing exports. This proposal belongs to the category of superlatively civilized projects of this government which is so concerned with justice. Russia had not, on the other hand, adhered to the Brussels convention on sugar, whose object was to abolish the sugar cartels.

We ask if this policy will not come to a general disillusion analogous to that produced by sugar. The large producing states have ended by recognizing that the best thing to do was to completely suppress the artificial system they had painfully created. But metallurgy and the sugar industry do not resemble each other in any way: sugar is manufactured more or less everywhere under identical conditions and is directed to the domestic economy which can have only a slow and regular progress; metallurgy is an industry subject to violent crises, an industry which must quickly satisfy large demands and which can find in newly developed countries unforeseen outlets when these are diminished in the normal clientele. Because of this uneven progress, export of metals cannot be supported by rewards voted by a parliament. It is necessary that commercial corporations be able to appreciate without delay the interest that a transaction presents and that they consent to necessary sacrifices to help the internal market.

The German cartels find themselves in conditions that, from this perspective, are inferior to those of the American trusts. However colossal they are, these trusts are managed like a small business placed in the hands of a single owner. The German cartels, especially in export agreements, can adapt much better to circumstances. But it does not seem impossible that the Germans will also obtain results allowing a sufficient independence to the central offices.

We do not always take sufficient account of psychological conditions in examining these problems, because we treat them more as political questions than commercial ones. Prestige plays a large role in getting orders from new countries. For example, there is no small advantage to the German rolling mills in having their series of iron beams accepted as scientific.[19] In order to compete against them in foreign markets, certain French mills have had to change their laminating cylinders. In Germany, as in the United States, the great preoccupation is to eliminate England. This is quite obvious in written works on this question of competition, in the midst of much oratory. The English have accumulated a great deal of wealth abroad, and this has for a long time given them the prestige that belongs to the wealthy merchant-usurer whom the poor peasant assumes has an intelligence often quite superior to his own. The English have long had an incontestable superiority from the point of view of mineral wealth. But on this point, America is in the process of greatly surpassing them, while, besides, the progress of science has worked to reduce these natural advantages because there is an ever-decreasing consumption of coal per ton of metal produced and because we now know how to exploit those mines that were heretofore difficult to utilize. The English builders have an advantage over those of the Continent because the large-scale manufacture of textiles began there long before it was ever thought of in Europe. They have been able to acquire a remarkable practice in the use of iron in machines and in building. Today they would be somewhat behind their competition because they have not kept abreast of the advances in science. Their steam engines and especially their locomotives no longer have the slightest reputation.

The Germans and Americans presently demonstrate an impressive awareness of the conditions of the modern struggle. They have understood the importance of the role of public works in the basis of prestige. The glory of Rome derived in large part from its aqueducts. The English contractors have left bad reputations everywhere they have gone; almost all the railways they have built have demonstrated the incompetence and often the improbity of their engineers. In mastering the Asian railways, the Germans propose to become the masters of commerce in that region. Americans sell bridges in British colonies at a more favorable rate than the English.

These two enterprising peoples even dare to try to bring competition to the country that was long the *terra classica* of all economic production. After the great engineers' strikes, American machines were introduced in England, and there is no doubt that they will end by occupying a predominant place despite the extreme repugnance felt by the English worker for changing something in his routine. Nowadays American capitalists find it easier to undertake operations in England than in their own country because they do not encounter as much competition that is enterprising and capable of following modern movement. Thus, in the area of electricity, the English have remained behind their rivals, and this inferiority is especially noteworthy since it was often the English who renewed the science of electricity during the nineteenth century. But it is foreigners who have understood the practical importance of their research.

The sacrifices the cartels may often make selling to the English consumers lower-priced products than those produced in England will not be lost for the future, since they constitute the best advertising imaginable for destroying the old prestige of British industry. Speaking only a few years ago in an Oxford lecture, Thorold Rogers joked about the fear produced by the invasion of German goods. Speaking of the semiembossed leather imported from Pomerania that came "to offer itself to the more skillful hands of the English worker," he said,[20] "I was happy to learn that a section of the German race had succeeded in inventing something besides metaphysics and advanced diplomas." It was on this biting tone and with such happy self-assurance that spoke one of the most eminent representatives of English liberalism! The English liberals find it hard to believe that their island is not predestined to produce the best things that other countries vainly try to imitate. Just as Gladstone is, in their eyes, the greatest genius of modern times, so for them British industry is incomparable.[21] Thus the English are asleep, lulled by the tales that flatter their pride. Filon said that it is a "king people" that dies through its mania for greatness and no longer wants to work (*Débats*, 19 June 1900).

Notes

In this part I make extensive use of the excellent work of Paul de Rousiers: *Les Syndicats industriels de producteurs en France et à l'étranger* (Paris: A. Colin, 1901). We must be highly mistrustful of the majority of the publications devoted to these questions: one finds more nonsense than reason in them.

1. In most of France, doctors are paid *a lot* for their practice (when they retire or leave).
2. L. Reybaud, *Etudes sur le régime des manufactures; Condition des ouvriers en soie* (Paris: Michel-Lévy Frères, 1859), pp. 231–32.
3. De Rousiers, *Les syndicats industriels*, pp. 222 and 237.
4. Ibid., pp. 228–30.
5. Ibid., pp. 228.
6. Ibid., pp. 218–21.
7. Ibid., pp. 206–8.
8. Congress on Grain Sales held at Versailles in 1900, p. 118.
9. Georges Villain, *Le fer, la houille, et la métallurgie* (Paris: A. Colin, 1901), p. 181.
10. J.J. Rousseau, *The Social Contract*, Book I, ch. 6.
11. *Journal des économistes* (December 1901):354. At that time, unrefined sugar went for 25,25 francs on the Magdeburg market.
12. It has also been calculated that in 1900 the steel wire cartel lost 878,000 marks on its foreign sales and earned 1,700,000 marks in Germany. It is always an atrociously expensive system. *Journal des économists* (September 1904):472.
13. De Rousiers, *Les syndicats industriels*, p. 176.
14. Sayous, *La crise allemande de 1900–1902: Le charbon, le fer, et l'acier* (Paris: L. Larose, 1903), p. 287.
15. Ibid., pp. 349–52.
16. *Journal des économistes* (April 1902):109.
17. Molinari notes that the German manufacturers have moved their factories to Holland because of this situation. *Journal des économistes* (September 1904): 474.
18. Sayous, *La crise allemande*, p. 287.
19. De Rousiers, *Les syndicats industriels*, p. 261.
20. Thorold Rogers, *The Economic Interpretation of History*.
21. In England one cannot come to admit that the admirality cannot find good domestic boilers and is obliged to buy them in France.

CHAPTER TWO

In the preceding chapter we have seen how the cartels are tied strictly to their governments' foreign policy, and how they constitute a type of reenforcement for protectionism. They are unable to practice the system of double pricing if they are not strongly defended by a customs tariff, which allows them to impose burdens licensed by legislators on their compatriots. Thus the cartels are auxiliary powers whose importance is enlarged or restricted by the state by means of its tariffs. According to many, this is an abnormal situation which should disappear on the day the public acquires a more complete knowledge of the natural order suitable to prosperous societies. Many fine souls think that the great unions (whether of bosses or of workers) should be formed without ever being subordinated to the actions of the state. "In themselves," says Paul de Rousiers,[1] "these unions are a normal manifestation of industrial freedom and the freedom of association." Only political abuses can make the unions oppressive. But can they be entirely determined by private law?

We shall now examine the question in a purely theoretical way and ask ourselves if the cartels depend solely on private law or if they are connected at some point to the general interests over which the state has custody. If it is so, it becomes difficult to admit the hypothesis of a complete separation between cartels and politics. To resolve this problem, we must go back to the economic conditions on which private law is based and to the considerations I have often presented on this mixture of wills that gives the economy an appearance of physical movement. When there is only chance involved in details, the whole would appear to be determined because each particular force is drowned in an ocean of forces independent of one another.

It is only in modern times that the economy has taken this form and has then been able to become scientific. But already in antiquity there were a few analogous phenomena: in the markets frequented by small peasants and country artisans, buying and selling ended up by combining in such a way as to produce average prices, around which all transactions were united. These markets were also courthouses, since the disputes relative to the operations of buying and selling had to be judged in an impersonal way and since, finally, many others had to be treated as well. There a truly abstract law was created, that is, obligations that did not recognize men except in their unique role of "accidental bearers of juridical rights." The concrete beings having continuity disappear: one is a lender one day, the next day he presents himself as a proprietor; a certain partialized farmer will become an artisan, farmer laborer, etc. There is no longer any continuity in the persona, which decomposes into a discontinuous succession of apparitions of small machines to which are attached certain labels designating the various roles they represent with various claims. The internal effusiveness of duration is suppressed, as Bergson's disciples say, and is substituted by movements regulated by several springs independent of one another. We pass to complete objectivity. Everything becomes automatic.

It is often said that Roman law owes its success to a quality of abstraction that renders it so perfectly fit to express the relations that exist in a mercantile society.[2] This law has pushed for the double principle of the analysis of actions and of the settlement of claims. One can even compare it, in certain old forms, to a mathematical operation. There are closely observed "functions of procedure" whose properties are known like those of mathematical functions.[3] One cannot proceed in a court of law if one is unable to represent the facts by means of these instruments. As in physics, one cannot resolve problems if one has not come to give to empirical laws a form which includes certain functions. The experimenter begins himself to anticipate a certain number of mathematical operations, among which one should be chosen. If he cannot, with a convenient approximation, employ functions that lend themselves well to calculation, his work remains useless.

Just as mathematical physics suppresses "physical causation,"[4] so the civil code of a mercantile society seeks to reduce everything to accounting considerations among men who meet without knowing one another except by the nickname given them momentarily by reason of the right they have over things. The tribunal is not concerned with knowing the consequences of the sentence being pronounced. This judgment will become mixed with the infinity of forces that act in the world, and its consequences disappear in the whole in the same way as do the consequences of these forces. We will have to avoid the desire to make a decision as a sovereign king would, judging one case after another with a certain feeling of equity. He will pronounce himself according to a reasoning, applying the ruling that was proposed to him in its most general sense.

Rarely can we know the true intent of the legislator. When this argument is invoked, it is only for the purpose of better understanding the power of the limits that are applied and in view of *determining the general direction*. One should not, with the pretext that one knows the true purpose of those who have drawn up the law, adopt irrational interpretations of the law. This procedure, which is often vaunted as legal progress, as an attenuation of excessively rigid rules, as "a socialist way of adjudication," can only produce the perversion of the average order the law aimed to create.[5]

To know the thought of legislators means knowing what, on average, would be the effect of a proposed regulation whose purpose is the general interest. There are cases in which the coincidences between this typical result and well-rendered judgment are poorly made. There can also be cases in which the result is completely opposite to what was expected. But this difference should not concern the judge, who is unconcerned with consequences, leaving the average sought to pure chance.

All this can be summarized in the following formula: the economy is the case of detail and apparent necessity in the whole; private law is "juridical blindness and mechanics." It is useless to say that, as in all human matters, this is true only to a certain degree; the legislator almost always allows the judge a certain right of judgment. The reliable magistrate uses this right prudently, but for the philosophy of private law, we must take the most absolute formulas to perceive the notion well.

To these two economic and juridical systems applied exactly to one another is juxtaposed everything that belongs to the farsightedness of a human reason that is perfectly enlightened and capable of understanding well, in every particular case, the conditions that correspond to the general interest. No philosopher has expressed more forcefully than Hegel the antitheses that exist between the economic realm of fatality and the domain in which the intelligent action of the state is exercised. According to Hegel's definition,[6] "the state is the social substance that has attained consciousness of itself." Earlier he said:[7] "The social substance as immediate or natural spirit is *the family;* the relative totality of reciprocal relations of individuals as independent persons contained in a general form, is *civil society*; the substance that has consciousness of itself as the unfolding spirit and forming an organic reality is the *state*." Civil society is economic society considered with the means of coercion that ensures its order. In it is found[8] the mechanics of necessity and the state appears here only as police. This Hegel calls the "external state." Here the generality is formal since it does not depend on an internal principal but on a legal constitution.

Vilfredo Pareto has regrouped a certain number of Hegelian formulae that at first sight seem repugnant and obscure, but which offer a satisfactory meaning when one reflects on the opposition that Hegel illuminated between the two modes of conceiving society. On the one hand, the economic world is a mass of particular forces, something like an organized nature retained in a figure by coercive forces; on the other hand, the state is a thinking being which wills and realizes rational goals.[9] For example, Hegel says: "The state is the reality of the moral Idea, the moral spirit as far as it is substantial will, apparent, clear to itself, that thinks itself and knows itself, and which fulfills what it knows in proportion to what it knows. . . . The state represents everything that is rational in itself and for itself. . . . The state in itself is the moral whole, the realization of liberty."

If this formula illuminates well the opposition of which I have spoken, it also has the grave disadvantage of tending to give to the will of the chief of state an exaggerated extension while it restricts the law too much. An old Catholic tradition compels us to consider that everything that relies on public law in some way is practiced by a delegation from the central power. Catholics always ask themselves whether the action whose outline appears in society is "legitimate"; and no power is legitimate except through its union with the regulatory center, in the same way that a priest is not truly acting in a priestly way if he is not in communion with the visible head of the church. When there is no explicit transmission of authority from the center to the outer regions, at least we need the prince's control and implicit consent. Enlarging the principles of pagan Rome, Christian Rome has made every organization that is not deeply unified very difficult to comprehend, and consequently we have a tendency to concentrate public law in the organization of the state.

Hegelian thought depends a great deal on the governmental ideas of the eighteenth century which found their complete expression in the monarchy of Frederick II, whose influence on all modern political theory is enormous. It is a secular and quasi-atheistic renovation of papal government. All information should reach the prince, and all initiative should originate with him or be in close contact with his initiatives. Frederick is Prussia who recognizes its path and follows it with constancy and wisdom; Frederick is the Hegelian state.

By virtue of unitary theory, it is said: Education can be practiced only by virtue of a delegation from the governor or at least with his permission. Religious associations cannot be created to form a Catholic state opposed to the secular state. If the latter accepts them, it is because it needs their services and can transform them into useful auxiliaries. If the government is not yet at the stage of giving education and assistance to all those who need them, the government can resort to these associations but treat them only as agents. If there are too few parish priests, not enough to preach to everybody, we can permit the existence of monastic orders of preachers, but these would only be tolerated, and they could never exist by virtue of law. Our ancestors believed that no association should be tolerated in a free country, and the law of 18 August 1792 applied this principle, suppressing every teaching, charitable, or pietistic congregation, be they secular, ecclesiastical, or lay. There must remain no obstacle to the manifestation of the general will as conceived by Jean-Jacques Rousseau. When we abandon these old ideas to place ourselves on the ground of factual observation and philosophic studies of law, we recognize that there are things that do not fall into the domain of private law. There are those that escape this mixture, where the particular will is cancelled and where, as a consequence, the imprint of a persistent will can be recognized. When an end is pursued with conscience and perseverance by a group that is *not* confronted by an antagonistic force sufficiently numerous or powerful to drown the group's actions in the ocean of actions; when there remains a trace capable of being related to the personality of the actor, then we pass into public law, at least in part. We are no longer in the presence of an accidental and impersonal phenomon, of a fragmentary action which does not have an author, so to speak, since juridical masks pass successively over a thousand representations. We know that there is a determined author that acts according to a plan; his movements would announce his personality, even when he does not make it known to us; we always avoid designating him with a legal sign, we give him his name.

The adversaries of freedom of instruction have observed that in France schools can no longer be the object of provisions of private law and that it is wrong to speak of freedom in this subject. Aside from the state institutions, they say, there no longer exists anything but a tiny number of private institutions, and that these are still in full decline. Very soon we will be confronted with a choice between state colleges and schools on the one hand and those of the religious institutions on the other. These latter, being animated by the same spirit obeying a single authority and modeling themselves on each other, constitute in fact a single organization—the teaching church.

There is no mixing of several antagonistic forces in this competition. There are only two currents left: those of the church and that of the state, which remain indefinitely separate. Vainly would the houses founded by secular priests or even by lay Catholics pretend to constitute themselves outside the system and claim their freedom. The universities answer that their authorities wear masks and that they are nothing but branches of the congregations. Whatever their label, their adversaries claim to be able to give them their true name (the congregation) and treat them according to the nature revealed by this true name. From this it comes about that, after having abolished the schools belonging to religious congregations, the French government is on the verge of establishing a monopoly on education.

The question of associations could not be brought back completely to problems of private law. For a long time French laws have contained the belief that it is not possible to allow limited liability corporations to be formed freely. The law demanded a decree emanating as a consequence of an opinion of the Conseil d'Etat, and a government commission was charged with supervising their direction. This question gave rise to a profound discussion at the time of the editing of Napoleon Bonaparte's commercial code. It was thought that the bankruptcy of such corporations had too great an influence over public credit and over the wealth of many individuals to consider their existence irrelevant to the public good. After the great capitalist combinations multiplied and liquid capital was readily available in the country, it was no longer thought useful to treat limited liability corporations as exceptional institutions, and government is no longer concerned with them. They are powers dissimilar and numerous enough that their effects are countervailing. They can be treated according to simple regulations of private law.

The last law passed in France on nonprofit associations (1 July 1901) divides associations into two distinct categories: in the first group are collected all those associations not directly dependent on the church and these are treated as isolated individuals; in the second group are the religious congregations that the state subjects to a severe control while rendering their formation very difficult. The first group is treated almost completely according to principles of civil law, and the second in conformity with the more strictly unitary rules of public law.

It is hardly necessary to observe that the limits of civil and public law become blurred, and it is impossible to have either pure civil law or pure public law—types that I have given here for clarity. The French government does not grant legitimacy to any corporations except those which appear worthy of its solicitude. The German civil code allows associations without economic purposes to be established freely with a simple declaration. But if there is an economic purpose, the civil personality can be acquired only with the consent of the state or by virtue of the law that takes this particular kind of association into consideration. Foundations acquire civil personality only with state authorization (Articles 21, 22, 43, 80, 87).

According to these principles cartels fall largely under the domain of public law. They are organized to abolish economic anarchy, that is, the fatality that rules production, and to lead industrial society to a reasoned existence. If they realized completely the program their defenders propose, the essential bases of private law would disappear. Therefore public opinion was not mistaken when it regarded industrial agreements as having the effect of creating new authorities side by side with the state, authorities that some people want to subordinate to that of present government. Other people would want to see them develop either side by side with government or combined with it in some way.

Private and public law are not formed in the same way. It has often been maintained that private law results from a slow, barely conscious evolution, or again from the almost mechanical pressure of the economy. Public law requires a clear doctrine based on observation and principle. These theories are not absolutely true, but they are useful to show the difference between the two processes. We practically rediscover the Hegelian conception. The social reformers who begin with a statist conception and who hope to generate the economy and private law by means of public law, consider themselves as fully conscious organs of society who do the thinking for it. After the Prussian ideal appeared old-fashioned and parliamentary corruption showed that democratic government is even more incompent than the old enlightened despotism in directing industry, ethical reformers often propose to find means of governing things in that very organization of industry. The cartels allow them to conceive a social system with a new appearance.

If one assumes that industrial agreements are completely developed, one can regard any category of producers as forming a separate society having its own economic domain which chooses representatives to establish its internal rules and defend its interests against the outside. All these groups have interests opposed to one another. In order to reconcile these opposed interests it would be necessary to gather delegates of groups in mixed commissions. There would be a state of coal mines, another of suppliers, another of rolling mills, etc., and finally a general metallurgical state.

This constitution would greatly recall those of the ancien régime, and it is obvious that those of the ancien régime were at least inspired by ideas analogous to those of other times. The diverse orders did not come together to legislate, but to discuss administrative and especially financial questions. The king convoked the Estates General when he needed money, and it was a question of knowing how they would divide exceptional burdens among the various groups. The Estates General were unions of cartels that had to deliberate on economic interests. It is therefore quite natural that we find in so many modern books a conception of cartels that reproduces the political organization of the past.

Those who extol the union of cartels usually don't want to admit the perfect analogy that exists between their projects and those of the past.

It would be impossible to refuse to give a place in the estates general of industrialists to representatives of the workers. When we take this factor into consideration we can get a still better account of the nature of the system. Workers' unions would go there for the purpose of demanding sacrifices from the capitalists, and with the threat of using the power that results from striking, constrain the capitalists to accept those sacrifices as the lesser evil. Their role would closely resemble that of the old royalty which always demanded and consulted the Estates General not so much over whether to make expenditures as over how to divide them.

The experience of the last few years demonstrates that the workers are trying to push industry into the path of the organization of the Estates General. As soon as the working class ceases to be revolutionary, it imagines industry as being in a form that is best suited to its customs. Not having anything to direct in the economic order, it conceives things under the rudimentary form that is suitable to a meeting of comrades. If it is a question of knowing how to arrange a holiday, it is natural that there should be voting and, if necessary, appeals to the intervention of third parties to reconcile uncompromising opinions. The heads of workers' corporations would like every industry to be represented by a board of directors, and they cannot understand the difficulty of this. During the last French miners' strike, the Workers' Federation presumed to force the coal mine owners' committee to deal with them, although this committee was a simple office of technical information.

Governments are disposed to pushing industry onto this path, considering the function that they assume when large strikes occur. It is much easier for the government to discuss with a committee than with an isolated owner. Obliged to intervene as peacemakers, governments must take great account of the wills emerging from the conflicting parties that can provoke disorders.[10] It is with the threat of insurrection that governments move, and if the labor unions firmly demand that the capitalists unite, it is necessary to give in to them. They also try to get the producers' union to become permanent and enter into relations with the labor union. Here then is the principle of the Estates General.

When one laments the organization of cartels in Germany, the defenders of cartels reply that anyone can organize like the manufacturers. There was a question of forming unions of cartels to ensure the passage of raw materials to various groups of factories for transformation under suitable economic conditions. There are even merchants' agreements to form associations to defend their interests. It is difficult for consumers to unite freely; but the government can intervene to give them "indirect representation." It can require industrialists to enter into discussions with the representatives of a certain number of large cities where consumption is important. It can also take a direct part in the life of cartels, imposing direction on them, and this has been proposed in Germany.[11]

The project of a general delegation of producers and consumers is very fashionable today. It comes to us from Germany, and this is as it should be, because the parliaments there are not so much political bodies legislating to obtain a certain national ideal as they are medieval-style diets in which one undertakes diplomatic discussions among plenipotentiaries and which come to establish compromises among various interests.[12] The negotiations the German center undertakes with the government regarding any important vote shocks anyone accustomed to the usual theories of parliamentary regimes.

The progress of protectionism tends to introduce the same customs in all parliaments; interest groups are formed, among which favors are exchanged. Not long ago the Reichstag was accused of having become a stock exchange during the discussion of protective tariffs. The same phenomenon occurs everywhere. Only in Germany, the parties being better disciplined than in France, their divisions depending on local conditions and parliamentarianism having recent importance, questions of interest appear more easily on the surface without any veil.[13]

Notes

1. De Rousiers, op. cit., p. 287.
2. "Not in vain had generalized jurisprudence preserved and commented over the ages that Roman law which was, is and will be the typical and classical form of law for all market societies, until communism removes the possibility of buying and selling. (Antonio Labriola, *Del materialismo storico*, p. 85.
3. Jehring, who often insisted on the decomposition of the proceedings, appears not to have noted the analogy between law and mathematics.
4. Let us note in passing that this is one of the most important Newtonian theses. Newton says, *"Vir ium causas et sedes physicas jam non expendo."* *Principia*, definition 8.
5. The French socialist newspapers often attack the Court of Cassation completely mistakenly. A case in point is a remarkably stupid article appearing in Jaurès's newspaper *L'Humanité* (30 March 1904). Applying a law of amnesty voted in 1904, the Court is accused here of not taking into account the *intentions* that the Chamber of Deputies had shown in 1904 in rejecting a proposed modification of another law of amnesty! The author is a university professor and one of the strongest pillars of French socialism.
6. G.W.F. Hegel, *Phenomenology of the Mind*.
7. Ibid., pp.
8. Ibid.

9. Vilfredo Pareto, *Les systèmes socialistes*, Vol. I, p. 315.

10. The minister of public works admitted artlessly to the Chamber of Deputies, defending a bill for the improvement of miners' pensions: "We just missed being thrown into very grave events. . . . In order to give a solution to the conflict and to have authority over the workers, *we have negotiated with those who most particularly represent the workers.* We have kept our promises." *Petite République* (2 March 1902).

11. Sayous, *La crise allemande,* p. 364.

12. I have already noted the great importance of this consideration in my *Essai sur l'église et l'état* (Paris: Jacques, 1902), p. 48.

13. We must never forget that, if parliamentarianism has partially deserved the eulogies given it by liberal theorists, this occurred as a result of accidental circumstances, which made parliament's tribunals in which general political ideas were discussed. It seems to me that there were no parties similar to ours in antiquity: there is in parliamentarianism a mixture of spiritual ends and material interests that most often makes the study of modern history quite difficult.

CHAPTER THREE

I have lingered on the preceding schema only to improve our understanding of what is occurring in the world today. Perhaps there will never be the corporate estates general. Nevertheless, one finds at any time in discussions among interested groups an image of this constitution. Besides we must not forget that the *unofficial* institutions are much more important than the *official* ones. There is not the least need for example, for a law determining the function of the state in strikes, for governments to intervene in them as arbitrators, imposing their will to a greater or lesser extent. We should cast a quick glance at what the German cartels teach us from the perspective of the internal economy. In the first chapter of this part, I considered them as auxiliaries of the German government in its foreign policy, in its active protectionism,[1] and in its efforts to bring about the extension of commerce beyond its borders. We shall now examine how they direct production and local consumption.

It often happens that consumers are made to pay much more dearly for an article than it is worth, in order to offer another at a good price. Thus in Germany, industrial alcohol is sold at a price that could not allow any profit and that probably produces losses, while later producers compensate for it in high prices for drinking alcohol. This can only be done with state approval, which establishes a fiscal system adapted to that purpose and so that there is an advantage for agriculture in the development of distilleries. The state could do directly what the cartel does indirectly by giving rewards to one producer and taxing another. But it is certain that the cartel is better than bureaucracy at the active advertising necessary to make the consumer of alcohol enter into industrial practice.

The cartels also play an important role as auxiliaries of German protectionism,[2] disposing themselves in such a way as to *put the tariff laws into operation*. At all times one laments that the protective tariffs are no longer effective and especially that they no longer produce results at the end of a relatively brief time when protectionism has given a slight boost to production. Farmers greatly lament the insufficiency of tariffs on grains, and ask the government to favor the export of their grain to raise the price and put tariff laws *into operation*. Paul de Rousiers tells us[3] that without the opposition of the firm of Darblay, the French paper mills would have succeeded in understanding how to operate the laws. He maintains[4] that the metallurgical cartel allowed industry to earn more profits from protection.

The history of the Port of Marseilles gives us a similar example and shows what can result from competition under the rule of a high tariff.[5] Following the 1900 strike, the dockers' wages having been brought to six francs a day, a considerable migration occurred. Instead of working five or six days a week, the workers generally worked three. Their weekly income, which had been 25 to 30 francs, declined to 18 francs. Governments can only regard industries en bloc with respect to foreign countries. They cannot regulate production legislatively; they need to find technical bodies of such a kind as to follow movements closely and complete their work. It is therefore quite natural that in Germany cartels have been viewed in a good light by the authority that strives to ensure a satisfactory level of profits to all branches of national production.[6] De Rousiers strongly insists on this point.

While in America the trust has been helped by *corrupt public powers*, in Germany the cartels have been helped by *honest public powers*, but powers subjected to a tradition of paternalism.[7] In regard to the agreements among coal producers and locomotive and railway car manufacturers, Paul de Rousiers says: "Here are three industries in which the existence of cartels has been favored or determined by the state." When attacks were made in the legislature against the coal cartels, the government has candidly taken their defense.[8]

The vices of protectionism should be found in the cartels having social conservatism as their purpose. They serve to maintain, at the price of very grave sacrifices, businesses that competition would have abolished. An industrial organization that is not in condition to withstand a struggle against adversaries of the first order is kept alive at a very high price. In America an energetic selection process took place, and only iron manufacturers of an exceptional strength are still on their feet; while in Germany they are living in deceptive security. This regime, says Paul de Rousiers,[9] "prepares a dreadful future for the branches of industry to which the government momentarily assures security. It is perhaps the least noticed and probably the gravest of its defects." He concludes:[10] "This renders German industry a bad service on the eve of unavoidable universal competition."

These considerations by a sagacious observer are most important. They show us that in cartels are found defects manifested in businesses that are closely controlled by the state. Here a certain carefree satisfaction is produced that is quite the opposite of the true tendencies of capitalism.

The anticapitalist vices of the cartels appear most clearly, perhaps, in their everyday commercial practices. Most often they do not try to foresee the tastes of their clientele to help develop consumption. Sayous says[11] that a merchant would lose his clientele if he proceeded with the same disregard cartels show their customers whom they regard too much as subjects. The same author thinks that the policy of high prices too frequently practiced by cartels can constitute a grave harm for Germany.

After the period of high productivity, businesses hoped that the Essen cartel would provide them with cheap fuel:[12] "The country had greatly suffered from the lack of fuel and from its high price. After the situation became normal, the cartel was unable to give back a little life to industry. The French cartel saw justly that it would not go back to quantity if it had lost in another area. But this is not the point of view that an economist concerned with the general interest should share. Woe to the peoples who will defend such a policy independently;[13] they will see their outlets closed."

Villain thinks that all the fine declamations by the defenders of cartels are pure hypocrisy; it is a matter of placing the buyer at the discretion of the seller. I do not dwell on the aggressive clauses that are introduced into contracts[14] because one could respond that these are abuses that will disappear when strongly constituted unions of buyers could oppose sellers' syndicates, or at least in cases in which there were mixed commissions. But it is more useful to note that the cartels do not deal with everyone in the same way; they operate as parliamentary parties do, and grant favors to people they fear.

When it is difficult to satisfy everyone, the cartels reserve the high-quality merchandise for certain clients and impose onerous conditions on the others. For example, the Hayange and Rombuch foundries, both in Lorraine, were sold coke of a markedly different quality, because the Hayange belongs to the powerful Wendel family.[15] Thus the regime of cartels tends to introduce a type of feudalism into industry, because the prosperity of an enterprise would no longer depend on technical science, on business ability, or the strength of capital, but above all on the rank the masters occupy in the social hierarchy. The bourgeois idea relies on the perfect objectivity of business relations. There is no need to conceal that these feudal tendencies can exist in a democratic society as in any other. The patronage of influential politicians or the support of well-paid petty politicians produce the same hierarchical result.

During the last German crisis no one saw the cartels distinguish themselves through their science of prediction, and Villain notes[16] the harm of leaving the industry of a great country at the mercy of sovereign committees that take themselves for infallible authorities. I do not know what the exact idea is that this authority wanted to express; but it is obvious that his criticism means that *industry suffers* by being *governed according to the principles of the state.*

The cartels were supposed to regulate production in such a way as not to be taken unawares by spells of too much activity or depression. This problem was insoluble and as a consequence, much of the criticism directed at the cartels does not quite hold up. They are criticized for not having done perfectly a job that no one could do reasonably. Their mistake was in having announced with great fanfare that they would be the saviors of industry. The cartels had the illusion that the "special science" of the German universities had spread profusely—an illusion which we find in the social democrats. In Germany it is assumed that "the anarchy of production and of distribution"[17] should lead to the ruination of England. But the experience acquired through the practice of cartels bursts all these soap bubbles and demonstrates that in the present state of the world the problem of the regularization of production resembles that of perpetual motion.

I am truly amazed when I see that Kautsky does not benefit from this experience and regards the disappearance of crises as a simple matter.[18] The question will be resolved in the twinkling of an eye, after the socialist parties are in power; nothing is more urgent and at the same time more simple. It is enough to prescribe to each factory what it should produce; we could object uselessly that consumption is variable,[19] but it varies because of the alternating activity and rest in industry. Today it is assumed that these alternations will be suppressed. Hence, everything being regulated, it will be easy to have regular production everywhere. This is a fine tautology. The author correctly observes that "it is the iron industry in particular that occasions crises," but he does not ask who occasions the crises in the iron industry. At least for France, state intervention has had a considerable influence on the upheavals in metallurgy in the last twenty years.[20]

In this study Kautsky shows himself a provincial petit bourgeois.[21] Since consumers who live on small incomes are highly routinized, he cannot understand that there are excesses in production and that these would occur whatever system is adopted by the management of the enterprise. A family living solely from the products in its own possession does not know crises but only the stages of existence.[22] However, if the family intends to make improvements in cultivation methods and gets the help of neighbors and then the operation fails or is obstructed by the weather—we have a phenomenon greatly resembling a crisis. There is only one way to avoid it: nothing will be improved if there are not sufficient savings put aside and if experience has not shown the absolute safety of the operation. In a word, we will follow in the footsteps of those who have a small income, and the snail will become the emblem of the socialist regime as Kautsky seems to think.

Crises do not have an invariable pace, and today we know that there are different types of crises. They are now much less upsetting than in the past.[23] But it is not by dreaming of the patriarchal life of a fossilized past that we will be able to think of means of lessening the ills that are the counterpart of the spirit of initiative. At the risk of passing, as Bernstein puts it, "for a bird of evil omen," I find that the experience of the cartels shows that the difficulties of central management would be enormous.

Sayous thinks that the concentration of operations can have the effect of increasing panic in a crisis:[24] "One of the significant consequences from tight producers' agreements is that of changing perspective; of concentrating buying and selling to the point of making people lose their heads when needs are strongly felt. The producers' syndicates appear full of evils in an atmosphere like ours where truth is so frightening and where the mass is composed of 'lambs of Panurge.' "

We can go further than this author and give psychological causes a greater role in the perils produced by concentration. We know that almost all speculators succumb on account of a veritable "logical madness." They want to follow their ideas logically, and after having good luck on their side for some time, end up by having the reverse. In normal commerce subjected to competition, there are many particular tales of success and failure that cancel each other out. The cartels concentrate all wrongs in the same direction and reject all countervailing efforts. The "logical madness" becomes much more serious insofar as these efforts are united and receive impulse from men with a stronger personality and more knowledge.[25]

Kautsky is among those who think that social democracy possesses an economic science of a higher order. Unfortunately he has always failed to tell the public what this science is. Without fearing to slander Kautsky, we can assert that this science is borrowed from the German ethical economists and from the old utopians. Every time we study Kautsky's thought, we find the utopian and the petit bourgeois German in him.

The ethical economists have as their ideal fixed prices, which allows them to imagine a perfectly stable society, just as Kautsky does. The long-term contracts concluded by the cartels appear to them an approximation of this ideal regime and, for that reason, they generally defend the cartels. This type of contract presents great dangers from the point of view of prices. When there is a shortage of materials, this is ordinarily verified, because new and exceptionally favorable investment opportunities exist, and because then the industrialists who undertake these new enterprises hope to realize greater profits thanks to which they pay higher prices. As for needs of a secondary order, they are temporarily ignored. This is what happens when a large regulatory market exists. But with treaties covering periods of several years, factories that are not engaged in operations that yield extra profits continue to receive materials and are able to satisfy secondary needs, while others are denied material and are obliged to provide for themselves in a highly restricted market.

Certain German cartels have tried to regulate market prices imitating what certain producers do to force retail merchants to keep only the slightest profit for themselves. In a circular of 20 February 1900, the cartel at Essen *ordered*[26] the coal merchants to serve preferentially their old clientele and to raise prices only as much as the cartel had raised them. Later it inserted a clause in the contracts specifying that the Essen Chamber of Commerce would arbitrate buying and selling prices. It prohibits[27] factories from selling at cost the fuel that is delivered to them. That prevents the factory having great needs from being able to satisfy them with the help of other factories with less pressing orders. It does not appear that the cartels found any means for constituting the regulative and distributive mechanism of prices. All their regulations had the effect of making more difficult the activity of those workshops that had pressing orders. In many cases, one consents to paying higher prices only to satisfy the clientele. These establishments were obliged to provide for supplementary fuel outside the cartel on an artificially restricted market.

Many socialists do not understand this mechanism despite its great simplicity. As an example of this failure of comprehension, I will cite a speech given by Rouanet against the monopolists in which he denounced the Longwy cartel.[28] He lamented that cast iron climbed to 60 francs per ton after 1898 while the increase of the price of coke justified almost an increase of around 13 francs. He exclaimed that "such facts cannot occur without Parliament, without the legislator, without public power intervening." He asserted that the Longwy cartel withheld "all the raw material, the bread of life of every industry that served cast iron." Rouanet's statistics are not precise,[29] but it is very curious that in his chauvinistic ingenuousness he believed that the Longwy cartel set the price for the entire world. The importance of French metallurgy is not that great.

What did Rouanet want to say? Perhaps that King's Law, which was limited to representing price variations schematically,[30] should be replaced by a law voted by Parliament. Yves Guyot says[31] that in 1893 workers chided him for not wanting to "abrogate either *the law* of supply and demand or the iron law of wages," Rouanet has not shown himself markedly superior to the ingenuous interlocutors of Yves Guyot. He thinks in the same way as his old friends from the *Libre Parole*.[32] Rouanet ended his speech with an appeal to the principles of the revolution which would not wait long to be seen intervening in price fixing. "It will be," he said,[33] "the honor of democracy and of the revolution of having brought into the world the idea of justice in economic and social relations. . . . I ask you to remain in the conditions of equality before the law that have been posed by the principles of 1789 and which you have the duty to apply in 1901." What can this mean?

In his posthumous article on value, Engels explained[34] how exchange was for a long period dominated by considerations of labor time. "How would [artisans and peasants] have been able to exchange their products other than in relation to the labor performed? . . . Do we think perhaps that the peasant and the artisan would have been so stupid as to exchange the product of a labor time equal to ten hours for another product which took a single hour?" It is on this analysis that he based his assertion that Marx's law of value was generally accepted by the end of the fifteenth century. In this system, all buyers make the exact estimation of what behooves the seller according to the time employed; this is a regime of economic equality. Rouanet confused it with the equality of the law proclaimed in 1789.

Many Catholics, great admirers of the Middle Ages, reason like Rouanet and think that natural justice is violated as soon as the producer receives more than his cost augmented by a slight profit. Nevertheless, the wisest people would agree to price increases during crisis. But this augmentation ought not to result from the blind action of competition; it ought to be just compensation for a supplementary effort, and one should be able to calculate the precise value of this reward. King's Law ought to be reformed to satisfy the demands of equity.

The problem posed by ethical theorists resembles that of determining the height of the ship's main mast by knowing the age of the captain. Georges Renard has given us a solution for wages, and it is useful to recall it here to show how the modern economy is understood by the "scientists" of reformist socialism. This professor of belles lettres asks himself how should incomes vary according to craft: quite a few professions requiring little daily labor attract many people; other, less attractive professions demand much labor. Renard decided that the price of a day's work ought to be proportional to the square of the duration, and proves that with this formula one will calculate the painfulness (*penibilité*) of every type of occupation.[35]

It is useless to dwell on these stupidities. I would not even have mentioned the ideas of Rouanet and Renard if I had not found them in perfect agreement with the tendencies that result from the general use of cartels. The similarities between cartels and political organizations obscure economic questions. A legislative act is made to last for a long time to satisfy needs that do not vary over a long time, in order to formulate a public medium. The contemporary economy, which is continually revolutionized by inventions and called upon to satisfy limitless demands, escapes all legislation. The activity exerted on prices by the cartels is so unfavorable to the progress of large-scale industry that some powerful enterprises try to avoid all new economic developments. Paul de Rousiers[36] was told that the Krupp works have a marked superiority over much of their competition. It could happen that in trying to favor the middle positions, the cartels find themselves in a position of having forced German metallurgy into entering the path of more concentration.

These great isolated establishments represent capitalist principles, and among them are produced inventions that are difficult to introduce in factories obligated by ties to the producers' syndicates. Every invention of some importance brings difficulties in the functioning of a cartel. As Paul de Rousiers says:[37] "As long as the producers' syndicate has existed, none of the factories that have entered into it have realized a notable advance in manufacturing and remain secret. A trust can find itself fortified by a fortunate invention . . . especially if it avoids letting the public know about it. A cartel is destroyed by an adventure of this type."[38]

Notes

1. Recall that we must always distinguish between two protectionist policies, one which has the purpose of conserving (which we can call "passive" protectionism) and another which has development as its object ("active" protectionism).
2. See the observations of G. de Molinari in the *Journal des Economistes* (February 1904):312 (September 1904):471.
3. Paul de Rousiers, *Les Syndicats industriels*, p. 190.
4. Ibid., p. 266.
5. *Musée Social*, (July 1901):302, col. 1.
6. Paul de Rousiers, *Les Syndicats industriels*, pp. 280–87.
7. Ibid., pp. 134–42.
8. Ibid.; Villain, *Le fer, la houille*, pp. 151–55. The Prussian government,

great proprietor of coal mines, profits from the artificially high prices of the cartels. Recently it has nevertheless clashed with this coalition when it wanted by buy the *Hibernia* in order to make itself more independent of the coal cartel. Raffalovich says that this is the first conflict produced there. *Economiste français* (18 February 1905):216, col. 2.

9. Ibid., p. 179.
10. Ibid., p. 182.
11. Sayous, *La crise allemande*, p. 95.
12. Ibid., pp. 160–67, 342.
13. It appears that the author believes that the international agreement could change this situation and allow for price regulation without competition.
14. Sayous, *La crise allemande*, pp. 199, 345.
15. Ibid., p. 95.
16. Villain, *Le fer, la houille*, pp. 160, 186, 207.
17. Georges Blondel, *L'Essor industriel et commercial du peuple allemand*, 2nd ed. (Paris: L. Larose, 1899), p. 5.
18. *Mouvement Socialiste* (1 March 1903):386.
19. Ibid., p. 392.
20. *Saggi di critica del marxismo*, p. 371n.
21. Ibid., p. 321 (*From Georges Sorel*, p. 172).
22. This expression is from Le Play. These "phases" demand the intervention of the master who aids his client. See my *Introduction a l'économie moderne*, p. 55.
23. Sorel, *Saggi di critica del marxismo*, pp. 370–76.
24. Sayous, *La crise allemande*, p. 185.
25. The experience of the large American operations gives evidence of this "logical madness." The most able speculators commit senseless acts when the crisis becomes grave.
26. Sayous, *La crise allemande*, pp. 158–59.
27. Ibid., p. 169.
28. *Revue Socialiste* (April 1901):481–83. Rouanet is a "specialist" in such questions; in *Introduction à l'économie moderne* (pp. 327–28) I spoke of his campaign against a sugar merchant that he accused of cornering the market.
29. Cf. Paul de Rousiers, *Les Syndicats industriels*, pp. 225, 227.
30. Note that, according to this law (which resulted from observations of current grain prices in the eighteenth century), a deficit of ten per cent produces a price increase of thirty per cent, and a deficit of twenty per cent results in an eighty per cent increase in prices. Sorel, *Saggi di critica del marxismo*, p. 347.
31. Yves Guyot, *L'Economie de l'effort* (Paris: A. Colin, 1896), p. 253.
32. Rouanet's relations with *Libre Parole* have endured for a long time; Drumont reminded him of this at the session of 24 March 1900 and often his newspaper turned on such questions. When Rouanet took charge of the report on the inquiry into the Panama affair, the *Libre Parole* published documents that could not have been provided by anyone but the teller, and this publication was all the more deplorable insofar as it implicated people that the inquest did not even consider.
33. *Revue Socialiste* (April 1901):485.
34. *Devenir Social* (November 1895):718.
35. This brilliant discovery was published in *Revue Socialiste* (January 1898).

Millerand having become a cabinet minister hastened to give Renard a professorship of economic history at the Paris Conservatory of Arts and Crafts. He would have done better to give him a chair in French grammar. The invention of the word *pénibilité* is well deserving of such a reward! Reform socialism truly has a peculiar touch for putting everyone in the job that suits his talents!

36. Paul de Rousiers, p. 181. In France, de Wendell has not entered the construction beam syndicate (p. 257).
37. Ibid., pp. 118–19.
38. It seems that the last German agreements have nevertheless gone further than the old ones. Raffalovich says that the steel *cartel* includes 90 percent of the manufacturers while the American trust controls only sixty per cent. *Economiste français* (18 February 1905):216, col. 2.

CHAPTER FOUR

As soon as we make a study of cartels, we find ourselves comparing them to the life of political parties. This comparison does not rely only on the ideological dependency, established in the previous chapter, between the cartels and public law, but rather on the analogies that exist in the mechanisms of operation and which in turn generate analogies in customs. The resemblance between cartels and political parties is great, and so, at any given instant, it is useful to pass from one system to the other to interpret the economy by means of politics or vice versa.

At first it seems strange that interests *can* combine in an agreement, when we are used to seeing them abandon themselves to ruthless battles. The same difficulty exists for the economy and for politics. In politics it is very easy to find explanations. Agreements arise from two causes: (1) from permanent bodies which ensure administrative continuity and form what is called "the state" in the strictest sense of the word; (2) from the substitution of discordant forces with other forces that supposedly represent them.

By the sole fact that men have agreed to enter into a deliberative assembly, they unconsciously subject themselves to the obligation of establishing agreements among themselves or at least of accepting what will be done.[1] This necessity of agreement is much stronger still when there is a directing committee which is the materialized unity and which labors to produce solutions. It would not have any reason for being if there were not solutions! The committee, a type of mediator, strives to convert those who hesitate and tries to make apparent the advantageous side of certain ancillary consequences—and often the decision is made for reasons of this type. Parliamentary experience proves that cabinet ministers exert a strong influence in order to unite the parties. Therefore, responsible cabinet ministries constitute a fundamental organism in our political life and ensure to the governments a tradition that would seem at first glance inconceivable given the brusque variations of popular instinct.

The masses are always greatly different from their representatives. What is dominant in the existing relations between these two groups is not the dependency of the ruled in relation to the rulers. It is the *admiration of the electors for the elected.* This phenomenon occurs especially in democracy: the workers have a superstitious veneration for their representatives, whether they fear them or whether they are dazzled by their ability, eloquence, and boldness. Generally it is a bad calculation that makes many conservative politicians accuse socialist parliamentarians of having too many relations with the official world. They thereby only develop the sentiment of admiration that the deputies inspire in their electors. Their elected deputy must be a strong man, because the wealthy bourgeois accord him so much honor!

Aristocracies are less easily led than the working class, because they do not have such a sentiment of respect. Consequently, they allow less freedom to their representatives. Nevertheless, despite their stubborn spirit, even the agrarians have ended almost always by admitting that their deputies can accept compromises. At present there are, among the great landed proprietors, many of great agronomical understanding who impose themselves on their country neighbors and who realize the importance of the general progress of the industrial economy. When a man abandons old agricultural practices to adopt new procedures, he largely avoids agrarian prejudices. The landed proprietors, feeling that there is something to be done, are disposed to accept the impulse of the personality who seems able to show them by example what can be attempted in agriculture.

The great English labor unions give us notable examples of the forms that the relations between the representative and the represented mass can take. In the cotton industry close, amicable relations were established between the union leaders and the owners[2] which produced agreements analogous to those made by the manufacturers joined in a cartel. Quite wrongly it was believed that this system could be generalized. Everything relies on a *psychological accident*: the complete confidence these workers have in the man who leads them and whose directions they follow. From time to time this fragile relationship weakens, and it is then necessary to allow the instincts free rein. The leaders then follow the masses and strikes break out. When workers are discouraged, they ask to be placed under the direction of leaders again; but the moral authority of these leaders is greatly shaken, and if the old discipline is to be restored, the owners must agree to give prestige again to the union functionaries. The conciliation committees serve this purpose, presided over by the country's leading personalities.

Sometimes it is thought that the state could use its administrative machinery to facilitate the agreements between workers and capitalists. The experience of mixed councils where delegates from both sides are seated beside high government functionaries proves that conflicts are almost always less irreducible than might be believed at first sight. Administrative action is especially strong when it takes the form of an office bound to an industrial parliament and having the air of depending on it. The labor bureaus are thus much more effective than simple ministerial bureaus would be.

In some industries, capitalists have introduced mixed councils. At Mariemont, J. Weiler appears to have obtained remarkable results. The publications devoted to this curious institution show us that the workers' delegates are *unofficial worker-leaders*, and that the great difficulty for the capitalists consists in giving them enough authority over the men who regard them as representatives.[3] The Catholics would not seem to have proceeded very tactfully in their attempts to organize the workers: workers' delegates appear too much to be auxiliaries of the clergy, and the clergy appear too much to be the capitalist police force.

Until now, the most successful system is that practiced at the coal enterprises of Pas-de-Calais in France. They have a fairly good understanding with the labor leaders, and agreements are reached so that the leaders always look as if they are battling victoriously in favor of the workers. They are allowed to pronounce inflammatory harangues against capitalism on the condition that socialism does not penetrate the country. They are granted concessions so that the miners are persuaded that without their leaders they would not obtain anything. Their recommendations are, on the whole, treated carefully, and workers who wish to rebel against the labor union are persecuted. At the head of 1,900 workers united in the trade union, Basly governs despotically 45,000 miners of Pas-de-Calais. The last strike broke when he judged it useful to break the line of defense of the authority of the Commentry Congress. It was terminated at his will, and, in the spring of 1903, the government placed the armed forces at his disposal to help put down those socialists who attempted to act. Never has the separation of the masses from their representatives been so forcefully marked.[4]

The practice of agreements between cartels of owners and of workers tends to transform the ideas that formed the very basis of socialism. Marx believed that the working class was the only class capable of unifying itself, and that it would be confronted with a capitalism increasingly divided by competition.[5] Today the capitalists have organized themselves in a methodical way. Many people estimate that the organization of the capitalists is progressing much more quickly than that of the workers, and ask that the same state, taking the cause of the weak to heart, give a constitutional charter to the workers' cartels to oppose the cartels of the heads of industry. Thus the natural movement of things would produce the complete opposite of what Marx imagined. As for the ideas, they would also have changed a lot!

The hope of an imminent revolution disappears as soon as one assumes a power as formidable as that of the capitalist cartels. Workers' delegates who enter into consultative councils or who find themselves in continual business relations with the capitalists' unions feel a sort of amazement in discovering that capitalism is not so old and worm-eaten as they had been told. They make sad reflections on the weakness of the unions they represent and ask themselves how they could change their unions into an organization as formidable as that of the bourgeois class. They become timid and, as a consequence of these reflections, there begins to emerge in them a tendency toward reformist or state socialist ideas.

They become aware that it is not as difficult as they had thought to obtain improvements of details; that capitalism does not form an irreducible bloc; and that many owners' representatives are inclined to find a basis of agreement. The surprise they feel when these facts appear clearly before their eyes is great, and from then on they do not cease changing. Seeing that things do not go at all as the socialist theoreticians had said they would, they assume that the error of their old teachers stems from a poorly conducted experiment. If one did not believe in the possibility of reform, they say, it is because there are bad means in trying to deal with the bosses; it is because good means were not used to arrive at an agreement; and finally their own awkward practices are justified with false theories. Through the consequence of an easily understood mirage effect, labor leaders admit that if the capitalists and public functionaries manifest tendencies toward conciliation and agree to negotiate, this depends on their personal abilities. So after the former revolutionaries have had some contact under these conditions with those whom they regarded as irreducible enemies, they have a natural feeling of pride and set themselves to despise the revolutionaries who remain outside the reformist movement.

The workers are perhaps more sensitive than anyone else to the slightest improvement of their lot, because their life is extremely uniform. As soon as the capitalists make small concessions to them, or a cooperative procures them a small saving on their consumption, they are disposed to believe that the world has entered a new life and that, in the long run, there is no progress to which one cannot aspire. Many union leaders cease completely to think according to their old principles after successes obtained from reformist practices justify the attribution of salaries that permit them to live comfortably. They are very sensitive to the respect that the "able bosses" have for them. When they think of the distance they have traveled, they have no doubt of the inevitability of indefinite progress.

The theory of progress was asserted in the eighteenth century in analogous conditions. Following a long depression, prosperity returned, and marvelous scientific discoveries filled everybody with hope. The literati, who were first regarded as diversions for the people and the princes, in the meantime discussed practical politics and were listened to by statesmen. They hoped that they were not very far from the moment when it would finally be recognized that it was necessary to place public affairs in the hands of capable thinkers who could be discovered without passing through the administrative and judicial hierarchy. Their situation was analogous to that of a part of the present leadership of the workers' unions. They had no doubt of the indefinite progress of the world when they thought of the homage rendered them by high society.

In this way people come to develop a reformist outlook against which the partisans of the old revolutionary viewpoint have undertaken a very unequal struggle, in which, at least in France, they will not have the upper hand as long as general conditions remain the same. It does not appear that Kautsky has escaped the influences of reformist socialism. He no longer has faith in the class struggle as he once believed in it. It is his turn[6] to reproach the capitalist class for not showing more sympathy for the workers. It is his turn to note[7] with a certain conceited satisfaction the reintroduction of socialists into the salons they had so often frequented before 1848—to make[8] the proletariat the most solid support for the arts. Would we not believe that he had borrowed ideas from Jaurès, when he promised[9] us an "empire of force and beauty worthy of the ideals of our most noble thinkers"?

In this polemic, the advantage rests with the reformists, not only because they are supported by general sentiments, but again because their adversaries are obliged to place themselves on grounds favorable to the reformists and to accept reformist principles in part. The question is discussed as if one had to choose between two solutions: one completely violent,[10] the other completely pacifist. It is assumed that history can be constituted in two ways, and it is asked which is the most economical way to obtain the most advantageous results: improvement of working conditions, better utilization of the means of coercion possessed by the state, changing institutions with the goal of enlarging the role of the representatives of the working masses.

Kautsky tries to convince the reformists by placing himself on the very ground of material interests. He wants to prove to them that the best thing is to continue the "tactics" long adopted by social democracy. His argument is beside the point. He asserts that one cannot expect to suppress bourgeois institutions by means of agreements with other classes. Everyone agrees with him. "I desire only one thing," says Kautsky,[11] "seeing whether those who believe that the great difficulties of the transition from capitalism to socialism have already been surmounted are correct in their views. . . . Unfortunately, it is impossible to be of this view. The gravest, most painful struggle remains to be done: it is the struggle for public power. It will be long and bitter, and we must employ all the force and energy at our disposal." Thus, conciliation with the bourgeoisie would be a bad judgment. Why not try to obtain the whole instead of contenting ourselves with a part?

But this conquest of public power is made gradually, and it is made more easily insofar as one utilizes the results acquired through exerting an influence on the people by pointing out the *successive effects* of its electoral endeavors. It would take heroic courage on our part not to take advantage of the partial advantages that power procures. To place the electoral struggle as the highest priority is to concede to the reformists the most essential part of their program.

Participation in politics, in any form, is a great harm for socialism, because this participation leads men to give importance only to wheeling and dealing. In bargaining both the revolutionary and the juridical spirit are extinguished at the same time, and this Kautsky does not seem to understand.[12] Kautsky endeavors[13] to demonstrate that the material advantages acquired by the working classes are not as great as is generally asserted. These are idle debates, because the notion of class struggle depends on moral causes, and class sentiment can develop at the same time that workers' living standards improve either in an absolute or relative way.

The whole question is whether the workers accept the principle of hierarchy more easily now than they once did. The manner in which many union leaders exercise their functions—and they often form a new petite bourgeoisie—shows that hierarchy is no longer so repugnant to many proletarians. The more easily the intelligent workers can obtain social positions that give them prestige among the bourgeoisie, the more the revolutionary spirit is extinguished. Progress in the conquest of public power and in the organization of collective bargaining works to produce this result.

Socialist sentiment is extremely artificial. It was Marx's great mistake not to insist on this principle. This sentiment relies on reflections that have nothing to do with necessity. Being a class sentiment, it contradicts that natural instinct that causes us to take up our defenses directly against the men who oppose us. Demagogues have much influence on the people when they denounce the misdeeds of certain individuals and concentrate all the popular anger on a representative personage. It is much easier to make the poor understand that their ills depend on Rothschild or some other Jew than to explain to them the economic basis of the class struggle. Socialism has something that is both instinctive and intellectual, while anti-Semitism is entirely instinctive.

The reformists try to obtain concessions from industry leaders and say that the more these leaders are shown to be conciliatory, the more they will work to abolish the feelings of hatred between industrialists and workers. Most often the opposite occurs. If the capitalist grants the request of honorable or pious people, the workers think that he must have recognized the immorality of the regime to which he had long subjected them. From then on they suspect his good faith in all circumstances. If there is an arbitration exercised by people outside the trade, the intellectual authority of the boss disappears—we are convinced that he is an imbecile. There is no greater damage for the head of a business than to be regarded as ignorant. Finally, if political intervention puts an end to the conflict, the workers think that with force one obtains everything one desires and that the purpose of reformism is to treat capitalists as vanquished. These phenomena do not ordinarily happen with this clarity, because many other sentiments come to mix with these so as to modify or even hide them. Generally, the politics of bargaining reaches more or less the same results that the most uncouth demagoguery could attain: hatred, contempt, or envy among men.

Man is not naturally moved to love his neighbor and attribute good sentiments to him. Ordinarily we attribute to him everything that is most wicked in ourselves, and we are brought to hate those who bother us when our spirit is not dominated by strong principles of action that impose themselves on the conscience in a tyrannical way. Catholics are right when they assert that something other than reasoning is needed to make peace reign among men. But their influence has always been weak. Socialism produces results of an entirely different value: it popularizes the idea of economic fatalism. The bosses cannot act in any other way than they do; they are almost totally unresponsible for the existing order; the world cannot be changed in accordance with the goodwill of the bourgeoisie. It therefore becomes absurd to hate a particular member of the bourgeoisie.

In place of the vital competition between individual men, socialism substitutes the class struggle. Better still, the struggles fought on democratic grounds (and especially in the Greek *polis*) were hardly anything but vital conflicts, wars of the poor who wished to confiscate the wealth of the rich. We have here an excellent criterion for separating the democratic spirit from the socialist idea. When socialist sentiments weaken, everything is done in terms of immediate and particular material interests; class struggle vanishes from our consciousness. But the phenomena that are produced when this happens are no longer those that would be produced if man had remained in his natural instinctive state. Every retrogression of the intelligence toward instinct contains a sort of corruption that the old moralists had recognized perfectly: man becomes more evil, more sophistic, more skeptical, moving through a temporary intellectual stage in which he is incapable of remaining.[14]

During the passage through revolutionary socialism, the worker is completely transformed: his spirit has lost all confidence in the mystical veils that first disguised the brutality of economic relations; the mind is sharpened and has discovered the importance of economic motives in the world; the idea of demolition of the social order, that should be replaced by free cooperation without bosses, is imposed as a law of reason. When degeneration occurs, the mystical veil is not reconstituted. All humanity appears dominated by interest. All the instincts of resistance, of opposition, and of war that were first evoked against the capitalist *class* are now concentrated entirely on the one *person* of the boss.

It is easy to illustrate to any intelligent reader these general observations with many examples: *the degeneration of socialism is accompanied everywhere by a moral decadence*—at least in our democratic countries. The Catholics have often noted the horrible *lack of conscience* they found among old revolutionaries who, discouraged and disgusted, came to the church. They have not always interpreted the facts well and believed that this phenomenon was the consequence of Marxist materialism when it was simply the result of the ruination of revolutionary ideas.

The psychological and moral problem to which I call attention is of major importance for the future of the modern world. It is hoped that it will be studied closely, at least by the distinguished men who in Italy are at the head of social Catholicism. They know socialism and can appreciate the causes which ruin moral sentiment in the popular classes. This ruination dominates today the question of reformism and constitutes the great danger of what are called the "new methods."

Jaurès and his friends make magnificent homilies to the beauty, duty, and regeneration of humanity; but all this changes nothing in the morality of the individual. Does he not himself give us the odd spectacle of the impotence of this idealism which he teaches with such fanfare? Several years ago, the *Petite République*, when he was its chief editor, had a clothing business which was often denounced as being based on the "sweating system." It has been proved that this newspaper had "inadvertently withdrawn" a rather round sum of money from the donations on behalf of the Creusot strikers.[15] It appears certain that, before publishing Jaurès's articles in favor of Dreyfus, the administrators of this journal had exacted strong subsidies from some Jews.[16] Jaurès was not moved: political necessities dominated everything for the man who posed as the stubborn defender of truth! He finally deserved to be called "leader of the informers" (*Rappel*, 20 November 1904), having shown such ardor in defending the ignoble police proceedings of Combes.[17]

Notes

1. A unique example of this psychological phenomenon is found in the Algerian Kabalye. Everything is decided in a village general assembly, and majority rule is unknown there. Nevertheless, things end by establishing agreements or by nominating an arbitrator whose decisions are always obeyed.
2. Paul de Rousiers, *Le trade unionisme en Angleterre* (Paris: A. Colin, 1897), p. 322.
3. Cf. J. Weiler, *La grève de Mariemont et les conseils de conciliation et d'arbitrage*, pp. 11, 14, 16.
4. In the *Voix du Peuple,* organ of the General Confederation of Labor, we find numerous details on Basly's struggle against the revolutionaries. In the issue of 20 December 1902, we read that at Lens (the city in which Basly is mayor) some Parisian delegates could not find a room because everyone feared the terrible Basly. In the issue of 4 January 1903 we read that Basly is mad with rage and every day insults and defames the unionists who come from Paris to make revolutionary propaganda.
5. Paul de Rousiers, *Le trade unionisme en Angleterre,* p. 322.
6. *Mouvement Socialiste* (15 October 1902):1851.
7. Ibid., p. 1844. Cf. *Communist Manifesto.*
8. Ibid., p. 1842. This passage is very important. First, because it shows that the author does not intend to break completely with the bourgeois ideology; second, because it is the confession of the intimate sentiments of German social democracy. They would like to enjoy bourgeois luxury. We could ask ourselves whether Kautsky only desires to be a teutonic Jaurès, but German high society rejects the social democrats.
9. Ibid. (1 March 1903):418.
10. For many revolutionaries the question is of knowing how much time it will take to produce the transformation. They intend that it be produced during their lifetime. They think as the Israelites thought before the belief in immortality had become preponderant among them.
11. *Mouvement socialiste* (15 October 1902):1889.
12. We can add that the practice of mixed commissions on which the bourgeoisie and the workers are seated produce the same consequences; indeed, this does not depend on a mysterious ideological cause but on the mechanism which serves to produce agreement.

13. *Mouvement socialiste*, pp. 1834–41. I do not see very clearly that one could compare the third class railway carriage of today with that of fifty years ago. How many comfortable bourgois travel in third class!
14. I think that we should follow this order of ideas (at least partially) when we study the psychology of the bad priest. If the public scorns the priest who had abandoned his vocation, this is not due to Catholic prejudices but to very serious reasons based on the observation of the harm caused in people by keeping company with bad priests, in whom the instincts have triumphed.
15. In *Petite République* (28 March 1901) Jaurès recalled that he had been condemned for having supported the Carmaux strikers and said: "This is our well-known way of robbing the strikers"; the day before the newspaper had announced that it gave back the 2300 francs, "lost," one knows not how.
16. The fact has been told in *Libre Parole* (25 October 1900). From various parties I have had information agreeing with this account which, on the other hand, has not been denied. *Libre Parole* undoubtedly received its information from the Guesdists; it *alone* gives complete and precise information on the Guesdist congresses that are closed to the outside.
17. Fournière, another apostle of idealism, veteran of fantastic socialism, the true successor of Malon, has no minor admiration for the sychophants. It is true that General André had nominated him for a professorship at the *Ecole Polytechnique*, and that, in order to be able to find employment for him, had suppressed the course in geodesy at that school (and would have abolished the course in astronomy if the Institute had not protested so strongly). We have here again a socialist who has made his own little social, practical, and personal revolution.

CHAPTER FIVE

We now need to examine what influences are exercised on the economy by democratic, moral, and religious forces which presently impel the world into the path of agreement, thanks to the propaganda made in favor of the ideas of moderation. I have called attention elsewhere[1] to a theory of Marx of capital importance and which is in full contradiction with the tendencies discussed here: "The evolution of the conditions of existence for a large, *strong*, concentrated, and *intelligent* class of proletarians comes about at the same rate as the development of the conditions of existence of a middle class correspondingly numerous, *rich*, concentrated, and *powerful*." The parallelism established by Marx is very noteworthy and impresses everyone who knows what enormous value Marx placed on parallelism in his doctrinal expositions. Revolutionary socialiam cannot have as its ideal to moderate the progress of capitalism. There are never sufficient productive forces and the capitalist class is never rich or powerful enough.

Against those who signal the danger in which democracy puts the development of capitalism, we would be tempted to cite the example of America where a uniquely daring capitalism coexists with democratic institutions. When speaking of the United States, we must take account of this exceptional fact for a democracy: that the actions of the public powers are quite limited; private initiative is considerable, on the other hand, and in an infinity of cases compensates for the neglect of the state. De Rousiers observes[2] that Americans are in the same situation as a ship's captain to whom one says in the middle of a storm that his cook robs him: this detail would be of little interest to him. Politicians are universally known as rascals, but they have the ability not to interfere too much with the progress of business. The country earns a great deal of money, and the malfeasance of politicians is exerted particularly on the public treasury. It is also their lot to accept bribes to vote for protectionist legislation. But Americans seem convinced that protectionism is at least temporarily necessary to increase the wealth of the country.

De Rousiers has understood[3] with great perspicacity that behind democratic political forms there is an aristocracy of ability and of energy

289

in civil society. We are not dealing with an aristocracy of birth here, but of a class of men who attain the highest positions, direct all the great businesses, and see their supremacy accepted by everyone. Nowhere is inequality greater than in the United States and nowhere does it seem more natural to the citizens. It is the latter which characterizes first and foremost an aristocratic society.

We need not be surprised if the theories of Henry George, which have had such success in England, have not encountered success in their land of origin.[4] They have been relished only by people who have not been able to succeed in creating for themselves an independent situation "while those who succeed—and these are numerous in the United States—remain hostile to their propaganda." The system of this celebrated reformer was directed against men who based their fortune on the rapid increase in land values. "It costs nothing to condemn vigorously land speculation, when one is sure of never being able to practice it, as is the case with many Englishmen. On the other hand, an American always cherishes the hope of some boom."

Wealthy society has the sentiment that it is an aristocracy because it makes great sacrifices to ensure[5] "the administration of a quantity of general interests insofar as they are revealed." De Rousiers has shown the difference between this *aristocracy of power* and our *aristocracy of weakness*, emphasizing the care with which the great American foundations are administered.[6] "One thing is to give some sum of money in a bequest, another is to create a durable institution. In the United States, the true aristocracy maintains and elevates itself through the real services that it renders to the whole nation."

While the American is consumed with ambition for power, the European democratic classes are inclined to simple tastes. The workers would be satisifed (when socialism does not transform them) if they always had assured and suitably paid work that allowed them to afford some recreation. For them, everything would seem to go well if the state slightly redistributed wealth, taking away some superfluous money from the rich to create social welfare institutions, and gave work in times of unemployment. The workers hardly conceive of anything else than a passive protection. Every sudden change of equilibrium upsets their misoneist instincts, and what appears marvelous to the capitalist entrepreneurs of America is almost an injustice in their eyes.

In 1848 Proudhon forcefully explained the true tendencies of our democracies:[7] "The system fallen upon hard times," he said, "could be defined thus: the government of the society produced by the bourgeoisie, that is by an aristocracy of talent and fortune. The system toward whose creation democracy is at this moment working can be defined in the opposite way: the government of society by means of an immense majority of the citizens who have little talent and no wealth at all." He cited a curious circular directed to the teachers by the minister of public education, to oblige them to run for election to the Constituent Assembly:[8] "The greatest error of the rural population," says the minister, "is to believe that to be a representative one needs to have *education* and wealth. The majority of the assembly plays the part of a jury: judging with a 'yes' or 'no' vote. . . . It only needs honesty and common sense. This is the fundamental principle of Republican right."

Proudhon, bringing out the strange declarations of this document, wants to prove that democracy does not like the control of government to be carried out by men of talent. Experience also teaches us that assemblies constituted in this way do not listen much to the elites and impose their instincts. Frightened by the disorder created in those periods by the preponderance of instincts, he said:[9] "Democracy closes the factories, reduces compromises to nothing, puts commerce, industry, and the state in bankruptcy." And, at the end of his work:[10] "Thirty days of dictatorship have laid bare the impotence and the inanity of democracy. All that it possessed of old memories, philanthropic prejudices, communist instincts, discordant passions, sentimental phrases, and antiliberal tendencies has been displayed in a single month. It has borrowed some of its ideas from utopianism and from *routine*; it has consulted the empiricists and the charlatans." What we have seen since 1848 has only confirmed the judgments brought by Proudhon on the perils of a government dominated by instincts and which has economic mediocrity for its ideal.[11]

Several years ago the United States became acquainted with the dangers presented by democratic instincts. The Democratic Party of William Jennings Bryan just missed imposing complete upheaval in economic relations with the free coinage of silver. De Rousiers thinks[12] that the defeat of this candidate was due to the defection of many Democrats, frightened by the consequences of such a policy. A Catholic tenant farmer, a strong partisan of Bryan, was highly indignant to see Archbishop Ireland speak in favor of gold: "The poor," said this good Democrat, "expected that if a bishop had to declare himself for a party, this ought to have been the party of the poor people's money." In this matter the archbishop showed great courage, breaking with the prejudices and errors of his constituency. We know that this is difficult.

European democracy finds repugnant one of the most important ideas on which modern capitalist production rests. It does not want to admit that the inventor is rapidly despoiled of the fruits of his invention, which is of use to everyone—imitators, competitors, and finally to consumers, passing through intermediaries of every order. When the worker is despoiled of the improvements he has brought to his mode of work, the injustice appears enormous. It seems to the democracy that he acquired through his ingenuity *a right to property* that cannot be taken away from him without committing a true theft. The bosses never cease thinking up ways of bringing the workers to accelerate production, and, when these results have been obtained, they reduce the price of labor in such a way as to despoil the workers of the right to their invention.[13] Such a practice goes directly against this democratic postulate: the law ought to establish a correction of economic relations to favor the poor. Here the law lets the poor lose the fruits of their labor without any possible resistance. The progress of production violates the very justice that ought to consolidate the small improvement realized by the worker, thus giving satisfaction to his mediocre ambition.

If the modern economy would conform to the *proprietary instincts of democracy*, any improvement realized in production (whatever its origin) ought to benefit the worker in the improved craft. According to an idea of Proudhon already mentioned,[14] there is a newly opened territory, and democracy wants to reserve it for the poor. It seems monstrous that the rich should take possession of this windfall to increase their wealth, which is already too great. An almost identical instinct is found among the agrarians, in whose eyes all progress should translate into an increase of income from the land. These are very primitive sentiments which show how much democracy is incapable of comprehending the capitalist economy.

The capitalists would not ask anything more than to consolidate to their benefit the advantages of new inventions. But they cannot easily succeed, and accept as hard necessity the competition which prevents such consolidation. The workers do not want to accept the lowering of their economic situation as a fact of life. The mobile scale is not suitable to them. For this reason the corporate possession of inventions would have in the economy a completely different result from appropriation by the inventor, and would hinder the progress of production.

Another condition closely joined to the preceding one is no less opposed to democratic instincts. It is that of the continuous increase of labor and especially of the attention of labor. There is no popular instinct more powerful than that which pushes man to laziness. Democracy especially regards man as obliged to occupy his time in politics and has never understood the law of labor. About forty years ago, Corbon forcefully[15] inveighed against the prejudices of the people who regarded labor as degradation and idleness as a superior situation. As for Corbon, he thought like Proudhon that the historical movement did not lead to a life devoted to thought and contemplation:[16] "Of all the errors that could ever cross the mind for an instant, I know of none more enormous than this. The truth is that, the more one augments the power of the instruments of labor, the more man comes to be enmeshed in increasing activity. . . . The most advanced nations are those that work the hardest."

Proudhon, Buchez's old collaborator, again expressed an idea that conforms very little to democratic inclinations when he said:[17] "It is good work that represents the end, and good harmony the means. Thus, for the revolution as for the church, fraternity, even if universal, is therefore secondary." Democracy places things in reverse order: when democrats can interfere in industry, it is almost always to inconvenience the capitalists under the pretext of protecting the poor against the scourge of large industry. Democracy is resolutely conservative, while, according to Kautsky,[18] socialism recognizes the necessity of allowing ills to be produced that are inseparable from economic progress.

Democracy does not act in this way alone: it is strongly supported by the moral tendencies of our time. Almost invariably we find professional moralists in associations formed by "friends of the people" for the purpose of struggling against capitalism. All modern philosophical thought seems dominated by the Kantian thesis that we must never regard man as a *means* but always as an *end*. It is not very difficult to see how this formula has owed its success to the existence of the regime of manufacturers. In this period the worker was an *animal trained to exercise* virtuosity and treated accordingly. He replaced mechanisms that no one yet knew how to construct. I shall not return to this question that I have already treated in part I of this work (chapter 7). The results obtained were so deplorable that the moralists believed that they ought to formulate a doctrine that directly opposed these industrial practices that reduced man to the level of an instrument.

Today we still read many declamations against any comparisons between labor and a commodity. The importance of this protest escapes most of the authors who formulate it. They repeat a thesis that had been produced by the miserable conditions of the working class at the time of manufacture. In this period there would always have been too many hands ready to work, and one could *sacrifice them* without committing any guilty improvidence. It seemed that industry consumed human flesh as it consumed coal, without having to concern itself with the origins and conditions of formation of this "raw material." It is against this comparison that the old philanthropists protested, because they did not want to accept the comparison of labor to a commodity. The old philanthropic literature often refers to the "homicide industry." As

Marx says:[19] "We heard how overwork thinned the ranks of the bakers in London. Nevertheless, the London labor market is always overstocked with Germans and other candidates for death in the bakeries." He compared the procedures adopted in the past in England to those of slave traders among whom there was a maxim that "the most effective economy is that which takes out of the human chattel in the shortest space of time the utmost amount of exertion it is capable of putting forth."

Many of our philanthropists write as if this situation still existed. It is true that, according to many polemicists, it would exist in a good number of philanthropic establishments. The exploitation of poverty among Catholic workers has often been denounced, and the trials endured by the *Bon-Pasteur* in France demonstrate that the slave tradition is still found in these establishments. But one would not regard them as representative of modern industry. The moralists often imagine that the capitalist baths must be infinitely harsher than the houses maintained by people with a tender heart and devoted to a life of charity. This is a grave mistake! Presently Christianity is quite involved in all sorts of philanthropic activities, and it is often difficult to separate what belongs to Christianity from that which depends on morality and democracy.

To better understand modern religious sentiments, we should recall the effect that the dreadful carnage of the revolution and the Empire produced on our ancestors. It seemed then that the world had become pagan again and that human life did not have any more value than it had at the time of the ancient Romans. A great disgust is felt for these human sacrifices accomplished under the pretext of great undertakings. Tolstoy's current publications are animated by this spirit that penetrates all the Christian revival: the horror of ruthless domination which sacrifices anything to a political ideal. Previously, Christians and Jews had cursed Rome for the same reason, and it is therefore not without motive that Tolstoy claims to interpret the true Christian spirit. Living in a deeply despotic country, he is moved as much as the ancient Christians by the oppression of the military yoke that crushes the tender soul, but his books do not seem to have any other value than the literary. It does not appear that Tolstoy has exerted the slightest influence; but the success of his works shows there is an accidental agreement between his reminiscences and the general conditions of European thought.

We must give an entirely different importance to the renewal of the Christian spirit that has created so many small Protestant churches and so many new Catholic devotions. At the end of the Imperial War, man felt oppressed by the burden of capitalist fatalities and asked if the new economic barbarism was not as homicidal as war. There were no longer parades, glory, or patriotic songs that served to hide the horrible situation of the victim. Man descended into himself and then heretofore slumbering mystical sentiments were reawakened. A miracle was needed, a direct and perceptible contact with God, to escape the present misery. This explains the extraordinary importance of the apparitions of the Virgin Mary which have made the nineteenth century an "era of Mary." The mediocrity of this devotion to Mary has often been noted. In its origins it was able to appear as an effort of the spirit upset by the sight of horrible spectacles, to find refuge in the queen of purity. But the period of this heroic devotion has passed. The apparitions have long ceased to occur, and what is seen today contains many inspidities. At a later time Lourdes will be regarded as suitable to characterize the manner in which our century has understood human destiny. It is closely related to the aspirations of our democracy as much as with the new Catholicism.

Zola had an exact appreciation of these sentiments when calling Bernadette[20] the "new child Messiah, come to comfort the wretched, charged with announcing to men the religion of divine justice, equality before miracles, upsetting the laws of *impassible nature*." The great success of this new messianism would be incomprehensible at a time in which men did not feel the need to find a refuge against the fatality of the economy. The rigidity of natural laws is intelligible and interesting for only a small number of people; but that of the economy is felt by all and provides us with the experience of "impassible nature." Christianity illuminates the infinite value of the humble servant of God, of the brotherhood of Jesus, of the poor whose laments will never be in vain. Kantian morality resumes this thesis with a more modern determination. For democracy it is a matter of safeguarding the dignity of the sovereign. The miserable and almost animal life of the citizen seems inadmissible to the literati who take Athens for their life model.

These three principles are united to oppose the theory of those who maintain that it is necessary to tolerate the present evils because they will produce a better future. Is it possible to sacrifice the sovereign, man, and even the brother of Christ in view of a future *material progress*[21] that nothing guarantees? It is with reference to the present that the question should be put, if we are to take account of the three principles. Capitalist fatality ought to be combatted because it puts "undeserved ills" on a class of the population that cannot be sacrificed to a problematic felicity promised to the men who will come to benefit from the labor of present generations, in some distant time, and who perhaps will not have any relationship with those who suffer today. Finally, democracy, morality, and Christianity ask the heads of industry to justify their position of leadership with a conduct capable of evoking admiration, that they have usurped without any authorization from civil and religious powers. It is very easy to see that the heads of industry are neither Greek heroes, nor pure souls, nor saints.

The system I have just summarily described can be called the "ideology of supreme ends," since it always regards man as devoid of economic necessity and pursuing an ideal end: the realization of the laws deducted from his superior nature. This system is opposed to economic society and to everything that immediately depends on it, that is to civil law and to the *liberal state*. In previous centuries this system took other forms, but there has always been that opposition more or less. Precisely because of the contradiction noted here, governments that have claimed to set the foundation for realizing this ideology of supreme ends have been frightfully authoritarian, since they have not been held back by any juridical or economic considerations. Thus the church often advised persecutions that had the most sorrowful influence on the countries the church dominated. Renan has often observed that the Jews were never so prosperous as when they no longer had the possibility of applying their theocratic legislation.

In this system we must consider democracy independently of the economic constitution which, according to what we have seen, serves as the basis for the Declaration of the Rights of Man. It has often been demonstrated that this declaration, treated as a purely abstract rule, is irreconcilable with regular government. Therefore we need not be surprised if it can be upheld with solid arguments: that democracy is both the inspiration of the Napoleonic Code and that it is anarchic. We should never lose sight of this secondary characteristic when we wish to understand modern history, since a principle that renders all public law an impossibility translates in practice into despotism.

Philosophers have made great efforts to hide the existence of the contradition. Since it is repugnant to them to admit that contradictions can coexist in this way, they have incorporated the system of supreme ends into the doctrines on the state, on law and on the economy.[22] Their error is much easier to excuse insofar as it corresponds to the general aspirations of our time. The present world wants to believe that it acts according to highly distinterested principles—which show some hypocrisy but especially a great blindness and an incredible weakness of character. The world does not want to understand this. For many years it was believed that capitalism was too powerful to have to take account of religious, philanthropic, or democratic fantasies. It was believed that the world had its destiny fixed in an immutable way through the progress of capitalism. Experience has disappointed those who were lulled into this illusion.

Not many years ago it was maintained that the Protestant countries were predestined for economic progress. Certainly they have long occupied the predominant place at the head of the capitalist countries. The causes of this superiority have not been well determined until now. It appears most likely that early Protestantism was greatly imbued with the spirit of discipline, thus adapting perfectly to the regime that needed an iron discipline to force workers to work in a regular way. Protestantism disorganized the old Catholic notion of charity that was so favorable to laziness. It taught and propagated the dogma of the obligation to work, strongly bound to the idea of original sin, while developing in a senseless way the idea of predestination. It removed any scruples from the judge in charge of ruling on the fate of the discontented.

Protestantism certainly eased the task of a society that wanted to push workers into factories, but well deserved the inexorably harsh criticism that Marx often directed against it.[23] Protestantism refashioned a Christianity imbued with Roman law and with the idea of the state, greatly favorable to the princes and the oligarchy. But there had to come a day on which the Christian foundation would reappear and then the old Protestantism would collapse.

Today everything has changed considerably: the Catholic and Protestant nations are similar from the industrial point of view, and England, more than any other country, would seem to have lost the feeling for the old capitalist necessity. "The English people," says Max Nordau,[24] "found its national ideal in the temperance societies, charity works for the redemption of prostitutes, and in a puerile worship." We should keep these harsh words in mind to understand the emotion that imposes itself on England during a major strike. Public opinion instinctively goes to the poor without knowing what consequences would result from its sympathetic movement. But can one really have less *pity* for workers than for prostitutes?

Modern protectionism is in the mainstream of this ideology. It transforms the state into a benefactor for all those who have no confidence in their personal strength and who deserve its support for the excellence of their own sentiments. The cartels reinforce protectionist policy and make the providential action of the state even more felt. Finally, the new tendencies impose on people social peace, the moderation of desires, and the respect for weakness, which lead to viewing agreement as the highest social duty. At the same time, they remove men from endeavors that can upset the whole economy.

The conclusion of these reflections is that the cartels cannot have the same function in France that they have in Germany. In this country power is still entirely imbued with the sentiment of its superior force; it understands its function in the same way as the old sovereigns who launched their people onto the path of progress at the beginning of modern times. As long as there are men conserving the traditions of Frederick the Great at the head of Germany, the cartels can be directed in a moderate spirit, but they will not be allowed to favor too much the lazy tendencies of their members. Neither does it seem that German social democracy is animated by the same spirit that dominates the popular parties in France. It is, in some way, penetrated with the sentiment of responsibility that is incumbent on it as the heir apparent of capitalism. It does not want to compromise the inheritance with imprudent acts. In it we find something of the spirit of the Prussian monarchy.

Notes

1. *Saggi di critica del Marxismo*, p. 29; citing Marx, *Revolution and Counter-revolution*.
2. Paul de Rousiers, *La Vie américaine: L'éducation et la société* (Paris: Firmin-Didot, 1899), pp. 216–17, 225.
3. Ibid., pp. 135, 179; *La Vie américaine: Ranches, fermes, et usines* (Paris: Firmin-Didot, 1899), p. 321.
4. *La vie américaine: L'éducation*, pp. 279–80.
5. Ibid., p. 162.
6. Ibid., pp. 152, 166.
7. Proudhon, *Solution du problème social*, in the complete works (Paris: A. Lacnoix, 1868), p. 60.
8. Ibid., p. 58.
9. Ibid., p. 76.
10. Ibid., p. 86.
11. In France, democracy and anti-Semitism have more or less the same conceptions. In *Libre Parole* (11 June 1902) we find great praise for a discourse by Léon Bourgeois which affirmed that "one could no longer tolerate the power of money accumulated in a few hands." It was, said the journal, "an anti-Semitism of the best and purest kind." In *Libre Parole* (27 November 1904) the Socialist deputy Veber was congratulated for having praised the Leuger administration in Vienna.
12. Paul de Rousiers, *La vie américaine: L'éducation*, pp. 206–08.
13. Yet it is quite rare that something does not remain for the worker in these businesses.
14. Proudhon, *General Idea of the Revolution in the Nineteenth Century*, English trans., p. 221.
15. Corbon, *Le secret du peuple de Paris*, 2nd ed. (Paris: Pagnerre, 1863), pp. 74–75.
16. Ibid., p. 385. Cf. what Proudhon says in the *Contradictions économiques*, Vol. II, pp. 367–73. From this he concluded on the possibility of limiting the population automatically, because, thought he, labor can only advance hand-in-hand with chastity. In *Justice*, he modified this thesis which seemed too physiological to him. In *La Guerre et la paix* (Book IV, ch. 2) he again returns to the aggravation of labor.

17. Ibid., p. 358.
18. Kautsky, *Politique agraire du parti socialiste*, pp. 25–28.
19. Marx, *Capital* (Modern Library ed.), p. 293.
20. Zola, *Lourdes* (Paris: Charpentier, 1894), p. 582. For several years, Protestant pastors, and especially Vilfredo Monod, have made a great to-do about a new messianism that they preach; they claim to realize the "kingdom of God" right now on the earth. I ask myself whether these preachers have not simply borrowed this idea from Zola.
21. The Middle Ages were greatly concerned with laws condemning thieves to death. The ruin of the Hohenstaufen family was attributed to the fact that they had put such a law in force, and that they had therefore put on the same scale the *life* of a man and *material possessions*. J. Clarus, *Receptarum sententiarum*, lir V, furtum. In the eighteenth century, Brissot's protests again responded to the same sentiment. Lichtenberger, *Le socialisme au XVIII siècle*, pp. 413–19.
22. I believe this is all that this ethical economics consists in, an economics with which we have been deafened for several years and whose banner serves to cover intellectual commodities that are sometimes of poor quality. See ch. 9 of Pareto's *Les Systèmes socialistes* cited above.
23. Marx cites in *Capital* (pp. 793–94, n3, Modern Library ed.) a curious speech delivered in 1698 in the Scottish Parliament. The orator said that he was "a Republican on principle" and demanded the restoration of serfdom for the 200,000 beggars in the country. On the same page we find mentioned a memoir on landed property written in Queen Elizabeth's time that Marx notes as a manifestation of the Protestant "spirit." In using the word *spirit* (in quotations) there is an ironic intent. Marx regards Protestantism as full of hypocrisy.
24. Max Nordau, *Paradoxes psychologiques*, French trans. (Paris: Alcan, 1897), p. 86.

CHAPTER SIX

According to Kautsky,[1] contemporary capitalism displays a characteristic somewhat unforeseen and unique, and which we must emphasize if we want to understand the present trends in socialism. Industrial capitalism, that had a preeminent place in England, is found ever more subordinated to finance capitalism. America, with its enormous trusts, shows this subordination in a particularly surprising form: the industrial bourgeoisie was pacifist, disposed toward concessions to the workers; contemporary capitalism has come around to violence; it is allied with the great landed property to demand a strong government, solid armies, and conquests. The two allies intend to drive back every development of social legislation.

Such a development differs completely from what Marx regarded as fundamental in his theory. According to the master, the triumph of industrial capital over the old forms (commercial and usury) was definite. Among many important passages I will cite only the following two: "Interest-bearing capital, or, as we may call it in its antiquated form, usurer's capital, belongs together with its twin brother, merchant's capital, to the *antidiluvian forms* of capital, which long precede the capitalist mode of production."[2] "In modern English history, the commercial estate proper and the merchant towns are also politically reactionary and in league with the landed and moneyed interest against industrial capital. . . . The complete rule of industrial capital was not acknowledged by English merchants' capital and moneyed interest until after the abolition of the corn tax."[3]

Marx's description corresponds more or less to Kautsky's: the old capitalist forms are allied with large landed property. The evolution is asserted by Kautsky as being a purely empirical fact; but it is clear that he does not conceive the existence of any cause capable of bringing to the foreground what was once obsolete in economic history. Kautsky appears to believe that this renaissance of finance capital, by intensifying social conflict, will have the effect of making the revolution more certain. But he does not ask whether such a revolution would correspond to Marx's ideas and why the old socialists, who had the most violent forms of usury capitalism under their own eyes, had no idea of Marxist theory.

Although I had not planned to deal with the question of trusts, I find myself led here to examine it under an entirely different aspect from the point of view of their relation to Marxist hypotheses. Many Marxists imagine that the trusts occur as an excellent manna from heaven that Providence would envy—to allow them to demonstrate the illusions of the reformists and to prove the exactitude of Marx's revolutionary predictions. It would seem more reasonable to think that, if capitalism will really regenerate taking forms that it had assumed in its infancy, the time for socialism has not yet come, and that we shall wait a long time while the new evolution can mature. We would also ask if there are not some laws of revival analogous to those that Vico uncovered which ensure capitalism an indefinite series of regenerations.

If things come about as Kautsky says, we must abandon the Marxist theory on the passage to socialism.[4] Industrial capitalism should indeed prepare for the conditions of free cooperation that socialism hopes to realize—the authority of the master during this period is based on the technical organization of production—the business is ever more governed by *internal forces* and there comes a time in which the authority of all external powers (that is the owner) will appear completely useless. If things come about as Kautsky thinks, the *economic bridge* between the two successive societies is broken: there may be a wide-reaching revolution, but it will be the product of force pure and simple. This will be an idealistic revolution made by men located outside of production, for the purpose of suppressing the authority of men also located outside of the business establishment and for substituting themselves for them. The proletariat will only have changed masters, and the revolution will benefit only a new oligarchy.

In primitive capitalism what is especially obvious is, on the one hand, the separation that exists between the industrialists and those who think for them, and on the other, the strong cohesion of all these categories of capitilists around the state. We find the same phenomena today in Kautsky's description of modern society. The great landed property of which he speaks is replete with feudal memories, because, as he says,[5] this class aspires to become court functionaries, and introduces its own sons "to careers as army officers, to which the sons of the bouregoisie seem less suitable." Clearly he is thinking here of the German Junkers. When great property restricts itself to the cultivation of the soil and finds n this cultivation sufficient resources for prosperity, it is not too states-nanlike and demands only tranquility. When great proprietors are very ich, we can verify two very different cases: either they exert a noticeable pressure to influence the government toward a policy of conquest, or they have no other ambition than to spend their income in the big cities. The phenomenon noted by Kautsky depends on the position that the nobility occupies in the army; it intends to exert an influence on the state by dint of its military importance. The function of great landed property is obviously not therefore the same in all countries, and Kautsky makes the world too much like Prussia.

Near the state live the great speculators who form the financial aristocracy that, according to Kautsky, tends to govern the modern world. They possess all the concessions, monopolies, loans, and colonial businesses that alone can give enormous profits today. We see reappear much of the old buccaneering that signaled the origin of modern times. In America, these pirates need the state to obtain protective tariffs and organize profitable railway service. Without these two auxiliaries the trusts could not have been established.

Financiers have only a limited taste for business conducted in a regular way. They need new business opportunities in which they can exercise their particular talent for usury combinations. Once the stocks are sold to the public, business administration no longer interests them very much.[6] The great Israelite bankers would accept with pleasure a system that permitted them to pass on to the state the enterprises from which they had withdrawn abundant commissions. The railway shares no longer give fruitful speculative opportunities after there are no more mergers to effectuate. The bankers would not see any inconvenience in redeeming railways over to the state. Financiers like to see their money moved around frequently, because they have always had magnificent opportunities to offer to simple-minded bourgeois. The ransoming of the railways would produce, as most conversions do, a shift of securities, and would allow for the hope of some good profit. I do not believe that the men of the Stock Exchange are hostile to heavy taxes on inheritance. They observe that the law on inheritance makes men much more prudent. America is the country blessed by financiers, and there no one counts on inheritance.

Our financiers no longer uphold good state administration as much as good administration of industrial enterprises. What they need are politicians able to understand the "great ideas," who ably manage large amounts of money, and who launch the country on the road to expenditure. The ministries of the Second Empire suited them marvelously. They became reattached to the Third Republic when Gambetta launched them on the road to profitable affairs. They are quite disposed to accept Jaurès's socialism, because it promises them fruitful harvests. Here is a declaration published in the *Petite République* for 29 August 1902 over the signature of the chief editor: "We aim indefatigably at progress in any form. We will not speak of economies that we know are impossible. But we will say to governments: look for new sources of revenue for your budget; look for them where you are sure to find them, from the property owners. Our formula is not: 'let us economize.' It is '*let us spend*' for the general good at the expense of the privileged."[7]

Parliamentary socialism harvests the inheritance of the old democracy. Here is a notable passage written by Proudhon in 1848 that would be applicable to our times:[8] "Money, money, always money; here is the sinew of democracy as of war. Give large sums of money to democracy and it will do what you want. Money for the deputies, money for the sick, money for beggars, money for the talented, the artists and the literati, for all those who will be friends of the government, or friends of the friends of the government. But of the means of obtaining all this money Lamartine does not speak; it is the only thing he forgets."

At the beginning of modern times, the absolute powers had an enormous need for money. The present democracy finds itself in the same condition; it scorns the old parsimony of governments dominated by landowners and industrialists. Financiers take on their old function of money lenders because of the prodigal policy on which we are launched, although their relations with the state are quite different from those of the past.

We must place here the class of intellectuals whose importance Kautsky has not fully appreciated. Men who live by science, the arts, or the press, who were once parasites of princes, now place themselves in the service of those parties that can pay them. Kautsky observes[9] that they are in all camps, but he could add that the greatest of intellectuals are inclined toward the camps that might be in power tomorrow if they are not yet coparticipants in authority. The true function of the intellectuals is to advise, entertain, or celebrate statesmen. If there are many who come to socialism, it is because on this side the competition is less active and the benefits more sure.[10] The Dreyfus affair revealed to many intellectuals the *monetary value of their talents*. This affair was inflated like stock issues on mines in the moon. In both camps there were very few who did not receive the "just deserts" for their speeches.

At the beginning of modern times, the state and the financiers were what directed the world toward the new life. If at the present time these two great forces, allied once again, take over the direction of the industrial world, we must not expect to see anything but authoritarian state socialism come about. The transition would be all the easier insofar as the politicians and financiers resemble each other in an amazing way.

Their intellectual level is not greatly different; their morality is generally fairly base; experience shows that politicians easily become distinguished financiers. Business would not be conducted worse under parliamentary control than under bankers' control.[11] Many good people who have not lost their illusions about representative government think that public opinion would rise more easily against the abuses committed by government minsters than against those of the stock exchange parasites. This shows that in the honest bourgeoisie there is at the same time a deep anti-Semitism and a certain fondness for statist solutions.

We go back to the ideas of 1848[12] for several reasons: the three sentimental principles—democracy, morality, and Christianity—are now much more powerful than at that time, and all three lead men to surrender to the state. Finance has taken on such great importance in the world that it often conceals industrial development to the eyes of the public. The mechanism of the state has so increased that an enormous mass of interests is connected to it and sees no future except in its extension.

In such conditions, Marxism finds itself in very bad health. It is attacked even in its basic ideas by those who profess to defend it; hence the Marxists are the most eager to point out to the people the absolute domination of the financiers without doubting that their speeches result in making the workers understand that the true solution to the present ills would consist in the rapid elimination of the financiers. Therefore, their polemic tends toward state socialism, which they pretend to hate. But it is not enough to have a horror of a solution; it is prudent not to do anything in order not to make it inevitable.

Many people think that the cartels, by bringing the capitalists together, create insurmountable obstacles that were not predicted and which will arrest all the normal progress of the working class. Such seems to be Kautsky's opinion.[13] If labor unions cannot develop as Marxist theory assumed, we must abandon the idea of a transformation from capitalist to proletarian administration. Therefore, only an act of state intervention can modify the present regime, replacing the present rulers designated by the capitalists with new ones, dependents of the state. We will return once more to the pseudosocialism organized by authoritarian democracy.

I believe that Kautsky is mistaken and Marx was right when he regarded the capitalist class as very difficult to unite: not being heads of enterprises, the workers are not subjected to the necessities of competition like their bosses, whose interests are manifested as contradictory every day. Observations of every period show that common peril may not produce union, and that an oligarchy is all the more divided the more the insurgents are strong and close to an assault. When there is such an imminent peril, the most shrewd members of the oligarchy either go over to the enemy or do their best to make an individual peace.

The Catholics claim that the mystical veil of religion can hide the antagonisms of an accidental and material order resulting from competition and thus favor agreement with a view to higher ends. This assertion seems highly contestable. For the capitalists to form "a head and a heart" it is necessary that universal peace be conceivable. The promoters of social catholicism never separate *peace* among the classes from *accord* inside the same classes. The *idea of this peace* is indispensable for making this *accord* intelligible. We do not go from the particular to the general, from the individual to persons of the same profession, from the professions to classes, and from this to society—thus generating unity by means of multiplicity. The mind goes through exactly the opposite process. It departs from the idea, that is, from the universal, from what is farthest from its practice, in order to control and direct it according to its conformity with the universal.[14]

But what if we encounter a blank? What if we come up against an absolute impossibility, for example if the working class angrily manifests its will not to accept any proposition of social peace no matter what the proposed conditions? In this case the movement will be interrupted and common sense will show that all unity is impossible. Thus we perceive in a new light the revolutionaries' function: by preventing the working class from accepting the idea of social peace, they prevent the idea from dominating the minds of the capitalists and impose an insurmountable barrier for the enemy classes to reach an accord among themselves. Revolutionary propaganda, by uniting the working class, divides the capitalists.

Consequently, will the reformists' tactics not have the result of facilitating agreements among capitalists? This seems probable, since then the hiatus noted above will no longer manifest itself so obviously. Universal peace will no longer seem absurd. The financiers can then intervene, come to terms with the representatives of the democratic state for the purpose of imposing arrangements on the industrialists. Finally reformism, by giving to the bourgeoisie the idea that it can still last a long time, blocks many desertions from its ranks and increases its courage. The day the working class comes to believe in the long-range durability of capitalism and in reformism, it will tend to divide into crafts and pursue divergent ends. This phenomenon has often been noted. The revolutionary principle is the only one capable of uniting the proletariat.

Notes

1. *Mouvement Socialiste* (15 October 1902):1850–58.
2. Marx, *Capital* (Moscow: Progress Publishers, 1966), Vol. III, p. 593. Italics added.
3. Ibid., p. 327n.
4. Sorel, *Saggi di critica del marxismo,* pp. 349–54.
5. *Mouvement Socialiste* (15 October 1902):1853.
6. Paul de Rousiers cites this unique fact, that the shipping trust acquired some ships, having already had a number of years of service, at 500 francs per ton of displacement, while English builders sell new ships at 280 francs. *Journal des économistes* (March 1904):426.
7. After having reproduced this very important declaration in *Pages Libres* (21 March 1903) they added: "We therefore need not be surprised (as Drumont is every day) at the sympathy for parliamentary socialism shown by many people on the stock exchange and in banks; but as far as I can tell, Guesde inspires as much fear and hatred in them as Jaurès inspires admiration and confidence."
8. Proudhon, *Solution du problème social*, p. 75.
9. *Mouvement Socialiste* (15 October 1902):1843.
10. The great development of present anti-clericalism shows us how eagerly the intellectuals launch themselves on paths that seem profitable to them.
11. In certain circumstances, this sentiment is also manifested in America. *Débats* (23 March 1905).
12. Hence it is extremely important today to re-read Proudhon's effective critique of democracy in the *Solution du problème social*: he denounces its authoritarianism. How many times could we repeat with him, while reading the discourses of Jaurès: "always the same representative prejudices, always the same cult of the *multitudes*, always the same palliatives of philanthropy" (p. 75).
13. *Mouvement Socialiste* (15 October 1902):1843.
14. There is no way to raise ourselves from observation and empiricism to the categorical imperative by means of an inductive procedure. It is only the datum of this imperative that allows for reasoning on moral life in Kant's system. In the same way, the idea of class struggle is a datum of socialism, a datum that can be justified to a certain degree, making it intelligible by pointing out its economic bases and proving its historical function.

CHAPTER SEVEN

We cannot regard finance capitalism as belonging to a unique type; it is almost always mixed with commercial capitalism. They are "twin brothers," as Marx says. Moreover, it is not manifested in the same way in countries where the spirit of initiative is extinguished and in those in which it emerges. America and Germany are new countries which have begun production with extraordinary splendor; they cannot be compared to France and England.[1] Apropos of interest-producing capital, Marx made some observations of great importance for our subject:[2] "The villainies of the Venetian thieving system formed one of the secret bases of the capital wealth of Holland, to whom Venice in her decadence lent large sums of money. So also was it with Holland and England. By the beginning of the eighteenth century, the Dutch manufacturers were far outstripped. Holland had ceased to be the nation preponderant in commerce and industry. One of its main lines of business, therefore, from 1701 to 1776, is the lending out of enormous amounts of capital, especially to its great rival England."

When the industrial spirit is exhausted, we see capital search for new and profitable remuneration. Financiers scheme to offer the public investments for capital that can appear more advantageous than the usual ones. One of the simplest procedures consists in acquiring factories in particularly prosperous foreign countries. A foreign exchange agent in New York told Paul de Rousiers:[3] "Syndicates of small English capitalists come here to buy already established and fully functioning industrial businesses; but the money they bring allows the Americans to launch new businesses under the rule of private firms."

The operations practiced by the great American financiers, the organizers of trusts, present a completely different character. It is no longer a question of contenting oneself with mediocre profits abandoned by adventurous Yankees, but of realizing exceptional profits. This does not occur in sleepy countries, but in those in which the spirit of enterprise is very ardent. The enormity of this operation has deceived many people about the true nature of trusts. It is believed that everything that is large belongs to a superior order (through analogies with the great nations, the great spinning mills, and great metallurgical furnaces), and the trusts have been regarded as the *terminus ad quem* of capitalist evolution. Americans, whose national pride knows no bounds, have been quite happy to possess a capitalism that is more capitalist than that of the English, which has led many of their writers to extol the effects of trusts. There is nothing new in all this. The trusts are the old mergers repeated on a larger scale than in Europe. The difference arises from the fact that America has at its disposal much more money than did European financiers fifty years ago, from the fact that the natural resources of the country are enormous, and from the fact that technical progress allows them to create concentrated enterprises of which no one had any idea before.

I have noted elsewhere[4] that these operations belong to the category of usury. They often do not differ at all from the old usury, since in many cases they translate into a simple spoliation of modest holders of capital to the benefit of the builders of mergers. In America usury capital seems less oppressive than in Europe because many great trusts are directed by captains of industry who are powerful creators of productive forces. Ordinarily we are used to seeing in usury a simple exploitation[5] which ruins production and prevents all progress. It is the general circumstances which make the difference: the financier and the usurer belong to the same type. In America the trusts are tolerated much more easily insofar as the country is very rich,[6] the opportunities for enrichment more numerous, and the directors of the trusts are very prudent. The country does not have much occasion to lament its usurers (this occurs especially in the petroleum trust). But very often the trusts are simple speculations that bring a temporary disturbance and end in noisy catastrophes.[7] In these instances their usurous character is obvious.

The German cartels are much less dominated by the usurous spirit of the trusts. De Rousiers has strongly insisted on their commercial character. He offers the opinion[8] that they correspond to a need for "commercial concentration" that can be satisfied without the enterprises being united in the same hands. He says: "The German cartel is not like the American pool, that is, it does not arise by chance in the present history of industrial concentration, an ephemeral combination imagined by a captain of industry in order to serve his designs for conquest. Rather, it is an organism which develops in a favorable atmosphere and which changes—but all of whose changes are progressive."[9] Thus the cartel develops on an entirely different level from the trust and is not designed to coincide with it. "It is an alliance," he continues, "in which everyone preserves a certain freedom of action, and a temperament more or less disposed toward the economic struggle. The trust, on the contrary, is the result of a life or death struggle."[10]

Commercial capital lends itself much more easily to agreements than does financial speculation. A large speculator generally tries to crush his associates while a merchant can live with them under the regime of corporative pricing agreements. Past experience shows that such arrangments can be maintained until the time comes in which the great money handlers intervene in order to wreck everything. De Rousiers observes[11] that the German cartels almost always manifest a conservative spirit, moderate desires, and an absence of a taste for domination and exclusivism.

Precisely because of these less savage characteristics, the cartel is less bold than the trust and has much less sharply defined tendencies. This explains why so many authors have been mistaken in describing cartels, sometimes nearly identifying them with the trusts when the usurous spirit dominates them, sometimes nearly comparing them to a simple sales agreement when they are especially concerned with the increasing prosperity of one branch of production. De Rousiers has rightly observed that to understand American business we must take careful account of the American character, and it is useful for us to dwell for a moment on this point because people do not always pay enough attention to the moral causes of economic institutions.

"Only fifty years or so ago," says our author,[12] "the almost completely agricultural nation contained only independent producers. Few people managed businesses or enterprises of others, there was little great wealth, and many farmers. Such was the condition of the new Britain at that time. Independence was the general rule." This population arose from a selection made in the class of English yeomen. The lifestyle these yeomen had followed for a long time developed the sense of personality to the highest level. Still today, the true American[13] is concerned only with his wife and children, who constitute his entire household. The idea of a large family and, more so, the idea of a clan are completely foreign to him. The men of New England continue to play a dominant role in American life. They have abandoned agriculture because it no longer yields anything.[14] But their tastes have remained strongly agricultural. Doctors, lawyers, and businessmen told de Rousiers that they had a strong taste for farming.[15] "Nine times out of ten, the great Western landowner comes from the Eastern states. He is a Yankee who has become temporarily, perhaps, a farmer, but who nevertheless occupies an exceptional position in the new territory. It is he who maintains the national feeling and imposes it on other emerging groups."

We should attribute great importance to these assertions by a sagacious observer like Paul de Rousiers. We are in the presence of a population that has preserved to the highest degree the rural, *combative, and dominant characteristics* which give them a certain resemblance to the old feudal knights. An old civil war colonel could say to de Rousiers:[16] "We are an imperious race." When we fail to take account of this fact, we cannot understand America. The Yankee is a man of the isolated household who works to be the sole master of his chosen domain, be it a piece of land or an industry. He does not intend to remain under the control of another man and feels confident enough "to try his luck."[17] Every entrepreneur is convinced that he can become a millionaire, as so many others have succeeded in doing.

We find among Americans the instinct of isolation so strong in all primitive populations[18] and which has so often led our peasants to refuse to enter into an association capable of improving their lot, and which renders them mistrustful of every invention. But in America this instinct is quite different from that of primitive men: it is the manifestation of the faith of entrepreneurial man in his own genius. He is not misoneist, he is overwhelmed by the desire to do great things. The American fears being disturbed by ties that the German, on the other hand, seeks out enthusiastically. The instinct of association is very old in Germany; it is highly probable that it emerges from a feeling of weakness and that its origins were servile. We know that communitarian forms have generally had an origin of this kind in Europe. The extreme discipline that has unceasingly been practiced in all German society could only develop this instinct.

In Germany the ground was perfectly prepared for the cartels. Nevertheless there had been spirited opposition, until the spectacle of prosperous agreements convinced the industrialists that practices of this type could be usefully applied to capitalism. Probably they would not have succeeded in uniting the Westphalian mines in 1893 if there had not been a notable transformation in the state of property,[19] and if many small concessions had not been absorbed by larger ones. It was very difficult to establish the sugar syndicate, because many manufacturers belonged to associations of proprietors who were afraid of vast combinations.[20]

A superficial observer would not fail to conclude from these facts that association constitutes a superior form of economic activity, since the opposition encountered by the cartels arises especially from heads of small industry who are less educated than others. On the contrary, it seems infinitely probable that strict solidarity, complete association, and the community of a very large number of interests belongs to a very primitive civic body.[21] In any event, we find these characteristics in humble civilizations. We also find them in convents which exist outside of civil society and law; and they were regarded as admirable by the ingenuous creators of utopias. Everything allows for the thought that the association that does not take over the entire human personality and which is concerned only with fragmentary interests, respecting the complete liberty of each individual, is the truly superior form.

Americans practice association on a grand scale; but association among Americans is conceived very differently than in Germany: it does not have the purpose of directly satisfying economic ends; it does not disturb individual activity; it does not have rules or militaristic customs. "It can," says Paul de Rousiers,[22] "subsist intact and without tyranny despite the most serious divergence of viewpoints among association members in regard to objects outside its purpose." In conclusion, the phenomena of trusts and cartels are dominated by historical conditions. The classical forms described ought to be observed in America for trusts and in Germany for cartels. We can identify the former with usury capital, the latter with commercial capital, that is to say, with the two sister forms of ancient capitalism. It is curious that Germany at the time of the Renaissance reveals many traits similar to those of contemporary America. This comparison, which is taken from the elements of analysis in Jansenn's work, seems highly instructive to me, because it shows us how the rapid expansion of wealth affects a country. Until recently, Germany had a great reputation for the abilities of its miners and metallurgists. All during the Middle Ages they made incessant technical progress.[23] At the end of the fifteenth century, the discovery of rich silver lodes made Germany into a sort of European Peru. New cities grew up with great rapidity. The depreciation of money was felt before the American influence was even apparent.[24] The miners' banking agents had enormous sums at their disposal.

Le Play observed[25] that the art of mining held a kind of fascination for the human mind. Although subterranean exploitation, when well managed, gives only mediocre profits, "the expectation of the unknown and the struggle with fate" give such great satisfaction that sometimes fruitless labors are undertaken for many generations. It appears that the search for precious metals produces a kind of intoxication in the human spirit. When the old moralists denounced the crimes caused by the desire for gold, their heads were filled with historical legends regarding the struggles between miners looking for gold and warriors looking for treasure. The Norse and Homeric poems have shown what part of the vision of gold has played in the passions of primitive men. In the adventurous character of the American there is something of the ancient hero. This should not be attributed to ethnographic causes but to the intoxication with metallurgy. At the end of the fifteenth century, the Germans were also completely intoxicated by the vision of precious metals, and the narratives of that time do not show much moderation in the conduct of their bourgeois aristocracies.

Eneas Sylvius (Pius II), who was a conscientious and very perspicacious observer, admired[26] the German cities and was amazed at the extensive freedom that reigned there. This seemed all the more amazing because in the Italian republics one was subjected to the most severe servitude. There is an analogy with contemporary America here, and this great liberty of the citizens should be compared to the truly American spirit of enterprise of German merchants of that time, just as servitude in the Italian republics compares to the decline of the Southern republics. The eccentricities of luxury in America are also found in this Germany of old. We are told[27] of shirts threaded with gold, of gold threads adorning women's hair, of gold horse bits, of the abundance of precious dishes, of diadems, worn by women, similar to those of the statues of saints. Fashion changes instantaneously and extravagantly; the women begin to show off men's hairstyles and spend part of their time drinking rare wines and in the baths. The interiors of merchants' houses are sumptuous.

Capital was abundant and able financiers knew how to centralize it. The renowned Hochstetter of Augsburg was the Péreire of his day. By associating with him, several people had earned enough money so that everyone brought him his own capital. There were small depositors of ten florins; he had to pay up to a million florins a year in interest.[28] He cornered all sorts of markets such as ash timber, wine, and grain; he adulterated spices; but his abilities did not preserve him from ruin; he lost 800,000 florins and died in prison. He had bought 200,000 florins worth of mercury, and the discovery of new mines caused him to lose a third of his money. A boat loaded with spices sank; a convoy from Holland was plundered; his son and son-in-law lost fantastic sums in gambling.[29]

The discovery of new commercial routes to India had transformed the old merchant habits.[30] To work for Lisbon, it was necessary to have considerable capital and a house in this city. The spice trade became the monopoly of the big enterprises. At the diet of Innsbruck in 1508 it was said[31] that commerce turned out to be impossible for those who did not possess at least 10,000 florins. It was claimed[32] that to compete with Hochstetter it was necessary to have 100,000 florins at one's disposal. The big capitalists[33] sent agents to buy merchandise in foreign countries or at the port of entry; offers of a price higher than the current one were widely practiced;[34] contracts with producers were made to ensure buying privileges; spices, metals, and wool were objects of monopolization against which the diet of Cologne in 1512 pronounced the confiscation of wealth; in 1508 an Austrian diet at Innsbruck listed the monopolies in metals, cloth, sugar, spices, grain, livestock, wine, leather; it also dissolved an association formed to monopolize soap. It does not seem that this legislation was any more efficacious than the American antitrust laws, and it was noted that the authorities in the big cities were accomplices of the monopolists. We could multiply the points of comparison and the analogies would turn out to be ever more surprising. Germany, profiting from rapidly acquired property, could see finance capital despotically governing economic life.

In comparing American history with that of old Germany, we are less surprised at the facts that occur under our eyes. This comparison leads not only to regard the American phenomena as no longer the *terminus ad quem* of capitalist economics, but to think that they could very well be only an accident in a development that would remain true to Marx's general concept. I believe that we should abandon Marx's excessively strict ideas on capitalist development and that we should consider that in all times there has been a mixture of the three forms of capital, in the same way that there is always a mixture[35] of particularism, collectivism, and communism. It is exterior circumstances which cause sometimes one form, other times another to become preeminent. Theory agrees with the best contemporary research on primitive institutions. There is no single schema of unique and therefore necessary development for arriving at the establishment of private property and the monogomous family. There are various paths of development, and in these paths there are oscillations.

Several years ago, when communal property was discovered in several areas, there was a pragmatic recognition that they were vestiges of primitive times. But today closer study has shown that the so-called survivals of this type often took shape in modern times. Thus De Laveleye is greatly mistaken on the *dessa* of Java; the Dutch socialist Van Kol[36] has shown how, after 1830, the government had established "for political motives, the communal possession that today governs half the cultivated land in Java."

But from the fact that there is not an *absolute law* of development, we must not conclude that there is not a *relative law*, that in a system of production highly developed in a technological sense[37] we can no longer return, at least in a complete and lasting way, to the forms of capitalism that Marx regarded as outmoded in the contemporary world. If we could be completely sure of such a law, we would already have obtained a notable result from the socialist point of view. The entire Marxist conception of the emancipation of labor relies on the hypotheses of the "stages of capitalism."[38] Here we could not invoke the help of social myths to correct errors of fact, if there were any. At this point we have penetrated the economic-historical roots of Marxism, and it ought to be definitely scrapped if the theory of stages of capitalism were false.

I call the attention of Marxists to the importance of studies dealing with this scale. It would be most useful in particular to try to explain the *apparent* renaissance of usury capitalism. I believe that among the causes of this we could note the following:

1. Nowhere in Europe has progress been as complete as Marx assumed. The wealthy have always preserved an enormous influence in the world. It is much easier to lead medium or small capitalists astray in a financial matter than in an industrial one, whose range escapes them. Many of the great money managers are in the same position, and they do not know how to venture into purely industrial innovations. We therefore can understand that buying stocks with a view to their future price increase is tempting to many, as much in a bold society (like the United States in which well-directed enterprises can reach high levels of development) as in a timid one content with small improvements in income designed to compensate for losses derived from conversions of old stock.

Mergers succeed especially when one expects a great deal in the near future. Such was the case in France fifty years ago; I have already said that the American trust only reproduces known phenomena (strongly enlarged). Every time an era of prosperity appears to begin, the small and average-size capitalists allow themselves to be deluded by sweet promises made by those who want mergers, and these mergers can end in fantastic wealth. Here sentiment dominates over reason;[39] a successful trust produces many other trusts which fail, just as the success of the Suez Canal allowed the mounting of the Panama affair.[40]

2. American speculators acquire vast territories in the Far West and resell them several years later, after having exploited them, without profit and even at a loss. European financiers operate in the colonies; they are able to obtain vast concessions there and establish business firms capable of producing vast and rapid profits, with the intention of selling them as quickly as possible to well-to-do entrepreneurs. All European states have been quick to conquer savage countries with as much enthusiasm as they had in the seventeenth century. The need for colonial products obtained at the very lowest prices and destined for a very extensive clientele has attracted the attention of financiers, while the industrialists hope to find new outlets in that region. Colonel policy is very suitable to the often-noted alliance between the territorial nobility and financiers that takes place today. It satisfies the need for military glory that has not ceased to exist in Europe. The French people do not know very well whether it has been very glorious to vanquish the Hovas

and the inhabitants of Dahomey, but they like to hear about victories.

3. At the beginning of the modern era, the state wanted to develop industry because it needed money. Our democracy is no less hungry for gold than the ancien régime from which the traditions were inherited. Never in France have people spoken so much of the need to develop the economic sphere of the nation as they do today. The economic power at the disposal of the state is limited. It can perfect what I have called[41] "the mechanical apparatus of the economic environment"; it can still have a great influence on the very organs of production by favoring capitalist accumulation. We see many old procedures reappear: protectionism, colonial conquest, favors that recall the old privileges (as happens with the German cartels).

The great development given to public works has been the most abundant source of greater wealth in all European countries where industry is not very far advanced. In Rome military works and provisions had already had great importance, as Guilielmo Ferrero has shown many times in his work *Grandezza e decadenza di Roma*. To achieve maximum results, these operations require that there be a close agreement between the political and financial worlds. This agreement, which existed in Rome, is still found in our times. As in the past, the avant garde parties are not the last to profit from this alliance (which in France produces various comical effects).

The intervention of the state in the economic field has been largely responsible for the development of usury capitalism we have seen in our times. If they still put any value in Marxist theory, socialists should be more concerned with this fact than they have been until now. In a thorough study one should take account of the effects produced by a prolonged period of peace such as we have enjoyed since 1871. Russia has been the only great European power to have started a war in the last thirty-five years (aside from the Boer War, which has been a farce). For France this prolonged peace has been a cause of moral and intellectual weakness, as well as economic weakness, the spirit of enterprise having become less virile.

No one doubts that this situation will not last indefinitely; a small matter would be enough to reawaken the warrior sentiments in France, and such reawakening would produce an upheaval throughout Europe. A great war would have the effect of suppressing the causes which today tend to favor the taste for moderation and the desire for social peace. The future does not seem lost for the Marxists; but they would do well to reflect on what constitutes the originality, force, and philosophical value of the principles their master has handed down.

Notes

1. Kautsky commits this error and says on the contrary that the situation in Germany can indicate England's economic future. *Mouvement Socialiste* (15 October 1902):1857. He regards social phenomena too much as physical things in the process of change, following a unique law, and he does not take sufficient account of history.
2. Marx, *Capital* (Modern Library ed.), pp. 828–29.
3. Paul de Rousiers, *La Vie américaine: Ranches,* p. 350.
4. Sorel, *Saggi di critica del marxismo,* p. 342.
5. Marx, *Capital* (Moscow ed.), Vol. III.
6. Trusts are tolerated in the same way as politicians. Thus in the great cities where luxury industries exist, certain workers' corporations can obtain exceptional working conditions that are paid by an economically insignificant luxury.
7. Paul de Rousiers has analyzed these disasters well in *Les industries monopolisées aux Etats-Unis* (Paris: A. Colin, 1898).
8. De Rousiers, *Les syndicats industriels,* p. 276.
9. Ibid., p. 160.
10. Ibid., p. 125.
11. Ibid., pp. 156, 157, 160, 279, 130, 108.
12. De Rousiers, *La Vie américaine: Ranches,* p. 281.
13. Ibid., pp. 137, 145.
14. Ibid., pp. 263–65.
15. Ibid., p. 111. Cf. pp. 120–22.
16. Ibid., p. 305. Cf. *Les syndicats industriels,* p. 278.
17. *La Vie américaine: l'éducation,* p. 19.
18. It is very strange that among the Athenians commercial societies were rare. Guiraud, *La Main d'oeuvre industrielle dans l'ancienne Grèce.,* p. 90.
19. Grüner and Fuster, *Aperçu historique sur les syndicats de vente de combustibles dans le bassin rheno-westphalien* (Paris: Comité Central des houillières de France, n.d.), pp. 14–15.
20. De Rousiers, *Les Syndicats industriels,* p. 150.
21. Professor Flach emphasizes these facts in the course of his lectures at the Collège de France.
22. Paul de Rousiers, *La Vie américaine: l'éducation,* p. 170.
23. Jansenn, *L'Allemagne et la Réforme,* French trans. (Paris: Plon, 1897), Vol. I, pp. 340–44.
24. Ibid., p. 384.
25. Le Play, *La Réforme sociale en France,* 5th ed., Vol. II, p. 117.
26. Jansenn, *L'Allemagne et la Réforme,* p. 384.
27. Ibid., pp. 362–66, 343.
28. Ibid., pp. 385–87. Jansenn noted that at that time with 12 florins one could buy three fat oxen (p. 363).
29. Ibid., p. 388: they say, 30,000 florins in one night; they gave feasts that cost from 5,000 to 10,000 florins.
30. Ibid., p. 381.
31. Ibid., p. 384.
32. Ibid., p. 387.
33. Ibid., p. 382.

34. Ibid., pp. 383–85, 387.
35. *From Georges Sorel*, pp. 145–47.
36. Rienzi (Van Kol), *La propriété foncière à Java,* p. 13. Extract from *Revue Socialiste* (1896).
37. The arrest and retrogression of development that was ascertained in previous times could depend on the fact that industrial technology was still in its infancy.
38. *Saggi di critica del Marxismo*, pp. 340–351.
39. Financial speculation is closely related to the instincts, and industrial enterprise to reason.
40. After all, it does not seem that the Suez business has been conducted with more probity and intelligence than the Panama affair.
41. In the preface to the *Historire des Bourses du travail* by Fernand Pelloutier (Paris: Schleicher, 1902), p. 12, and in the *Introduction à l'économie moderne*, pp. 129–42.

CONCLUSION

In the course of this long work of inquiry and discussion it has often been necessary to stop and examine many points of detail which our predecessors have not illuminated; from these have come many digressions. In concluding it would be useful to present an overview and propose some advice to socialists who believe that Marxism still has a role to play in the world. I shall not return to the question treated at the end of the preceding chapter, and I will assume that the scale of capitalism conforms closely to Marx's conception. I therefore go on immediately to the notions of determinism and freedom that Marx created in observing what was happening in England. Three orders of phenomena impressed him:

1. In England, for centuries, various social groups have been in a condition of struggle and have ruthlessly pursued their own particular ends without bothering about the consequences their conduct could have on the fortunes of the country. Their interests, their ambitions, or their rancor take precedence over any patriotic sentiment. And yet no other nation plays such a powerful industrial role. Capitalist prosperity can thus go hand in hand with complete social insolidarity.

2. The class which created the wealth of England had much to complain about with regard to the conditions that politics had created for it. The parasitism of landlords and their minions that had to be supported by means of rich sinecures;[1] an incoherent administration that was unintelligent and too often dishonest; slow and costly justice; outlandish parliamentary corruption; incompetent governments—these were the most characteristic conditions of English life. Nonetheless, the whole world envied England. Thus we must admit that capitalism has such power that it can triumph over all obstacles. All the more reason to come to its aid.

3. English industry having had at its disposal abundant capital, enormous outlets that a very extensive maritime commerce had opened to it, and a technology of a heretofore unsuspected sophistication served by very favorable mineralogical conditions, modern capitalism had come to be regarded as infinite. The men who managed enterprises were not

genuises; the peculiar power of modern industry has become independent of individuals.

Absolute social insolidarity, the all-powerfulness of capitalist initiative, and the infinity of production were regarded by Marx as principles which no longer had to be investigated. It was useless to know the causes which had brought about the position of English industry. He believed that the same situation would be found everywhere that capitalism developed. The ideology of inevitability and freedom was constituted on these foundations.

a) In competing against one another, capitalists produce a set of phenomena with all the aspects of a natural aggregation; we do not see a trace of individual wills in it. Thus is found in society a "world of inevitability" in which all individuals must submit to the general laws which govern the capitalist element under pain of ruination. Neither the state nor socialist organization can do much of anything about this bloc. It even seemed that inevitability was always increasing, for the progress of capitalism in Marx's time did away with all the obstacles that the laws, family traditions, and local and ethnic reasons had been able to oppose to it. On the other hand, with competition becoming more and more imperative, and with inventions revolutionizing technology always more rapidly, the capitalists became more alert to discovering improvements in equipment, in the use of material, or in the organization of labor. The perspicacity of capitalists could be regarded as a natural cause of the acceleration of movements which tend to make this world fatality more blind. This doctrine rests on many hypotheses and notably it assumes that industrial capitalism triumphs definitively over the old forms. It demands that the industrial spirit never waver for a single moment. It takes no account of the continual expansion of the modern state which advances hand-in-hand with that of capitalism.

b) To this world of increasing inevitability is opposed the world of freedom in the process of formation; confronting disunited capitalists are proletarians who work to unite. Those who are oriented toward a socialist life without masters, rebel against the masters who create the material conditions of a prodigiously rich society. The proletarians who are first disciplined for labor in the workshop by the authority of the capitalists will finally acquire a clear consciousness of relations, either between workers and tools, or among the worker-producers themselves. In this way they will attain reasoned liberty; but they will not attain it inevitably. They will have to want to become reasonable and seek the means to realize their hopes.

Here Marx's research was most imperfect. Living in a country imbued with Christianity, it does not seem to have occurred to him to ask what was the influence of moral education on the English working classes. Contemporary observers credit a large part of the progress accomplished in this country to nonconformist communities.[2] Neither did he think about the relationship between his conception of the class struggle and national traditions. He did not foresee that this conception would have great difficulty in being accepted.[3] Finally, he spoke and acted as if the socialist word, dropped in the midst of workers engaged in corporative conflicts with their bosses, was enough to produce the organization of the proletariat. He conceived of this organization under the form of adherence to an agitation directed by politicians. We know today that the problem is much more complex than Marx suspected. At least three conditions must be fulfilled: (1) that the proletariat create institutions in which it can do without the help of men outside its class; (2) that through moral striving it acquire a clear consciousness of personal responsibilities and demand from its functionaries a virtue superior to that of bourgeois functionaries; (3) that all its activity have as its origin and goal the class struggle. These conditions are difficult to fulfill.

c) Between these two worlds exists the area in which the state moves. This state has sometimes been regarded as subject to determinism, sometimes as free. Marx was disposed to the first view because in England power greatly depended on businessmen, and because parliaments seemed to him to register compromises resulting from a combination of individual wills analogous to what results from free competition in the economic arena.[4] In contrast, Lassalle regarded the state as a free force capable of smashing capitalism. He was thinking of Prussia, where the tradition of Frederick the Great still persisted and where the king was never very seriously bothered by parliamentarianism. Marx assigns the state a spiritual role; the state can give to the proletariat the means of creating its own culture. But in the *Critique of the Gotha Programme* he wants the state to subsidize schools without directing them. Marx's idea is relevant today because many socialists regard public instruction as a proper state function.

Declaring that the proletariat would soon be in a position to reverse capitalist domination and that a revolution would intervene before social relations were transformed, Marx estimated that the future society would regulate the remuneration allotted to its members according to the principle which now (approximately) regulates salaries. This thesis appeared to him to unfold from historical observation. It rendered all research on future law useless and did away with utopias. In practice, this result could be obtained in several ways; Marx always avoided pronouncements on the forms to be adopted. But according to his successors, free competition would intervene to ensure the satisfaction of all the needs of various occupations and to proportion wages to labor.

It matters little that the revolution did not materialize as Marx visualized, provided that the organization of the workplace not be changed to the point of abolishing what Marx considered essential. So long as the labor contract remains for sale and that this sale is made on a free market, the average remuneration conforms to Ricardo's ideas and the classes are independent of one another. Marxism is not shaken by the error committed on the revolution; the revolutionary period plays no part in socialist thought. For the sake of exposition, the revolution can be conceived as catastrophic without the least inconvenience.

The catastrophic conception of revolution can be preserved as a social myth, joined with the idea of the general strike. There remain many vestiges of utopianism in the writings of Marx and Engels, and it is by no means certain that these have not had more influence in popularizing their doctrines than their scientific and philosophical elements. For many socialists, Marx is the man who has irrefutably demonstrated that capitalist wealth derives from a theft committed against the workers, the man who has proclaimed the necessity of a revolution more absolute than his precursors had ever dreamed, and who taught "creative hatred" to the workers.[5] Marxism was adopted by many revolutionaries because it appeared to be the most violent of the socialist doctrines, and if several of them allied themselves to Bakunin it was because he appeared still more violent than his rival.

People were thus led to conceive of Marxism as the theory of the new 1793 and to regard as essential a conception of the magical power of government force. It was a matter of seizing power and using it to change the world. This utopia, sustained by the bellicose ideas inspired by the legend of the Paris Commune, is not remotely Marxist. It is still maintained, especially in Blanquist groups in several cities. The day when the electoral arena was entered under the pretext of raising the revolutionary flag against the bourgeoisie, primitive utopianism was quickly transformed. There was no choice but to take advantage of various electoral successes obtained in elections; gradually the idea was introduced that it was necessary to conquer power in fragments at all stages. The inevitable catastrophe was then replaced by a progressive revolution which would be realized to the extent that elected socialist officials became influential political personages. Various stages could be obtained only by compromise. The accepted idea now was that the state could suppress capitalism by creating an industrial system seriously controlled by the progressive parties and that socialism ought to turn more to the benefit of the poor the production which had heretofore been too much to the benefit of the rich. The result at present is the total replacement of Marx's principles by a mixture of the ideas of Lassalle and democratic appetites.

While Marx wished only to concern himself with the organization of the *hands* of industry, the socialism which thinks of itself as following Marx is concerned with the *head* of industry. The conquest of political power necessarily leads to this return to utopian views. General causes have precipitated this movement toward degeneration and make a return to the old principles very difficult. Protectionist policies which are increasingly dominant tend to engender the notion of solidarity, and they would make no sense if we still conceived of industrial production as infinite. When socialism has been concerned with the countryside (for electoral purposes), it has recognized that neither production was infinite there nor was insolidarity. It has been asked why the benefits the state dispenses to certain social groups are not spread to everyone, and the socialist deputies have judged that their role was especially to appeal to the benevolence of the state in favor of their poor electors.

The cartels have not only reinforced the notion of solidarity, but have popularized the idea that things would go much better if, instead of being abandoned to the hazards of individual initiative, they were managed by economic estates general. Conflicts between workers and capitalists could also be settled by mixed commissions such as those which exist between competing capitalists, thanks to the cartels. On all sides we have seen a surge of projects which have the purpose of introducing into the economy methods borrowed from politics.

We cannot overemphasize the tendencies toward moderation which make compromise so easy today. I have related these tendencies to three categories: democratic, moral, and Christian. Capitalists are becoming more accommodating and are more imbued every day with the necessity of fulfilling "social duty." Henceforth the great obstacle confronting socialism will arise from the idea of social duty. Workers appeal to the good sentiments of their masters, asking the latter to give them a better salary out of charity and accepting that their leaders treat them as children who must be indulged.

Too often strikes, which formerly gave birth to revolutionary ideas, have produced close relations between union leaders and the bourgeoisie with government support. Notions of economic inevitability, insolidarity, and class struggle all vanish. Supposedly there no longer are two strictly separated worlds, as Marx had imagined. The *science of the new socialists* recognize only one society divided into two parts, which sometimes has contrary interests but is united by a deep solidarity. Between these two groups there are ignorant, eloquent, and foolish idlers *who appeal to the general cowardice* to make the ferments of civil war disappear. The notion of class struggle, strongly attacked by the solidarity born of protectionism and rendered unintelligible by the formation of mixed institutions, now vanishes completely under the influence of the oracles of social duty.

If new beginnings only take place en bloc, as Vico believed, there would be few chances for a lasting renaissance of Marxism to come about. But each strike of any consequence can become a partial *ricorso*. The small socialist tide that it produces can be preserved and accumulated with others if socialists know how to direct them appropriately. It is this which gives such great importance to the Bourses du Travail and to the efforts of the anarchists (so hated by our parliamentarians) to maintain these institutions as organizations of rebellion.[6] We cannot say that Marxism has been given a death blow yet; but it is about time to examine a little more closely the means of allowing for the development of the revolutionary proletariat. The following advice could be offered:

1. In respect to democracy: do not pursue the idea of winning many political offices by joining ranks with every kind of malcontent; do not take an active part in anticlericalism; do not present yourselves as the party of the poor, but as the party of the workers; do not mix the workers' proletariat with public administration employees; do not pursue the expansion of the domination of the state.
2. In regard to capitalism: reject all measures which could restrict vigorous industrial activity even when they seem momentarily favorable to the workers.
3. In regard to negotiators (political or philanthropic): refuse to enter into any institution which tends to reduce the class struggle to a rivalry of material interests; reject all participation of workers' delegates in organizations created by the state or the bourgeoisie; limit yourselves to the labor exchanges and concentrate all workers' activity around them.

I conclude with a reflection which arose from my studies on the origins of Christianity. Christianity could very probably have obtained tolerance as did so many other exotic cults such as Judaism; but it sought to isolate itself and thus provoked suspicion and even persecution. It was intransigent church leaders who prevented the new religion from taking a normal place in Roman society. There was no dearth of wise souls who regarded as insane all those like Tertullian who did not wish to accept any conciliation. Today we know that because of these mad ones Christianity was able to form its ideas and become master of the world when its hour had come.

Notes

1. Thorold Rogers, *Travail et Salaires en Angleterre depuis le XIIIe siècle,* p. 265.
2. Paul de Rousiers, *Le trade unionisme en Angleterre,* p. 32-35.
3. In 1901, Hyndman, who was one of the veterans of the Social Democratic Federation in England, resigned from the executive committee saying that English workers had no class consciousness.
4. Laws made on the length of the working day in England are regarded by Marx as necessary or natural, because they do not reveal a plan. *Saggi di critica del marxismo,* pp. 81-82.
5. We know that this expression comes from Jaurès, who characteristically, clearly translates an instinct that he encountered in socialist groups. Creative hatred is the caricature of the class struggle.
6. What can we say of the labor exchanges founded by the prefectures? This has been seen, it is said, in Cherbourg in January 1904.

INDEX

Abnegation, 137
Adams, Brooks, 187, 191 n.10
Agriculture, 111-12, 114-15, 121, 214-16, 219 n.10, 221-27, 228 nn.2,3,5, 7, 229 n.18, 280, 311
Agronomy, 111-12, 114-15, 127, 280
Alcohol, 269
Algeria, 92, 93, 287 n.1
Alienation, 9, 10, 293-94
Anarchism, 61, 63 n.21, 74, 163 n.22, 186, 324, 326
Andler, Charles, 213
André (General), 288 n.17
Animal laborans, 29. *See also Homo economicus,* Labor
Anticlericalism, 68, 71, 178, 180, 181 n. 10, 183, 326
Anti-Semitism, 223, 285, 305; and social democracy, 298 n.11
Aquinas, St. Thomas, 56, 85 n.
Arabs, 98 n.12
Archimedes, 81
Architecture, 81
Arendt, Hannah, 29
Aristocracy, 280; French, 67, 70, 72, 90 113, 136; finance, 135-36; of workers, 194; Prussian 280; American, 27, 289-90
Aristotle, 11, 12, 27
Armenia, 223
Art, 30, 43, 95, 96
Assemblies. *See* Parliaments, Representatives
Astronomy, 12, 187
Australia, 84, 94, 98 n.11, 220 n.15
Austria, 298 n.11, 315
Authority: political, 29-30, 187; of science, 143, 189; feudal, 239; Napoleonic, 184; bureaucratic, 243-44, 302;

in Hegel 261-62; tirbal, 287 n.1. *See also* Politics, Myth

Babeuf, G., 51 n.15, 197
Bacon, F., 66
Bakeries, 294
Bakunin, 193, 194, 242, 245 n.13. *See also* Anarchism
Bank of France, 243
Bargaining, 20-21, 29, 214, 215, 234-36, 279, 284, 287 n.12; collective, 284-86
Basly, 242, 245 n.11, 281, 287 n.4
Berbers, 92
Bergson, Henri, 3, 9, 81, 86 n.19, 260
Bernard, Claude, 116 n.11
Bernstein, Edouard, 104, 217
Bible, the, 143, 185
Biological analogies, 205, 261
Bismarck, 12, 54, 212, 213, 217, 220 n.10
Blanqui, A., 36, 37 n.45, 324
Boer War, 317
Bonaparte/Bonapartism, 1, 12, 20, 113-14, 115 n, 126, 184, 264, 296; Louis Bonaparte, 41-46
Bonner, Charles, 132 n.14
Bonnier, Charles and Pierre, 159-60, 227
Boredom, 147 n.8
Boulanger, 1
Bourbons, 114
Bourgeois, Emile, 191 n.5
Bourgeois, Léon, 60, 69, 75 n.5, 213, 298 n.11
Bourgeoisie, 24, 29, 57, 63 n.21, 69, 73, 117, 132 n.13, 134-37, 142-46, 157-58, 160, 162, 167, 175, 194, 207, 243, 303, 306, 321
Bourses du travail (labor employment exchanges), 74, 326; official, 327 n.6
Brazil, 134

329